Oliver Dickinson has written a scholarly, accessible and up-to-date introduction to the prehistoric civilisations of Greece. The Aegean Bronze Age, the long period from roughly 3300 to 1000 BC, saw the rise and fall of the Minoan and Mycenaean civilisations. The cultural history of the region emerges through a series of thematic chapters that treat settlement, economy, crafts, exchange and foreign contact (particularly with the civilisations of the Near East), and religion and burial customs. Students and teachers will welcome this book, but it will also provide the ideal companion for serious amateurs and visitors to the Aegean.

CAMBRIDGE WORLD ARCHAEOLOGY

THE AEGEAN BRONZE AGE

CAMBRIDGE WORLD ARCHAEOLOGY

BRIDGET AND RAYMOND ALLCHIN *The Rise of Civilisation in India and Pakistan*

CLIVE GAMBLE *The Palaeolithic Settlement of Europe*

ALASDAIR WHITTLE *Neolithic Europe: a Survey*

CHARLES HIGHAM *The Archaeology of Mainland Southeast Asia*

DAVID W. PHILLIPSON *African Archaeology: Second Edition*

SARAH MILLEDGE NELSON *The Archaeology of Korea*

CAMBRIDGE WORLD ARCHAEOLOGY

THE AEGEAN BRONZE AGE

OLIVER DICKINSON
University of Durham

CAMBRIDGE
UNIVERSITY PRESS

Published by the Press Syndicate of the University of Cambridge
The Pitt Building, Trumpington Street, Cambridge CB2 1RP
40 West 20th Street, New York, NY 10011–4211, USA
10 Stamford Road, Oakleigh, Victoria 3166, Australia

First published 1994

Printed in Great Britain at the University Press, Cambridge

A catalogue record for this book is available from the British Library

Library of Congress cataloging in publication data

Dickinson, O.T.P.K. (Oliver Thomas Pilkington Kirwan)
The Aegean Bronze Age / Oliver Dickinson.
p. cm – (Cambridge world archaeology)
Includes bibliographical references and index.
ISBN 0 521 24280 0
1. Civilization, Aegean. 2. Bronze Age–Aegean Sea Region.
3. Aegean Sea Region–Antiquities. I. Title. II. Series.
DF220.D49 1994
939'.1–dc20 93-2666 CIP

ISBN 0 521 242800 hardback
ISBN 0 521 456649 paperback

WV

To Tania and Edmund, who have been living with this book for a very long time.

CONTENTS

ILLUSTRATIONS

(showing sources, where this information is not incorporated in captions. NB that scales cited in captions for objects may be approximate)

Figures

Plates

PREFACE

This book is intended to be a general introduction to the Aegean Bronze Age. The need for generalised coverage within this format means that no topic can be discussed in great detail, and not all have received attention; the reader is urged to consult other sources for more extensive discussion and richer illustration, particularly the works cited in the first part of the General Bibliography and the chapter bibliographies. The General Bibliography is obviously not comprehensive (this would require a book in itself), but lists relatively recent works of wide coverage and all other sources cited. Similarly, the chapter bibliographies are principally intended to provide references, generally used extensively in the text, for the main themes and sources of data. Citations have been chosen with coverage of previous discussion and accessibility particularly in mind, but more obscure sources have also been included because of their significance.

Creating a general account of the Aegean Bronze Age in a limited space has proved a far more difficult and lengthy process than I once envisaged, and I am still not satisfied with the result. I have certainly not had the space to mention everything that deserves it, and although I have tried to absorb the findings of the ever-lengthening series of important conferences covering various parts of the subject, some could only be consulted very recently and partially (especially Hardy 1990, and Darcque and Treuil 1990). As one who has specialised in mainland archaeology, I may have fallen into error over the interpretation of Minoan material, and I have felt obliged to take a provisional position, which many specialists may consider outdated, on some crucial questions of chronology. Thus this must, like all its predecessors, be considered a progress report, which will start being superseded as soon as it is published.

In attempting to synthesise the work of many specialists of differing theoretical approaches without having any particularly clearcut position of my own, I have given prominence to the viewpoints that I find most plausible, but have frequently qualified statements, to a degree that may irritate the reader. But I believe that this is absolutely necessary; the days are gone when the evidence of a few sites or finds could be blithely assumed to be typical of a whole culture. We are far less certain of everything than our predecessors often seemed to be, and continually ask new questions without having sufficient data to answer them.

The Aegean Bronze Age is a recognisable unit with a degree of internal coherence in the sequence of Greek development, although of course its societies inherited a great deal from their Neolithic predecessors and transmitted much in their turn to those of the succeeding 'Dark Age' from which Archaic Greece developed. To emphasise the element of continuity, I shall give brief coverage to Greece's earlier prehistory and refer on occasion to the Dark Age, but I shall be concentrating on a period stretching from the late fourth millennium into the eleventh century BC. I shall also be limiting coverage effectively to the region of the Minoan, Cycladic, and Helladic cultures in the southern part of the Aegean; the northernmost parts of modern Greece, the north Aegean islands, and most of the Turkish coastal areas are culturally separate and, although often demonstrably in contact with the Aegean cultures, have an essentially different history.

For a work of this kind it is scarcely possible to list every source of ideas and information. I extend thanks to all those who in the past have given me books, offprints or information, especially the following, who have also in many cases made useful comments on drafts of various sections or given other valuable help (see also Acknowledgements): Paul Åström, Robin Barber, Phil Betancourt, John Bintliff, Harriet Blitzer, Helen Hughes Brock, Cyprian Broodbank, Ann Brown, Gerald Cadogan, Hector Catling, Bill Cavanagh, John Chadwick, John Cherry, Pascal Darcque, Jack Davis, Katie Demakopoulou, Søren Dietz, Christos Doumas, Lesley Fitton, Lisa French, Lucy Goodison, Robin Hägg, Paul Halstead, Vronwy Hankey, Anthony Harding, Sinclair Hood, Alexandra Karetsou, John Killen, the late Klaus Kilian (whose untimely death is a great loss to Mycenaean studies), Imma Kilian-Dirlmeier, Dora Konsola, Georgios Korres, Olga Krzyszkowska, Robert Laffineur, Nanno Marinatos, Hartmut Matthäus, Bill McDonald, Manolis Melas, Nicoletta Momigliano, Christine Morris, Penelope Mountjoy, Lyvia Morgan, Jim Muhly, Wolf Niemeier, Gullög Nordquist, Tom Palaima, Alan Peatfield, Catherine Perlès, Mervyn Popham, Colin Renfrew, Bogdan Rutkowski, Jerry Rutter, Yannis Sakellarakis, Elizabeth Schofield, Cynthia Shelmerdine, Andrew and Sue Sherratt, Anthony Snodgrass, Christiane Sourvinou-Inwood, Ingrid Strøm, Gilles Touchais, Lucia Vagnetti, Ken Wardle, Peter Warren, Vance Watrous, Todd Whitelaw, Malcolm Wiener, Nancy Wilkie, Jim Wright and Carol Zerner.

I am extremely grateful to the Institute for Aegean Prehistory, New York, for a generous grant towards the cost of preparing figures, which has also subsidised the plates. The figures have been produced with great care and skill by Glenys Boyles, Head of Illustration and Design at the York Archaeological Trust, and Eddy Moth. I am indebted to Peter Clayton, F.S.A., for many of the plates; several others were prepared by Trevor Woods, photographer in the Department of Archaeology, University of Durham. Isobel Williams and Sylvia Stoddart, successive Secretaries in my Department, typed early drafts of several chapters. The University of Durham granted me terms of research leave in 1982, 1986 and 1990, during which parts of this book were written.

Finally, I should acknowledge the patience and understanding of Cambridge

University Press and my successive editors, Robin Derricourt, Peter Richards and Jessica Kuper.

Oliver Dickinson
September 1992

ACKNOWLEDGEMENTS

Acknowledgements for all plates and many of the figures are included in the captions; I am very grateful to the organisations and individuals named for providing and/or granting permission to reproduce them. But considerations of space make it impractical to include all acknowledgements for some multi-sourced figures in captions, and I therefore give thanks here to the following organisations and individuals in respect of these: Dr R.L.N. Barber (figs 5.2: 1–2, 4–6, 5.3: 6); Prof. P.P. Betancourt (figs 5.7: 1, 5, 7, 5.8: 1, 5–6, 5.10: 5, 5.11: 3, 5–6, 5: 13: 1, 4); the Managing Committee of the British School at Athens (figs 5.1, 5.7: 2–4, 8, 5.8: 2, 4, 5.10: 1–4, 5.11: 1–2, 4, 5.14, 5.15, 5.16: 5–6, 5.17: 4, 5.18: 6, 6.8: 1, 8.6: 7–9, 8.9: 1, 8.13: 4–5, 7); The Faculty Board of Classics, University of Cambridge, and Prof. P.M. Warren (fig. 5.21: 4–14); Dr S. Dietz and Mrs N. Divari-Valakou (figs 5.9: 1–2, 6–7, 5.12: 3); Yale University Press and Mr M.S.F. Hood for illustrations from *The arts in prehistoric Greece* (1978) (figs 3.2: 2, 5.22: 1, 3, 5.39: 1, 3–5, 7–8, 10, 5.40: 7–9, 5.42: 1, 5–6, 8); Dr A. Jockenhövel, Editor of *Prähistorische Bronzefunde* (figs 5.22: 4–5, 7–9, 5.23, 5.47a, 5.47b: 3–5); Profs J. Crouwel and R. Laffineur (fig. 5.12: 4); Prof. J.A. MacGillivray (figs 5.7: 6, 5.8: 3); Dr P.A. Mountjoy (figs 5.12: 1–2, 5–8, 5.13: 6, 5.15, 5.16: 1–4, 5.17: 1–3, 5.18: 1–4, 5.20); Dr G. Nordquist (fig. 5.9: 3–5, 8); Mr M.R. Popham (figs 5.10: 1–2, 4, 5.11: 2, 5.14, 5.17: 4); Prof. Lord Renfrew (figs 8.6: 9, 8.13: 4–5, 7), and with Methuen & Co. (figs 5.2: 3, 5.4: 2, 5.21: 1–3, 5.46: 2); Prof. J.B. Rutter (fig. 5.3: 4, 6–7); Prof. P.M. Warren (figs 5.1, 8.9: 1); Dr C. Zerner (figs 5.5: 1–5, 5.6: 1–2, 5).

A note on usage and nomenclature

Greek placenames are cited in a mixture of forms, in which I have been guided by familiarity and, for modern personal and placenames, closeness to the modern pronunciation. Unless otherwise indicated, common names like Akrotiri, Ayia

Irini, Ayia Triada and Palaikastro will refer to the best-known sites bearing those names; 'Myrtos' will refer to Warren's EM site at Fournou Korifi, 'Pyrgos' to Cadogan's mainly later site nearby.

It has proved convenient to have a single term to cover all the eastern countries with which the Aegean had links. I have preferred to follow logic rather than modern usage and call the whole region the Near East, including within this Egypt, Cyprus, and the territories commonly known to archaeologists as Anatolia, Syria, Palestine and Mesopotamia. These names will be used separately, where necessary, in preference to those of modern states.

ABBREVIATIONS

Periodicals

AA	*Archäologischer Anzeiger*
AAA	*Athens Annals of Archaeology* (Αρχαιολογικά Ανάλεκτα εξ Αθηνών)
AE	Αρχαιολογική Εφημερίς
AJA	*American Journal of Archaeology*
AthMitt	*Mitteilungen der deutschen archäologischen Instituts: athenische Abteilung*
AR	*Archaeological Reports* (supplement to *Journal of Hellenic Studies*)
ASAtene	*Annuario della Scuola archeologica di Atene e delle Missioni in Oriente*
BAR	*British Archaeological Reports*
BCH	*Bulletin de correspondance hellénique*
BICS	*Bulletin of the Institute of Classical Studies* (University of London)
BSA	*Annual of the British School of Archaeology at Athens*
CR	*Classical Review*
CAJ	*Cambridge Archaeological Journal*
Hydra	*Hydra, working papers in Middle Bronze Age studies*, coordinated by G. Nordquist and C. Zerner
JdAI	*Jahrbuch des deutschen archäologischen Instituts*
JFA	*Journal of Field Archaeology*
JMA	*Journal of Mediterranean Archaeology*
JPR	*Journal of Prehistoric Religion*
JRGZM	*Jahrbuch des römisch-germanischen Zentralmuseums, Mainz*
OJA	*Oxford Journal of Archaeology*
OpAth	*Opuscula Atheniensia*
PAE	Πρακτικά τής εν Αθήναις Αρχαιολογικής Εταιρείας
PZ	*Praehistorische Zeitschrift*
SIMA	*Studies in Mediterranean Archaeology*
SMEA	*Studi micenei ed egeo-anatolici*
TUAS	*Temple University Aegean Symposium*

Others

BA	Bronze Age
BP	Before present
CAH	*Cambridge Ancient History* (3rd edition)
CAH I–II, pl. ...	*Cambridge Ancient History*, Plates to Volumes I & II (3rd edition)
EB(A), MB(A), LB(A)	Early, Middle, Late Bronze (Age)
EC, MC, LC	Early, Middle, Late Cycladic
EH, MH, LH	Early, Middle, Late Helladic
EM, MM, LM	Early, Middle, Late Minoan
EN, MN, LN	Early, Middle, Late Neolithic
ha	hectares

INTRODUCTION

Only in the last century has it become evident that the past of Greece was immensely longer than the Greeks themselves imagined, and that it reached a peak of development that may reasonably be termed a civilisation during the Bronze Age, before declining into a long period of recession, the Dark Age, from which it finally emerged in the eighth century BC. This civilisation was partly contemporary with the early civilisations of the Near East, but unlike them it has no mass of contemporary documentation from which the outlines of its history can be reconstructed. Some have sought to extract a kind of history from the Greek corpus of legends. But no objective criteria for isolating genuine BA elements in this material have ever been established, and most treatments of this material make no attempt at source-criticism, so that 'traditional' status is attributed not merely to the legends themselves but to the learned speculations of Herodotus, the brilliant extrapolations of Thucydides, and the work of the late mythographers, which are in fact attempts at codifying and interpreting this material, no different in essence from those of modern scholars. Even the vivid and genuinely archaic setting of the Homeric epics demonstrably mixes elements of different dates, perhaps reflecting the Dark Age more than anything else. The only safe position to adopt has been enunciated by Forsdyke: 'Archaeological discovery may throw light upon the legends, but the use of legendary statements for historical interpretation of material records is a reversal of proper procedure' (1956: 166).

Thus, the Aegean Bronze Age is essentially prehistoric, accessible only through the methods of archaeology. The development of Aegean prehistoric archaeology has normally been recounted in terms of the sequence of major excavations and the controversies over their chronological and cultural relationships. Attention is less often focussed on the underlying preconceptions that determined the excavators' choice of sites and interpretations; yet these have shaped Aegean prehistory quite as much as the major discoveries, and some relevant comments will be incorporated in the following outline.

As is well known, Aegean prehistory was effectively founded by the excavations of Schliemann. His finds at Mycenae were so impressive that it seemed natural to apply the term 'Mycenaean' to the similar material found in the following years at many Aegean sites, and it was used in this way in the first great synthetic account (Tsountas and Manatt 1897), in which evidence for a pre-Mycenaean stage was already being cited. Schliemann's other significant excavations in Greece were at sites famous in Greek tradition, Tiryns and Orchomenos, but after him, although Tsountas conducted much further research at Mycenae, there were no conscious attempts to verify the legends. Rather, Tsountas showed a true archaeologist's interest in the evidence for material culture and development for its own sake, investigating first the pre-Mycenaean stage in the Cyclades, mainly through excavating cemeteries, and later the even earlier Neolithic stage of Thessaly, particularly at Sesklo and Dhimini. Other remains were investigated more haphazardly, as they attracted attention, particularly the monumental tholos tombs and other graves.

The first large-scale stratigraphical excavations in the Aegean were undertaken at Phylakopi on Melos in 1896–9 to study the relationship of Tsountas's 'island civilisation' to the Mycenaean. But important though these were, their results had already been eclipsed, by the time of their publication in 1904, by the great series of Cretan excavations which began in 1900. In the space of a few years the finds at Knossos, Phaistos, Palaikastro, Gournia and other sites had completely overshadowed all previous discoveries (Fig. Intro.1). The excavation of the palace at Knossos (Evans 1921–35) was the most spectacular and best publicised, and its excavator, Evans, swiftly produced a chronological scheme dividing the Cretan material into three phases, Early, Middle and Late, of a Minoan civilisation (named after the legendary king Minos), running nearly parallel to the tripartite division of Egyptian history into Old, Middle and New Kingdoms (Evans 1921: 25–7), with a preceding Neolithic period. This gained immediate acceptance and has effectively provided a template for all further classifications of Aegean prehistoric material.

The identification of a civilisation in Crete comparable with those of the ancient Near East had two effects. One was to concentrate attention on the more elaborate architecture and artistic products of this civilisation; the remains of the pre-palatial phases received less attention, except where they heralded the glories of the palatial age, and least attention was paid to the way of life at ordinary level. Boyd Hawes, the excavator of Gournia, enunciated principles that were a model for any period: 'We must know the standard of living as well as the aesthetic principles of a race, and to save our studies from becoming a mere discussion of styles, must keep in view the significance of the humblest articles of use' (1908: 29). But her example was not generally followed. In his survey of Cretan archaeology, Pendlebury was to call Gournia a town of farmers (1939: 191), but to show little interest in it, let alone in the 'humblest articles of use'; once the palatial age was reached, he invariably concentrated on the palaces when discussing architecture, and on the most elaborate fine wares when discussing pottery.

The second effect was more insidious, but a natural consequence of the links perceived with the Near East. Not only was the origin of Minoan civilisation explained through the diffusion of influences, if not actual populations, from the Near East, especially Egypt, but its structure was assumed to be essentially similar. Thus, terms like palace, king and town were commonly used, without

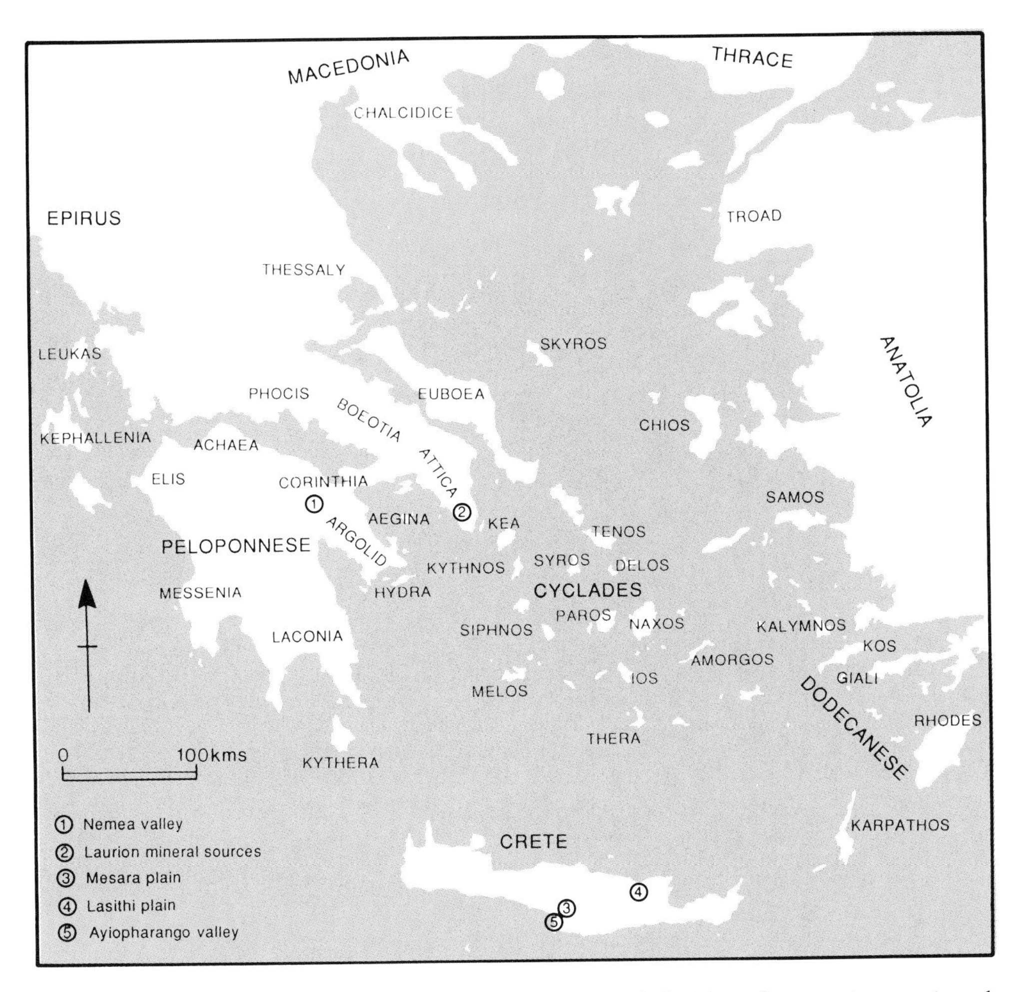

Intro.1 The Aegean, showing geographical subdivisions frequently mentioned in the text.

any defence of their appropriateness or any detailed exposition of social structure seeming necessary. Following Evans, Pendlebury imagined Minoan civilisation at its height as 'an ordered state with a highly centralised bureaucracy' (1939: 285), but beyond that little was said, and it is symptomatic that he could speculate on the Minoan mentality through analysis of art (275–6), while dismissing Glotz's attempt to reconstruct Early Minoan social organisation from its burial customs (279–80). Yet in many respects Evans's overall picture of Minoan civilisation was unlike the Near East, evidently deriving partly from wish-fulfilling use of the imagination (cf. Bintliff 1984: 35–6).

The establishment of Crete's primacy relegated 'Mycenaean' civilisation to provincial status and seems to have stimulated interest in the earlier phases on the mainland, which evidently had little to do with Crete, and especially in the

Neolithic period, represented by long sequences in Thessaly and central Greece. The problem of classifying the abundant mainland pre-Mycenaean material became increasingly urgent, but was solved for the BA by the excavations of Blegen at Korakou, upon which basis Wace and Blegen developed a 'Helladic' system designed to run parallel with the Minoan (Blegen 1921). Much of this terminology came into general use, but Evans and his followers persisted in describing all Late Bronze Age material in the Aegean as Late Minoan, and a bitter split developed over the use of the term 'Late Helladic' by Wace and Blegen to stress the individuality of the mainland material, over the chronology of major monuments at Mycenae, which Wace dated after the accepted date for the end of the palace at Knossos, and ultimately over the 'Greekness' of the mainland civilisation. For in a seminal article (Blegen and Haley 1928) it was argued that the ancestors of the Greeks arrived in the southern mainland at the end of Early Helladic and established the Middle Helladic culture; Late Helladic was argued by Wace and Blegen to develop from this under Minoan influence, whereas for Evans Late Helladic was merely provincial Late Minoan and thus could not be Greek, since the Minoan civilisation was not.

While there continued to be major work in Crete, Mallia and Ayia Triada being the most important new sites, there was increasing interest in large, multi-period sites on the mainland, whose excavators used the Helladic terminology while remaining non-committal as to the 'Greekness' of the later phases. Frequently this was combined with an attempt to investigate the site's cemeteries and view it in its geographical setting, as Blegen did at Zygouries (1928). This and many other excavations were in the north-east Peloponnese, the neighbourhood of Mycenae, with the result that this region became far better known than the rest of the mainland, although important material was also excavated in Boeotia at Thebes and Eutresis. Many Late Helladic cemeteries were discovered, and surveys in search of prehistoric sites were undertaken in several areas of the mainland and Crete. Much of the material thus uncovered was made accessible by swift publication, establishing many of the standard sources of mainland archaeology, particularly Prosymna (Blegen 1937), Dendra (Persson 1931, 1942) and Eutresis (Goldman 1931); but a great deal remained unpublished, and the Cyclades were largely neglected, although much work was carried out in the Dodecanese.

The most startling discovery of the period was in Messenia, a promising but relatively poorly known province, at Epano Englianos (Pylos). Here in 1939 remains of a palatial building were uncovered, in which were found tablets written in the last script used in the palace at Knossos, Linear B script. For many this must have seemed proof that Evans was right and that the Mycenaean/Late Helladic civilisation was Minoan; for others, especially Wace, it strengthened a developing conviction that the final phase of the Knossos palace was 'Mycenaean'. Ventris's decipherment of Linear B as an early form of Greek in 1952, now almost universally accepted, made clear that Wace and Blegen were essentially right to distinguish Mycenaean/Late Helladic from Late Minoan, and put an end to that controversy. It has also provided one of the most significant advances in Aegean prehistory, making it possible for the first time to use contemporary documents, however obscure, to improve understanding of the late palace societies. But it gave rise to a new controversy over the dating of the Knossos texts, and so of their context, which remains unresolved (see Appendix to Ch. 1).

Since the Second World War a mass of new archaeological evidence has been accumulated, often in 'rescue' excavations within modern Greek cities, as at Thebes (Symeonoglou 1985), or in surveys. Our knowledge of many well-known sites has been substantially altered if not transformed, and many more have been added to the list constantly referred to in discussion (e.g. Myrtos, Zakro, Arkhanes and Kato Symi in Crete, Ayia Irini and Akrotiri in the Cyclades, the Franchthi cave, Lerna, Lefkandi and Perati on the mainland). But the vast increase in data has only partly broadened its scope: many recent finds have related to the field of religion, including for the first time unquestionable remains of mainland and Cycladic religious sites, but most investigations have continued to focus upon palaces and other big buildings, large multi-period settlements, and cemeteries. Very few farmsteads or truly small villages have been excavated, although surveys have identified the likely sites of many such.

The growth of interest in survey has radically affected perceptions of the distribution of population and land-use in the BA, even though its incidence remains patchy and only recently has it begun to be conducted with much system. The traditional method of inspecting likely-looking mounds and high hills had an inbuilt tendency to overlook the truly small sites and dispersed indications of human activity; but 'intensive' methods have only been applied over limited areas, because of their expensiveness, and there is still debate over the legitimacy of drawing wider conclusions from samples, however 'scientific' their basis. The related topics of land-use and the basis of the economy have received much attention, especially in two published surveys (McDonald and Rapp 1972; Renfrew and Wagstaff 1982) and in Bintliff 1977. This long-overdue development has been aided by an increasingly systematic use of the sciences, especially geology, botany and zoology, to investigate the modern landscape and natural setting of sites as well as the remains from them.

In this context, much use has been made of analogy from the practices of traditional rural Greece, following a precedent established in the early days of Aegean archaeology, when archaeologists found themselves working in a countryside whose practices seemed rooted in the past and whose peasants could rapidly apprehend the purpose of excavated items, which matched their own implements and utensils. This approach has great potential if applied with proper rigour, but it runs the risk of underestimating structural differences in setting and society, not to mention the natural environment (cf. Halstead 1987b). Greek villages have for a long time been part of states of considerable size, and so have often been linked, however weakly, with a money economy and an international trade network. The effect that this can have on the agricultural economy can be perceived in the quite recent development of large-scale olive cultivation in the local economy of Karpophora in Messenia (Aschenbrenner 1972: 49–50) and inland Boeotia (Rackham 1983: 313, 331, 339). Socially, the differences may have been even more marked; for while BA religions could have had a pervasive influence on moral perceptions, their basis and value-systems were surely very different from those of Greek Orthodox Christianity (for whose effect on village society see, for example, Du Boulay 1974: 51–63, 101–6). There is not even an identifiable BA equivalent for that indispensable village institution, the *kapheneion!* The analogy may have most value, then, if confined largely to traditional crafts and agricultural practices, which may be suggested to have changed little, when applied to the same crops and livestock, until the advent of mechanisation.

Scientific analysis has provided data also on the sources of materials and on absolute dating, principally through the radiocarbon technique. A great deal of useful information has been produced, but often this seems to have created more problems than it has solved; the temptation to draw dramatic conclusions from limited evidence has not always been avoided, and methodology is still being refined in many areas. But this work has made a major contribution, not least by its stress on the proper quantification of data and the need for statistically valid samples.

But the most important change of all has been in the approach to explanation. Until the 1970s the most explicit general theories in use were those of Gordon Childe, who conceived the growth of civilisation in Europe to be intimately linked to the search for raw materials, especially metals, by the Near Eastern civilisations, in the course of which ideas and skills were spread from the Near East, and who developed the notion of the archaeological 'culture', a recurring assemblage of archaeological traits, as a means of classifying the material. Inevitably, Childe, and even more his successors, tended to assume that cultures were the archaeological expression of ethnic groups, so that their spread could be conceived in terms of population expansions. Thus the concepts of migration and diffusion came to play major explanatory roles in accounts of Aegean development and, combined with the tendency to treat the Greek legends as a respectable source of historical information, led to the 'event'-dominated accounts of the Aegean BA justly criticised by Snodgrass (1985: 35–6). But such explanations have been looking increasingly implausible, and more recently, in a series of seminal studies, Renfrew has attempted to formulate general theories to explain Aegean development in local terms. While these have in turn come under criticism from a younger generation of specialists, there can be no denying their enormous value, above all in emphasising the necessity of explaining all developments, including the introduction of foreign ideas and even populations, within the context of the continual processes of Aegean social development.

Much more work needs to be done before a new Aegean prehistory can emerge. The available data remain variable in quality, uneven in distribution, often poorly recorded, and limited in different ways. But in fairness to all my predecessors and contemporaries, it seems right to end this short account by emphasising that Aegean archaeology is an immensely rich and exciting field of study, constantly being renewed by stimulating discussions and new approaches.

Bibliography

Forsdyke 1956 rigorously analyses the supposed chronological and historical content of the Greek legends in their developed literary form. On the Homeric material see Dickinson 1986a, Sherratt, E.S. 1990 (with full bibliography), Whitley 1991.

Warren 1989, ch. 1 provides a useful short account of the development of Aegean archaeology; McDonald and Thomas 1990 is more extensive, but concentrates on Mycenaean archaeology.

For an introduction to Linear B see Hooker 1980, and for more detail, Ventris and Chadwick 1973.

CHAPTER 1

TERMINOLOGY AND CHRONOLOGY

Terminology

As already noted in the Introduction, it was Evans who introduced a tripartite system of classification to Aegean prehistory, a system that has become so popular that one might imagine that it was the natural and obvious way to classify material. Evans suggested as much in expounding it: 'This tripartite system, indeed, whether we regard the course of Minoan civilisation as a whole or its threefold stages, is in its very essence logical and scientific. In every characteristic phase of culture we note in fact the period of rise, maturity and decay' (1921: 25). As McNeal has observed (1975: 390), Evans is using a biological metaphor, but the suggestion that a tripartite system necessarily conveys images of growth and decay is surely wrong; it can simply model beginning, middle and end. Evans could not in fact adhere to the pattern that he suggested; he clearly did not regard EM III as a decline, described MM III as a 'splendid revival', and wrote of the early part of LM as 'the golden age of Crete, followed, after a level interval, by a gradual decline' (1921: 27). The model works better, though not altogether satisfactorily, for his view of the pottery styles by which these phases are largely defined; but this is, or ought to be, a separate matter. Unfortunately, Evans's use of the same terminology to denote both his phases and the material, particularly pottery, assigned to those phases, although open to obvious criticism (most succinctly, Renfrew 1972: 53–4, cf. also 1979), has become normal practice (Fig. 1.1 shows a developed form).

The tripartite system has many defects as a means of classifying Aegean BA pottery, which are no different in essence from those cited by D.H. French in his trenchant criticism of using a similar system for Neolithic pottery: 'It cannot include all the pottery groups found in Greece. As used, it does not indicate that the pottery so grouped may contain many elements. It does not allow for the adjustments and additions (to sequences and groups) which may have to be made as more research is carried out' (1972: 2). As a system of historical phasing it is even more clearly inadequate, as two examples plainly show. The rise and fall of the palace societies is evidently the most significant historical development of the Aegean BA; but the First Palace Period in Crete begins after the beginning of MM and ends before its end, while the Second Palace Period begins before the end of MM and ends with LM I. Secondly, it has been customary to detect three major historical divisions in the EBA, but the revised interpretation of the EC

Crete	Cyclades	Mainland
EM I	EC I	EH I
EM II	EC II	EH II
EM III	EC III	EH III
MM IA		
MM IB	MC	MH
MM IIA	(early)	(early)
MM IIB		(middle)
MM IIIA–B	(late)	(late)
LM IA	LC I	LH I
LM IB	LC II	LH IIA
LM II		LH IIB
LM IIIA1	LC III	LH IIIA1
LM IIIA2	(early)	LH IIIA2
LM IIIB	(middle)	LH IIIB1
		LH IIIB2
LM IIIC	(late)	LH IIIC
Subminoan		Submycenaean

Fig. 1.1 The tripartite system of classification, showing the most commonly used terms. (Mainly after Demakopoulou 1988: 27, with some additions.)

sequence by Barber and MacGillivray (1980) plainly identifies four; there being no scope for an EC IV, two phases which are not obviously successive statigraphically, have few cultural links, and have largely distinct distributions in the Cyclades, must be termed EC IIIA and EC IIIB. The system has in fact become a bed of Procrustes, to which the material must be fitted willy-nilly.

Nevertheless, some systems of historical phasing and material classification seem required. It is still not possible to use absolute dates, as McNeal hoped (1975: 400–1); even the tidy blocks of decades and centuries that are used by later historians can hardly be deployed when there are few if any fixed points. Rather, the basis for discussing development of any kind must be a relative chronology, based upon regional classification systems (cf. Warren and Hankey 1989: 2-3); the results can be correlated within broad phases that ideally should reflect stages in historical development, and if possible these phases can then be given absolute dates.

It can be conceded to defenders of the tripartite system that it is so familiar that it cannot easily be replaced. But there is no need to continue its use as the system of historical phasing, although its three basic subdivisions, Early, Middle and Late, remain useful in making broad general comments and definitions, and it is convenient to use phrases like 'in LM I' chronologically, as an abbreviation for 'in the phases characterised by LM I pottery'. But in general, for purposes of historical and chronological comment, I propose to use a system of five broad divisions that reflects the rise and fall of the palace societies, close to that favoured by Platon and others. Sometimes, but rarely, it may be possible to use an absolute chronological term, such as 'in the sixteenth century' (all dates will be BC unless otherwise stated).

The familiarity of the tripartite system also makes me reluctant to discard it totally for classificatory purposes. There seems no point in trying to replace the basic Minoan–Cycladic–Helladic division, or the well-developed sequence of Mycenaean pottery phases; the Minoan phasing, though still subject to considerable problems of definition between EM III and MM IIIA (see below) has also been in use for a long time. But there are strong arguments against the use of the system before the LBA outside Crete, because the material divides much more readily into groups that may overlap, mingle, and disappear without immediate successor in the material record, especially in the EBA.

For these groups I propose to use assemblage names, drawn as far as possible from those already suggested by Renfrew, Doumas, and D.H. French; but these will not be termed cultures, to avoid the overtones, especially the equation culture = people, that the word has so often attracted. To indicate their provisional and symbolic nature, these group names will be cited in inverted commas, e.g. 'Lerna III', and where these are absent the reference will be to the actual site, etc., from which the name has been taken. They are intended to provide immediately recognisable reference-points rather than precise definitions; hence 'Phylakopi I' will be used in the general sense indicated by Renfrew's and

Doumas's usage, since there is no obvious alternative, although strictly it refers only to the material of what is now defined as Phylakopi I, phases ii–iii. In order to make cross-reference easier, I shall also qualify use of these terms where it seems necessary (as in the section on relative chronology) with the term in the tripartite system to which it is attributed in Warren and Hankey 1989, thus 'Lerna III' (EH II). The result (Fig. 1.2) is less tidy, and potentially more confusing, than the traditional scheme, but for that very reason I believe that it will reflect the realities of our knowledge more accurately.

The local sequences and relative chronology

The relative chronology of the Aegean BA must be based very largely on the evidence of pottery sequences, themselves based on a combination of stratigraphical evidence and stylistic analysis. The exhaustive discussion of the material in Warren and Hankey 1989 (referred to for the rest of this chapter as Warren and Hankey), supersedes all previous work. Even so, it is necessary to point out that recent study of the Knossos deposits is pointing strongly to the need for reorganisation of the MM sequence. Momigliano's analysis of Knossos deposits traditionally assigned to MM IA distinguishes at least two groups among them, one which seems essentially identical with what has been termed EM III, the other with what, following MacGillivray's analysis, may be termed MM IIA (Momigliano 1991, especially 267–9). MacGillivray in fact equates what has been termed MM IB with MM IIA, and identifies MM IIIA as the last stage of the first palace at Knossos, combining MM IIB with material previously thought to represent the first stage of the Second Palace Period (1986, cf. Driessen and MacGillivray 1989: 99).

If accepted, these reclassifications would produce three major phases between EM II and MM IIIB at Knossos (EM III/MM IA, MM IB/IIA, MM IIB/IIIA). This would correspond much better with those distinguished by others in the development of pottery over the same period, especially in sequences outside central Crete (cf. Cadogan 1983: 516–7; Walberg 1987). There will almost certainly be argument over correlations and scope for renewed subdivision of such long phases (the possibility that intermediate stages could be recognised in material outside the palace was accepted in MacGillivray 1986), and any attempt to produce a uniform terminology for a period in which there is acknowledged to be considerable local variation within Crete (e.g. Cadogan 1988: 95–6) may ultimately be futile. The safest approach will be to use the traditional subdivisions from EM III to MM IIIA sparingly, and to accept that correlations with the Cycladic and Helladic sequences are less clearcut than has been suggested.

The student of the Minoan sequence is at least blessed with an abundance of stratified material to form a basis for classification and correlation. From this it can be seen that EM I and EM II are universal phases, though with local variations. At least one major phase should follow EM II, representing the late

Crete	Cyclades	Mainland	Period
EM I	'Pelos'	'Talioti' & 'Eutresis'	
EM IIA	'Kampos'		
EM IIB	'Syros'	'Lerna III'	Prepalatial Period
	'Kastri'	'Lefkandi I'	
EM III/MM IA	(gap?)		
	'Phylakopi I'	'Lerna IV' etc. MH (early)	
MM IB/IIA	MC (early)		First Palace Period
MM IIB/IIIA		(mature)	
	(late)	(late)	
MM IIIB LM IA	LC I	LH 1	Second Palace Period
LM IB		LH IIA	
	(LC II)		
LM II		LH IIB	
LM IIIA1	(LC III)	LH IIIA1	
LM IIIA2		LH IIIA2	Third Palace Period
LM IIIB		LH IIIB1	
		LH IIIB2	
LM IIIC		LH IIIC	
			Postpalatial Period
Subminoan		Submycenaean	

Fig. 1.2 Suggested sequences of the Aegean cultures, incorporating the terms used in this book (the MM IIIB/LM IA transitional phase is not shown). This figure is not intended to show precise relationships or lengths of time, but to give general indications.

Prepalatial Period, and the First Palace Period should, as indicated above, contain at least two more, while the phase defined as MM IIIB, because light-on-dark style is still very common in the decorated pottery, will represent the first stage of the Second Palace Period. A MM IIIB–LM IA transitional phase, incorporating some of what has in the past been classified as MM IIIB or LM IA, has recently been strongly argued for (Warren and Hankey, 61–5, updated in Warren 1991b); this is an example of the greater precision possible through the study of large deposits, but also of the infelicities that the tripartite terminology produces, though definition of this phase is useful in a period of important historical developments. The succeeding LM sequence (Warren and Hankey, 72–93) has few difficulties, since very similar wares can be found throughout Crete and the phases are almost as well defined, both stratigraphically and stylistically, as those of decorated Mycenaean pottery, with which they have many links. But it is not until LM IIIA1 that all parts of Crete were evidently producing variants of a single style, for the most characteristic LM IB wares seem to be products of Knossian workshops (cf. Betancourt 1985: 136–48) and although LM II has been identified as a distinct phase at Mallia and Kommos it is still largely defined on the basis of material from the Knossos region.

The situation in the rest of the Aegean is quite different before the LBA. Long stratified sequences are known from a number of sites, but there are demonstrable gaps in most of them and detailed publication is still awaited in several cases. The EC phases are particularly poorly represented, and have to be defined largely on the basis of cemetery material, while MC is represented largely by the material from two sites, Ayia Irini and Phylakopi. In fact, in both the mainland and the Cyclades some regions or islands are much better known than others, though EB groups covering most if not all of the respective territories can be identified. These show a considerable degree of homogeneity, but local variability becomes marked late in the EBA, when major sites can differ markedly in features of their sequences, and continues in the MBA despite the family resemblances detectable over each region as a whole.

The earliest identifiable EC group in the Cyclades will be termed ‘Pelos’ (EC I); other major groups, ‘Kampos’ (EC I/II) and ‘Syros’ (EC II) seem to follow in direct succession from this, but in all these cover a very long period and subdivisions may be isolated through more precise analysis. All have wide though not identical distributions in the Cyclades. At most EC sites and cemeteries nothing obviously later than ‘Syros’ can be identified, but at some a stage is found, as in Ayia Irini level III, in which ‘Syros’ pottery types are mingled with new forms that can be linked to the north Aegean and Anatolia; this will be termed ‘Kastri’ (EC III). This assemblage is being identified on an increasing number of islands; but it is still absent from Melos and the connection between it and the next clearly identifiable grouping, ‘Phylakopi I’ (EC III), remains quite unclear, since its sites, including Ayia Irini, are abandoned in their turn.

Phylakopi certainly provides an unbroken sequence from the time of its establishment as a major nucleated settlement (Phylakopi I, phases ii–iii) to the end of the LBA, and material related to one or more of its earlier phases has been found on several islands; however, Ayia Irini, re-founded at a time that apparently falls within the First Palace Period, differs from Phylakopi in aspects of its material culture, and the same may prove to be true for other islands when their material is better known. The occurrence in increasing quantities of Minoan pottery provides an external check on local sequences, and after the Second Palace Period the Cyclades effectively become a province of the Mycenaean culture sphere.

Until recently it was thought that the mainland EB sequence began with 'Eutresis' (EH I), recognised particularly in central Greece but also reported from the Peloponnese; however, Weisshaar has now identified a distinct complex of 'Talioti' pottery which is much better represented in the Peloponnese than 'Eutresis' and seems to be of comparable date (1990). How either of these relates to 'Lerna III' (EH II) is still not clear, but this is the next major grouping, which can be traced throughout the Helladic region south of Thessaly, where the occurrence of 'Lerna III' pottery at Pefkakia allows correlations with the local sequence. The sequences of Tiryns and Lerna will provide evidence for the internal subdivision of 'Lerna III', which must cover a very long period; once this is established it may be possible to trace the spread of 'Lerna III' over the Helladic region.

At a late stage of the EBA, the same Anatolian/north Aegean types that appear in the Cyclades occur at sites in Boeotia, Attica, Euboea and Aegina, usually mingled with 'Lerna III' types but in the earliest levels of Lefkandi in apparently unmixed deposits; hence this group will be termed 'Lefkandi I' (EH IIIA). Rutter has argued that many characteristic types of Lerna IV pottery derive from a fusion of 'Lerna III' and 'Lefkandi I' forms, a suggestion that receives considerable support from the stratigraphy of Kolonna on Aegina, where such a sequence can be observed; but at Tiryns there seems to be evidence for a layer containing a mixture of 'Lerna III' and 'Lerna IV' types. The complexities are great (see the discussion in Warren and Hankey, 35–42), largely because of the breakdown in homogeneity of pottery style, and only resolve themselves to some extent when it can be perceived that the 'Lerna IV' (EH IIIB) pottery assemblage is dominant in the north Peloponnese and Aegina, and the related 'Ayia Marina' (EH IIIB) assemblage in Boeotia and Phocis.

However, only at certain sites, notably Lerna and Lefkandi, is the transition to MH clearly covered in the sequence, and it has to be said that although 'Lerna IV' types and wares are clearly the direct ancestors of much of the standard MH assemblage, the process by which this spread over the central parts of the Helladic region remains obscure, as does the development of related wares elsewhere in the mainland, notably the south Peloponnese, where the sequence has a gap of unclear duration after 'Lerna III'. The MH sequence of Nichoria evidently begins very early ('Lerna IV' links have been postulated), but its pottery is not close to that of the central Helladic region, nor is that of Ayios Stephanos in Laconia, which can be linked to middle phases of Lerna V at earliest, and the establishment of correlations between these local sequences is still to a great extent a matter of informed guesswork. It is worth pointing out, since this point has not been perceived generally, that of the three layers attributed to MH at Eutresis only the first falls within the MH period, and this is very late, since it contains polychrome pottery; the occurrence of 'Mainland Polychrome' ware is a strong indication that the succeeding layers are contemporary with LH I. But with the development and wide spread of Mycenaean decorated pottery homogeneity returns, for the style perfected in the Peloponnese, whose centre after LH I was surely the Argolid, was followed throughout the region of Mycenaean culture for the greater part of the LBA, and even in the final stages cross-connections are readily apparent.

Correlations between the Minoan, Cycladic and Helladic sequences become progressively clearer through time; at first only broad general similarities can be traced, so that even the relative dates of inception of the BA sequences are hard to establish. 'Kampos' (EC I/II) types have been identified in 'Eutresis' (EH I) and nearly if not entirely pure EM I contexts, and these links are strengthened later, when exchange of 'Syros' (EC II), 'Lerna III' (EH II) and EM II artefacts, particularly pottery, and the common use of similar artefact types indicates that these three were broadly contemporary. Thereafter there seems to be a gap in links between Crete and the rest of the Aegean, for the widely spread 'Lefkandi I' (EH IIIA) types do not appear in Crete, and although there are well-known links in the MBA, it is here that the repercussions of any redefinition of MM pottery phases will be felt most. For much of what has been termed MM IA in the discussions (especially Rutter and Zerner 1984: 77–9, Warren and Hankey, 21) is later on Momigliano's definition, so that the chronological significance of the occurrences of Minoan and Cycladic pottery types in Lerna VA must be reconsidered. The best that can be suggested until the position becomes clearer is that the MB sequences of the three regions were roughly parallel; and continuing uncertainty over the nature of the structures preceding the major MM II complexes at Knossos and Mallia makes it safer to retain MM IA, as defined by Momigliano, in the Prepalatial Period.

Minoan influence on other Aegean pottery styles perceptibly increases towards the end of the MBA and is very marked in the fine decorated pottery of the Cyclades and the Mycenaean style of the mainland at the beginning of the LBA, which relate closely to the LM IA style. Thereafter correlations are generally easily established through the identification of imported pottery and Minoan, and later Mycenaean, stylistic influences over wide areas. The destruction deposits created by the eruption of Thera represent a useful fixed point, now coming to be regarded as a stage before the end of LM IA and LH I (cf. Warren 1991a: 30). Links between LM IB and LH IIA are also strong, and as demonstrated by the destruction deposits of Ayia Irini Period VII, which include several LH IIB types, LH IIB had evidently begun before the end of LM IB, though clear links with LM II can also be identified. Further cross-connections are perceptible in the LH IIIA and LM IIIA phases, but the earlier homogeneity within regions breaks down at the beginning of LM IIIB and during LH IIIB, and the correlation of Mycenaean and Minoan becomes less clear. In the Postpalatial Period styles become increasingly regional, although exchanges and cross-influences can be documented as late as LH IIIC Advanced, and ultimately connections between the local styles are so sporadic that relative chronology in the Dark Age is very frequently a matter for involved and inconclusive debate.

Absolute chronology

The traditional method of calculating a chronology for the Aegean Bronze Age, through establishing synchronisms with the historical chronologies of Egypt and Mesopotamia, has been gravely weakened in recent years by the doubts cast on the value or significance of the majority of these synchronisms. While there are good reasons for rejecting the proposal of P. James and his collaborators in *Centuries of darkness* for a radical reduction of dates by as much as two and a half centuries (see the review feature in *CAJ* 1 (1991) 227–53 and Manning and Weninger 1992), they draw attention to weaknesses and ambiguities in the traditional methods. It should be noted that even by the traditional methods no agreement has been reached upon the Near East's absolute chronology. Opinion is increasingly favouring the 'low' chronology, sixty years lower than the previously favoured 'middle', since it seems more compatible with the latest lowering of Egyptian dates, but a case is still being maintained for the 'high' chronology, sixty years *higher* than the 'middle'; even for Egypt, the evidence could support two similarly divergent chronologies before the New Kingdom (cf. the papers and discussion in Åström 1987, especially Kitchen on Egyptian chronology, hereafter referred to as Kitchen).

The hope that radiocarbon dating could provide a reliable basis independent of the historical chronologies became difficult to sustain for the Aegean, when dates so often proved to be earlier than had been expected on the basis of correlations with the Near East, especially for the early LBA when these were thought to be quite tightly established. This was not entirely a new problem, for, when calibrated, radiocarbon dates for Near Eastern developments have frequently appeared too high, inspiring Mellaart's proposal to raise the 'historical' chronologies to accommodate them (1979); but his arguments concerned earlier periods than the LBA, and were heavily criticised. To reconcile the conflict for the Aegean LBA, a higher and longer chronology for the earlier phases has been suggested (Betancourt 1987; Manning 1988), partly through taking a different view of the synchronistic evidence, partly through using scientific evidence to place the eruption of Thera around 1630/20, instead of a century or more later. Some of the supporting arguments, involving supposed correlations with acidity peaks in Greenland ice cores and 'frost events' in Californian trees, have already been abandoned by Manning (1990), who bases the scientific part of his case essentially on the radiocarbon dates from Akrotiri, the majority of which undoubtedly suit a later seventeenth century date; he discounts Olsson's argument (in Åström 1987: 18–22) that all these dates may have to be rejected because the eruption itself could have affected the carbon content of samples.

These arguments have been extensively criticised, particularly by Warren, but it is clear that the synchronistic data are often ambiguous. But one point that does not seem to have been answered by Manning (Warren and Hankey 1989: 145) deserves repetition here. It is that in the earlier 'Keftiu' tomb-paintings (below, ch. 7, p. 248), datable to the reigns of Hatshepsut and Tuthmosis III, the 'Keftiu' are dressed in a style that can be readily paralleled in Second Palace Period representations, whereas in slightly later paintings, apparently dating to the reign of Tuthmosis's successor Amenophis II, a kilt comparable to that shown on some figures in the Knossos Procession Fresco, thought to be LM II in date, is shown. It is impossible to square this with Manning's chronology (cf. Fig. 1.3), by which the Second Palace Period, and indeed LM II, should have been over before the reigns of Hatshepsut and Tuthmosis III began (probably in 1479, certainly not before 1490, according to Kitchen, 40–1), and this remains a great difficulty in Manning's case.

The problem may ultimately be resolved through the construction of a complete dendrochronological sequence back from historical times. For the present, I have decided to accept the position adopted in Warren and Hankey, which is to make use of radiocarbon dates for the third millennium and earlier, where they are available, and to use absolute dates linked to the 'low' chronology for the second millennium; but I also show in Fig. 1.3 the alternative chronology proposed by Manning for the relevant phases. Since Warren and Hankey give extended treatment to the material, only a broad outline will be presented here, and Fig. 1.3 is designed to give a general impression.

For the beginning of the BA there is no evidence apart from that of radiocarbon dates (Warren and Hankey, 120–1). The general tendency of these is to suggest that the latest Neolithic material falls in the earlier fourth millennium and the local BA sequences could begin well before 3000 BC. This view is supported by consideration of the dates from Myrtos in particular, which suggest a beginning for EM IIB before 2500 (Whitelaw 1986). Such a dating gains general support from synchronisms with the Near East, especially Egypt (Warren and Hankey, 125–7), and radiocarbon dates from 'Lerna III' contexts give

Fig. 1.3 Suggested outline of absolute chronology. The lay-out is formal, and not intended to represent spaces of time accurately; for closer assessments see the text. The spacing of dividing dashes, or absence of them, indicates the reliability of the evidence for the placing of subdivisions.

Notes. 1. The earliest phases may well begin before 3300 BC.

2. LC II–III are shown after Barber 1987, fig. 22.

Date B.C.	Crete	Cyclades	Mainland	Manning's sequence for later BA (1988: 56)
3300				
3200				
3100	EM I	'Pelos'	'Talioti' & 'Eutresis'	
3000				
2900	– – – – – –	'Kampos'	– – – – – –	
2800	EM IIA	'Syros'	'Lerna III'	
2700				
2600				
	– – – – – –			
2500				
		– – – – – –	– – – – – –	
2400	EM IIB	'Kastri'	'Lefkandi I'	
2300	– – – – – –	– – – – – –	– – – – – –	
2200		(gap?)	'Lerna IV' etc.	
2100	EM III/ MM IA		– – – – – –	
			MH (early)	
2000		'Phylakopi I'		
1900	– – – – – –		MH (mature)	
1800	MM IB/IIA, MM IIB/IIIA	MC (early)		MM III/MH III
1700	– – – – – –			LM IA/LH I
	MM IIIB	MC (late)	MH (late)	
1600	– – – – – –	– – – – – –		LM IB/LH IIA
			– – – – – –	LM II/LH IIB
1500	LM IA, IB	LC I (LC II)	LH I, IIA	LM/LH IIIA1
	– – – – – –	– – – – – –	– – – – – –	
1400	LM II,IIIA1		LH IIB, IIIA1	LM/LH IIIA2 LM/LH IIIB
	– – – – – –		– – – – – –	
1300	LM IIIA2, LM IIIB	(LC III early)	LH IIIA2, IIIB1, IIIB2	
1200	– – – – – –	(LC III middle)	– – – – – –	
	LM IIIC		LH IIIC	
1100		(LC III late & final)		
	– – – – – –		– – – – – –	
1000	Subminoan		Submycenaean	

generalised support for transferring this kind of dating to the Helladic and Cycladic sequences. Thus the middle stages of the EBA can be spread over the greater part of the third millennium. But there is less certainty about when they end, although the sequence of radiocarbon dates from Lerna itself, going through to early MH, suits placing Lerna IV in the last centuries of the third millennium.

The problem over the definition of MM phases affects all arguments relating to the chronology of the MBA, particularly since few useful radiocarbon dates are available after the beginning of the period and many of the relevant items are from 'MM IA' contexts, which may actually be later. Rather more helpful is the discovery of pottery of clearly First Palace Period styles in a series of contexts in Egypt and at Beirut whose date range runs from a fairly early stage in the Twelfth Dynasty into the period of the Thirteenth Dynasty (Warren and Hankey, 134–5). This provides general support for dating this period to run from the early or middle nineteenth to the earlier seventeenth century. Radiocarbon dates from Phaistos and Ayia Irini (Warren and Hankey, 128) fit within this range. But despite demonstrable links between the Tôd Treasure and First Palace Period pottery (Warren and Hankey, 131–4), the equally clear links between two Tôd kantharoi and one of transitional MH/LH date from Peristeria, with other considerations (most recently Laffineur 1988), make it impossible to accept that the material can be associated exclusively with the reign of Amenemhet II (1917–1882 or 1875–40, Kitchen), so that this link remains chronologically unreliable.

If MM IIIA is to be considered the final phase of the First Palace Period, as argued by MacGillivray (1986), the finding of a stone lid bearing the cartouche of the pharaoh Khyan in a context of this date would be of some significance. On the most recent dating for Khyan (1648–30 or 1637–19 in Kitchen; Warren and Hankey, 136) this would bring the end date of the First Palace Period down towards 1600, and so conflict completely with the Betancourt–Manning chronology. But it must be admitted that the contextual material has never been fully published and analysed, and it may be best to suspend judgement on this piece of evidence.

In comparison with the earlier periods the LBA is relatively straightforward, although its beginning cannot be very closely fixed. That LM IA began before the Eighteenth Dynasty of Egypt (1550 or 1539, Kitchen) is suggested in particular by the presence of apparently MB II Syro-Palestinian stone vessels at Akrotiri, although these could have survived for some time; certainly, a date in the first half of the sixteenth century might seem to follow. A series of links between the time of Hatshepsut and Tuthmosis III (1479–25, Kitchen) and the LM IB, LH IIA, and LH IIB phases (Warren and Hankey, 141–6), though not unassailable, is cumulatively impressive, and such a connection would fit well with the later synchronisms between LM IIIA1, LH IIIA1, and the reign of Amenophis III (1390–52, Kitchen), and late LH IIIA2 and the reign of

Akhenaten (1352–36, Kitchen). These phases, then, are likely to have covered much of the fourteenth century, and the transition to LH IIIB may have occurred within Akhenaten's reign or not much later (Warren and Hankey, 146–54), so that LH IIIB had begun by 1330 or soon afterwards. LH IIIB also has considerable associations with the reign of Ramesses II (1279–13, Kitchen), but may extend to the end of the Nineteenth Dynasty (1186, Kitchen). Radiocarbon dates from the destruction levels of Mycenae and Pylos could certainly fit a time around or slightly after 1200.

Thereafter, fixed points are almost impossible to identify; the best is the discovery of pottery classified as LH IIIC Middle at Beth Shan in contexts that may have a link with the reign of Ramesses VI (1143–36, Kitchen) (Warren and Hankey, 164–5). Many indications, including cross-connections between the Cypriot and Aegean sequences, suggest that the Postpalatial Period was of considerable length; though there is still considerable disagreement, LH IIIC is now generally taken to end well after 1100, perhaps even after 1050.

Appendix: the last palace at Knossos

The date, relative to the LB sequence, of the destruction of the last palace of Knossos is one of the most important unresolved questions in Aegean prehistory. Whole books have been written on the topic, and further data which have or may have a bearing on it are still being uncovered. Essentially, the dispute is between those who favour what has become a standard view following Popham's work (1970), placing the destruction early in LM IIIA2, equivalent to an absolute date somewhere in the second quarter of the fourteenth century, and those who favour a date within or at the end of LM IIIB, so probably somewhere between the middle and end of the thirteenth century (Hallager 1977; Niemeier 1982). There is, however, a middle view which would place the destruction late in or at the end of LM IIIA2, thus quite late in the fourteenth century (cf. Hood 1971: 149–50), and for a variety of reasons this is beginning to look like a reasonable compromise.

I do not believe that the problem can ever be conclusively answered through re-examination of what has been reported of the stratigraphy and contents of the Knossos palace itself; too much remains a matter for speculation, such as the attribution of the masses of plainer pottery discarded in the original excavations. Rather, I feel that the most important question is, which period seems more likely as the time of the major functioning palace demonstrated by the contents of the Linear B texts, which indicate that it was the administrative centre of a state with interests in much of Crete?

To summarise very briefly, there is considerable evidence for the continuing wealth and importance of Knossos in the earlier part of the Third Palace Period, covering the LM II and IIIA phases. This is a time of elaborate tombs and rich burials, especially in the neighbourhood of Knossos, of the renewal of many frescoes in the Knossos palace, of strong Knossian influence on pottery style throughout Crete, and of continuing links of importance with the Near East. In LM IIIB a wholly different picture is symbolised by the complete disappearance of Knossian influence on Cretan pottery (cf. Watrous 1984b); in fact, Crete appears to have broken up into several distinct if related pottery-producing regions, of which Khania appears the most important. Knossos itself seems an impoverished settlement, without evidence of important buildings, tombs or foreign contacts to compare with other surviving Cretan sites, particularly Khania, let alone with the major Mycenaean sites.

Simply on the basis of this comparison, I find it impossible to believe that LM IIIB was the period represented by the Linear B texts; if it was, some special explanations of the problems outlined above are surely required. Because of important finds dating as late as LM IIIA2 at sites within the suggested territory of Knossos such as Arkhanes, Ayia Triada and Kommos, I believe that the palace may have survived later into LM IIIA2 than suggested by Popham, and that at least some of the 'Reoccupation' material in the Knossos palace therefore belongs to this final phase, which would explain some reported associations of 'late' pottery with Linear B tablets. But this can only be a provisional position; the demonstration of clear links between the Linear B texts of Khania and Knossos would inevitably argue for dating the last palace at Knossos to LM IIIB.

Bibliography

As indicated above, Warren and Hankey 1989 covers the whole topic in detail; pp. 137–48 discuss the evidence for the earlier LB phases' absolute chronology, attempting to answer the arguments of Betancourt and Manning for a longer chronology, cf. also 214–5 and Warren 1991a: 34–6.

CHAPTER 2

THE NATURAL ENVIRONMENT AND RESOURCES

The climate, landscape and natural resources of Greece must always receive attention in any discussion of its history, for they have an important bearing on the direction in which societies can develop. In particular, climate, soils and water supply determine which farming practices are most likely to succeed. These are unlikely to have been the only factors that influenced development; there may always have been social reasons why some resource was not fully exploited or land was relatively wastefully employed, for if one thing is clear from the mass of ethnographic data it is that human groups do not organise their lives solely with regard to cost–benefit ratios. But neither are they usually wilfully stupid in matters of their subsistence, and it is reasonable to expect that the communities of Greece will have made a conscious effort to suit their practices to the land and climate.

The Greek landscape is dominated by the mountains and the sea (Fig. 2.1). The mountains ensure that overland travel, whether within the mainland and islands or to the rest of the Balkans, is often arduous, at worst too difficult to be normally contemplated, and they are so extensive that on average less than a third of the land-surface is now classified as arable, though much more can be used for other purposes, especially pasture. The percentage of 'natural' arable may originally have been 50% or more in favoured areas, but this would include marginal, often remote land as well as what has now been affected by erosion. The most notable difference in terrain is that in the northern mainland there are extensive plains; elsewhere, ranges of mountains and lower hills dissect the country into innumerable small patches of coastal or upland plain and valley, on both the mainland and the islands. The prominence of the mountains reflects the Aegean's position in the zone between two great plates of the earth's crust, the Eurasiatic and African, whose constant confrontation has been, and is still, responsible for a great deal of tectonic activity, which mostly takes the form of earthquakes but also includes volcanic eruptions in an arc across the south Aegean, especially on Thera. This activity has resulted in a quite complex distribution of different types of rock, although limestones and related rocks of varying ages are dominant except in the volcanic areas, where a range of igneous rocks is to be found.

While tectonic activity was in remote geological time responsible for the subsidence that formed the Aegean sea, it is only likely to have had local effects in recent times; the submergence of ancient remains is probably more often due

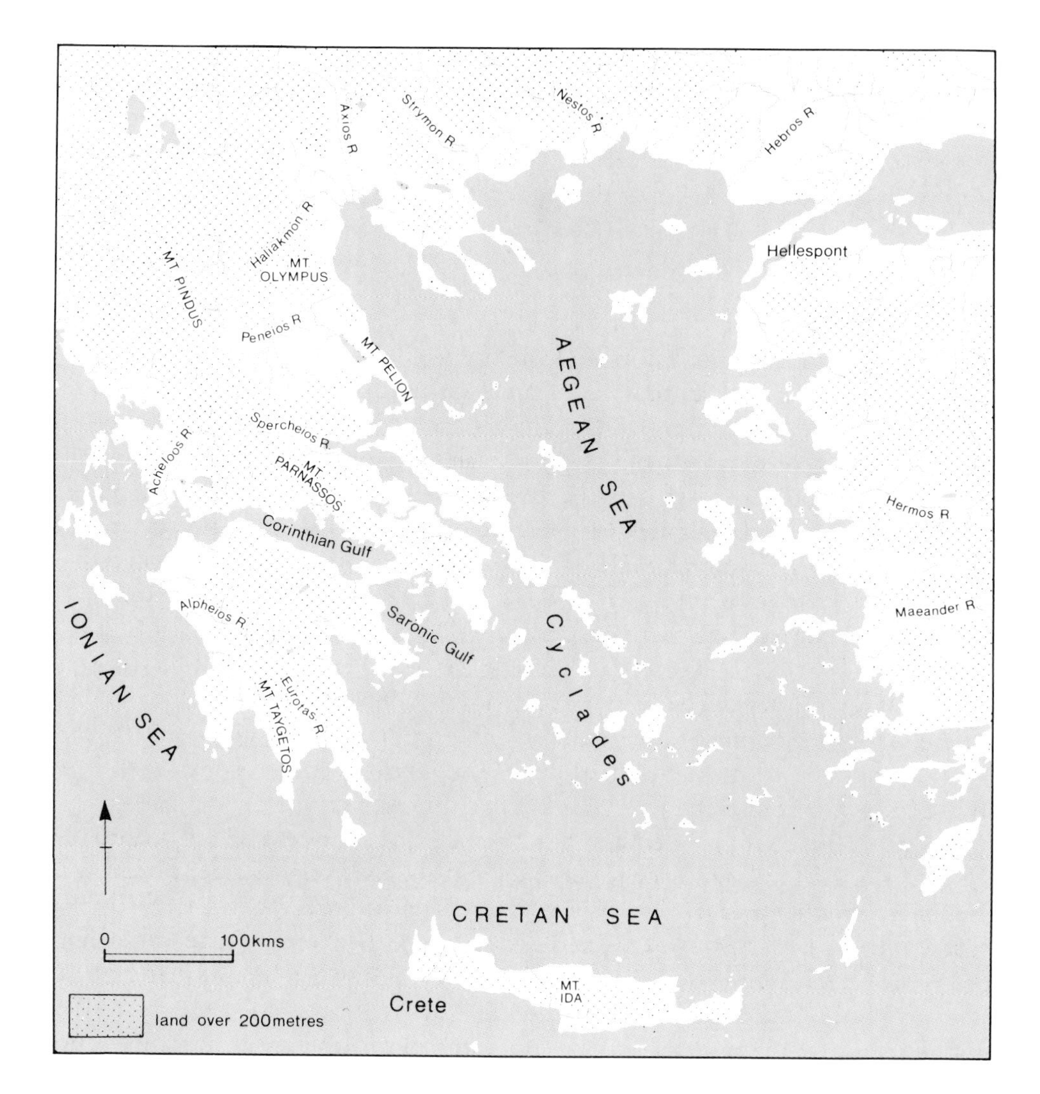

Fig. 2.1 Physical map of the Aegean.

to a continual rise in sea level which has been going on since the end of the last Ice Age, when many of the present islands were joined to the mainland or to each other. Nowhere in the southern mainland is now more than 60 km from the sea, which makes great inroads into the land-mass, virtually cutting it in two at the Isthmus of Corinth. But this ensures that the climate is milder than would otherwise be the case, and the sea in general provides an easier means of travel than the land in the right season, though storms dangerous to small boats can arise at almost any time. Chains of islands make it possible, when the wind is in the right quarter, to cross from the mainland either directly to Anatolia or south through the Aegean to Crete and then up to Rhodes and along the south

Anatolian coast to Cyprus and the Near East; either way, land need not be lost sight of, except when travelling from Melos or Thera to Crete, and innumerable bays and inlets provide sheltered spots where boats can be beached for the night, though good harbours are rare. Since currents run naturally westwards along the south Anatolian coast, it is easier for boats to come from the east than to go there, but other currents can carry them directly south-east from Crete to Egypt and also up the west coast of the mainland to Italy.

The Greek climate does not seem to have varied greatly since the end of the Ice Age, although a period of unusually high rainfall may have immediately succeeded it; if anything, conditions for most of prehistory may have been slightly warmer and drier than at present (against claims of a drastic shift in rainfall patterns near the end of the Bronze Age see Sandars 1978: 20, with references). The semi-arid Mediterranean climate is prevalent, characterised by long, hot, dry summers, and cool, largely frost-free winters when most of the rain falls, but the northernmost parts of the mainland have a more continental climate, with greater extremes of heat and cold and more rain; the western side of Greece also receives more rain than most of the mainland, and the islands receive least of all. The effect of these variations is not conspicuously great – for example, the olive may be grown in most parts to an altitude of 700 m – but in combination with local geology they will produce a variety of terrains, which in turn should support a variety of types of natural vegetation. The regions of classic Mediterranean climate certainly seem to have offered the environment most favourable to Bronze Age development.

Recent studies are laying emphasis on the significance of local conditions and the evidence for local sequences of erosion and alluviation, which runs counter to the general models that used to be proposed. Thus, it no longer seems likely that the woodland zonation shown in Renfrew 1972, fig. 15.1 covered the entire Greek landscape after the Ice Age, or that there were only two universal phases of erosion which produced the 'Older Fill' and 'Younger Fill' (as proposed in Bintliff 1977, following Vita-Finzi). The topic of erosion has occasioned much controversy, but increasingly it is being argued that neither human activity nor natural forces like rainfall have had such major deleterious effects on the environment as used to be suggested. Over-intensive use and/or poor management of hill land certainly might create conditions for dramatic episodes of erosion, which unusually severe storms or other natural causes like earthquakes could precipitate, and such episodes are attested. But when population contracted and outlying areas were abandoned the vegetation was given a chance to regenerate, and the soil to stabilise again, and new deposits of fertile land developed, so that damage was not irreversibly cumulative (cf. especially van Andel *et al.* 1986 on the southern Argolid sequence).

The original soils of Greece were created by weathering of the largely limestone rocks. The reddish 'Older Fill' soils represent widespread and massive erosion during the last Ice Age; they will have been reasonably fertile originally but often contained a considerable admixture of rocks. Far better are the light 'rendsina' deposits, interpreted as the relics of brown woodland soils, which seem to have been recognised as most fertile by early farmers and are widespread on flat terraces and gentle slopes in important areas of prehistoric settlement like Crete and the Peloponnese. But the best modern soils are the product of the 'Younger Fill' alluviation, which seems to be a feature of Roman and mediaeval times. Although there are instances of earlier erosion, even in the later EBA in the Argolid, Bintliff's contention (1977, Ch. 2), that the 'Younger Fill' must be discounted as a feature of the prehistoric landscape seems to hold good. Attempts to estimate carrying capacity or reconstruct patterns of land use on the basis of recent evidence are therefore likely to be inherently flawed.

Bintliff has pointed out (1977: 100–4) that the 'Older Fill' soils are likely to lose nutrients in a semi-arid climate and will become progressively less productive; so too will the more fertile soils if intensively worked over long periods. Thus, even if erosion was not produced by original agricultural practices, it could have resulted from attempts to intensify use that were not combined with practices like terracing. Erosion would have been most severe on steep slopes; but it has been estimated that all the soil eroded from the southern Argolid slopes could not, when in place, have produced a depth sufficient to support dense woodland (Van Andel and Runnels 1987: 152–3). The original vegetation, as in many other parts of Greece, may have been a patchwork of steppe, grassland with some bushes and trees, and woods in the better-watered areas, with scrub ('gariga') on the barer hills (cf. Payne 1985: 225, arguing from the Mesolithic fauna from the Franchthi cave; and Rackham 1982: 188, 193; 1983: 346). Dense woodland may only have been found in the areas of higher rainfall in northern and western Greece.

Removal of this original 'wildwood' to clear land for agriculture and provide building timber, fuel, etc., would have given scope for the macchia or maquis type of vegetation to develop, which as argued by Rackham (1983: 347) would have ultimately contained a much more varied and, for human purposes, useful range of plants. It is characterised by evergreen species which can resist the effects of browsing by animals more easily than most of the original species, providing that grazing is not too intensive, and can in fact, if properly managed, provide a self-replenishing source of fuel and fodder (Rapp and Aschenbrenner 1978: 56–7). But it may not have been as water-retentive as the original woodland, and in this respect woodland clearance may have had deleterious effects. There are many examples of ancient wells that have dried up, and while sometimes this may be due to tectonic activity it may often testify to a lowering of the original watertable. However, this does not seem to have been a major factor in the prehistoric period, and it is unlikely that water would have been required in truly large quantities except at the biggest settlements, since irrigation is not thought to have been widely practised.

The evidence from carbonised wood and pollen samples that relates to the prehistoric vegetation is scanty and its interpretation has been disputed. But it seems that originally deciduous trees may have been far more widespread, as indicated by the largely pre-Neolithic sample from Ayia Galini in south Crete, which has been too arid to support them in more recent times (Rackham 1982: 193–4). Evidence of various sorts from the mainland, including samples from Lerna, Tiryns and Nichoria (Nordquist 1987: 20; Shay and Shay in Rapp and Aschenbrenner 1978: 53–4), and the identifiable types of wood named in the Pylos Linear B texts (Ventris and Chadwick 1973: 135), suggest that many deciduous trees were still available there in the BA, including ash, boxwood, buckthorn, elm, horse-chestnut, hornbeam, maple, oak, poplar, willow and perhaps yew. But other evidence suggests that the types of tree characteristic of the modern Mediterranean environment were already becoming dominant in some parts: evergreen varieties of oak, olive, pine, and the bushy varieties common in maquis are often reported, and cypress and fir are particularly identifiable in Crete (Shaw 1971: 135–6), where they remained common until relatively recently. The representations of landscapes in frescoes, especially those of Akrotiri on Thera, similarly have a Mediterranean look: trees are rarely realistically depicted, but pine and fig can be identified at Akrotiri, cypress and olive in Minoan representations, and palms, which still survive rarely in south Crete, are found in both sources.

Apart from fig, olive and vine, several other types of fruit- or nut-producing tree or bush are native to Greece, including the almond, cherry, pear, pistachio, walnut and wild strawberry (a common maquis plant), while Lerna has evidence of either plum or sorb apple. These could have supplied tasty supplementary foods to vary the diet, although it is unlikely that any were common in the early woodland. The main value of most trees will have been in providing wood and green shoots that would be useful as fodder; but it should not be forgotten that oak acorns could be eaten by humans as well as pigs (cf. the Arcadians' epithet 'acorn-eating', Herodotus I.66), and that pine resin could be a valuable resource. Smaller food plants could grow in open areas: wild barley, oats, lentils, vetches and coriander are all attested from pre-Neolithic Franchthi deposits, and flax, whose seeds contain oil and whose fibres are the raw material for linen, from Neolithic Servia. But the characteristic herbs and edible plants of later Greece are mostly hard to identify and will only have become common with the spread of maquis vegetation. One might well expect that wild garlic and onions, the variety of plants now generically known as *khorta*, and herbs like basil, mint, oregano, rosemary, sage and thyme were used once they became available; the saffron crocus, shown in some famous frescoes, is also a native plant. Some of these appear in the Linear B texts in connection with making perfumed oil; others have medicinal qualities, real or supposed, or may be used for dyeing. Such properties need not all have been discovered in prehistoric times, but it is still likely that wild plants were collected on a greater scale than the evidence can indicate (cf. Nordquist 1987: 30–1).

The richest evidence for fauna comes from mainland sites. In this field the evidence from bones is likely to give the most reliable picture, since depictions can conflate features of different animals and focus on uncommon types like the lion; even so, some bones may have reached their findspot inside traded skins. The animals most frequently hunted for food are red deer, wild boar and hare; also attested are wild cattle, roe deer, fallow deer (perhaps not native, cf. Halstead 1987a: 95), rabbit and ibex/agrimi. As well as their meat, these could provide hides and skins, and domesticated cattle and pigs could be bred from local wild stock; red-deer antlers could be used as digging sticks, agrimi horns in bow-making (Wachsmann 1987, Ch. VI), and horn cores generally as pressure-flaking tools in manufacturing stone blades (Blitzer 1991: 37). The mainland has also produced evidence of a range of mammals that are now barely found, if at all; probably none were ever very common, except the fox, but if not hunted simply to control predation they might have been sought for their skins and sometimes have been eaten. Apart from the fox, the badger, bear, beaver (only in northern Greece), beech marten, lion (certain at LH Tiryns, Von den Driesch and Boessneck 1990: 110–11), lynx, otter, weasel, wild cat and wolf are found. Many kinds of bird, desirable for their plumage if not meat, have been attested in different samples, including many types of water bird and predator, also pigeons and rock partridges. The small amphibians, reptiles and rodents that are still common and are attested in the richer samples could have been eaten, particularly the tortoise, as also forms of land snail.

The sea could also have been a significant source of food. Many of the present range of fish have been identified, especially the migratory tunny, and depictions are common in Minoan art, but fish bones are not found in great quantity after the Neolithic period (this may simply reflect the fact that few bone samples have been recovered by wet-sieving, the most reliable method, but see Payne 1985: 223). The commonest marine creatures represented in site-material are in fact edible molluscs, including the dye-producing murex and related types; but these are generally so few, compared with the enormous numbers needed to produce much purple dye, that it is hard to accept them as evidence for a significant purple industry, though they might well have been used to produce small quantities (cf. Barber 1991: 228–9).

As regards raw materials, Greece is not well supplied except for workable clays and stones. Some of the most valued or useful materials have few natural sources: in the Aegean, obsidian comes only from Melos and Giali in the Dodecanese, emery from Naxos and Samos (Warren 1969: 160), rock crystal from Crete, the best white marble from Paros, Naxos and Attica. Metal sources are also sparsely distributed, though recent research is improving our knowledge: Laurion in Attica is now known to be a source of copper as well as silver-bearing lead, and several of the Cycladic islands have one or both, notably Siphnos (silver/lead) and Kythnos (copper). Some copper sources in Crete could have been exploited with BA technology, and reports of copper, silver and even gold in Laconia are being taken seriously, though details are still scanty. It is possible that these metals were also found in other small sources that have been worked out, but tin must always have been imported, and it seems out of the question that the Aegean could have been self-sufficient in copper or gold by the LBA. Some ores like malachite and azurite provide colouring materials, which can also be found as earths.

Overall, Greece can never have been a remarkably well-endowed or fertile country. Its climate makes drought a constant threat, an untimely rain or frost can ruin a crop, and poor to bad years are frequent. Many sources, ancient and modern, emphasise its relative poverty and the frugality required. Yet to suggest that its communities were permanently living on the edge of famine (as is the tendency of, for example, Sandars 1978, Ch. 1) is surely going too far. The archaeological record suggests long periods of relative stability and even modest growth in prehistory, as history does later, which could hardly have been sustained under such conditions. The citation in this connection of data from later mediaeval times does not allow for the great increase in the human and animal populations by that time and the effects of many more centuries' exploitation of the land, as well as of warfare on a scale dwarfing anything that can be imagined for the BA. It seems more reasonable to suppose, with Warren (1989: 35), that in the more fertile parts of Greece a relatively low population could, with careful management, not only survive but prosper in moderation. Whether the limits were exceeded at any time in the BA must be a topic for later discussion.

Bibliography

General discussions relating to the Aegean BA normally include comment on the geography, climate and vegetation (most recently, Faugères in Treuil *et al.* 1989, Introduction, A); for much detailed discussion, see Bintliff 1977, Chs 1–4, and for stimulating comments Sandars 1978, Ch. 1. See also, on the tectonic background, Shelford 1982: 74–6; on rising sea level since the end of the Ice Age, Van Andel and Shackleton 1982; on erosion and alluviation, Davidson and Tasker 1982: 92–3; and on their relationship to the vegetation cover and its original nature Rackham 1982, 1983 (especially 339–47; primarily relating to Boeotia).

Native Aegean flora and fauna are much discussed in Morgan 1988, Chs 2–3; see also on flora, Renfrew, J.M. 1973; on fauna, Payne 1985 and Halstead 1987a: 74–5; and on marine creatures, Gill 1985.

See Stos-Gale and Gale 1984 for the most up-to-date comments on Aegean metal sources; Gale and Stos-Gale 1986: 96 for more detail on potential Cretan copper sources; Jones 1986, Ch. 3, for clays; and Warren 1969, Ch. III on the remarkable range of stones available in Crete, with some comment on other parts of the Aegean.

CHAPTER 3

THE FIRST HUMAN POPULATIONS

Hunter-gatherers

Information about the earliest stages of human occupation in Greece is still scanty, although increasing with new excavations and surveys. Finds are richest in northern Greece, which has produced the only certain Lower Palaeolithic remains, dating before 200,000 BP (notably the skull from a cave at Petralona in Chalcidice, Gamble 1986: 159–60), and many Middle Palaeolithic finds (c. 55,000–30,000 BP), especially in Thessaly (cf. Runnels in French 1990: 50–1) and Epirus. Middle Palaeolithic finds also occur in the northern Peloponnese, and the distribution of Upper Palaeolithic finds is very wide, extending to islands adjacent to the mainland which would have been joined to it at the time of lowest sea level during the last Ice Age, around 18,000 BP; but there is still no agreed evidence from the Cyclades, Dodecanese or Crete. The Franchthi cave in the south Argolid is particularly remarkable for its series of occupation phases, ranging from the Upper Palaeolithic to the end of the Neolithic (Jacobsen 1981), and is so far unique for the information it provides on the millennia between the end of the Ice Age and the spread of the farming economy.

The sites identified include caves, rock shelters and open sites by lakes and rivers. These would have been occupied temporarily by groups moving around a territory to make the best use of its food resources. Hunting and trapping would have provided the basic diet, since the Ice Age climate would not favour food-producing plants and trees, although some plant foods would be available in the summer. Probably such groups would have been extremely small: on modern analogies, a size of about 25 would have been average (Gamble 1986: 50), but the users of the Klithi rock shelter in Epirus might have numbered no more than 15, and all eastern Epirus might have had a population of only 50 (Bailey 1986: 34–5). But these would have had extensive networks of contacts; it has been estimated that a total contact population of 200–400 would be required to give every member of a group an optimum chance of finding a marriage partner (cf. Gamble 1986: 50–1), and forming relationships with other groups by intermarriage would help to provide some security against local disaster (cf. Gamble 1986: 54–6, 58). Little more can be said, except that the limited range of stone tools shows parallels with neighbouring parts of Europe.

The warming of the climate and recession of the ice brought considerable changes, as the low-lying plains which extended far beyond the modern coastlines of the Mediterranean became submerged. Franchthi was reoccupied around the twelfth millennium and the remains suggest activity at most seasons. A wide range of food sources was being exploited, including fish, land and sea molluscs, and wild cereals, pulses and nuts, as well as deer and other game, which were probably becoming scarcer; this has more than technical interest, for it undercuts the still popular assumption that hunting was virtually the only source of food before the introduction of farming. Fish might have been caught close to the shore, but other evidence suggests that there was sea-going of a sort, for obsidian identified as coming from Melos has been found in the cave. Although this early boating might have involved no more than paddling a canoe along the coast and across straits between islands larger than the modern ones (cf. Broodbank and Strasser 1991, fig. 1), it required the development of new skills and adventurousness of a kind that might have attracted even more prestige than hunting large and potentially dangerous animals.

The next major stage, running from the late eighth through the seventh millennium, saw further changes, most notably a considerable increase in fishing. There is also an increase in the evidence for the exploitation of wild plants, barley, oats and pulses; it is even possible that some had been virtually domesticated. This is the first evidence from Greece that can be compared with the long phase in the Near East in which the farming economy was developed, which starts as early as 9000 BC or before. But it is not enough to support any theory of the purely local development of farming techniques, and although Jacobsen suggests caution in the use of hypotheses of migration and diffusion to explain the appearance of the farming economy, the arguments for these remain strong.

The introduction of farming

The earliest farming settlements identified so far in Greece are at Knossos and in Thessaly, dated by C14 around the beginning of the seventh millennium. They were on previously unoccupied sites, in positions suggesting that they were founded by experienced farmers who could recognise the soils with best potential (Jarman *et al.* 1982: 146–50). Moreover, of the dominant species in their economy, wheat, barley, sheep and goats, only barley had been previously exploited, at Franchthi, and sheep and goats derive from a wild ancestor thought not to be native to the Aegean. There are also changes in the typology of chipped stone tools (Perlès 1988: 484–6), and new crafts were introduced. The predominance of sheep, a general feature of early farming settlements in southern Europe, is especially noteworthy, since these would not be best suited to a terrain that would have had considerable woodland, especially in northern Greece; it may be considered one sign of the artificial nature of the environment that was being created (Perlès 1992).

All these features would be appropriate to new colonists; but it is not easy to identify their source, which might well have differed as between Thessaly and

Crete, for there are noticeable differences in material culture. Western Anatolia seems a reasonable possibility: comparably early sites have yet to be identified there, but the presence of bread wheat at Knossos, a hybrid quite possibly developed in Anatolia (Renfrew, J.M. 1973: 202–3), suggests a link, and certain types of artefact, with the common use of mud-brick for building, suggest general Near Eastern connections. But the Aegean sites have other features which are hard to parallel in the Near East, and certainly the settlement of Knossos must have required careful planning and considerable familiarity with sailing distances and possible landfalls in the Aegean (Broodbank and Strasser 1991).

The foundation of Knossos was a unique expansion of human society into the Aegean, and in many respects it remains strongly individual (Broodbank 1992). But the discovery of obsidian here, as at the Thessalian sites, suggests their participation in a network of sea-borne contacts through which this was disseminated. Indeed, Perlès has argued powerfully, on the grounds that the stones used in the early communities are very largely exotic and artefacts were often evidently introduced ready-worked, that they were not acquired by direct procurement but by exchange with specialists, particularly a sea-faring group that she argues to have worked and disseminated obsidian for a long time (1990). On these grounds, the argument that these early settlements were involved in 'trade' seems very strong, though it is still implausible that this could have been the prime reason for establishing them (Van Andel and Runnels 1988: 236–8), and many exchanges may still have occurred in the context of relationships established through exchange of marriage partners, as already hypothesised for the Palaeolithic.

Although the earliest farming settlements on the mainland may well have been founded by colonists from Anatolia, it is easiest to interpret their spread as the result of local expansion and the acculturation of the previous population. The arguments for continual new influxes of population characteristic of Weinberg 1970 are based mainly on supposed links in pottery style with very distant cultures, such as the Halafian of Syria–Mesopotamia, and seem inherently unconvincing, since they imply movement over great distances into already occupied territory, at a time when modes of transport were few and primitive. Natural disasters may have prompted the abandonment of some sites and movement to other regions, but at first there was plenty of room and surely no need to attempt to take over land occupied by others. The network of inter-settlement contacts which has been postulated, which would have been continually expanding with the foundation of new settlements, is the most plausible medium for the transmission of new skills and technological developments, new types of artefact, even social and religious ideas.

The Neolithic period lasted from the seventh millennium to the fourth in the Aegean, but does not require extensive coverage in a book intended to concentrate on the BA. Yet some consideration must be given to it, for it saw the establishment of a way of life, based on the farming economy, which was to endure into and beyond the BA, and many of the characteristic features of this way of life continued with little essential change. To discuss them briefly is to introduce topics that will continue to be relevant, the patterns of settlement, resource exploitation and social organisation. The perceptible changes in material culture take place within a framework that only altered very slowly. For a long time, the northern mainland was the most advanced region of the Aegean, often in contact with the rich cultures of the northern Balkans and showing signs of development beyond the smaller and sparser settlements further south (Fig. 3.1). Indeed, the earliest settlement in the Cyclades may not have been founded much before 5000 BC, and the spread of settlements here and in Crete is essentially a feature of a later period still. The relatively scattered nature of settlements encouraged the development of regional cultures, despite the potential for

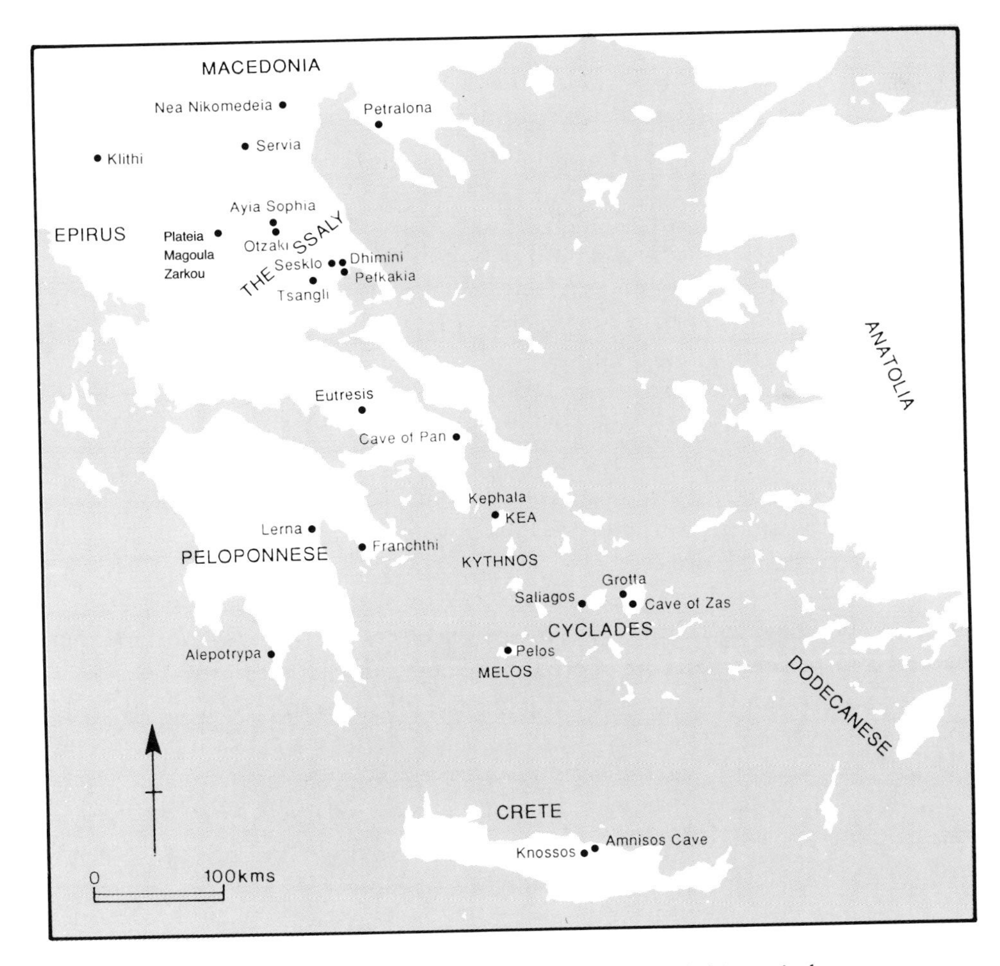

Fig. 3.1 Important sites of the Palaeolithic to Neolithic periods.

pan-Aegean links provided by the network of contacts already mentioned, but the differences are unlikely to have extended to the basic way of life.

Settlements

The majority of Neolithic sites were in open positions, often on ridges or knolls, situated by a lake, a river or the sea. Some caves were used, but these are most evident in later stages, when they may have had a special function. Apart from caves and the temporary stone-working sites represented by concentrations of tools and wastage, the only identifiable type of site is the farming village. These were small, covering at most a few hectares, and would have ranged from a few households to some hundreds in population (an average of one hundred per ha is often suggested, but may be too high). Some were relatively short-lived, but most were clearly intended to be permanent, being occupied without apparent break for many centuries.

The intention of permanence is evident from the buildings, which are generally substantial, several metres to a side, and built of durable materials. Wood seems to have been specially favoured at northern sites like Servia, where it provided a framework for walls of mud-coated brush or reeds as well as for the roof, and planks for the floor, but the building with walls of mud in layers (pisé) or sun-dried bricks, on a low stone foundation, was to become standard. Wood was still used for some structural features in such buildings, but floors were of stamped earth or sand; roofs, which might be pitched or flat, were of thatch or brush, coated with mud plaster to make them waterproof, and a similar coating would be applied to the walls. Such buildings can be found free-standing or built onto one another in the style common in the Near East; normally they seem to have been single-storeyed, but cellars have been identified at Servia, and one type of house with inner buttresses may have had a gallery and been entered, with the help of a ladder, via the roof, as again at some Near Eastern sites (Fig. 3.2: 1). Their size and plan suggest that such houses were used by nuclear families rather than more extensive groupings.

The mud-brick village has endured to the present day in the Near East, and was typical of farming cultures over a very wide area. It has the characteristic that the surface is constantly rising, because of the accumulation of mud washed off buildings by winter rain, general settlement rubbish and the remains of levelled or abandoned buildings; hence, artificial mounds quickly develop, reaching a height of many metres in some famous cases. The floors of the buildings were constantly being relaid, thus eventually narrowing the space between floor and roof, and for this and other reasons houses must have been rebuilt every generation or so, either on the levelled remains of their predecessors or on another site, while the old building was left to crumble, as sometimes in the Near East today. Features such as cooking installations and storage pits seem originally to have been outside, but changes involving moving them into an enclosed yard or inside the house can be perceived; these could reflect social developments weakening the communal spirit and pressure to share food argued to have existed originally (Halstead 1989: 73–7). The published evidence relating to such features is still rather limited, however, and the significance of the variation between sites where houses seem randomly distributed and those where they are tightly packed and replaced one another on the same plots is not clear.

Surrounding a site with ditches or sometimes stone walls, as at Sesklo and Dhimini, also seems to be generally a late feature, but its interpretation in defensive terms is questionable. At Dhimini, the many circuit walls may reflect settlement divisions, and Hourmouziadis considers the structures to fall into groupings representing domestic complexes (1979; cf. Halstead 1981b; 1989: 76), whereas Halstead interprets an arrangement of central court and 'megaron' house at Dhimini, Sesklo and other Thessalian sites as *prima facie* evidence for the development of hierarchy (Halstead 1989: 75). Such central buildings might equally (or also) have served as ritual centres; but whatever their function, they seem to represent a purely Thessalian development.

The economy

The plant remains from settlement strata indicate that from the beginning forms of wheat, barley and pulses, including lentils, peas and vetch, were grown. The evidence once taken to suggest that all were sown together, to ensure some return whatever the climatic conditions, is now thought open to other interpretations, but the decision to grow a variety of crops almost certainly reflects a strategy designed to spread the risks of crop failure and perhaps to produce a sequence of harvests so that no crop need be stored for too long. Concern with storage may explain the continuing popularity of the more primitive forms of wheat, einkorn and emmer, over the bread wheats, because the former can be stored in spikelet form that is more resistant to disease and insect infestation, although it is harder to process; they are also less demanding in soil and water requirements. The pulses require more work than cereals, but have a characteristic likely to have been noticed, that of renewing nutrients in the soil. Improvements over the Neolithic period are difficult to identify, but six-row barley replaced two-row, a clear gain since the requirements were identical but the yield far higher, and beans and chickpeas seem to have been introduced from the Near East.

The livestock pattern is dominated by sheep and goats; cattle and pigs are always represented, but are generally rarer. Halstead has suggested an interesting model whereby herding on a small scale, primarily for meat products, could be a significant element of the farming system (1981a; 1989: 70–1). This would involve an intensive 'garden' style cultivation of small fields, in which cereals and pulses were grown in rotation, or alternating with fallow periods, and the livestock, especially sheep, were pastured on the stubble and fallow areas to manure the fields. Such a system is argued to maintain the productivity of the fields for a very long time, contributing to the stability of the early settlements. Certainly, such practices would suit the small scale of the settlements and the labour output that they could have sustained.

Suggestions that the sheep were transferred to upland pastures in the summer, on the transhumance system, not only presuppose the existence of such pastures, which more probably were created in historical times (Halstead 1987b: 79–80; Cherry 1988: 15), but would require that several adults, probably men, were absent from the settlement for much of the year to guide and protect the flock. Given the probably small numbers of sheep, this seems an inefficient use of their time and, like the suggestion that agriculture was practised by the women alone, leaving hunting and stock-rearing to the men, inherently implausible. For, to judge from the bone remains, meat in any form seems to have been very much a supplementary food, compared with the cultivated crops, and it is reasonable to expect that the major effort of all members of the community who could work would be concentrated upon the crops, especially since preparing and tending fields with no more than digging sticks or hoes would have been fairly arduous in the Aegean region.

Whatever the precise methods followed – and they might have varied somewhat in different parts of the Aegean – they were evidently successful, since many of the original settlements survived and new ones were founded, indicating an increasing population. Indeed, it is likely that there was often surplus food, since the commonly attested dogs would have had to be fed on scraps, and, if modern practice is any guide, farmers would have sown enough to produce a crop larger than they needed if all went well, to minimise the risk of hunger if the level of yield was poor, as might be the case only too often because of variations in the weather. Halstead has argued that the exchange of food surpluses was one means by which settlements kept themselves and their neighbours in being, effectively, and that this led to a system of deferring repayment by 'social storage'. As the land began to be filled and new settlements had to be established in less favourable situations, this could have fostered the growth of some households' and communities' fortunes at the expense of the rest, as these accumulated promises of repayment for food which might have to be made in the form of labour. An elite could have developed that increasingly controlled the type of farming carried on through its control of labour; and as settlements grew larger they might have altered their practices to make use of more land with the increased labour available. In such ways, inequality could have developed within and between communities. Such arguments seem plausible, although they can give the impression of an inexorable process; yet Sesklo, for long one of the largest Thessalian settlements (Catling 1973: 21), was abandoned for a considerable period, and others did not maintain the prominent position evident in LN into the BA. Moreover, it has yet to be shown that this process took place outside Thessaly, for example at Knossos, which also grew to a considerable size but did not found dependent settlements, as far as can be seen (Broodbank 1992).

It is possible that in the later Neolithic more specialised pastoral groups developed, which made use of the caves identified as in use in various parts of Crete, and also in some parts of the mainland, when moving sheep around; Halstead has also suggested the development of specialised cattle-herding groups in well-watered western Thessaly. These groups would have to be imagined, like their historical counterparts, as existing in symbiosis with the agricultural communities, exchanging their specialised products for storable foods and, perhaps, artefacts and materials. The possibility is an intriguing one, but more evidence needs to be produced in its support.

Crafts

The craft range practised in Neolithic communities was considerably wider than previously, but, as in earlier times to judge from modern ethnography, adults would normally have been expected to have some competence in quite a range of crafts that are now mostly practised by specialists. Stone-working, especially the production of chipped stone blades, may have been practised by special groups (above, p. 32). But the majority of specialists will have been people who showed particular aptitude for some craft, picked up knowledge and techniques from relatives or neighbours, and passed them on in the same way, but did not expect to practise their skill full-time, let alone make a living by it; rather, they may have been expected to use their skills for the community, in a spirit of cooperation and reciprocal aid that may have been the dominant ethos. Similarly, building houses and even the processes of agriculture may have been undertaken jointly by whole communities, or at least groups of relatives or neighbours. But individual households may have been expected to be self-sufficient in a range of household items including clothing, utensils and simple implements, in normal circumstances.

The skill of stone-working was certainly greatly expanded: not only were implements of many kinds produced from chipped or ground stone, but also querns, vessels, figurines (*CAH* I–II, pls 19a, 23e–f), beads, pendants and other ornaments, and what look like stamp seals, though these were commoner in baked clay (*CAH* I–II, pl. 19b), a material also used for others of the above and for items like sling bullets, spindle whorls, loom weights and, most of all, pottery. Bone and animal horn were commonly used for pointed implements, antlers particularly as picks/digging sticks, and shell, especially spondylus, was used for ornaments. An even wider range of items will have been made from organic materials that have not survived, although pottery has preserved impressions of textile, wickerwork and matting: these include hide, perhaps already being worked into leather for some items, linen and other items made from vegetable fibre, perhaps some wool (but see Barber 1991: 23–8 on the lack of woolliness of early sheep), and above all wood. A range of dyes and paints could have been made from coloured earths, vegetables and minerals (cf. Barber 1991, Ch. 10 for dyes), and furs and feathers could have been employed to ornament persons and objects further.

In this connection the use of two copper ores, azurite and malachite, in evidence at early Knossos, may provide part of the background to the development of metalworking. This was clearly established in northern Greece well before the technical beginning of the BA, and might well have spread from there or from western Anatolia to the southern Aegean. The early items produced were mostly small copper trinkets and implements, including simple flat axe-heads, but rare gold and silver ornaments have been recorded, and both copper and lead were found at the late site of Kephala on Kea. Some persons in the Aegean had probably acquired much basic knowledge concerning metal ores, smelting and casting by the end of the Neolithic; but this was a craft that required expert knowledge more than any other, and its practitioners are likely to have been few at first, and might well have been prospectors and miners as well as smiths.

Although there are reports of possibly experimental pieces from Sesklo (Catling 1978: 40), potting in general appears as a developed craft, if still somewhat rudimentary in its techniques and knowledge of the properties of clays, and its products quickly became one of the commonest classes of finds at every site (Fig. 3.2: 2–7). Originally the level of production was low, requiring little equipment and no kiln (Jones 1986: 773–7), and the range of shapes simple, dominated by bowls and jars; these always remained the commonest forms, later supplied with lugs for transport or suspension, and some later vases have band handles. From an early stage attempts were made to enhance the appearance of the pottery in various ways, especially by decoration with added clay, incision, impression or paint. Ultimately, some very time-consuming decorative processes were developed, not all of which are yet understood, and pots often seem to have been decorated individually, emphasising the special and non-domestic functions of pottery for much of the period. Wares clearly intended for domestic use, of thicker fabrics often containing much temper and with heavy burnished slips, only appear at late stages; such fabrics would be more durable, heat-resistant and watertight, and become much more common than fine decorated wares. (This section owes much to comments in Perlès 1992.)

Social structures, beliefs and contacts

Little can be said on these topics that is not ultimately based on informed speculation, derived from knowledge of how similar small-scale societies have worked in recent times. Archaeological evidence for such features as the distribution of tasks and roles between the sexes, clan or lineage groupings, and the nature of any leadership exercised is difficult to identify unambiguously, let

Fig. 3.2 Examples of Neolithic house-plans, pottery and figurine.
1 MN, Otzaki. 2–5 MN, Tsangli, Tsani, Chaeronea and Lerna. 6, 7 LN, Dhimini and Sesklo. 8 EN, Nea Nikomedeia. Scale for 1 1:400, for 2–7 mostly 1:6, for 8 c. 1:4. 2 courtesy of Yale University Press and Mr M.S.F. Hood; 3, 4 and 7 drawn by J. Blécon, courtesy of Presses universitaires de France.

alone evidence for religious beliefs and practices, and interpretations can all too easily be governed by preconceptions. The related beliefs in the worship by Neolithic communities of a 'Mother Goddess', the domination of society by women and their responsibility for agricultural work are still not dead, although the arguments for these positions, separately and together, are weak and often tendentious. It seems more reasonable to follow the approach of Treuil (Treuil *et al.* 1989: 143) in supposing that the tasks requiring greater physical strength, which would include the heavier agricultural and craft work, were allotted to men, but much other craft work and most of the child-rearing, to women, who would also work on the land as much as their other work allowed. Hard evidence to support such a division is not easy to find, but it fits recorded patterns of human behaviour in hunter-gatherer and simple farming societies.

As already indicated, the village communities are likely to have functioned much more as units than as groups of independent households, and their ethos would probably have stressed the values of cooperation and sharing, but they will have been large enough to require some kind of leadership. On ethnographic analogies (cf. Orme 1981, Ch. 3), this could have been displayed in limited spheres such as ritual or the settling of disputes, or exercised more generally in 'getting things done', through example and the influence gained by success, generosity and force of character. This kind of position would resemble that of the 'big man' (Orme 1981: 139–41, cf. also Whitley 1991: 348–52). But archaeological evidence for this kind of position, normally achieved in the prime of life but not necessarily retained until death, let alone passed on, is not likely to be easily found, though it might be detected in such features as unusually big houses. The very uneven distribution of fine pottery at Sesklo is plausibly interpreted as evidence for developing inequality between the households of a settlement and the emergence of an 'elite' of more fortunate farmers, who might be bringing others into dependence upon them. Such a situation could produce 'big men', or even hereditary chiefs, but there is simply not enough analysis of this kind to show whether this was a general or local phenomenon; the scanty and very variable Neolithic burial evidence does not provide any obvious support for theories of a 'chiefly class' (but cf. Halstead 1989: 75 on Ayia Sophia).

Again on ethnographic analogy, the part played in the life of the communities by ritual and ceremony is likely to have been large, and one in which leaders of any kind might be expected to be active, but patterns of ritual activity are not easily traced. There is no evidence for large-scale ceremonial sites, such as are found in some Neolithic cultures; but when so few settlements have been extensively investigated the existence of communal cult structures or sites can hardly be confirmed or denied. Deposits of ash and bones at supposed altars or hearths or in pits have been interpreted as evidence of sacrifice, but the best argument for ritual sites relates to those caves which are extremely difficult to approach, as many are (C. Perlès, pers. commun.), and contain finds which are of an unusual nature (Cave of Pan, Marathon; Cave of Zas, Naxos) or were found in remote

Pl. 3.1 Foundation deposit of figurines, Plateia Magoula Zarkou. Courtesy of Dr K. Gallis.

parts of the cave (e.g. at Amnisos); but systematic study of such material remains to be done. Goodison's argument that the early evidence is compatible with 'animistic' religion, which recognises spiritual forces immanent in natural phenomena such as rocks, water, trees, animals and heavenly bodies (1989: 10, cf. xiv), could suit the diffuse and scanty nature of the finds, including those most commonly associated with religion, the figurines.

There is certainly no reason to focus solely on female figurines, and interpret them as evidence for worship of a 'Mother Goddess', when they are only part of a range that includes humanoid males, animals, models of buildings and furniture, and hybrids (*CAH* I–II, pl. 22a–b), and have been found in a variety of contexts including burials, the central building at Nea Nikomedeia (Fig. 3.2: 8) and a foundation deposit at Plateia Magoula Zarkou in Thessaly (Gallis 1985) (Pl. 3.1); they may not occur at an even rate throughout the period (as at Knossos, where they are heavily concentrated in EN II, Broodbank 1992). They could have played many roles, in initiation rites, sympathetic magic, ceremonial exchanges, contracts and other types of activity that might have a ceremonial element; some may represent spirits, ancestral or otherwise, or even gods, but the basic analysis of types and contexts largely remains to be done. In sum, this is an area where very little can be said with any confidence (but see the Introduction to Ch. 8).

The same is true of burial customs, for remarkably few burials have been found. The majority of identifiable graves are simple pits, cut within the settlement area, rarely holding more than one burial; small children might be buried in pots. The graves were normally small, and the dead, perhaps for this reason, laid in a contracted position; they might be provided with goods like pots and implements. A development of the late phases is the establishment of cemeteries outside the settlement; in two well-known Thessalian cases these consisted of jars containing cremated remains, while at Kephala on Kea there are stone-built tombs containing inhumations of the traditional kind. The idea of such cemeteries may have spread from further north in the Balkans, but there is little positive evidence. Some caves were used as burial sites, as at Franchthi and at Alepotrypa in the south Peloponnese, where considerable quantities of human remains and some unusually fine goods have been found (Papathanasopoulos 1971; Lambert 1972). This custom is also found in Crete, where it was to have a longer period of popularity, but, as with the use of caves generally, the social context is not clear.

As already stated, there is good reason to suppose much exchange, especially of lithic products and materials, which may have involved both social alliances and distribution by specialists. It is tempting to envisage networks of ceremonial gift exchange parallel to those attested ethnographically behind the distribution of unusual artefacts. Certainly, such contacts sometimes cover remarkable distances, as in the case of that documented by Aegean spondylus shells in the Danube area (Renfrew 1972: 444) and a gold strip from the Cave of Zas on Naxos, which can be paralleled in Macedonia and the rich cemetery of Varna in Bulgaria (Zachos 1990: 30). Melian obsidian was ultimately reaching sites all around the Aegean, including those well away from the coast, and may have become a commodity for exchange in an almost commercial sense, although in the later stages of the Neolithic there is more evidence for its procurement in the raw form and local working, at least in the coastal regions (Perlès 1990: 28–34).

The possibility that inter-settlement contacts were not always friendly deserves consideration. Especially where settlements were close together and population was increasing, rivalry and competition for resources might result in warfare, the role of which in asserting and strengthening group identity means that it can be institutionalised very easily, even if it takes a largely ritual form (Orme 1981: 198–9). The rarity of identifiable weapons in the archaeological record is not a strong counter-argument, for these would be necessary for hunting and defence of livestock against predators, purposes for which it is evident that more than the rare sling bullets and projectile points that have actually been identified would be needed. The obvious answer is that weapons such as spears, bows and arrows, and clubs were often entirely of wood, perhaps armed with typologically undistinctive pieces of stone or bone or with animal teeth, or given fire-hardened points; no doubt, the stone-headed axes could also have been used, at need. The possibility that warfare in the form of raid and counter-raid was endemic, as in some societies described by Orme, cannot be ruled out but seems unlikely, given the shortage of evidence suggesting any preoccupation with defence; occasional skirmishes seem more plausible, but the abrupt abandonment of some communities may reflect unusually ferocious episodes.

The settlement of the Cyclades and the final stage of Neolithic

Leaving aside Maroula on Kythnos as of uncertain date (Cherry 1979: 28–32), the earliest proved settlement in the Cyclades is on the islet of Saliagos, originally part of Antiparos, founded late in the sixth millennium or early in the fifth (Evans and Renfrew 1968). Various indications suggest that fishing was prominent in its economy and may have been a motive for its foundation, since it is sited in a good fishing area, but the settlers farmed and raised livestock also. The lithic assemblage can almost all be paralleled on the mainland, but links with the east Aegean have also been noted (Sampson 1984: 240, 245). The settlement may well have played a part in cross-Aegean exchanges and thus have drawn upon different traditions, but it was probably founded from the western side of the Aegean.

Until recently it seemed that there was an unbridgeable gap between Saliagos and the 'Final Neolithic' site of Kephala on Kea (Coleman 1977). The situation has now changed considerably, with material identifiable as Late or 'Final' Neolithic reported from several islands (Cherry 1990: 164–5). The material from Naxos is particularly striking. Traces of an extensive settlement at Grotta have produced pottery that can be linked to that of Saliagos, but seems more advanced, while the rich stratigraphical sequence in the Cave of Zas begins with a phase that seems more advanced still, succeeded by a level that has 'Final Neolithic' links, though showing many differences from Kephala; this in turn is succeeded by one of essentially 'Pelos' character (Zachos 1990). The earlier levels contain material showing wide connections, including the gold strip already mentioned, a range of copper items, and pottery types that have links with the east Aegean.

This evidence emphasises that the settlement of the Cyclades took place within a network of Aegean-wide connections, which may have partly determined its progress; it certainly cannot be explained any more in terms of a simple migration of population from Anatolia, but Anatolian pottery types like the rolled-rim bowl occur widely (Warren and Hankey 1989: 9–10) and it might be premature to rule out any Anatolian involvement (see Phelps in Jones 1986: 375). However, the Cyclades-wide 'Pelos' group has a very distinctive character that must surely reflect its development within the Cyclades. A similar point may be made for the earliest BA groups of the mainland and Crete (Warren 1973b: 41–3 presents the best argument for some migration into Crete, cf. Warren and Hankey 1989: 12, 14 on Anatolian links). Linking the appearance of metalworking with migrants, as used to be done, is also unnecessary, given the evidence for its development in the north and the spread of metal items well before the end of the Neolithic. But the search for metals might have been a factor in the settlement of the Cyclades, although this remains unlikely for Crete: metal sources reported, especially near the Mesara (Branigan 1970a: 78–9), have been largely discounted in recent work, and can in any case have nothing to do with the expansion of population in east Crete which began at this time. One result of expansion in the south Aegean was the eventual eclipse of the previously important regions of northern Greece. They remained well settled, but show little sign of BA developments on the scale identifiable further south, although some may have reached a considerable size (Halstead 1989: 75 suggests 25 ha for some by the end of the second millennium), nor are there indications that they had wide influence. Notable sites like Pefkakia seem to derive their importance from their coastal position; more and more, connections by sea seem to be crucial in fostering development, and the growing importance of Crete made the southern half of the Aegean its cultural heart.

Bibliography

The most useful discussions available are Weinberg 1970, the relevant sections in Renfrew 1972, the papers in Theocharis 1973, Theocharis's contribution to Christopoulos 1974, Jacobsen 1981, which summarises the Franchthi sequence, and Treuil *et al.* 1989, Book I, Ch. 1. For a recent account of a Palaeolithic site see Bailey 1986. On the colonisation of the Greek islands see Cherry 1990: 158–73, and on that of Knossos, with general reflections on Neolithic colonisation, Broodbank and Strasser 1991. Halstead 1981a and 1989, and Broodbank 1992 provide stimulating discussions of economy and social developments, though concerned specifically with Thessaly and Knossos; on craft specialisation and exchange see Perlès 1990.

CHAPTER 4

SETTLEMENT AND ECONOMY

Introduction

All pre-industrial societies had as their essential basis the successful exploitation of the land. In the case of the Aegean BA, it may be suggested that this was even more dominant than in the contemporary Near East, in that the Aegean societies remained basically small-scale throughout their history, and the total proportion of their populations not directly involved in some form of farming was insignificant; it is extremely unlikely that fishing could have provided a base for the economy of any major site (Halstead 1981a: 335 n. 2; 1987a: 81). Of course, there were craft specialists, but, as will be argued in Chapter 5, most of these will have practised their craft part-time and also worked land, as specialised pastoralists are likely to have done, to judge from modern parallels (Blitzer 1990b: 38). Only specialists directly maintained by elite households, palaces or religious institutions could have practised their craft full-time, and these can hardly have been numerous enough to have had a significant effect on the economy of settlements where they were based. If there were professional traders, these would have dealt largely in agricultural products and may have owned estates, as often in recent societies; certainly, priests and other socially significant figures are recorded as holding land in the texts, and this is likely to have been their main source of wealth.

But if exploitation of the land was the most important activity of Aegean BA societies, data throwing light on it are hardly copious. Fewer analyses of plant and animal remains have been published than for the Neolithic, and they are particularly rare for regions of great importance like Crete and the Peloponnese. The distribution of sites is still patchily known and their nature a matter for debate; most data in any case derive from the substantial multi-period sites rather than the small, shorter-lived sites that intensive surveys are identifying in increasing numbers.

Crops and plants

As in the Neolithic period, the BA settlements evidently cultivated a range of cereals and pulses, probably as before to minimise the risks of a poor year. The evidence from some sites suggests concentration on barley, but wheat is widespread, and in the Linear B texts is the staple for issuing rations. The dominant form of wheat is emmer, surely for the same reasons as before (p. 35), but pure samples of bread wheat have been identified. The only new crop appearing is millet, but this is found at few sites, mostly in northern Greece; it probably failed to become a staple, as it appears to have done further north in Europe, because of its vulnerability to drought. All the pulses previously recorded are found; vetch was stored in some quantity, but may have been only animal fodder.

The major BA development in farming was the adoption of orchard husbandry, which was evidently of interest to the palaces. The signs later used for olives, olive oil and figs already occur on a Phaistos tablet that must be of First Palace Period date, and the Linear B texts of Knossos and Pylos record large orchards and vineyards and the issue of figs, olives, olive oil and wine. As noted in Chapter 2, the olive, fig and vine are all native to Greece, but their early history is varied: wild grapes and figs were certainly collected in Neolithic times, but there is little trace of olives. The now classic argument developed by Renfrew (1972, Ch. 15) is that domesticated forms of all these were established in the Aegean in the EBA and that, because they need not compete with the crops for land, they allowed an intensification of production that provided commodities for exchange and was one of the mainsprings of cultural advance and prosperity.

The arguments used to support this theory have recently been subjected to extensive criticism (Hansen 1988), and certainly the number of early finds that might indicate domestication is few, particularly for the olive, and supporting arguments are often inconclusive. But it is evident that to base arguments purely on surviving remains of olives, grapes or figs, when so little systematic attempt was made to look for them in the excavation of many important sites, is to take too narrow an approach. The case is best when different kinds of evidence point in the same direction, as at Myrtos, where there is a reasonable case for some olive and vine cultivation in EM II, and Kommos, where olive cultivation seems to be well established by MM I, on evidence cited by Blitzer (n.d.). Blitzer has argued strongly for the early if small-scale establishment of the domesticated olive in Crete, partly on the grounds that establishing extensive olive groves, such as could have produced an exportable surplus by the LBA, would have taken far longer than has been allowed. Crete also had early contacts with the Near East, where the olive seems to have been domesticated before the end of the fourth millennium. One may nevertheless wonder how early the domestic olive was established outside Crete.

Evidence relating to the vine is more extensive: although Hansen is not convinced by arguments for domesticated grapes at fourth millennium Sitagroi, it includes what appear to be the remains of pressed grapes in a Myrtos pithos and a large sample of grape pips from Lerna IV, at least some of which are defined as domesticated; grape pips also occur at MM Knossos and Phaistos and several MH sites, and are found widely in the LBA. But perhaps the best argument for early domestication in the Aegean, and familiarity with wine over a considerable area, is the great increase in the popularity of drinking vessels and jugs in the EBA. These were often produced in elaborate forms and wares, even in metal, and this has been plausibly taken to reflect their use in a ceremonial and prestigious activity, drinking alcohol (Sherratt, A.G. 1987b), which in the Aegean context would surely be wine. Since there is no evidence for wine containers likely to have come from the Near East, this must have been locally produced. Thus, the more attractive wine may have been produced in quantity before the more generally useful olive oil, which has high nutritional value and uses in cooking, lighting, the treatment of wool and cloth, and as a perfume base and soap substitute. But this need not be surprising if drinking wine had strong associations with status. That the fig had also been domesticated, at least in the palace economies, is made clear by the textual evidence; figs are listed as rations, probably in the dried form which concentrates the energy-producing sugar, in the Linear B texts.

An important point that relates to the olive especially, but also to the vine and fig, is that they require an input of labour for many years before they reach maturity and begin to yield significantly, and establishment on a large scale demands considerable effort over a long period. One is bound to question how many households or communities will have had the resources, let alone the will, to undertake such long-term tasks; it is surely hardly to be expected where communities were small and/or short-lived. Moreover, considerable storage facilities would be needed if production was on any scale, and these are not often identifiable outside the palaces and comparable buildings; Myrtos is an early exception, but even here not many more storage jars were found than in the modern village president's house reported by Kanta (1983: 157–9). This is a matter on which better data are needed, but it is worth considering the possibility that only the palace economies exploited orchard husbandry on a really extensive scale; however, there is no reason to suppose that they monopolised it.

Other trees may well have been domesticated: almonds and pistachios have been found stored at Ayia Triada and Akrotiri, and the latter seem to be recorded in large quantities at Knossos. Plants attested at least once by finds or the texts and likely to have been cultivated include celery, garlic, lettuce, onions, and many herbs and spices (Chadwick 1976: 119–21), and saffron is shown being gathered on Knossos and Akrotiri frescoes; but cumin and sesame, both recorded, have Semitic names and may have been imported from the Near East, or grown only in palace gardens. Gathering still supplemented cultivation, especially on the mainland where stores of the oil-bearing seeds of thistle and flax, as also of white mustard, have been found. Flax, the raw material for linen, was also cultivated, but the fibres are usually processed in water, which would not have been abundantly available everywhere. Many communities in Messenia are recorded as paying a tax, probably in flax fibre rather than linen, and substantial quantities are involved, of which the palace received most; some of the resulting linen could have been exported (Robkin 1979).

The exploitation of animals

Changes taking place in stockbreeding during the fourth millennium in the Near East have been presented as a 'Secondary Products Revolution' almost as significant as the original domestication of plants and animals (Sherratt, A.G. 1981). These involved a move from exploiting animals primarily for meat to breeding for the intensive production of milk and wool, and to provide draught animals. The new pattern of breeding should require that a much greater proportion of animals was allowed to live to a relatively advanced age; in particular, many more males should survive, as castrated draught oxen or wool-producing wethers. But a major difficulty remains, whether bone remains recovered from site-excavations will reflect such practices, or simply relate to the meat part of the diet, and the possibility of complex patterns like that tentatively suggested for Nichoria, where sheep may have been reared for wool, but goats preferred for meat (Mancz 1989: 210), cannot be discounted. Certainly, at several sites, including Lerna and Argissa, animals continued to be regularly slaughtered at a relatively young age throughout the BA (cf. Halstead 1987a: 80); only at Myrtos, where the sample is not very large, and the Menelaion, as reported (Catling 1977: 27), has a 'secondary products' pattern been detected, while at Tiryns cattle, sheep and goats were most often slaughtered when relatively mature, and a mixed pattern of use seemed likely (Von den Driesch and Boessneck 1990: 96–8).

The texts provide better support for the notion of intensive 'secondary products' exploitation. In Linear A texts there is not much indication of interest in livestock except at Ayia Triada, which may have been a centre of wool production, but the Linear B texts from Knossos certainly demonstrate the rearing of sheep for wool on a very large scale (something like a hundred thousand sheep are enumerated for central Crete alone). The flocks of Pylos were differently recorded, but were considerable, and as at Knossos there was a substantial textile industry, which presumably made use of their wool; substantial quantities of wool are also recorded at Mycenae and smaller quantities at Thebes. Other livestock are also referred to, but rarely in great quantities, though nearly two thousand goats and over five hundred pigs are recorded in one set of Pylos texts, with only eight cattle (Ventris and Chadwick 1973: 198). The Knossos texts also refer to goats and pigs in some numbers, but rarely to cattle; what must be teamed pairs of oxen are recorded, generally in small numbers, including four named pairs at Knossos itself (Ventris and Chadwick 1973: 208–13). But it is unlikely that either the texts, or the relatively low numbers of cattle bones at Nichoria, reflect the whole picture: cattle are notably well represented at Tiryns, and the general taxation records of Pylos, which show that 234 hides were expected yearly from the whole territory controlled (Chadwick 1976: 127), imply herds of some size.

Teams of oxen might have been used for pulling either ploughs or carts and waggons, though neither are at all well attested in archaeological material. There is a single model of a low waggon from Palaikastro, and the Greek terrain has been thought inappropriate for wheeled vehicles, but they would have been the best means of moving the massive stone blocks and timbers necessary for various forms of construction, as in later Greece. Figurines representing yoked pairs of oxen, which it is reasonable to associate with the plough, have now been identified at Tsoungiza, of 'Lerna III' date (Pullen 1992); but a rare Mycenaean figurine type that shows a man driving a single ox (French 1971: 165–6) more probably represents the driving of an animal to sacrifice than ploughing, and incidentally provides a reminder that cattle could be bred for non-functional reasons. The Tsoungiza evidence suggests that perhaps Halstead is being too pessimistic in supposing that plough teams were very rare, even in the palaces' own economies (1981a: 330–2; cf. 1987: 82). But ploughs may have been rather primitive; the only bronze ploughshare fragments identified are of probably Cypriot type, in the late Athens and Anthedon hoards, and even these might be scrap metal (Catling 1964: 81–2, 298).

The horse can be used singly as a plough animal in Greece (Aschenbrenner 1972: 57), but more probably horse and donkey were both used principally as pack animals at first, and later for riding and, in the case of horses, pulling chariots, as both the representations, from early Second Palace Period contexts onwards, and the Linear B texts suggest; rare horse and rider figurines suggest that the horse was being ridden by late Mycenaean times. Usually neither is commonly represented in bone samples, presumably because their flesh was not normally eaten or their hides used, but late Mycenaean deposits at Tiryns contained relatively many equid bones, including some identified as mules (Von den Driesch and Boessneck 1990: 93 Tab. 5, 102–3, 141–3). Probably they reached Greece by different routes. The donkey was originally domesticated in the Near East and first appears in the Aegean in Lerna III; more or less contemporary finds at Troy suggest that it reached the Aegean via Anatolia. Although finds are rare except at Tiryns, it seems a reasonable supposition that donkeys and mules had become common pack and riding animals by that time.

The horse, apparently first domesticated on the Russian steppes (Renfrew 1989: 202), is reported from EB contexts in Macedonia (Ridley and Wardle 1979: 229) but no further south before the MBA, although some bones of EH III date from Lerna and Tiryns might be horses rather than donkeys. The first certain horse bones, apparently from a pony-sized breed, come from MH contexts at Argissa, Nichoria and Lerna, of which only the Nichoria context is certainly early. There are some indications in Mycenaean material of a larger breed of horses, but the majority are still small. By this time the horse's associations seem exclusively aristocratic, and herds may have been maintained by the palaces solely to provide chariot-teams. But this association with the chariot was established long after the horse's first appearance in the Aegean, which must be firmly separated from the dramatic 'Indo-European' overtones that it used to have; its introduction is in fact unlikely to have had any appreciable social or economic effects.

Other domestic animals certainly existed. Remains of dogs are quite common, and evidence from mainland sites suggests that they were frequently eaten, but the cat is rarely attested and not certainly domestic (Morgan 1988: 42); it might have been introduced from Egypt. It has been claimed that some Minoan seals show domestic geese (but see Morgan 1988: 64), but there is no reliable bone evidence, nor for domestic ducks or pigeons, and finds of chicken bones are most likely to be modern intrusions (most recently, Von den Driesch and Boessneck 1990: 114–16). Finally, tangible evidence for the domestication of the bee, which would have flourished most in maquis vegetation, is provided by a plausible beehive from Akrotiri (Doumas 1983: 119 fig. 19) and references to honey and perhaps bee-keepers (literally, honey-men) in the Linear B texts (Chadwick 1976: 124, 126).

Evidence relating to wild animals can also be considered under this heading, since it will include deliberate hunting for food, hides and furs as well as the control of predators and crop-threatening creatures. At Knossos, products of the agrimi are listed, and professional hunters appear to be named at Pylos, but this is unlikely to have been a significant economic activity. But the mainland bone samples include respectable numbers of wild animal bones, although they form a small proportion of the total. It has already been suggested in Chapter 2 that the original range of fauna was richer on the mainland, and their natural habitats may have come under less pressure than in the islands; indeed, the clearance of woodland may actually have been favourable to deer, which prefer more open conditions. Certainly, these, especially red deer, were commonly hunted to the end of the BA, as were wild boar, and in smaller numbers hare and fox. Wild boar would have been particularly in demand once the helmet plated with boar's tusk became a prestige item; it has been calculated that, according to the number of zones of plates, anything from thirty to seventy-five pairs of tusks would have been needed for a single helmet (Morgan 1988: 112). Finally, as already noted, fishing is better attested from artistic representations than from actual finds; this may well largely reflect the methods of data recovery used, and perhaps also a failure to discover areas of fish processing, but it would be unwise to assume that fishing was an important economic activity at any settlement.

Settlements and their social setting

It has been a common assumption that all identified sites were farming settlements, and hence significant conclusions have been drawn when they are found on poor land (e.g. Sandars 1978: 77). This is a reasonable working hypothesis, but other possibilities are worth noting, which might be considered particularly when sites are found in unsuitable locations for farming (in fact, only ten of the

Messenian LH sites were on notably poor land, cf. McDonald and Rapp 1972: 182, Table 11-1). Such possibilities include ritual sites and guard posts, which might be expected to show special features in configuration or remains, and the seasonal or temporary camps of hunters, woodcutters, craft specialists who might wish to work close to good fuel supplies, such as potters and smiths (for possible smiths' sites in Pylian territory see Chadwick 1976: 141), and herders, the last being the most likely to have been common.

The size of the group represented by a site is another factor of considerable importance to its interpretation in agricultural terms. In general, the arguments presented in previous sections suggest that the average settlement would, as in Neolithic times, have concentrated on growing cereals and pulses (which are labour-intensive if grown on any scale), with some vegetables, and tending a modest quantity of livestock, while orchard husbandry, the intensive exploitation of livestock for secondary products and the growth of rare crops on any scale would have been practised mostly at large settlements, and perhaps only by the richest households in these, and, in the palace economies, on lands owned or controlled by the ruling elite.

Absolute population figures will rarely be mentioned below, because the few data collected are mostly 'soft', relying on formulae, inevitably disputable, for converting estimates of site extent or numbers of buildings into numbers of persons. The point is discussed at some length by Wiener (1990: 129–33) in connection with the island towns, which may well have been more intensively occupied than the majority of mainland settlements of any period. The smallest such towns may have had populations of several hundreds, while the average farming settlement may have consisted of a few score and the smallest of only one or two households; but really large concentrations should have had populations well into the thousands. The populations of the largest states and regions would then have been counted in tens of thousands at most, and the maximum of forty thousand suggested for Mycenaean Messenia in Carothers and McDonald 1979 may still be too high. No doubt many of the smaller 'cities' of the Near East whose capture is bombastically recorded by conquering kings were of similar size to the larger Aegean settlements; but the difference between the greatest of these and the cities of Mesopotamia and Egypt should never be overlooked, nor the fact that many significant settlements, described as 'large' in comparison with their Aegean contemporaries, fall within the range allowed for a village in Early Dynastic Mesopotamia (Renfrew 1972: 240). Such differences in scale between the Aegean and the Near East must have found their reflection in the organisation of communities and in society as a whole.

In what follows the nature of the sites and, where possible, indications of their relationship with each other will be concentrated upon and the question of their farming economy not referred to further, except where some particularly significant evidence requires mention. Excavation and survey are providing increasing detail on these topics, and it is evident that almost from the beginning of the BA there is much variation between regions (Fig. 4.1). In Crete there are clear signs of a developing hierarchy of settlements at an early stage. Knossos already seems the biggest, perhaps extending over 5 ha at the beginning of the BA, but Phaistos, Mallia and Mochlos can be recognised as substantial centres of population on the grounds of the spread of EB material or the size of the cemetery (Whitelaw 1983: 337–9). The social structure of these settlements remains obscure, however: Branigan's attempt to identify 'mansions' in the Vasiliki 'House on the Hill', traces of comparable structures at several sites, and the Myrtos complex (1970a: 42–51), is very doubtful, not least because of renewed investigations at Vasiliki. Here the 'House on the Hill' plan has proved to be a conflation of adjacent buildings of successive phases, one preceded by a comparable building on a different alignment, and remains of similar buildings are found

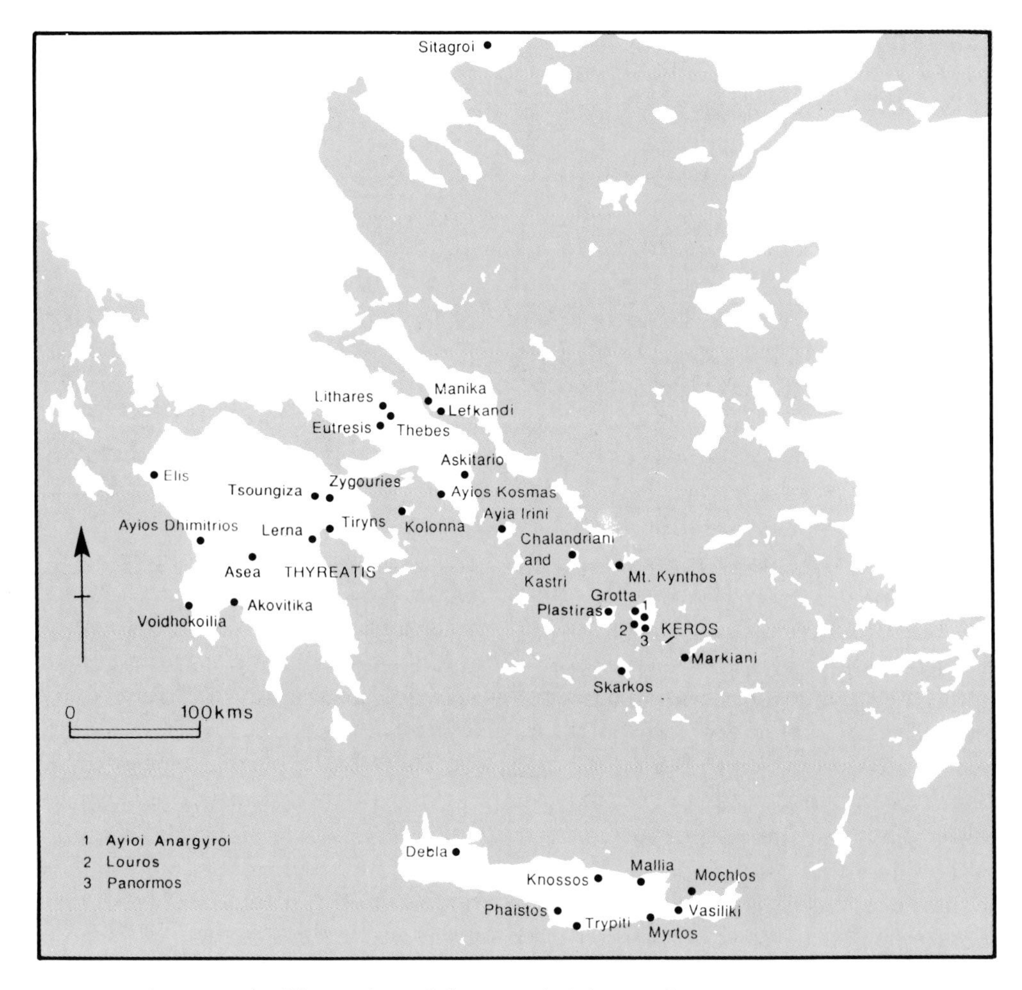

Fig. 4.1 Significant sites of the Prepalatial Period.

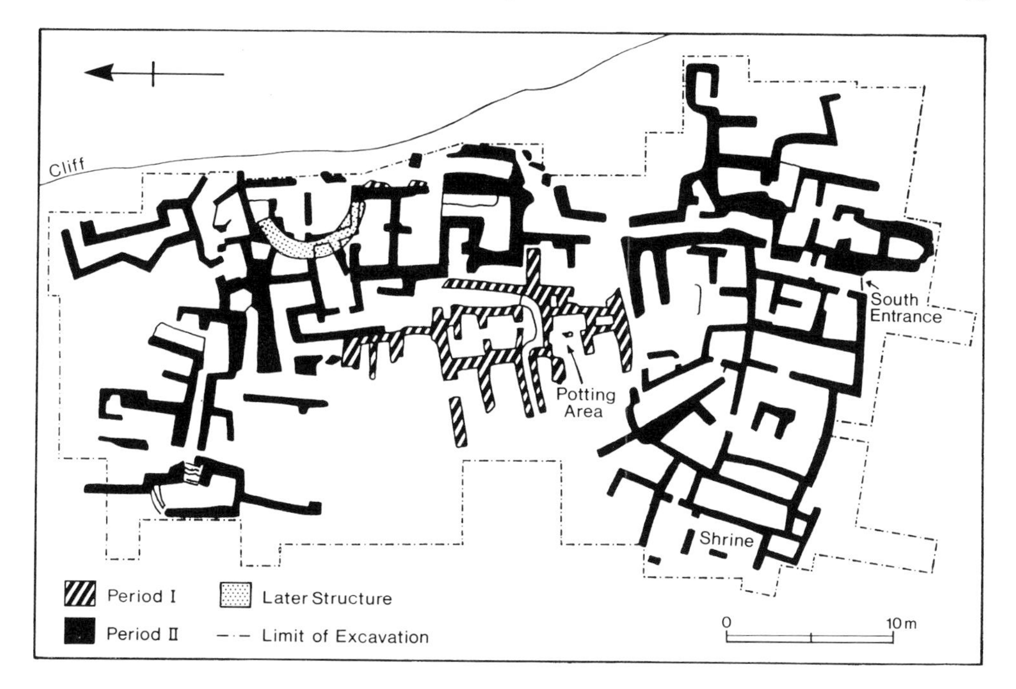

Fig. 4.2 Plan of Myrtos. Courtesy of Dr T. Whitelaw and Prof. P.M. Warren.

elsewhere on the site in each phase (cf. Catling 1976: 31, fig. 42, and *PAE* 1980, pl. IB′, reproduced as Warren 1987a, fig. 3).

Whitelaw more plausibly interprets Myrtos (Fig. 4.2) as an accumulation of household clusters, each with its cooking and storage facilities, added to each other in chronological sequence as the number of families to be accommodated grew to a maximum of five or six (1983: 323–34). There may have been a similar development at Vasiliki, although the structures are considerably more regular in layout. At Trypiti at least eight separate houses, consisting of a few rooms, have been distinguished, on either side of a central street (Fig. 4.3), but there is no suggestion that these were built in sequence (Vasilakis 1989, Catling 1989: 101). Like the Myrtos clusters they presumably held a single family each; a circular tomb identified nearby should have served part of the community. In the Ayiopharango valley, the data suggested a scatter of farmsteads around larger village-like settlements (Blackman and Branigan 1977: 69–71; Fig. 4.4), which mostly have one or two associated circular tombs. The small groups of circular tombs spread through the Mesara and its neighbourhood should indicate the presence of comparable small villages; Whitelaw's argument that each tomb was used by only one or two families begs questions (Branigan 1987b; see further Ch. 6). In the Lasithi plain five sites smaller than Myrtos, thought to represent farming settlements, replaced fifteen, even smaller, interpreted as possible herders' camps, during the EBA (Watrous 1982); the former might consist of only one or

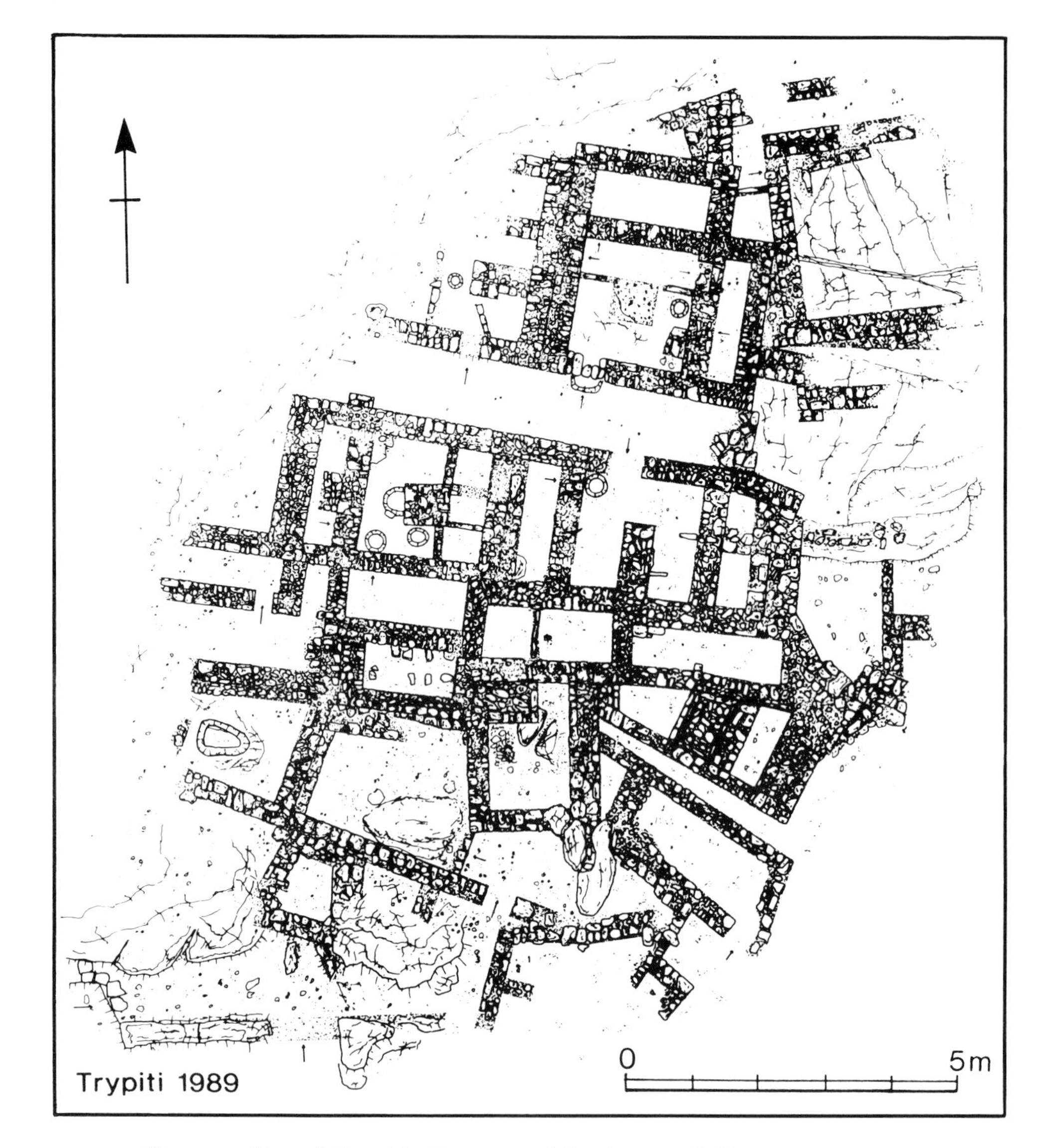

Fig. 4.3 Plan of Trypiti. Courtesy of Dr A.S. Vasilakis.

two farmsteads, while the latter might have resembled Debla in west Crete, where only two or three single-roomed structures were found and the bone material strongly suggested a seasonal herders' site (Warren and Tzedakis 1974).

In sum, it seems likely that in Crete there were only a few widely scattered 'large' sites with populations of several hundred. Much commoner were small villages, consisting of less than ten households, and in some areas smaller sites still might be single farmsteads or seasonal herders' camps. These could in some cases be satellites of a central village, but there seems no reason to credit even the

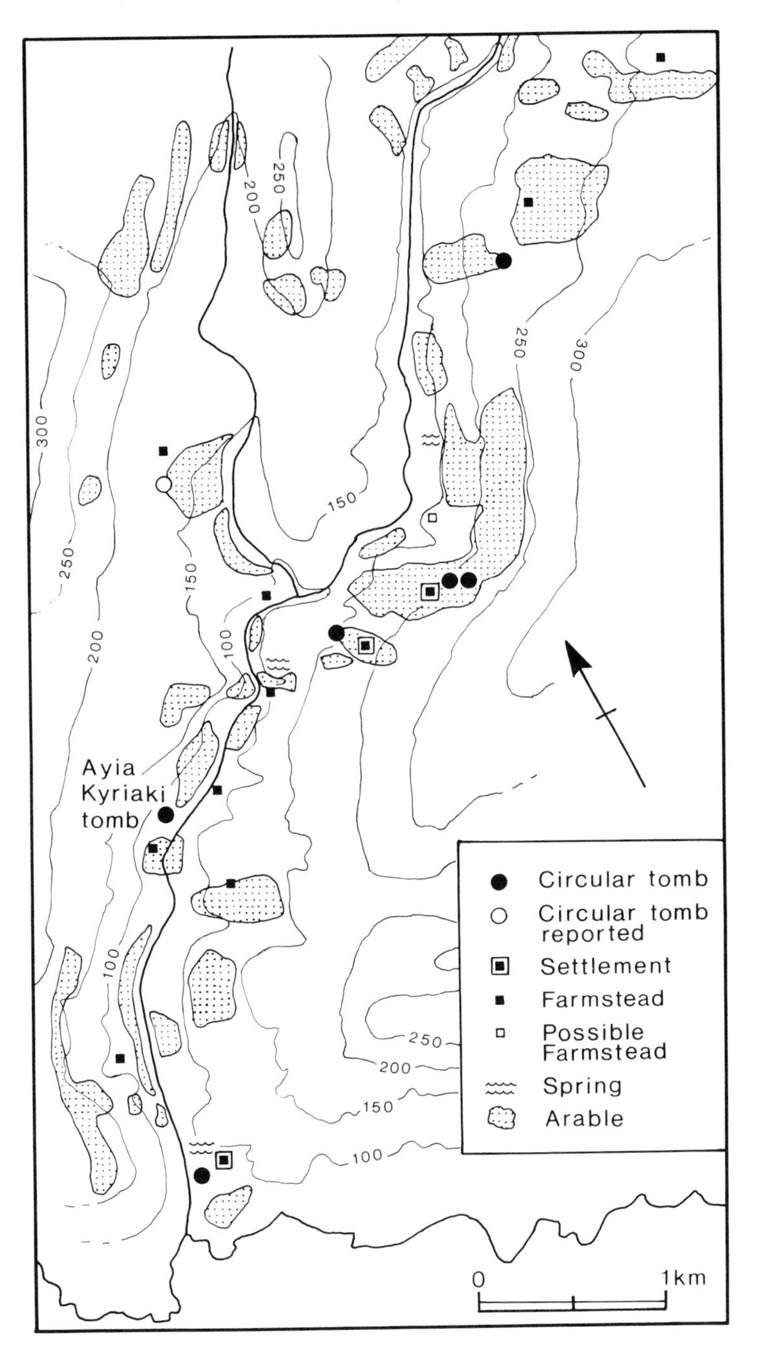

Fig. 4.4 Site distribution in the Ayiopharango valley. Incorporating information supplied by Dr T. Whitelaw.

largest sites with control of extensive territories. In the Cyclades the general impression given by the scanty traces of settlements and the size of cemeteries is that most EB settlements were not only of this very small kind, but often short-lived; some cemeteries contained material of several successive phases, but this could well reflect renewed rather than continuous use. Halstead has suggested that a scattered pattern of very small settlements widens the range of subsistence options (1987a: 82), and certainly some such explanation seems required for what looks like a widespread pattern, also traceable in parts of the Helladic region, especially Euboea, at the beginning of the BA. Later there are indications of nucleation: some of the 'Syros' cemeteries are extensive, particularly Chalandriani, and sites like Ayia Irini, Grotta, Mt Kynthos, Skarkos (Catling 1987: 49), and the fortified site of Kastri (Fig. 4.5) do seem to represent villages of varying sizes. But on other islands such nucleation only appears after the obscure stage that marks the effective end of the EC culture. Thereafter only a single substantial community can be identified on several islands, though there were clearly several on Naxos (Barber 1987: 71 fig. 51).

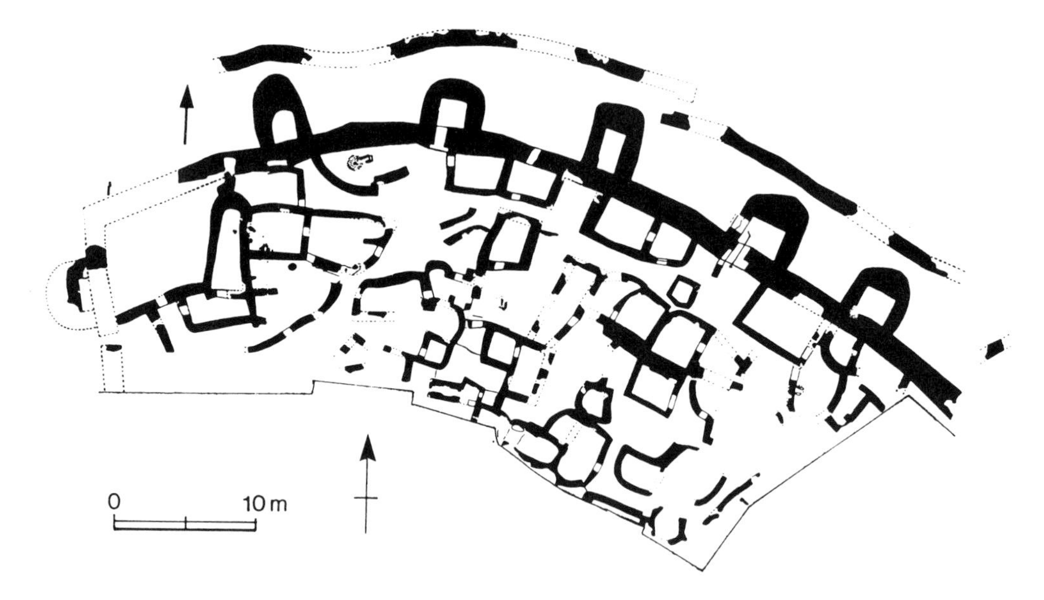

Fig. 4.5 Plan of Kastri on Syros. Courtesy of Prof. R. Hägg.

On the mainland and nearby islands excavations have almost always been at substantial, long-lived sites, but surveys have demonstrated the existence of numerous small sites. Some, as already noted, may represent a thin spread of farming population at the beginning of the EBA, which later became concentrated in villages; others seem to represent an expansion from these villages at the height of development in the 'Lerna III' (EH II) stage (cf. Fig. 4.6a). Several of the major village sites are larger than any in Crete, judging by the spread of

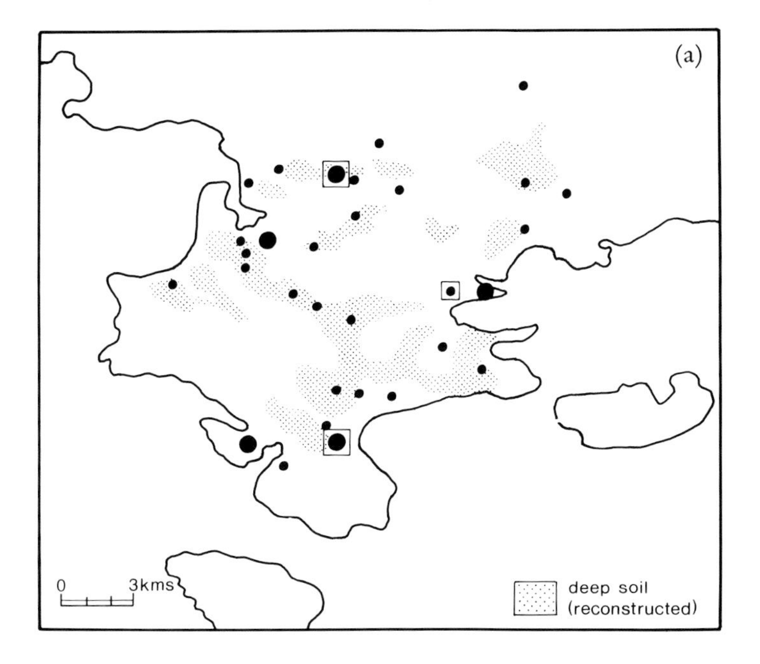

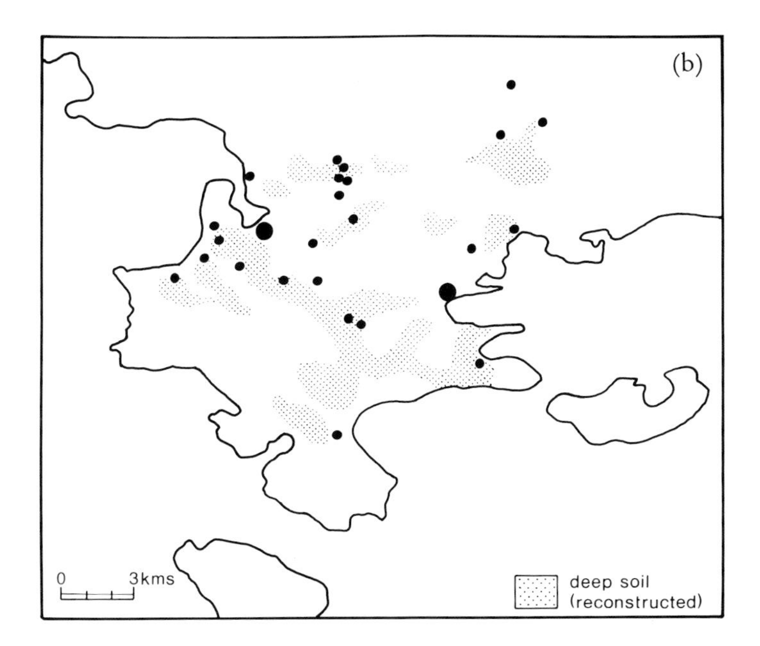

Fig. 4.6 Site distribution in the south Argolid in the EH (●) and MH (□) periods (a), and LH period (b). Adapted from *Beyond the acropolis: a rural Greek past*, by Tjeerd H. van Andel and Curtis Runnels, with the permission of the publishers, Stanford University Press. ©1987 by the Board of Trustees of the Leland Stanford Junior University.

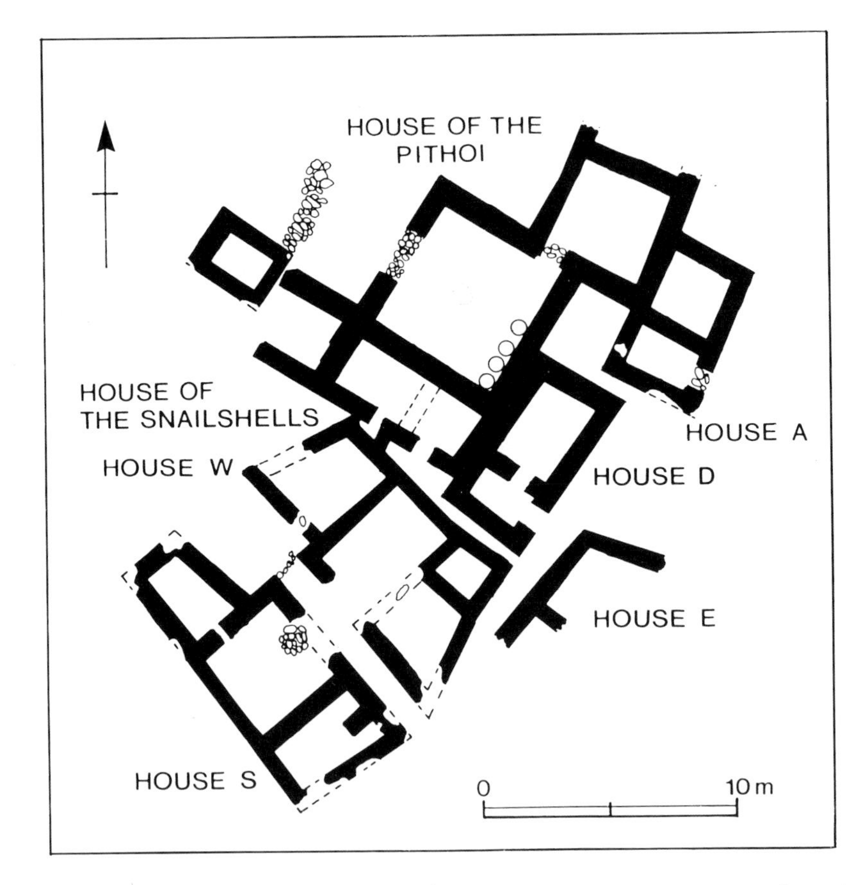

Fig. 4.7 Plan of 'Lerna III' buildings at Zygouries. Courtesy of Profs D.J. Pullen and R. Hägg.

material: Eutresis seems to have covered 8 ha in the 'Eutręsis' (EH I) stage, though less later, and big 'Lerna III' sites include Tiryns (6 ha) and Thebes (up to 20 ha) (Konsola 1990: 465), while Manika, which has a possible fortification, an extremely extensive cemetery and traces of a street plan, has been argued to cover 50 ha (Sampson 1986). But it has not been demonstrated that these sites were so extensive; more plausibly, perhaps, they consisted of separated groups of houses, as suggested for many Dark Age settlements, around a central nucleus. The smaller sites might have been tightly packed, with embryo street plans (Konsola 1984) like Zygouries (1.1 ha) (Fig. 4.7), Askitario (0.45 ha), and the early 'Lerna III' stage of Lithares (0.7 ha; Tzavella-Evjen 1985; Hägg and Konsola 1986, fig. 36); the fact that the last succeeded a 'Eutresis' settlement which may have covered 4 ha is a warning against making any assumptions about the direction development would take.

A notable feature of several 'Lerna III' sites is the appearance of monumental buildings and/or fortifications (Fig. 4.8). Mostly the buildings are of the 'cor-

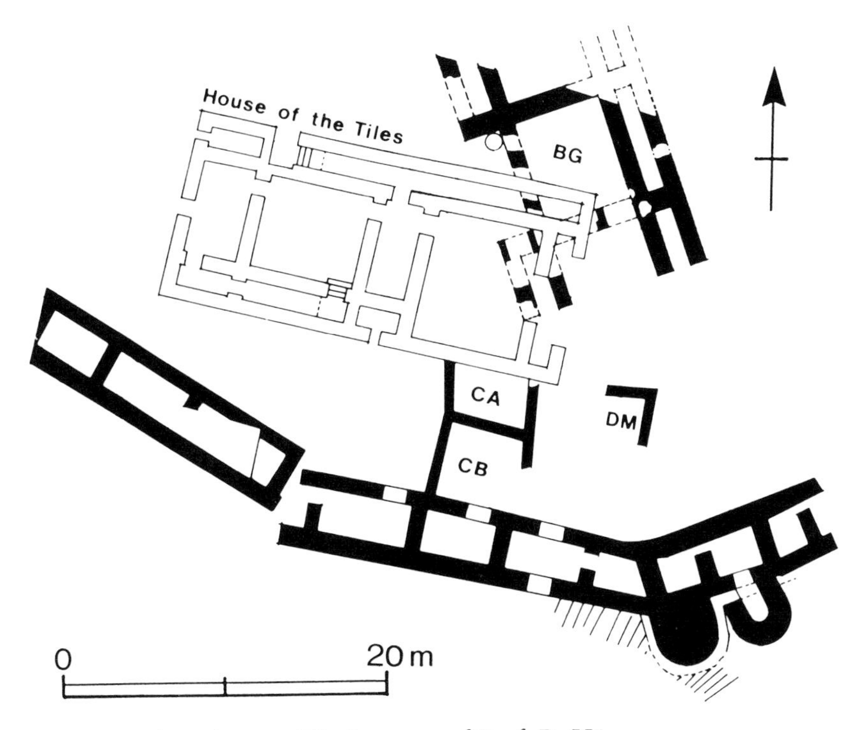

Fig. 4.8 Plan of Lerna III. Courtesy of Prof. R. Hägg.

ridor house' type, but the Tiryns 'Rundbau' should also be placed in this category. The temptation to attribute functions like those of palaces or temples to these buildings has proved hard to resist, but a recent discussion of EH architecture could reach no consensus on their function(s) (Hägg and Konsola 1986, 96); the 'Rundbau', however, is surely a public building (see Wiencke 1989: 503–5, where the features suggesting 'elite' use are stressed). The sites distinguished by such buildings, fortifications or other signs of significance such as the presence of valuable objects may have been becoming regional centres, even the capitals of embryo states, on the analogy of Troy; but the evidence from the succeeding stage suggests that everywhere except on Aegina this development was abortive.

A tendency of population to concentrate in substantial settlements can be seen to be common throughout the Aegean from the later EBA onwards, although in Crete this was combined with a pattern of small outlying settlements, which are not identifiable in the Cyclades or mainland; indeed, on the mainland the concentration seems accompanied by the temporary abandonment of some previously large sites and even whole territories, such as the Nemea valley and much of the southern Argolid (Fig. 4.6a). The mainland sites were made up of relatively large but simply planned buildings, often of the hall-and-porch or 'megaron' type (Fig. 4.9), but although they are substantial there is nothing to suggest that they were anything more than villages. No significant feature like a

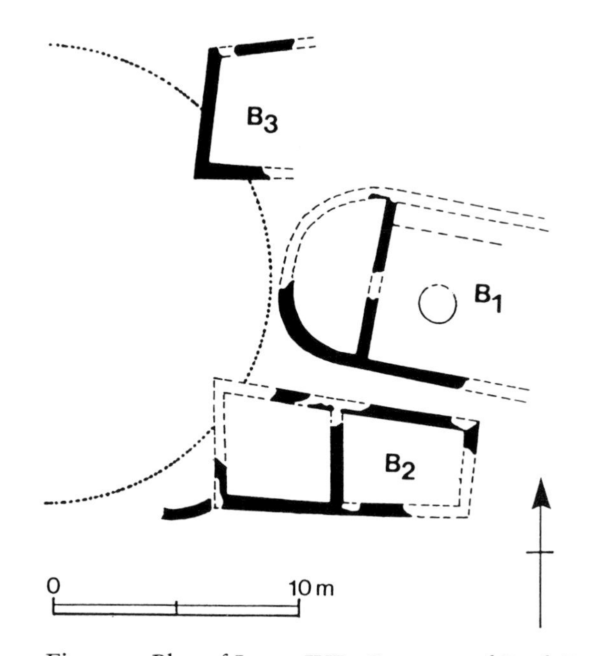

Fig. 4.9 Plan of Lerna IVB. Courtesy of Prof. R. Hägg.

fortification has been reliably reported (Darcque 1980: 32–3 persuasively suggests, on the basis of the stratigraphy, that the fortified village at Malthi is not MH but LH III). The total lack of likely intercommunal features such as ritual sites argues for a pattern of largely self-sufficient and independent communities, bound to each other by loose ties at best and having a relatively simple social organisation. In the Helladic region only Kolonna on Aegina looks a more complex type of settlement, which has clear affinities with the island towns (Walter and Felten 1981).

The most significant settlements of Crete and several other islands (Fig. 4.10) may reasonably be classified as towns, for they show notable similarities with the Near Eastern towns in arrangement, despite their smaller size. In general they are best known from their Second Palace Period phase, but signs of their town-like character are often evident earlier (cf. Phylakopi, Fig. 4.11, and Soles 1979 on Gournia). Their essential feature is a clear and fairly regular street plan which divides blocks of structures; in the Second Palace Period these can present a continuous facade to the street, but they may originally have been spaced. The street plan varies in appearance at different sites: sometimes it seems to focus on a public square or important building, sometimes simply to follow a line that serves as much of the settlement as possible (cf. Branigan 1972: 753–4 on Gournia, Palaikastro and Pseira, Figs 4.12, 13, 19). Alleyways run off to provide access to the interior of blocks and, not infrequently, routes for drainage channels or piping that ran from individual buildings to the main channels, which

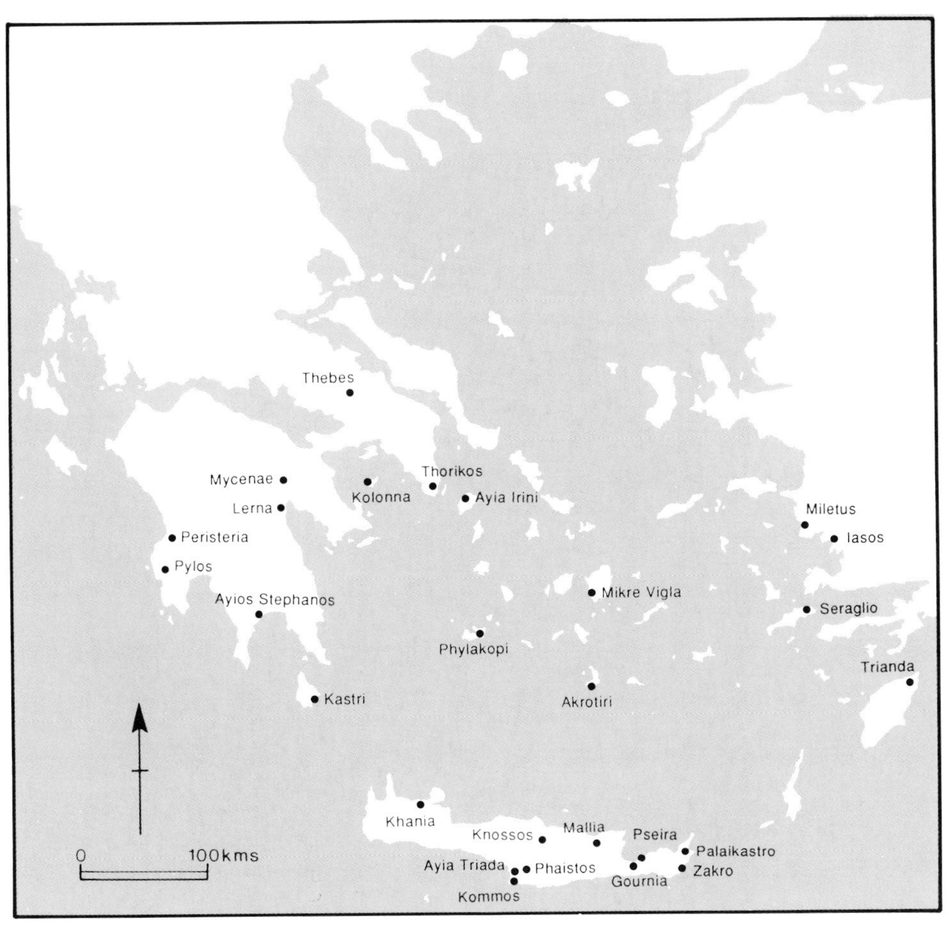

Fig. 4.10 Significant sites of the MBA and LBA.

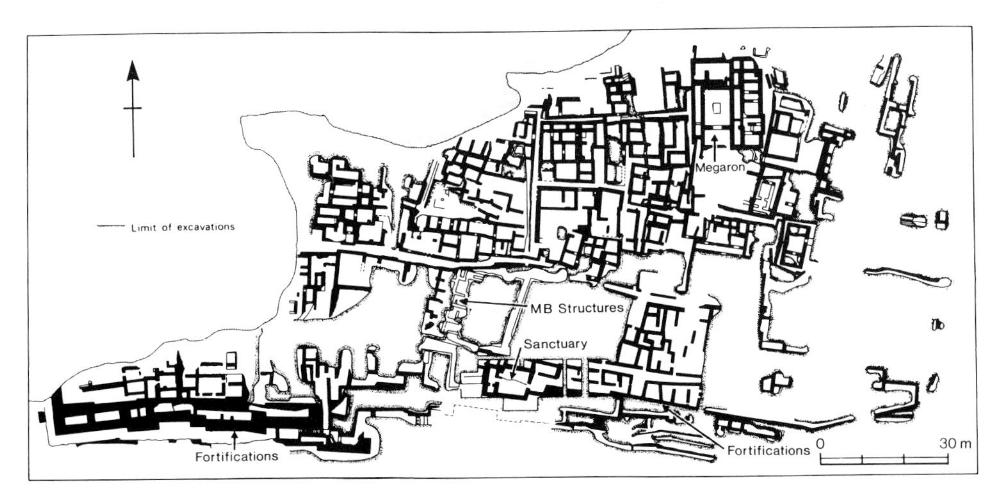

Fig. 4.11 Plan of LB Phylakopi. Courtesy of Prof. Lord Renfrew.

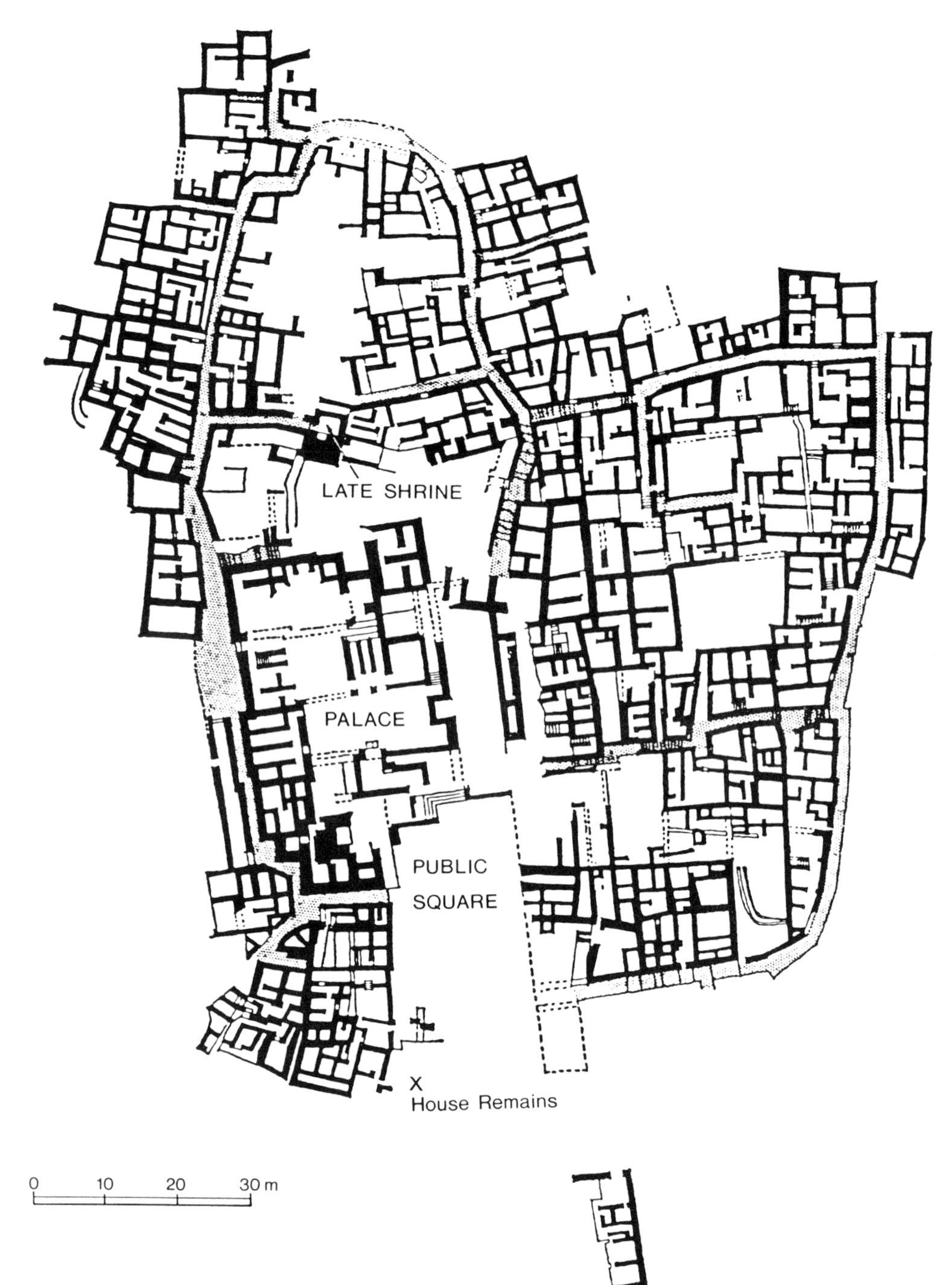

Fig. 4.12 Plan of MB–LB Gournia. After R.W. Hutchinson, *Prehistoric Crete* (Penguin Books 1962), p. 288 fig. 57, ©R.W. Hutchinson 1962. Reproduced by permission of Penguin Books Ltd.

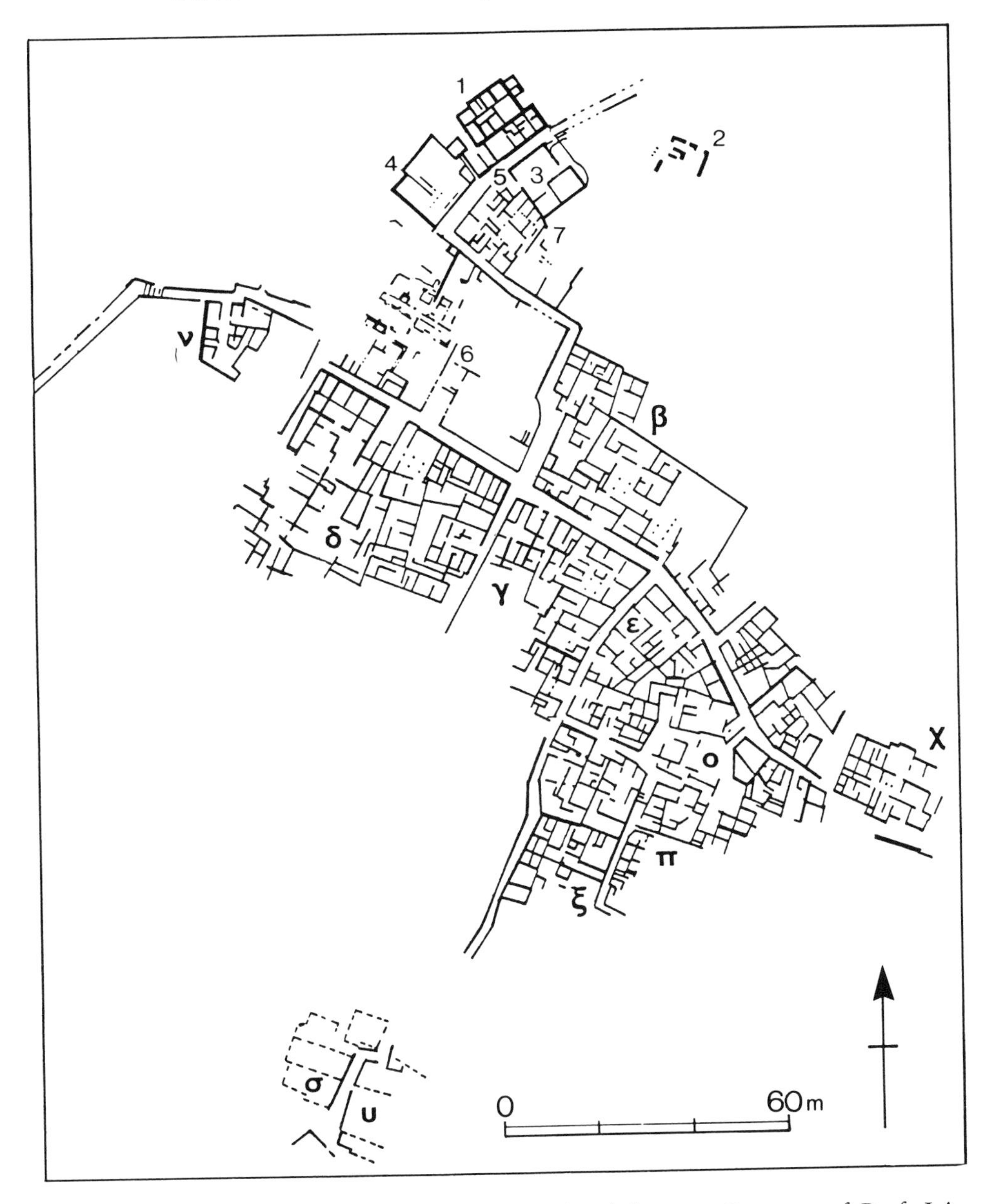

Fig. 4.13 Plan of Second Palace Period Palaikastro. Courtesy of Prof. J.A. MacGillivray and the Managing Committee of the British School at Athens, drawn by J. Driessen.

flanked the most important streets. At various points smaller squares or open spaces may occur. The houses vary in size, complexity, and architectural quality, but are generally multi-roomed and two-storeyed (cf. Figs 4.14, 15).

Palyvou's analysis (1986) of the Akrotiri layout (Fig. 4.16) demonstrates the

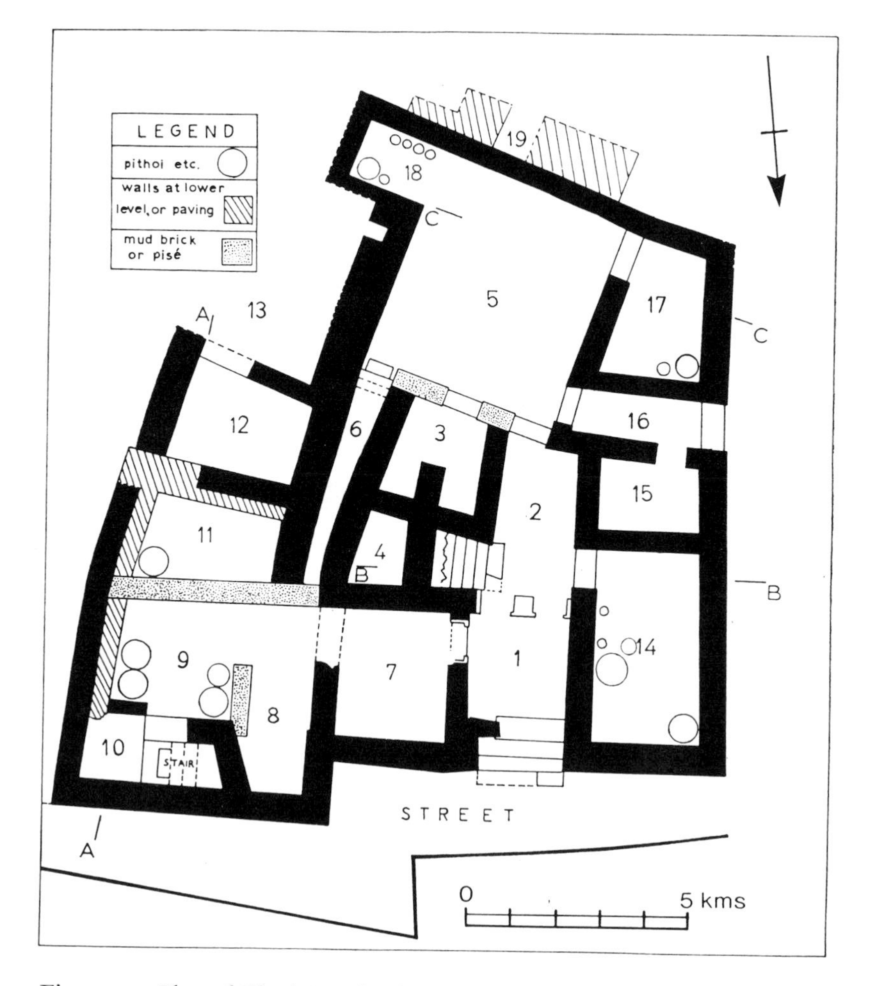

Fig. 4.14 Plan of Block N of Palaikastro. Courtesy of the Managing Committee of the British School at Athens.

likelihood of important underlying principles that may be considered a form of town planning and imply a degree of central control over building; this could even extend to the facades of houses, which show a regular system of projections and balancing insets along the main streets at Akrotiri. Overall, the impression is of a considerable degree of sophistication; the only feature of later Mediterranean towns which seems lacking is a public water supply.

Only the smallest examples demonstrably consist of a single group of structures, such as Ayia Irini (Fig. 4.17) and Kolonna (1 ha or less). Even at Gournia, whose central area is not much bigger (about 1.5 ha), there are indications of suburbs, separated by a natural dip in the ground, and many of the sites estimated to be really extensive, like Knossos (Fig. 4.18), Mallia, Palaikastro and Akrotiri (maximum areas suggested to be 75, 23+, 36 and 20 ha, respectively, in

Fig. 4.15 Restored house facades from the 'Town Mosaic', Knossos. After Evans 1921, fig. 226: a–b, i, q, u–v.

the Second Palace Period, Wiener 1990: 129–31), may in fact have consisted of a built-up nucleus surrounded by outlying villages, workshops and farmhouses. Except at Petras (Catling 1989: 106) there is no clear trace of a town wall in Crete, though there are various possibilities (see further Ch. 5, iv(b)), whereas Kolonna, Ayia Irini and Phylakopi were all extensively fortified on the landward side. The apparent circuit walls of the 'arrival town' on the West House miniature fresco at Akrotiri (Pl. 4.1) and the attacked town on the Siege Rhyton (Morgan 1988: 85–6) suggest that such walls may have been a common feature in the islands apart from Crete.

The towns are all likely to have functioned as 'central places' for their regions or islands, but some may have been primarily ports, like Pseira (Fig. 4.19), Mochlos and Zakro, and the greatest may be argued to have been the capitals of extensive territories and to have had lesser towns dependent on them. How such control came to be established, and why the towns developed in this way at this time, are not yet clear. A search for greater security may be part of the answer, but in Crete signs of troubled conditions in the late Prepalatial and First Palace Periods seem clearest in the east (e.g. the Pyrgos tower and cisterns, the fortified site at Ayia Photia, and the 'watchtowers'). The development may also reflect the

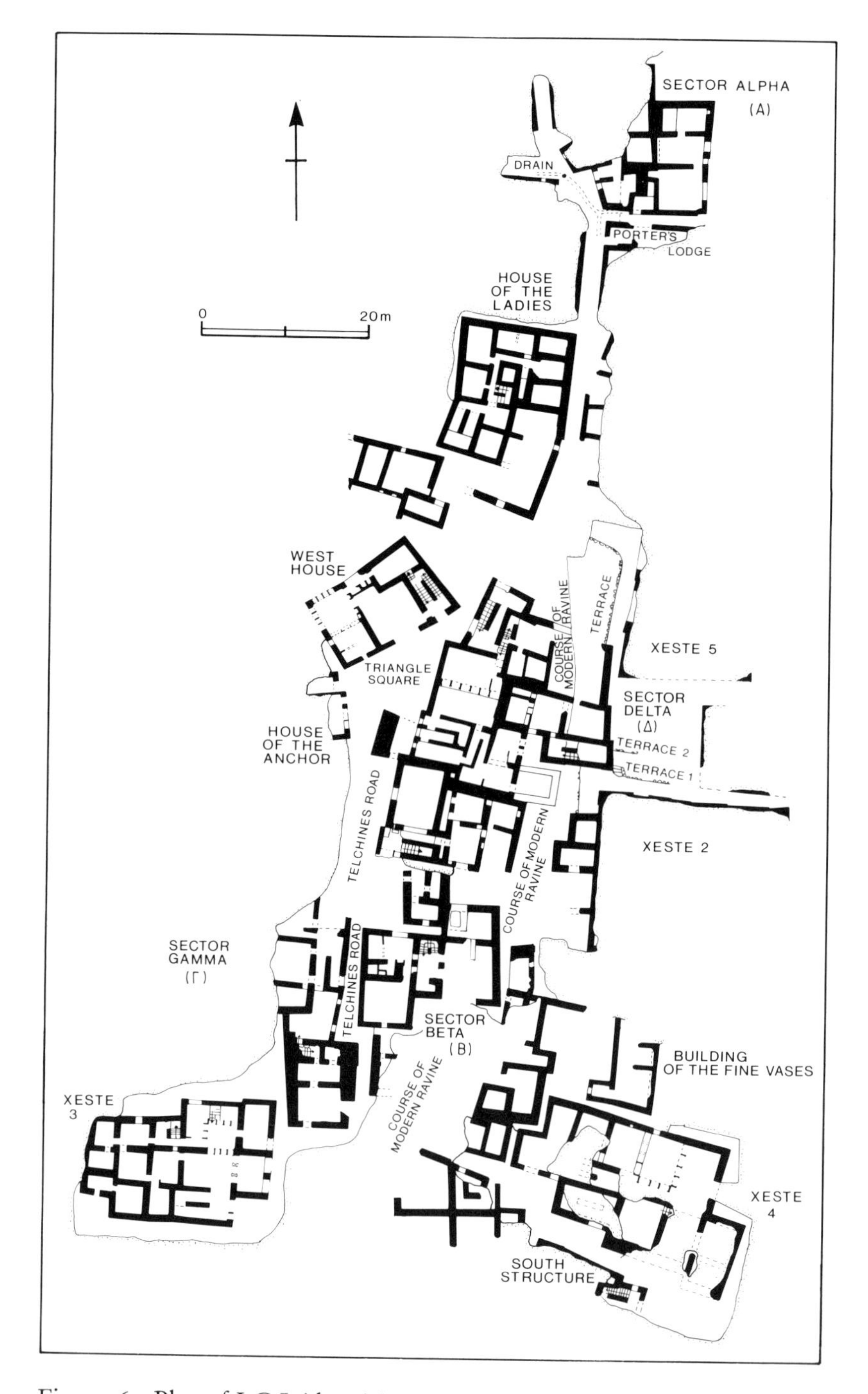

Fig. 4.16 Plan of LC I Akrotiri. Courtesy of Prof. C. Doumas.

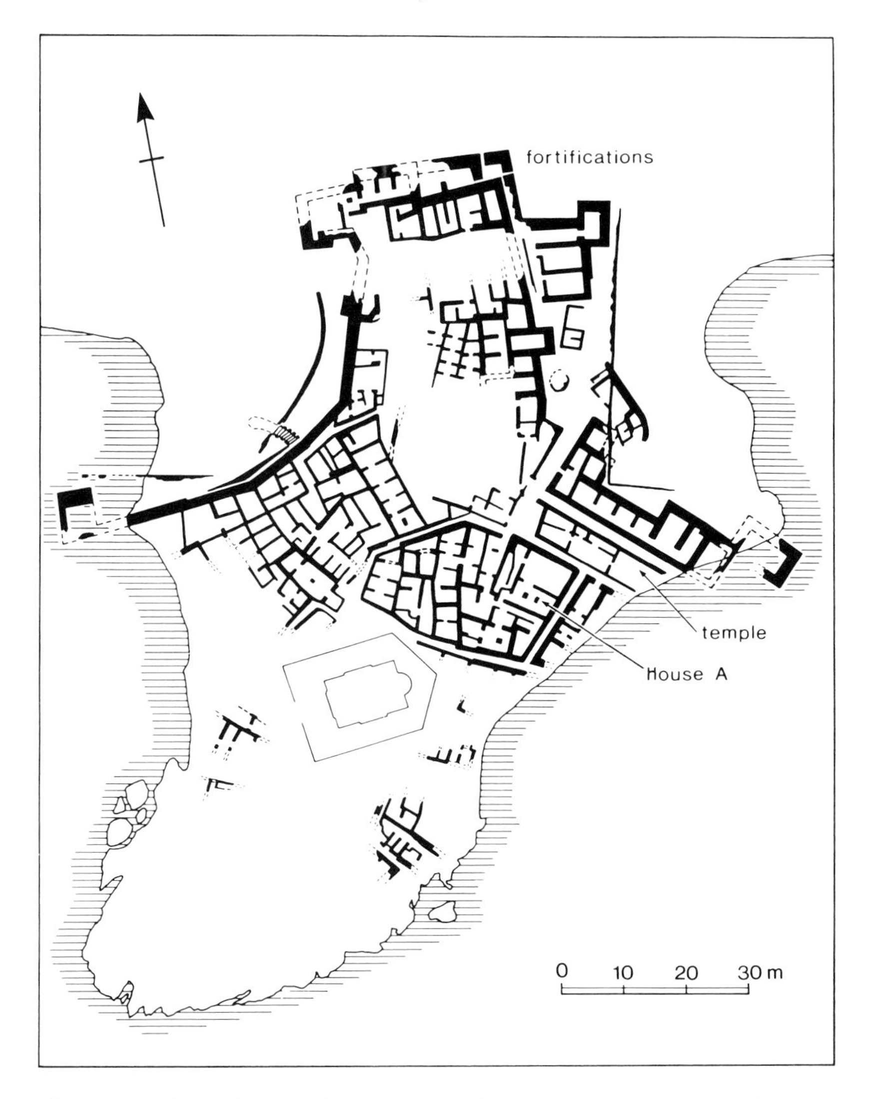

Fig. 4.17 Plan of Second Palace Period Ayia Irini. Courtesy of Drs R.L.N. Barber and E. Schofield.

strengthening of central authorities, for a likely administrative building is frequently identifiable within the towns.

It is in Crete that the setting for these towns is most clearly perceptible. Survey evidence indicates that sites of all kinds became more common in most regions, although the marginal Ayiopharango valley was beginning to be depopulated. Unfortunately, concentration on the larger sites has meant that the smaller remain poorly known. To judge from Xanthoudides's brief report of Kalathiana (1924: 84–5) and the scatter of substantial structures at Vasiliki (cf. Pendlebury 1939: 101, and the plans cited above, p. 53), their buildings might resemble the

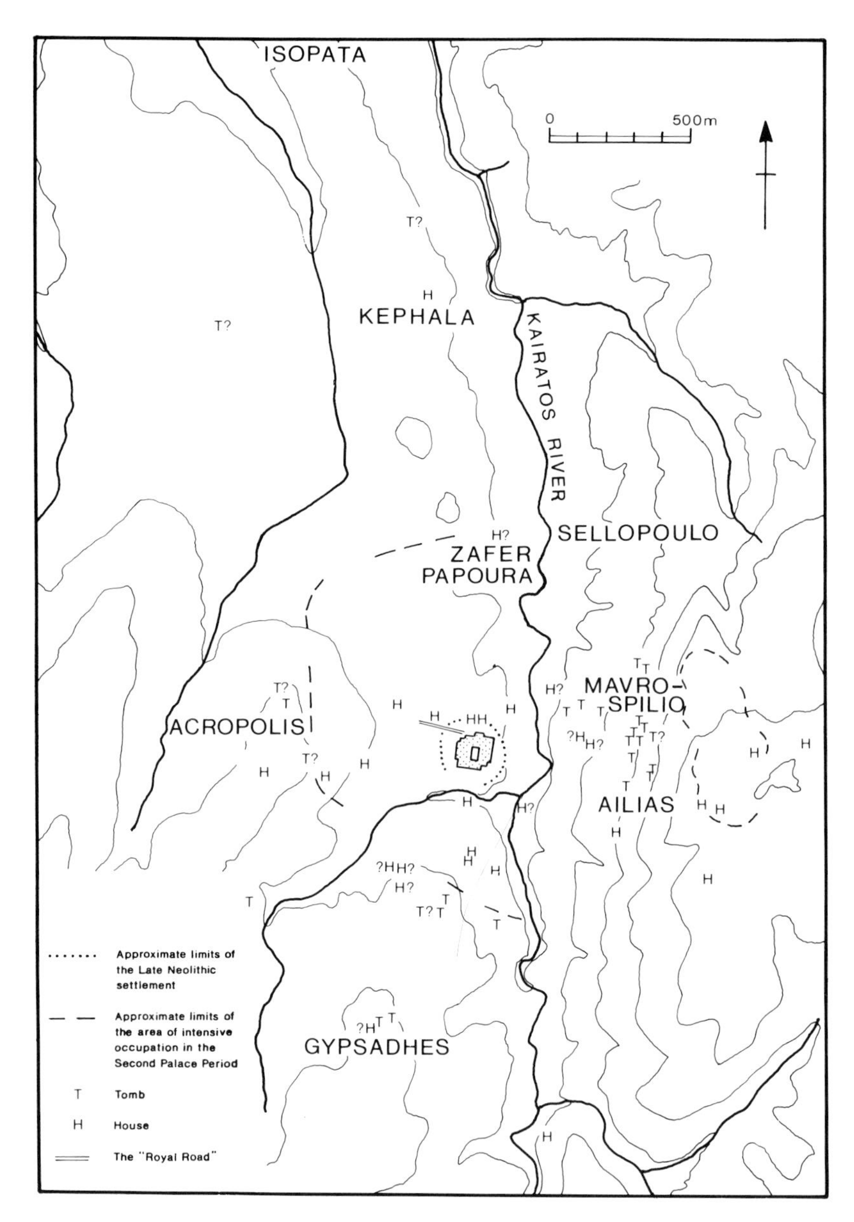

Fig. 4.18 The distribution of First and Second Palace Period remains over the site of Knossos.

simpler town-houses, and Pyrgos seems like a miniature town; both here and at Kalathiana evidence for one superior building can be identified, suggesting that the pattern identified in many towns was repeated in the more substantial villages.

Too great a distinction should not be made between towns and villages in

Pl. 4.1 The 'arrival town' on the West House miniature fresco, Akrotiri. Courtesy of the Faculty Board of Classics, University of Cambridge, and Dr L. Morgan.

terms of their activities; the majority of Aegean townsfolk probably owned and/or worked on the land, even those who were primarily craft specialists, priests or administrators. But the presence of such persons would be what made the towns 'central places', and any merchants would visit or be based in them. They may also have functioned as religious and ceremonial centres, but the most important Cretan religious sites seem to have been in the countryside or in palaces (see Ch. 8). Incidentally, the presence of many rural religious sites in east Crete, plausibly interpreted as serving local communities (Peatfield 1983: 273–4), argues against the suggestion that there was little rural population here in MM times (Driessen and MacGillivray 1989: 101–2).

Survey suggests further expansion of settlement in Crete in the Second Palace Period, to the extent that in some parts all agricultural land of reasonable quality may have been farmed (Warren 1984a; Fig. 4.20); the terraces and dams of Pseira (French 1991: 76) suggest an attempt to make maximum use of the land. Many small sites that could represent isolated farms have been identified, as also in the Dodecanese, now part of the Minoan culture zone (Melas 1985, 1988b); there are indications of a similar pattern on Thera (cf. Fig. 4.21 for a farm identified at Phtellos), but not Melos or Kea. Large structures, the so-called 'villas' (Cadogan 1976, Ch. 11; Hood 1983), are also a distinct type in Crete, which seem particu-

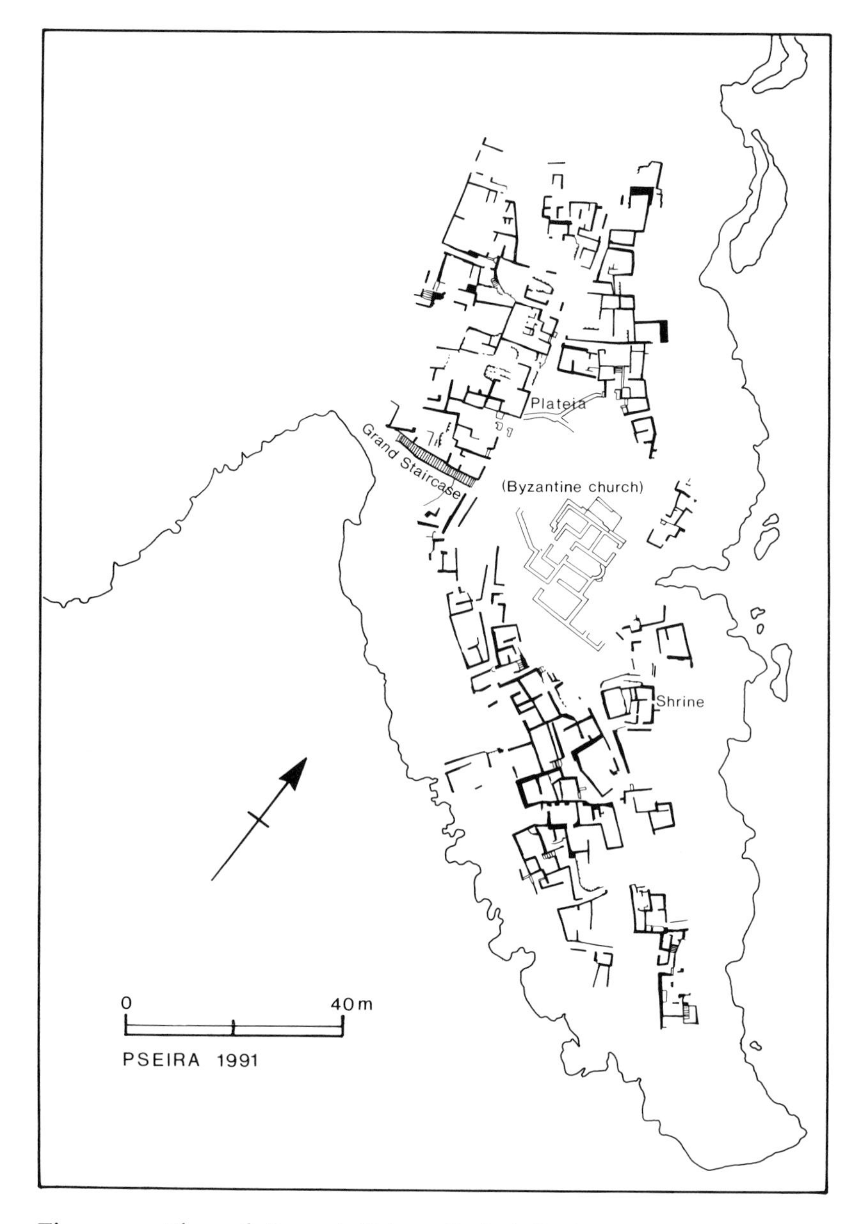

Fig. 4.19 Plan of Second Palace Period Pseira. Courtesy of Prof. P.P. Betancourt.

larly common in the east (Driessen and MacGillivray 1989: 103–4); but the suggestion of isolation implicit in the terms 'villa' or 'country house' may be inappropriate, for evidence of associated settlements, as at Pyrgos, is increasingly being detected (cf. Zois in Hägg and Marinatos 1987: 46 on Nirou Khani; Tzedakis *et al.* 1989: 63, n. 61). Nor is it clear that all examples combined the

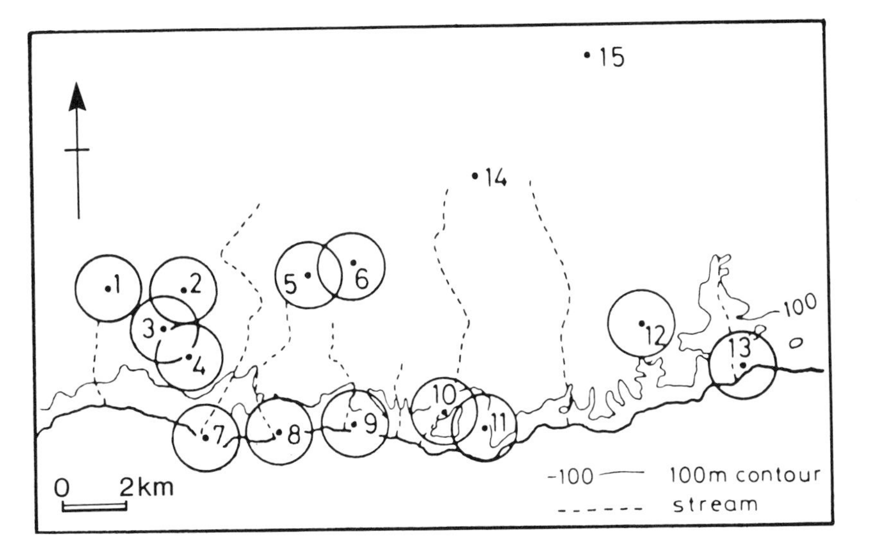

Fig. 4.20 Occupation in the south coastal region of Crete, south of the Lasithi Mountains, in the Second Palace Period. Courtesy of Profs P.M. Warren and R. Hägg.
Circles represent 1 km territorial radii. 1 Khondros (4 sites here). 2 Ano Viannos: Ligaras. 3 Ano Viannos: Galana Kharakia. 4. Mount Keraton. 5 Amiras: Khoroi. 6 Aghios Vasilios. 7 Trokhaloi West. 8 Trokhaloi East. 9 Arvi. 10 Kalami: Paphlangos. 11 Kalami: Psari Phoradha. 12 Gdokhia (approximate location). 13 Myrtos: Pyrgos. 14 Kato Symi sanctuary. 15 Selakanon.

functions of high-status residence and centre of administration, storage and ceremony; but excavation has often produced evidence of one or more of these functions, in the form of high-quality architecture and frescoes, suites of ceremonial rooms, Linear A tablets and groups of sealings, and considerable storage capacity. Their local importance is further suggested by indications that they were often placed to have a good view over a territory and be conspicuous within it, in this respect resembling peak sanctuaries.

Other evidence can be added to that for storage capacity to suggest that the 'villas' played a major role in intensive agriculture in their neighbourhoods. Wine and oil presses have been identified at Vathypetro, a wine press also in a building near Zakro, and at Pyrgos a tablet listing a quantity of wine has been found. This evidence may be linked to the general administrative interest in wine, olives and olive oil, as well as wheat, demonstrated by the ideograms used on Linear A texts throughout Crete (Palaima 1987: 304–5). The towns, which now reach their most elaborate phase, may well have had an 'upper class' of land owners with similar interests; presses have been identified at Palaikastro (Driessen and MacGillivray 1989: 106) and in greater quantity at Zakro, where it is suggested that the palace was supplied from the town houses (Chryssoulaki and Platon 1987: 84).

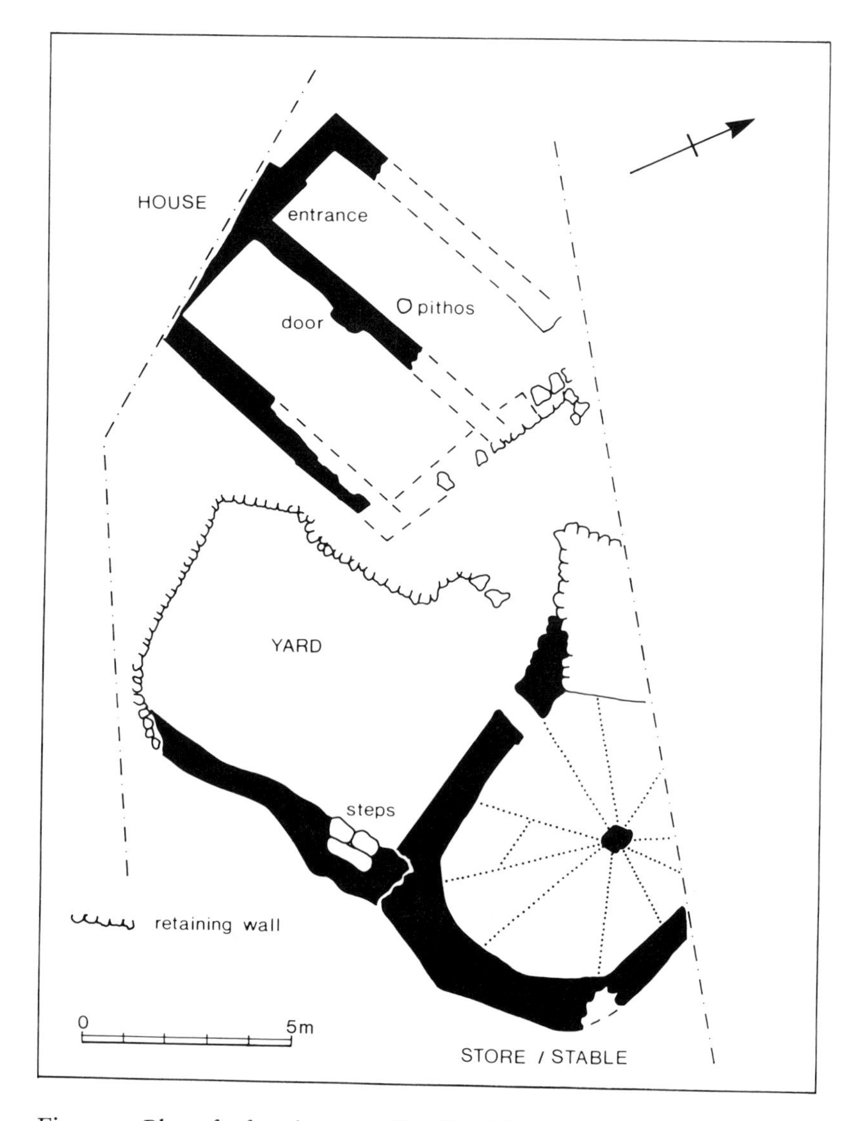

Fig. 4.21 Plan of a farmhouse at Phtellos, Thera. Courtesy of Dr R.L.N. Barber and Prof. C. Doumas.

Weingarten's painstaking analysis of the numerous sealings found at important sites (1986b, 1988, 1989, 1991) has produced valuable evidence for the existence of a network of connections between them, supplementing the evidence from the distribution of fine LM IB pottery and architectural refinements. In many cases such sealings seem to have covered the wrappings of folded documents, presumed to be of leather or parchment, while others were attached to containers, or may represent rations entitlements used by passing messengers. One major source, House A at Zakro, may have been like a customs house, monitoring the movement of goods inland from the port; an even larger group comes from the Ayia Triada 'villa', plausibly suggested to have become the administrative centre of the Mesara (La Rosa in Shaw and Shaw 1985: 47–50). The characteristic style of a Zakro seal-cutter (the 'Zakro Master', Weingarten 1986a) allows the identification of Zakro-made sealings at Ayia Triada, Knossos, Katsamba, and the Sklavokambos 'villa' west of Tylissos; other sealings that were probably made at Knossos with gold seal-rings have been found at Ayia Triada, Zakro, Sklavokambos, Tylissos and Gournia (Fig. 4.22).

Such evidence suggests regular and secure exchanges at various levels within Crete (Weingarten 1991) and might well be taken to imply that all these sites were included within a single administration, although the content of the transmitted documents remains utterly unknown, and could as well involve negotiations, contracts, etc. between different administrations as within a single one. The marked differences between the systems deducible at Ayia Triada, to which Khania seems close, although its sealings show few links with those elsewhere, and Zakro, which can be paralleled at Knossos, could be explained in terms of their different functions as sites. Certainly, sealed and often inscribed roundels are used in much the same way at all these sites (Hallager 1988). But there are no comparable sealings outside Crete, although Linear A tablets have been found at Ayia Irini (also a roundel) and Phylakopi.

The evidence for fortifications noted above suggests that conditions were not always peaceful in the Aegean, even in this period of prosperity. One source of potential danger may have been the growing power of mainland centres (e.g. Mycenae, Pylos, Peristeria; Fig. 4.23), which are most remarkable for what they lack, in comparison with the island towns. There is no sign of development towards a townlike plan or of monumental building, nor is there any trace of the administrative use of the seal or writing. The new ruling elite on the mainland are most clearly distinguished by their wealthy burials; their houses might be somewhat more elaborate than the average (some contained simple frescoes) and have modest storage facilities associated (cf. Kilian 1987b: 33 on Tiryns and Kakovatos), but there is nothing on the scale of the Cretan 'villas' or larger Cycladic town-houses. The sources of their wealth and the explanation for the massive growth in exchange of valuable materials that it implies remain problematic; certainly, there is nothing to associate it with an intensification of agriculture, and the possible growth in the population suggested by the reoccupation of some inland regions in the north-east Peloponnese (Wright *et al.* 1990: 641) cannot yet be shown to be a widespread phenomenon.

The major destruction horizon in Crete at the end of the Second Palace Period was followed by real decline. While there is evidence for continuing occupation of several town sites and, after a while, of further construction on a large scale at some, there are signs of declining standards, such as the failure to maintain the drainage system at Palaikastro. The Linear B texts of Knossos make clear that local centres played an important role in the administration of the state ruled

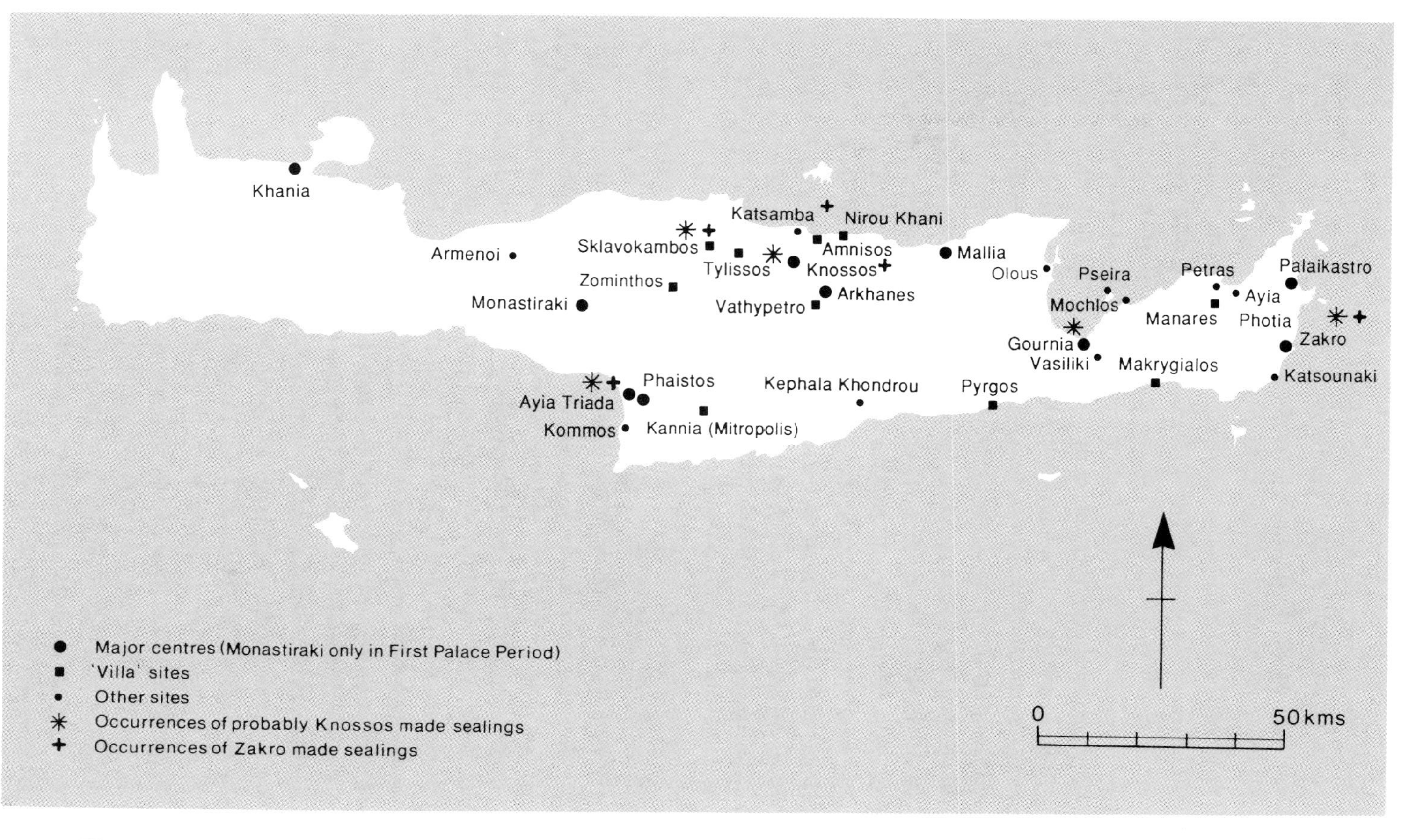

Fig. 4.22 Significant sites of the Palatial Periods in Crete.

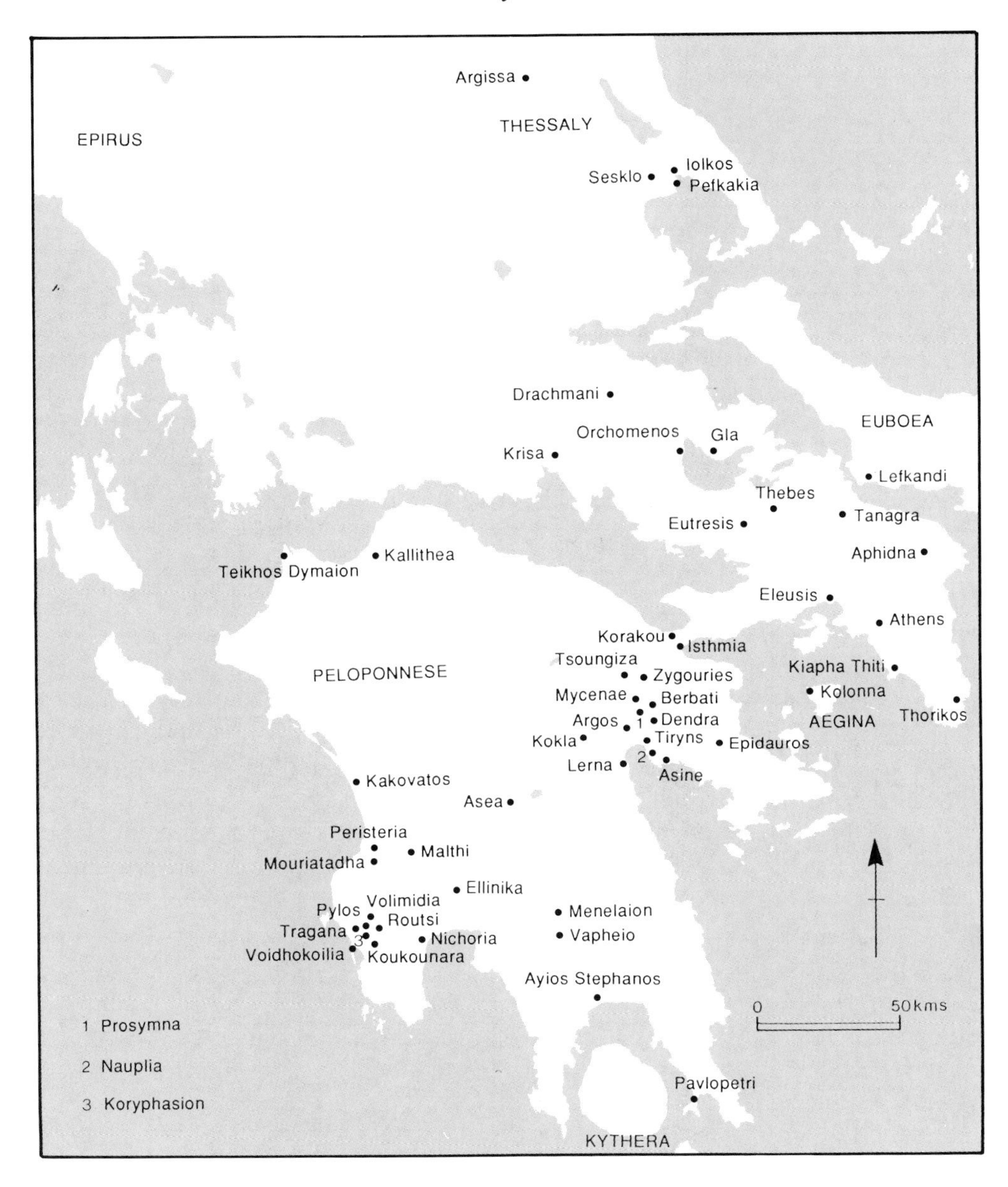

Fig. 4.23 Significant MH–LH IIIB sites on the mainland.

from there, which seems to have controlled or been influential in much of central and western Crete, though the relationship of western Crete to the centre is not wholly clear (Bennet 1987: 310). A combination of textual and archaeological evidence shows that among these were Tylissos, Kydonia (Khania) and Ayia Triada, which may be the *Da-wo* of the texts, while Kommos was a major port in south Crete (Shaw 1986). But 'villas' seem to have disappeared as a class, as did some towns and many of the small settlements, although there was still a considerable spread of large and small sites.

The texts provide precious glimpses of the economy of this final palace phase at Knossos. It is clear that herding sheep for wool was a major activity; large flocks were pastured in many regions, and it has been estimated that between a quarter and a third of the entire land surface of Crete would have been required for them (Bennet 1987: 309). Further, large numbers of women were maintained to produce textiles, presumably from this wool, being issued with rations at Knossos and other centres; quite probably they were producing not merely for the internal needs of the state but for export. Also, as noted above, many trees and vines were recorded, along with large quantities of olive oil, wine and wheat; one set of texts records quantities of wheat and sometimes other commodities received from the populations of various districts, which are plausibly interpreted as tax records, although the quantity recorded at *Da-wo* is so great that it may represent the entire harvest of the Mesara (Chadwick 1976: 117–18). Plainly, the palace economy had, if anything, become more intensive; there may have been greater emphasis on wool and textile production, and there seem to have been considerable changes in record-keeping (Palaima 1987: 305).

Whatever the cause of the final destruction of the Knossos palace, its consequences were less dire for Crete than used to be thought. In particular, it is becoming clear that Khania survived as a major palatial centre, continuing to use Linear B. Its influence is detectable in the wide distribution of its distinctive pottery, in the association of the widely distributed storage stirrup jars, apparently olive oil containers, with western Crete (although some might come from other centres in the west), and in the evidence for a pattern of substantial settlements with small satellites around Khania, suggesting a thriving rural economy (Moody 1983: 302; Lukermann and Moody 1985); a possible 'villa' has even been reported (Catling 1979: 42). This evidence for continuing prosperity can be paralleled in other parts of Crete. To some extent Minoan traditions survived, though domestic architecture was changing (Hayden 1987): the settlement of Kephala Khondrou has some resemblance to a town block, as also to Myrtos (Kanta 1980: 114–15), and the Postpalatial settlement of Karphi resembles a traditional town more than anything Mycenaean in its layout. There are other indications that Crete did not lose all its individuality at this time, so that to term it 'Mycenaean' is incorrect; but it did lose its position of cultural preeminence in the Aegean.

Settlement evidence from the other Aegean islands is not abundant, and although new settlements of substantial appearance can be identified, little can be said about most except that they tend to be in defensible positions and were sometimes fortified in the later Third Palace Period. Ayia Irini declined steadily, but Phylakopi seems to have remained a town, although eventually another substantial site was founded in southern Melos; the general pattern of population concentrated in a few major settlements apparently continued, for survey has failed to produce evidence of small sites. The Third Palace Period is represented in the Dodecanese largely by cemeteries, whose number, size and relative wealth should indicate the existence of several substantial settlements, particularly on Rhodes; but overall the evidence from the islands outside Crete is very unsatisfactory.

On the mainland, however, it is clear that the Third Palace Period saw the greatest expansion of settlement in the BA (Fig. 4.24). Surveys have presented a

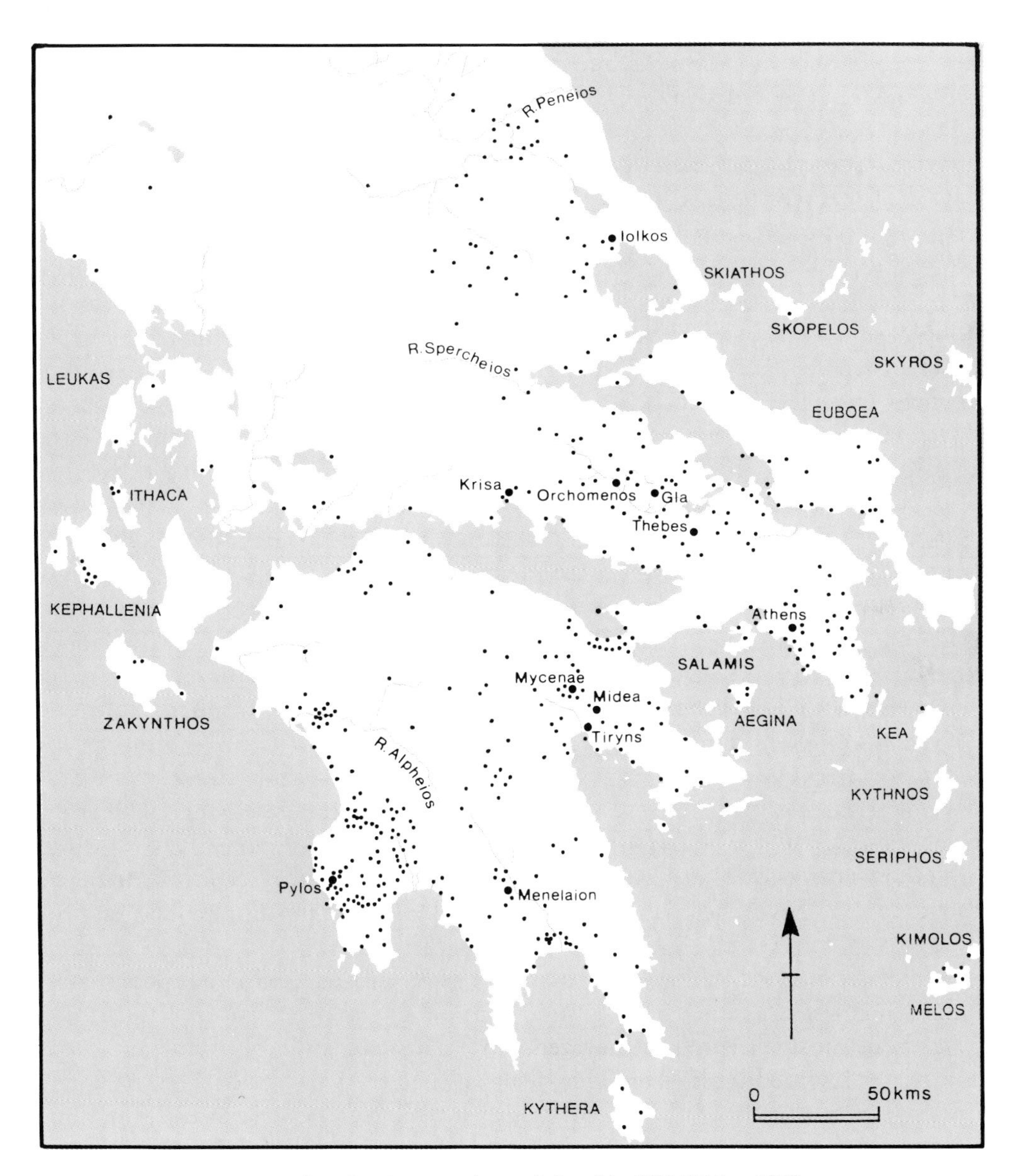

Fig. 4.24 Site distribution on the mainland in LH IIIA2–IIIB.

generally consistent picture of the establishment of many new settlements, ranging in size from likely villages to farmsteads; these may have been satellites of larger communities, but the patterns of relationship have not been studied much (cf. Fig. 4.6b). Such an expansion, comparable with those of 'Lerna III' (EH II) on the mainland and the Second Palace Period in the Minoan region, suggests an increase in population and a desire to exploit more of the land available (cf. van Andel and Runnels 1987: 315), probably both to support the increased population and to improve the economies of the states involved. For it is likely that the establishment of palace economies on the mainland is to be linked to this expansion, although the circumstances of their establishment and the nature of the link are not completely clear.

The presence of Linear B texts and inscribed sealings indicates that palace economies were established in the Argolid, centred on Mycenae (to which Tiryns may well have been subordinate, at least for part of the period), in Messenia, centred on Pylos, and in Boeotia, centred on Thebes, which may also have controlled much of Euboea. The existence of others may be hypothesised, as at Orchomenos (to which Gla might have been attached) and Athens, but it would be rash to assume that the whole Mycenaean world was organised in this way. Rather, less organised principalities, close in nature to their early Mycenaean predecessors, may have been normal in many regions.

Even at this most flourishing stage of the Mycenaean culture it is not easy to discuss the nature of the settlements, for lack of sufficiently extensive excavations; Tsoungiza is remarkable as a rare excavated example of a very small settlement, consisting of only two separated clusters of structures (Wright *et al.* 1990: 635). Even 'large' sites did not cover more than a few hectares in most cases: one of the biggest estimates is 8 ha for Tiryns, though if the whole Kadmeia at Thebes was built over, it would have covered some 30 ha, and a settlement with a regular plan close to Gla may have been even larger, though little detail has yet been published (Kienast 1987; cf. also Kilian 1988a: 133). Evidence of established street layouts dividing blocks of structures and containing drainage systems, as in the Aegean towns, occurs sporadically at best. Thus, on the Mycenae citadel drains are linked to specific buildings (Iakovidis 1983: 67–8), and elsewhere the LH IIIB blocks of structures on terraces, some with drains, such as the West House group and Panayia houses (Mylonas Shear 1987), seem to have expanded from original nuclei without any indications of constraints imposed by a prior town layout, and are intermingled with tombs (Fig. 4.25). At Nichoria the street lined with structures in Area III, which was laid out in LH IIIB, coexisted with a seemingly random scatter of houses in Area IV (Fig. 4.26) (Rapp and Aschenbrenner 1978: 120, 126–7).

Overall, Mycenaean settlement architecture does not seem very impressive, on present evidence. But this is not to say that Mycenaean settlements were completely without structure. On the contrary, there is a clear intention to reflect the social hierarchy in elevating the palace and sometimes other important structures at Mycenae, Tiryns and Pylos on an acropolis above the rest of the settlement.

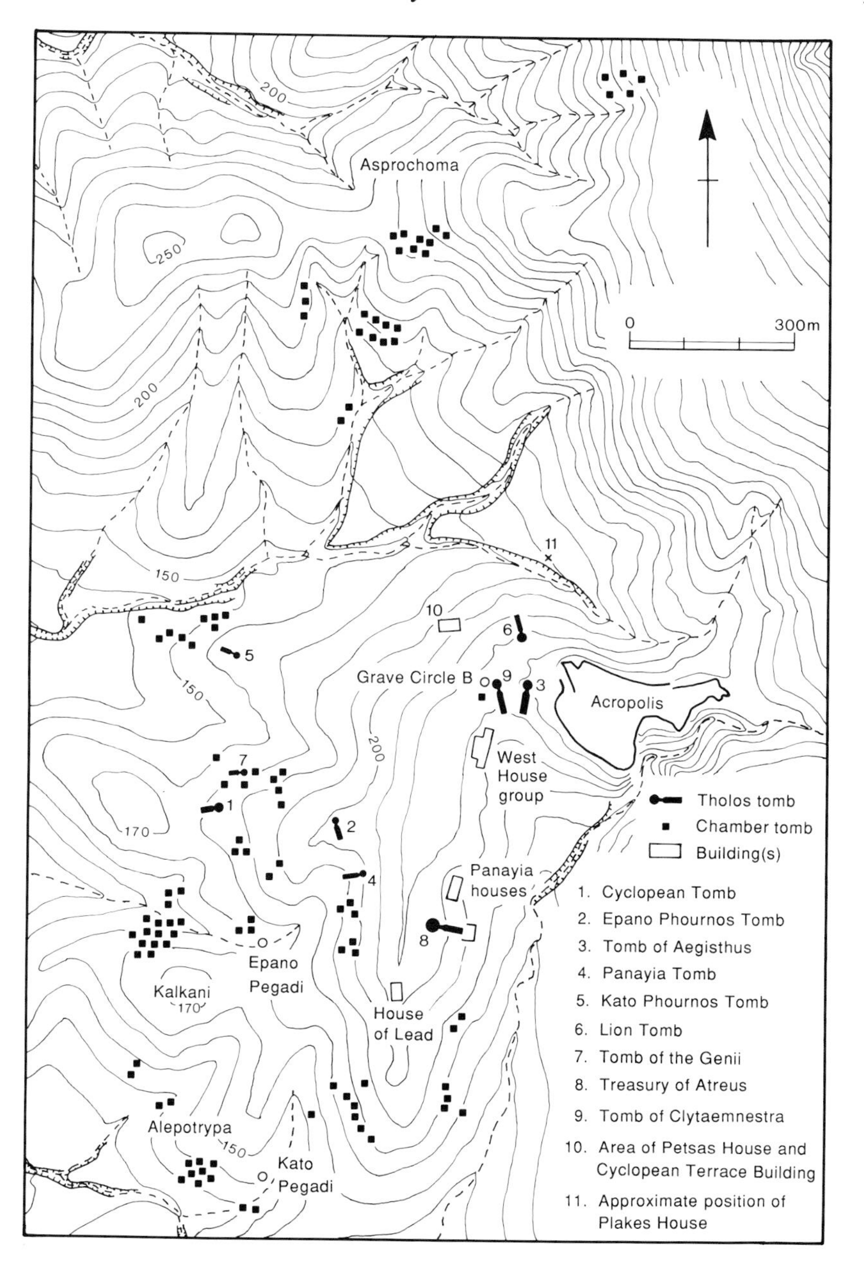

Fig. 4.25 The distribution of remains over the site of Mycenae. Incorporating information supplied by Dr E.B. French from the Mycenae Survey (AE and BSA).

This cannot be demonstrated at present to be a universal feature, but even where, as at Thebes, the whole settlement lay on the same plateau, the palace seems to have occupied the highest part. There is a very considerable gap in architectural quality between the palaces and average Mycenaean houses, which very often consisted of a few roughly square or rectangular rooms, rarely grouped in any distinctive fashion and less well provided with fittings than the earlier town-houses of Crete and the Cyclades. Some of the more impressive examples, which mostly belong to Hiesel's 'corridor house' class (1990: 111–55; cf. Kilian 1988c: 32), seem to be purely residential, like the Panayia houses at Mycenae; but the West House group are plausibly interpreted as a combination of residence, storehouses and offices (Tournavitou 1989b, 1990) and many others may not have been ordinary residential buildings. The excavations at Mycenae have in fact produced an unusually large number of such buildings; a wide scatter of fresco fragments at Thebes suggests a similar situation there, but this may well prove to be a feature of the greatest sites only.

The occurrence of fortifications has often been taken to indicate that warfare

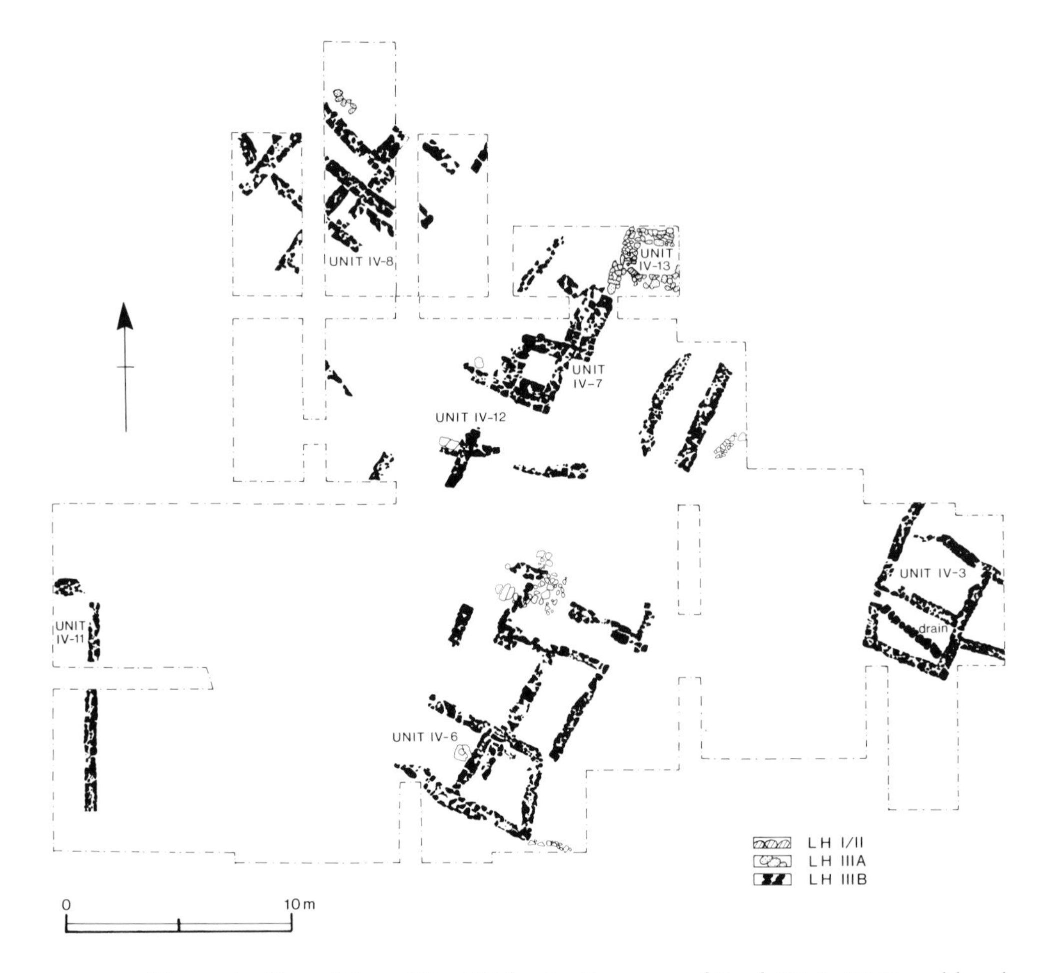

Fig. 4.26 Plan of Area IV at Nichoria. Courtesy of Profs W.A. McDonald and N.C. Wilkie.

was more prevalent at this time than earlier, but this is implicitly contradicted by the wide distribution of often tiny settlements, which argues for a general feeling of security, and by the evidently stable histories of most large settlements until late in the Third Palace Period. Until that stage, fortifications are notably rare, and of the certifiably early examples, those at Mycenae and Tiryns may have been intended to express power, that at Gla to be a centre of control, rather than to provide defence against a serious threat. Only later is this the apparent motivation for construction or extension of fortifications, the provision of accessible water supplies at Mycenae, Tiryns and Athens, and the enclosure of large open spaces, perhaps intended as refuges for local population and their livestock, at Eutresis and Krisa; and still no attempt seems to have been made to fortify such major centres as Pylos and Orchomenos.

The belief in the warlike propensities of Mycenaean society in this period seems in fact to derive largely from the belief that this society is accurately mirrored in the Homeric epics and other legendary material. But the world of Homer's heroes, in which wealth is essentially represented by livestock and movable treasures, and to acquire these by raiding is not thought at all reprehensible, seems completely at odds with the world of orderly taxation of territories' produce reflected in the Linear B texts. While raiding and piracy may have been practised in some parts of the Mycenaean world, just as they still were in parts of Classical Greece (Thucydides I.5), it is difficult to believe that they were encouraged in the palace societies; as Killen has argued (1985: 260), these show every indication of a strong centralised authority, which one would not expect to countenance such activities. Even when, to judge from the features just cited, there seems to be increased apprehension of attack in the later stages of the Third Palace Period, this is more likely to reflect interstate warfare than endemic raiding.

It has been common to lay stress on the palaces' control of the economy in their territories, considered to reflect their function as redistributive centres. It has even been suggested that they encouraged local specialisation in some forms of production at the expense of self-sufficiency, thus contributing to the collapse at the end of the Third Palace Period when the system broke down. But when scrutinised the evidence does not really support this interpretation. The territory of Pylos was divided into two provinces, headed by Pylos and a centre named *Re-u-ko-to-ro*, probably Leuktron (perhaps the site of Ellinika), each of which was subdivided into a number of districts for administrative purposes (Fig. 4.27); but the same six commodities are required from every district in regular quotas, which do not seem to reflect local specialisation but perhaps a system designed to produce more or less equal quantities from groupings of these districts. Remarkably, these commodities do not include any of the agricultural staples; in fact only two are identifiable, a form of woollen textile and oxhides, but the others are likely to be raw materials of some kind (Treuil *et al.* 1989: 496 notes as possibilities a herb, a spice, wax and honey, but cf. Ventris and Chadwick 1973:

THE HITHER PROVINCE (*De-we-ro-ai-ko-ra-i-ja*, 'on this side of Aigaleon'?)	*THE FURTHER PROVINCE* (*Pe-rai-ko-ra-i-ja*, 'on the other side of Aigaleon'?)
CAPITAL: *PU-RO* (PYLOS)	*Re-u-ko-to-ro* (Leuktron?)
DISTRICTS IN STANDARD ORDER (some name-forms in dative):	
Pi-swa	*Ti-mi-to-a-ke-e/Ti-mi-ti-ja*
Me-ta-pa	*Ra-wa-ra-tya*
Pe-to-no	*Sa-ma-ra*
Pa-ki-ja-ne	*A-si-ja-ti-ja*
A-phu	*E-ra-te-re-we*
A-ke-re-wa	*Za-ma-e-wi-ja*
E-ra-to/Ro-u-so	*E-re-i*, subdivided for taxation purposes into *E-sa-re-we-ja* and *A-te-re-wi-ja*
Ka-ra-do-ro	
Ri-jo	

Fig. 4.27 The administrative subdivisions of the Pylos state.

464–5). Flax production certainly seems to have been a speciality of some communities, since it was taxed separately, but these were quite widely spread; the sheep flocks of interest to the palace, however, were largely concentrated in three districts. Other indications of local specialisation are hard to find, and it cannot be assumed to have been general.

To judge from the Pylos archive and more fragmentary material from Mycenae and Thebes, the Mycenaean palaces certainly did distribute quantities of material: agricultural produce was given in rations and materials to workers, gifts, notably olive oil, were sent to shrines from the Pylos palace, and imported materials like bronze, gold and ivory were provided for craft specialists (but Smith 1991 argues that some smiths were not supplied with bronze by the state). They had a considerable interest in wool, and at Pylos in linen; many textile workers, some highly specialised, were supported to produce textiles at Pylos, and Thebes received quantities of wool not merely from its own territory, but, to judge from a tablet in the House of Shields, from Mycenae also (Tournavitou 1990b: 85). Evidently they also dealt in olive oil, both plain and perfumed: Shelmerdine has marshalled evidence to suggest that the Pylos palace was partly turned into a perfumed oil factory in its later stages (1985), and the large storage stirrup jars believed to be oil containers have been found in palaces and other important buildings at Mycenae, Thebes and other major sites, though many of these must have contained imported Cretan oil.

But the only agricultural commodities recorded as coming in to the palace or being handled by the administration are wool at Mycenae and Thebes, flax and some wheat at Pylos, herbs and spices in small quantities at Mycenae, livestock at Thebes (Piteros *et al.* 1990). Indications of where the palaces got their supplies of major agricultural staples are lacking, although it has been argued that territories close to the Pylos palace may have paid a tax in wheat (Killen 1985: 244). Thus the picture of the mainland palaces as clearing houses for all the produce of their territories is not supported by the data; it cannot be assumed that they would have been run on identical lines to Knossos, and the possibility should be considered that much of the orchard produce used by the palaces came solely from estates controlled by their functionaries. Indeed, the existence of olive cultivation on any scale in the palace economies has been questioned; but the C14 dates cited in the discussion of the pollen from the Osmanaga lagoon near Pylos (Wright in McDonald and Rapp 1972: 195–6) are uncalibrated and probably fall near or just after the end of the Third Palace Period rather than in the Dark Age.

But orchard husbandry was certainly not confined to the palace estates. One Pylos text, Un718, recording gifts to Poseidon from a particular district (Ventris and Chadwick 1973: 282–3), indicates that not only the *lawagetas*, apparently the most important figure in the state after the *wanax*, but an important landowner, *E-ke-rya-wo*, a community, and some kind of special estate were in a position to offer wine. In fact, *E-ke-rya-wo* is recorded in another text, Er880, as controlling two wheat estates, over eleven hundred fig trees and a similar number of (probably) vines, apparently in the same district (Ventris and Chadwick 1973: 267; Chadwick 1976: 117), and it is clear from the nature of other gifts on Un718 (cheeses, a bull, a sheepskin) that he controlled livestock. There are various indications suggesting that he was one of the leading figures in the state (but surely too casually named to be the *wanax*), and it is therefore of considerable interest to get this glimpse of the extent of his agricultural holdings.

The district in question may have been close to the palace, as those for which land-holdings are listed generally seem to be; but the palace's ability to get detailed information on a variety of topics clearly extended throughout the state, which undoubtedly testifies to its general influence. Other texts indicate that some officials travelled to inspect livestock and to acquire basic information on land-holdings; the most interesting series of texts, concerning the important religious centre *Pa-ki-ja-ne*, includes comments on local conditions which must reflect some kind of personal contact. As Killen points out (1985: 244) it is likely that the palace had some particular interest in the territories recorded, since they can only cover a minute proportion of the state's territory and clearly do not represent some surviving fraction of a state-wide survey. Hence it must be dangerous to deduce the complete pattern of the Mycenaean agricultural economy from them, as Betancourt's analysis tends to do (1976: 43–4); in fact, archaeology shows that pulses, never mentioned in the texts, were certainly stored in important buildings, providing just the kind of possible insurance against failure of the cereal crop that Betancourt believes to have been lacking. For the purposes of this chapter, the main interest of these texts lies in the glimpses they give us, however obscure, of systems of land-tenure.

It seems likely, from the small numbers of persons cited and lack of other place names, that the *Pa-ki-ja-ne* set relates to the community of that name rather than the administrative district of which it was capital. The site's religious importance may account for some peculiarities not found in the other land-holding texts, especially the major Ea set which relate to an unnamed area (Lejeune 1976), such as the prominent position of women in the land-holding structure, though none are named as primary 'owners', and the designation 'slave of the god' applied to many men and women. It seems reasonable to suppose that each named person, male or female, represents a household that included others who helped to work the land; in the case of what seem extensive holdings, one might infer the existence of dependent individuals or families as well, who provided extra labour. The introductory comment on one group of texts seems to refer to forty households, which would fit the total of persons named in this group, but in the whole *Pa-ki-ja-ne* set somewhat over eighty persons are named, so that the situation is not clear. A reason for suspecting that the account does not cover these people's total holdings is the small size of some, which are designated in two cases by the smallest measurement possible; but as the significance of the measurement remains elusive, this must remain a speculation.

In all the Pylos texts two main types of land are named, *ki-ti-me-na* and *ke-ke-me-na*; the second term is found also at Knossos and Tiryns, but at Knossos a different term seems to replace the first, a warning against presuming uniformity within the palace societies. The standard interpretation of these terms as meaning 'private' and 'public' land respectively has not gone unchallenged (most recently Carpenter 1983); but it does seem clear that *ki-ti-me-na* land is always associated with individuals, who may be termed *ko-to-no-o-ko* ('estate holder' or 'owner'), whereas *ke-ke-me-na* land can be at the disposal of the community (*damos*), groups of herdsmen, or sometimes individuals. Interpretations of *ke-ke-me-na* as referring to marginal land, only recently opened up, or fallow land seem quite plausible (interestingly, it seems to be available in much larger plots); but both forms are measured in terms of wheat seed. Killen has suggested that those who hold *ki-ti-me-na* land are in fact tenants of the state, receiving the land in return for services, but he acknowledges that this is only his preferred alternative, and that they may be owners of private land who have to pay a wheat tax (1985: 245).

Whatever the truth, it is worth noting that holders of *ki-ti-me-na* land include persons clearly described as craftsmen and herdsmen, especially on the Ea texts (Chadwick 1976: 115), who may be receiving land in return for their services to the palace or the community as a whole, but are not likely to be of high status, unlike *E-ke-rya-wo* and other named individuals. This is one of the indications that it is not possible to view Mycenaean palace society generally in terms of a peasantry dependent upon aristocratic landlords, although the existence of a dependent class is suggested by the fact that individuals like *E-ke-rya-wo* can provide men as 'rowers' (Ventris and Chadwick 1973: 186–8), and craftsmen and others can be tied to the *wanax*, the *lawagetas*, or the goddess Potnia (who may well be the 'god' of whom many *Pa-ki-ja-ne* persons are 'slaves') in some kind of bond.

But persons named as having an *o-na-to* of land from the 'owners' do not have this kind of bond to the 'owners'. This term, also used for land held from the *damos* or described as *ke-ke-me-na* or both, probably represents some kind of lease, but the terms of such leases are never stated. Quite frequently individuals hold an *o-na-to* from two or more 'owners', and some combine this with one or more holdings of *ke-ke-me-na* land. *Ke-re-te-u*, a man named in the Ea set, holds no less than seven plots of land in different ways (Ventris and Chadwick 1973: 260), which when added up represent a larger seed total than that for the estate of the *lawagetas* cited on Er312 (Ventris and Chadwick 1973: 266), surely suggesting that this is not the *lawagetas*'s only estate. The range of people who hold an *o-na-to*, whether from an 'owner', the *damos*, or persons who control *ke-ke-me-na* land, is wide: many are 'slaves of the god', some are religious functionaries, craftsmen, or (rarely) slaves of individuals, and some are the 'owners' themselves.

There are further complications: a kind of *o-na-to* called *ka-ma* appears to carry some special kind of obligation, which is recorded as not always being performed, and there is a type of land called *e-to-ni-jo* which may be free of all obligations, since there is a dispute between a priestess and the *damos* over whether a large plot of land held by her for 'the god' is *e-to-ni-jo* or an *o-na-to* of *ke-ke-me-na* land. Overall, it is evident that the system was complex and apparently offered scope for considerable freedom of action to those who were active in it, even if these were tied to a god or person; but it is not at all clear how large a proportion of the total population such people constituted.

The style of farming implied by the holding of several separate plots might resemble that common in Greece today in the use of different plots for different crops, but here the texts provide no information: wheat is the only crop mentioned in connection with land-holdings, but this may reflect a tax and have no necessary connection with the actual use of the land. So it is not possible to tie the texts to the scanty archaeological data, nor can the complex array of ranks and statuses suggested by the texts be distinguished in the relatively homogeneous evidence of houses and tombs. Overall, the archaeological evidence suggests a wide spread of mild prosperity, to judge from the common styles of house and tomb and the range and quality of artefacts in use, though study of skeletal material suggests common undernourishment (see further below), perhaps to be expected in a population dependent on farming in an often hostile climate. All sources imply that society was hierarchical, but in a complex way likely to have greater resemblances to the Near Eastern societies than to what can be inferred from the Homeric poems. It is noteworthy that religious functionaries and others tied to religion, the 'slaves of the god', participate in the system with the rest, and the recording of disputes and failures to perform obligations involving some indicates that the religious sphere was not separate from and beyond the control of the secular; the *wanax* may in fact have been the supreme figure in both (Kilian 1988b).

One problem with using the Pylos texts to give a picture of the average Mycenaean palace economy is that our information comes only from the final years of the Pylos palace society, when its economy may have been under strain. But it is worth noting that, even if the deficits recorded in the taxation texts reflect increasing difficulties in meeting palace demands, the provisions for deferring or even remitting part of the payment do not suggest that the system was, or was becoming, particularly harsh or grasping. This in turn would undercut one possible explanation for the collapse of the palace economies, the revolt of an overburdened peasantry, which in any case must seem implausible when there is no evidence for general taxation in the basic agricultural staples.

The signs of strain may rather reflect a situation that had been developing for some time, in which the palace elites were finding it increasingly difficult to acquire what they had been accustomed to acquire by trade, and, perhaps in consequence, tension and conflict were developing between the Mycenaean states, at least in some parts of the Mycenaean world. The already-mentioned increase in measures taken for defence, and the abandonment of part or all of some substantial sites before the end of the Third Palace Period, often following an episode of destruction, as at Mycenae, Berbati, Zygouries and Gla, together with other evidence like the apparent decline of Thebes in later LH IIIB, all suggest an atmosphere of growing insecurity, such as cannot be identified in the prelude to the earlier collapse of the Minoan palaces.

Whatever its causes, the widespread destruction horizon, particularly marked on the mainland, at the end of the Third Palace Period, did not mean the total collapse of organised society, any more than that at the end of the Second Palace Period. Some large settlements were abandoned or survived on a much reduced scale, but others continued in strength (Fig. 4.28). Tiryns is reported to have grown to some 25 ha, thus probably becoming the leading settlement of the Argive plain and its environs; important building activities took place on the acropolis, and the lower city was rebuilt to a townlike plan (Kilian 1988a: 135). There were other substantial sites, such as Lefkandi, which covered a hilltop of about 6 ha. The buildings in these settlements could be equally substantial, multi-roomed and sometimes two-storeyed, as at Lefkandi, though none are anywhere near the previous palaces in complexity and quality. But there is no evidence for the survival of small settlements, and over the Postpalatial Period the surviving centres dwindled to village size or were abandoned; the chequered history of Lefkandi suggests that they were liable to attack, perhaps because of their continuing prosperity. Their agricultural economy probably changed little,

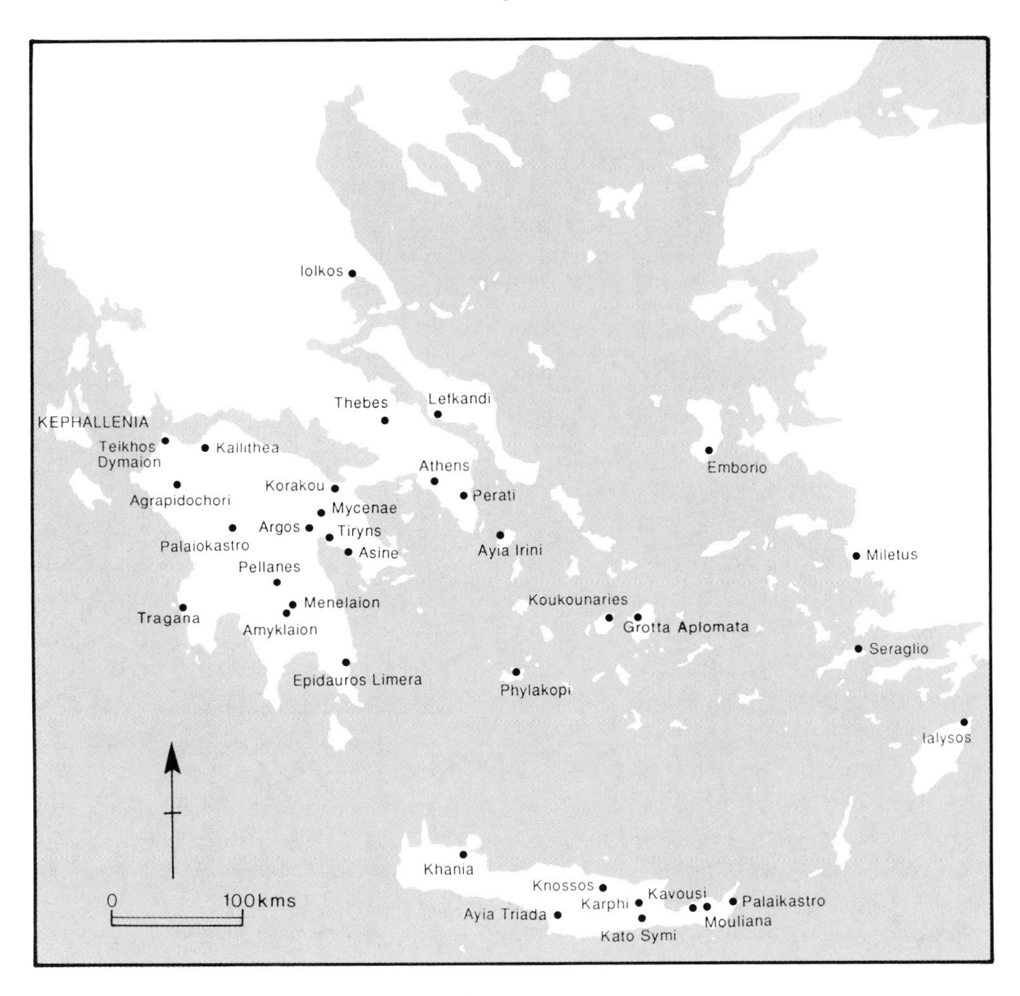

Fig. 4.28 Significant sites of the Postpalatial Period.

to judge from Kroll's analysis of Tiryns evidence (1984). The popularity of the small stirrup jar and its generally elaborate decoration certainly suggest that the production of fine, probably perfumed olive oil continued to be a speciality in several regions in Postpalatial times. But such stirrup jars now rarely travelled outside the Aegean, and the large storage stirrup jars have disappeared.

It has been suggested that the reason for the sparsity of identified Dark Age settlements is that the population scattered to archaeologically undetectable farms and hamlets; but the alternative view, that it concentrated at a few surviving settlements, is better supported by the evidence. Such settlements, though, seem to have been loose groupings of separate villages and hamlets with associated cemeteries, perhaps centring on the residence of a dominant family, made up of simple and unimpressive long houses and huts (cf. Kilian 1988a: 146–7 with fig. 19). Changes such as these surely reflect considerable social changes, but there is no reliable evidence for comparably radical change in the rural economy: the reported predominance of cattle bones in the Dark Age levels of Nichoria may suggest a local change of emphasis, but requires confirmation by further work, and certainly should not be used as a basis for general deductions. However, it may be hypothesised that agriculture was again directed mainly towards subsistence, and thus more towards cereals and pulses than the orchard crops which required such an investment of labour and time.

The people and their way of life

The amount of useful data about the demography and physical characteristics of the ancient Aegean populations is limited, despite the number of burials that have been excavated. The effort expended on measuring skulls in an attempt to distinguish human types and trace migrations seems to have been entirely wasted, though such study has provided other valuable data on sex, age, standards of nutrition, disease and even injury. Unfortunately, it was generally undertaken at the expense of study of other bones, and only a few large bodies of skeletal material have been evenly treated (most notably Angel 1971, on the mainly MH burials of Lerna).

Data on age suggest that life expectancy was low, at best averaging around 35 for men and 30 for women, and that few individuals reached their fifties, let alone their sixties. Such results have recently been treated with scepticism, on the grounds that they conflict with the laws of historical demography (Treuil *et al.* 1989: 142–3); but they differ little from what is suggested for Europe until relatively recent times and is still the case in many Third World countries. When medical knowledge is limited, hygiene rudimentary and antibiotics unknown, ordinary diseases and infections can frequently be life-threatening, and insufficient diet and a lifetime of hard physical labour will weaken resistance. Thus, there seems no *a priori* reason to doubt that children commonly died in infancy or childhood, and that many adults died in what would now be considered the prime of life, women not infrequently in or soon after childbirth. It may be noted that, to judge from the sample from the Shaft Graves studied by Angel (in Mylonas 1973: 379–97), even a better diet could not ensure a greater average longevity.

The latest survey of the Minoan material, by McGeorge (1988), indicates that signs of malnutrition, especially the markings in tooth enamel that indicate periods of arrested growth, are found in Crete (contrary to the results of earlier studies collated in Halstead 1977), but in the LM III cemeteries. They are apparently absent from MM contexts such as the Ailias cemetery at Knossos and Zakro burial enclosures (Becker 1975), although the latter has certainly produced evidence of dental disease and tooth loss comparable with what is found in the contemporary mainland material, probably indicative of a high carbohydrate diet. That some individuals, even at MH Lerna, nevertheless had good teeth could indicate that they came from families with greater resources, and, perhaps, higher status; McGeorge also notes exceptional cases of Minoan women who survived past 45 and had better teeth than younger women and better general health than their male contemporaries, both signs that might well indicate special status.

Study of the bones reveals common traces of arthritis and of 'rough country adaptations' appropriate to people who worked on the land and generally travelled on foot. Osteoporosis, a bone malformation, is quite often found, sometimes only as a trace; Angel's interpretation of it exclusively in terms of resistance to malaria is qualified by McGeorge, who suggests several possible causes. Healed and unhealed fractures indicate accidental and deliberate injuries, including those inflicted in battle (but 'parry fractures' in women are surely more likely to result from domestic violence); they are not very common, but some provide evidence of practical knowledge of bone-setting. There are also cases of deliberate tooth-extraction and very rarely of trephination, cutting a hole in the skull, which was presumably done to relieve headaches or mental disturbance by 'letting out evil spirits'. The general level of bone robustness provides indications of nutrition, often suggesting undernourishment.

All the large samples have produced very similar averages of height (as estimated by standard formulae from the long bones), around 1.67 m for men and 1.55 m for women, but with a range that in both sexes spreads over 20 cm around the average: thus, although there is a marked distinction, taller women overlapped with short men. In fact, despite the evidence for poor nutrition, these averages are only half a centimetre lower than in modern Greece; in both cases, the marked male–female distinction may partly reflect a socially instilled obligation to feed males of the household better than females, as in many Third World societies today.

The best guide to the appearance of the BA populations is provided by the LB frescoes; attempts to reconstruct heads from well-preserved skulls are still at an early stage (Sakellarakis 1991: 155 figs 133–4 show Anemospilia examples) and must reconstruct hair and colouring from representations. Frescoes normally show eyes and hair as dark (one girl in the Xeste 3 fresco has reddish hair), skin conventionally as red-brown on males and white on females, as in Egypt. All are comparable with the colouring used on later Greek statues and paintings, and suggest that the early populations were similar in complexion and colouring to the ancient, and indeed the modern, Greeks, whom they might equally have resembled in variety of physical type.

But hair is most frequently shown in long locks or braids, only occasionally as short and straight or curly. In fact, a complex sequence of hair styles has been identified for both females and males in the Cretan and Theran evidence (Davis, E.N. 1986b; Koehl 1986): in early childhood the scalp may have been completely shaved, then isolated locks were grown long, then hair was allowed to grow out but arranged in various styles. The context, generally ritual, and frequently elaborate dress and ornaments of figures shown in these ways, as well as the impracticality of the more elaborate arrangements of locks, strongly suggest that such styles, and the system of rites of passage and stages of initiation which they are suggested to reflect, were characteristic of an elite rather than the whole population. In fact, it may be argued that 'ordinary' Aegeans are very rarely represented, except, plausibly, in the 'towns' of the West House frescoes at Akrotiri (cf. Morgan 1988: 116–17 and Ch. 6 generally on the people in these frescoes). The male figures in Mycenaean frescoes, with unelaborated hair-styles, may also be reasonably close to reality, whereas the females may simply repeat a Minoan type in an exaggerated and perhaps misunderstood form (cf. Immerwahr 1990: 117). Further study of these inherently fascinating topics will undoubtedly yield valuable results.

A brief sketch may be offered of the round of work that would have occupied most people and shaped the year for all, for in a basically agricultural society the rhythms of the farming cycle would be paramount, determining when work is absolutely necessary and when there are slack periods for other activities such as building, craftwork or warfare. Here it seems legitimate to draw on modern evidence, since the climate and conditions have not altered markedly. The farming year begins in the autumn, following the first rains, with the clearing of fields preparatory to breaking up the soil with the plough or hoe. Cereals and most vegetables can then be planted, but peas and lentils are not put in until the spring, since they are very vulnerable to frost. Breaking up the soil and keeping it clear of weeds and undergrowth are constant and, before the advent of the plough, very labour-intensive activities; so too is the pruning of vines and olives. In fact, cultivating these together with a cereal leaves a farmer very few slack periods when other work can be done (Fig. 4.29; cf. Aschenbrenner 1972: 50–7 and Du

Crop	J	F	M	A	M	J	J	A	S	O	N	D
Wheat/ Barley					Harvest, thresh, winnow					Hoe, sow		
Olives		Hoe, plant, graft								Hoe	Harvest, press	
Grapes		Hoe, prune							Harvest, wine making			
Figs		Hoe						Harvest		Hoe, prune		

Fig. 4.29 Suggested distribution of major agricultural work with important crops, drawing upon Aschenbrenner 1972, fig. 4.2 and Du Boulay 1974, Appendix III. 'Hoe' has been written where these sources show 'plough', as probably the commoner method of ground-breaking and clearing; it may well have been necessary to hoe more often than suggested here.

Boulay 1974, Appendix III). The autumn is also a time for harvesting and if necessary processing fruit and nuts: figs may be harvested as early as August, but grapes normally in late September, eating olives in late October, and oil olives in November or December. But the main cereals are harvested in May or June, or in the uplands as late as July (Du Boulay 1974: 32), and the pulses a bit later; as much as a month may be taken up with harvesting, threshing and winnowing wheat with traditional methods.

What was harvested had to be stored as well as processed, of course, and here a problem is encountered. Evidence for storage tends to diminish through the BA, and most ordinary houses of the later stages contain remarkably little evidence for the amount of storage capacity that would seem to be necessary (for example at Nichoria only a single pithos, placed externally and so perhaps a water-butt, can be associated with most Mycenaean houses). But the significance of this is not clear, and it would certainly be unwise to suppose that this indicates central control of all storage and so of food supply. The explanation may be that perishable containers like wooden bins were used, or that unbaked clay bins, hard to detect in excavation, were far more common than the few reports so far would indicate, or that external storage structures have not been identified; also, some produce may have been simply heaped on room floors, and, finally, storage pithoi may simply have been removed when sites were abandoned in an orderly fashion, as many may have been.

Although a great part of what has to be done, work on the land is not the only constant requirement. Water and fuel are continually required, food must be prepared almost daily, and any personally owned livestock must be fed, watered and milked. In traditional rural societies some or all of these tasks have customarily been undertaken by women, helped by older children, in addition to making, repairing and washing clothing, bed coverings, etc., looking after children (but this can be delegated to their older siblings), collecting edible plants, fruit and nuts, and helping with the land work, especially at harvest time. The care of herded livestock might be the work of specialists, or perhaps be delegated to older children in secure areas where there was little danger of major predators or human raiding. The extent to which land work was the responsibility of individual households or shared among a community is quite unclear for earlier periods, but by the time of the Linear B texts the linking of land with individuals, presumably representing households, would suggest household responsibility. Kinsfolk and neighbours would no doubt help when they could in the expectation of receiving help in their turn.

Slack times and periods of bad weather could be used to repair implements and utensils or make new ones, refurbish the house by minor repairs and renewing plaster and earth floors, and for more strenuous jobs in which groups of families or whole communities might join, such as building a house, constructing a terrace wall or sheepfold, laying out a path or clearing a new field. Other variations in the routine would be provided by visits to specialists such as potters

Pl. 4.2 The 'flagship' on the West House miniature fresco, Akrotiri. Courtesy of the Faculty Board of Classics, University of Cambridge, and Dr L. Morgan.

and smiths, who might live at a distance, or to acquire commodities in local towns, or the arrival of itinerant specialists and traders at the settlement, and participation in a range of ceremonies. These would include family occasions such as weddings and funerals, religious observations confined to the household, and communal ceremonies and festivals involving the whole settlement or even a region, such as celebrations of important stages in the agricultural year, propitiation of the dead and honouring the community's ancestors, and the induction of new adults. One might also expect periodic assemblies to consider matters of common interest and settle disputes. On all occasions involving sizeable numbers of people, it may be noted, there would be opportunities for negotiating exchanges of goods or services, so that even if no markets as we understand them operated in towns, market-style bargaining would be possible. In the more organised societies requirements to provide work for the dominant institution, whether a palace, temple or elite household, might be a further call on time, and taxation of some kind would have to be paid, or negotiated over, at some time in the year; there might also be more need to travel to regional or national centres to deal with such matters and have disputes judged.

It seems very unlikely that the towns of the more organised societies in the Aegean had a very different style of life. Although more of their population will have been craft specialists, priests, administrators, etc., these will, as pointed out at the beginning, generally have worked and/or owned land. In a port activities connected with the sea would have taken on greater significance, such as the festival associated with the opening of the seaways in spring argued by Morgan (1988, Ch. 10) to be represented in the West House miniature fresco (Pl. 4.2), and in major towns and centres of organised states one might expect more numerous and elaborate ceremonies, including festivals concerned with the patron gods of the town or state and its rulers. But otherwise the natural rhythms of the agricultural year will have dominated life, as in the country.

Bibliography

For evidence relating to plants and crops see Renfrew, J.M. 1973, 1982, and Hansen 1988 (also on the vine and olive papers in Amouretti and Brun, forthcoming, especially Blitzer on the olive); on flax see Barber 1991: 11–15. For evidence deriving from animal bones see Payne 1985 and Halstead 1987a (to which add Mancz 1989 for Nichoria, von den Driesch 1987 for Thessaly, and von den Driesch and Boessneck 1990, the largest sample of all, from Tiryns), and for that from human bones Halstead 1977 and McGeorge 1988.

The amount of data deriving from survey is constantly increasing; Keller and Rupp 1983 provides a recent overview. Hope Simpson and Dickinson 1979 is a general summary of the evidence from the mainland, Kythera, Cyclades, north Sporades and Dodecanese to 1977; see also Blackman and Branigan 1977 (Ayiopharango valley), McDonald and Rapp 1972 (Messenia), Renfrew and Wagstaff 1982 (Melos), Van Andel *et al.* 1986, Van Andel and Runnels 1987 (south Argolid), Watrous 1982 (Lasithi), Wright *et al.* 1990 (Nemea valley).

Branigan 1972 includes many comments that can be applied generally to towns. On settlement representations in frescoes see Morgan 1988, Ch. 4, and 1990, Televantou 1990. Darcque and Treuil 1990 contains many papers on aspects of settlement.

Some useful recent sources for major sites and regions

(many older publications are cited in the Introduction)
Knossos: Hood and Smyth 1981.
Mallia: Van Effenterre 1980.
Phaistos: Levi 1976.
Ayia Triada: Watrous 1984a.
South Crete generally: Shaw and Shaw 1985.
Gournia: Soles 1979; 1991.
Mochlos: Soles and Davaras 1990; French 1990: 75; 1991: 74.
Pseira: Betancourt and Davaras 1988.
Palaikastro: MacGillivray and Sackett 1984; MacGillivray, Sackett *et al.* 1989, 1991.
Zakro: Platon 1971.
East Crete generally: Driessen and MacGillivray 1989.
Ayia Irini: Cummer and Schofield 1984; Davis, J.L. 1986.
Akrotiri: Doumas 1983.
Phylakopi: Renfrew and Wagstaff 1982, Ch. 4.
Trianda: Marketou 1988.
Kastri, Kythera: Coldstream and Huxley 1972; 1984.
Kolonna, Aegina: Walter and Felten 1981.
Mycenae: Wace 1949; Mylonas 1966.
Asine: Nordquist 1987.
Pylos: Blegen and Rawson 1966; Blegen *et al.* 1973.
Nichoria: McDonald and Wilkie 1992.

For Linear B evidence on the economy and land tenure, see particularly Ventris and Chadwick 1973, Chs VII–IX; Chadwick 1976, especially Chs 5 and 7; Killen 1985; Bennet 1988. Halstead 1988 summarises his 'social storage' theory, with criticisms of current views of the palatial economy.

CHAPTER 5

ARTS AND CRAFTS

(i) Introduction

In the past there has been a tendency to concentrate attention on the most striking and unusual classes of artefact, to the neglect of those classes which are actually much more common on settlement sites; even in the case of pottery, only the finest wares have received much attention until recently. This imbalance is beginning to be corrected, as it is realised how much information can be gained from detailed and expert study, even where the surviving remains are scanty, as with textiles (Barber 1991). But such developments are still in their early stages, and I must perforce follow my predecessors and concentrate attention on fields where much work has been done. After preliminary general comments I shall consider the data under headings that reflect classes of object more than their material, and attempt to identify general trends in the course of roughly chronological survey.

The surviving products provide the best source of information. Remarkably few workshops and work areas can be identified, and those that have been are often irritatingly uninformative. Deposits of wasters from kilns or of moulds from metalworking establishments are very rarely encountered. It may well be that the majority of workshops were situated on the edge of settlements if not outside them, like a kiln at Palaikastro (Davaras 1980), to be closer to supplies of water, fuel, and raw materials, and to lessen the risk of accidental fires and 'industrial pollution'; at all events, while small establishments specialising in luxury materials have been identified in and close to palaces, major potting and metalworking establishments have not, despite the general assumption that palaces maintained them.

The status of crafts and craftworkers

Though most of the material debris from settlements relates in some way to the practice of crafts, by no means all need have been the work of specialists. Three groups of crafts should be distinguished: the household crafts, of which most adults of the appropriate sex might be expected to have basic knowledge by their society; the crafts that required specialised knowledge but were widely practised, like potting and metalworking; and the crafts that were expensive in terms of materials and demanded exceptional skills, which would only have been patronised by persons of high status and institutions like palaces.

It seems very likely that only practitioners of the last group were truly professionals, who were able to work at their crafts full-time because they were directly supported by their patrons. Even these surely had to do more than produce luxury items; thus, palace potters would have supplied not only fine pieces in special wares but the mass of domestic pottery needed in such establishments. But the specialists whose products were needed among the ordinary population probably worked part-time at their craft and otherwise farmed land. Such a situation is widely documented in ancient and modern societies (cf. Kanta 1983: 159), is implied by Linear B references to craftsmen holding land, and must seem inherently likely, for otherwise their position could be extremely precarious (cf. Blitzer 1990a: 578 – life as a 'torment' for potters without sufficient land, even in a money economy – and 1990b: 38 for the dependence of specialist sheepherders on land for part of their subsistence).

Although, as society and its material culture grew more complex, specialisation developed in many crafts that were probably practised originally by many adults, the demand for most specialised work would be sporadic at best. Even smiths, whose skills are unlikely to have been known at any level by most adults, were probably part-time specialists in many cases, as Killen has argued for the numerous Pylos smiths (1979, but cf. Smith 1991); the demand for bronze items is unlikely to have been so constant as to provide them with sufficient work. Although they never figure in the land-holding texts, smiths are evidently liable to pay taxes in agricultural products, though they may have a privileged position in that these were often partly remitted (cf. Ventris and Chadwick 1973: 292–3, 296).

Only potters were producing a specialised product that was in continual demand on a large scale, as demonstrated by the quantities found at settlements of all sorts throughout the BA. Yet these too are unlikely to have depended on the vagaries of customer demand. More probably they had some kind of contractual relationship with households or communities to supply pottery at regular intervals, like the system operating in one type of Indian village society today (Miller 1981), and combined potting with farming, as the Indian potters and others operating at a small workshop level frequently do. Their relationship with farmers may have been symbiotic, in that they could use tree prunings and the sludge from olive pressings for fuel (cf. Matson 1972: 219), and would have concentrated partly, if not as much as recently, on producing storage vessels. Such local specialists were not divorced from the life of the farming communities, then, but intimately involved in it; indeed, they may have felt communal or family pressures to provide their skills or products without any immediate tangible return.

Nothing is less likely than that a significant proportion of the population ever left the land to engage in craftwork, as sometimes suggested. A wide range of crafts is indeed named in the Linear B texts, but on the above argument very few can have been practised full-time, and these would have involved very few individuals. The nearest to 'industrial' production that Aegean society came will have been in large-scale processing of the products of agriculture and stockbreeding, as by the large groups of women working in textile production recorded by the texts, who are surely palace dependants, if not slaves, and do not, therefore, reflect any real decline in the population engaged in farming.

In this connection, it is worth noting that making pottery, including fine wares, has been women's work in many societies; in the case of the Indian potters already mentioned, men make the pots but women decorate them. This is a reminder that we cannot necessarily make assumptions about the sex of specialists, or divorce them from their household backgrounds; indeed, the household rather than the individual may have been the unit of production in many crafts, especially pottery. That in the Linear B texts named craftworkers are always male (but one Knossian woman is named *ke-ra-me-ja*, 'potter', on Ap639) need imply only that they functioned as heads of households and directed the crafts, whoever did much of the actual work, a situation with many ancient and modern parallels.

Technology

There is not the space to discuss in detail how every category of artefact was made, even if this were always certain. But it does seem worth summarising the main technological achievements of the Aegean BA, even if many depended partly on advances made outside the Aegean. For in this field, at least, the Aegean can stand comparison with the Near East: its best specialists were capable of equalling and sometimes excelling Near Eastern work. But such specialists were probably much rarer than in the Near East, and some of the finest work may be the product of unrepeatable combinations of talented individuals, abundantly available materials and generous patronage. In the absence of one or more of these, highly specialised skills could easily disappear, as most had done by the end of the BA.

Many of the materials used for crafts in the Aegean were worked more or less in their natural state, and thus did not require very sophisticated technology, but simply skill and good implements. Bone, ivory and kindred materials fall into this category, as well as wood and to a great degree stone. But stone-working does require the use of an abrasive material and often of forms of drill, which in the most complex forms may have been mounted on stands, and bronze saws and chisels would be needed to dress large blocks. Working clay involves several processes, for it needs prior treatment to make it more plastic and firing to make products durable; if these are painted, the firing must be carefully controlled to produce the desired effect. But technology is seen at its most advanced in the working of metals, which had to be extracted from ores in most cases, and of glassy substances that had to be artificially created. Such work required the controlled application of heat at considerable temperatures and very often the use of varied types of mould, which themselves needed skill to prepare and use.

At the end of the Neolithic period metal objects were still few and simple, produced by hammering into shape or working a casting from an open mould, but already local copper-working was well established, rare lead and silver items suggest that Aegean sources were being exploited, and gold items occur. Great advances were made during the Prepalatial Period. Increasingly, weapons and tools were made of copper that was improved either through the inclusion of a percentage of arsenic (some perhaps present in the copper source, but some probably extracted somehow from arsenical ore) or through alloying with tin, originally in quantities less than the optimum (8–12%), probably because it was difficult to obtain. In both cases, the result was easier to cast and to work, and casting was further facilitated by the frequent incorporation of some lead; hence, more elaborate pieces could be produced in two-piece moulds, especially daggers with midribs and eventually decorative features in relief. Such daggers and similar types like knives, razors and scrapers were characteristically attached to their hilts by rivets, necessitating the development of efficient techniques for producing and inserting these.

More spectacular are the results of increasing expertise in producing metal sheet, foil, wire and rod, which were used in the production of a wide variety of ornament forms, as sheet was, rarely, for vessels and covers of dagger hilts. Crete, where gold was in frequent use, seems pre-eminent in this, though there is also mainland goldwork and the Cyclades have produced some fine examples in other metals. Sheet metal could be decorated with tracers and punches, the commonest motif being repoussé dots, and might be shaped over a former, while thin sheet or foil could be beaten around a copper or bronze item. Soldering may have been used on more elaborate pieces; there is no clear indication of the filigree or granulation techniques, well known in the contemporary Troad, but some Cretan pieces may be of late Prepalatial date.

Although few really elaborate pieces have survived, metalwork of the First Palace Period in Crete could attain very high quality, as not only the Chrysolakkos pendant but the fine Mallia weapons demonstrate; these include examples of gold plate hilt covers and pommel attachments, traces of the application of gold to a dagger blade (Quartier Mu), and rivets capped with gold or silver. Such cappings may often have been simply hammered over the rivet head or attached by an adhesive, but study in one case has demonstrated that they were fused on by a process similar to Sheffield plating, which requires both very pure metal and close control of temperature (Charles 1968; cf. Branigan 1974: 85; but this dagger probably dates to the Second Palace Period).

An important development of this time is the establishment of a local faience industry in Crete, which to judge from the number and quality of finds at Knossos was based there. Items from Prepalatial tombs may be Syrian imports, but the major group from the Vat Room deposit at Knossos, now dated to the First Palace Period, includes inlays and the arm of a figure that are surely local work. The processes involved in producing faience, a combination of silicates, sodium carbonate, and usually colouring material, are complex (Foster 1979, Ch. 1), and the technology was probably introduced fully developed by immigrant specialists, but it took an individual direction. Glass paste can be produced by similar processes, but it is not clear that any pre-LB finds are of this material, although MH beads have been so described (some are definitely faience, Banks 1967, Ch. VI). The more elaborate faience pieces must have been produced from moulds, now also in use for special forms of pottery like the relief-decorated pieces from Mallia (Poursat 1980, 1983: 278–9) and perhaps 'eggshell ware'. Another development that deserves mention is the inlaying of stone vessels with stone or shell, which may be seen as a precursor to a more general development of inlaying and perhaps also as an early example of a Minoan taste for contrasting materials.

The finds from Second Palace Period contexts demonstrate mastery of a wide range of metalworking techniques as well as the ability to produce and colour elaborate faience items, to carve vessels, sealstones and inlays from very hard stones, and to inlay elaborate objects with varying combinations of materials; a well-known example is the 'Royal Draughtboard' from Knossos, on which gold, perhaps silver, rock crystal, ivory and glass paste or faience were used (cf. Foster 1979: 92–5 for comparable pieces), and the item decorated by the faience 'Town Mosaic' inlays, also from Knossos, must have been a comparably remarkable piece of work (Foster 1979: 99–115; cf. Fig. 4.15). Study of the metal vessels has revealed the use of many different techniques, including the joining of separate pieces by soldering or small rivets, the incorporation of cast parts, especially handles (one or two vessels may have been completely cast), the strengthening of rims, handles and feet by the inclusion of cast copper or lead cores, and the decoration of surfaces by inlay, part overlay with gold or silver, and perhaps deliberate patination. The fine swords and daggers found principally in the Shaft Graves also display remarkable skill in the production of complex moulds for the relief decoration of midribs and blades, and in the covering of the hilt with repoussé-decorated goldwork or ivory hilt-plates decorated with gold pins; rivets were normally capped with gold or silver. There is little comparable in Crete, but some weapons and tools were decorated by incision, presumably being of softer metal than the incising tool; one example, the Lasithi dagger, is now dated between LM IB and IIIA (Long 1978), but some incision was used on the Anemospilia spearhead earlier (Sakellarakis 1991: 154).

The Shaft Graves also contain several examples of inlay in various forms. The use of lapis lazuli and rock crystal inlays on an extremely fine dagger hilt-plate of gold can be paralleled on some items of the 'Aegina Treasure', especially the rings, and on a ring inlaid with glass paste from a Second Palace Period tomb at Poros; some later rings and beads are also comparable. The techniques used on

Pl. 5.1 The Lion Hunt dagger, Shaft Grave IV. Courtesy of the National Archaeological Museum, Athens, and Dr K. Demakopoulou.

daggers (Pl. 5.1) and metal vessels were different. The most recent discussion, backed by scientific examination and analysis (Xenaki-Sakellariou and Chatziliou 1989), distinguishes the hammering of metal ribs, plates and cutouts into prepared matrices, found on a number of items, from the true 'metal painting' involving the use of niello, a complex mixture of silver, copper, lead and sulphur, as an adhesive, to hold on such cutouts, and as a decorative substance; layers of niello have even been detected on vase-surfaces, presumably intended to create a colour contrast. The technique involves applying the niello as a powder and then heating it; it will solidify around the cutouts when cold, and any excess can be removed by polishing. Niello was used similarly at an earlier date in Byblos, and it seems likely that knowledge of some basic techniques reached the Aegean from Syria. But there is still no trace of them in Crete, so that in the Aegean the technique was essentially developed at Mycenae in the Shaft Graves phase, though surely by highly skilled metalworkers who are likely to have come from elsewhere, if not from as far away as Syria. The heavy concentration of finds in the Argolid suggests that the art continued to be practised there for much of the LBA.

Other advanced metallurgical techniques observable in the Second Palace Period include the forming of gold seal-rings over a core of inferior metal, the making of ring bezels in different metals, the gilding of glass beads and stone vessels, and the provision of gold cappings to the perforations of beads and sealstones. The coating of clay vases with tin, evidently to give a bright silver-like appearance, is a later development, particularly characteristic of the earliest stage of the Third Palace Period but lasting beyond. Also characteristic of the Third Palace Period in general is the casting of relief beads in glass paste from steatite moulds (Pl. 5.20); gold examples of the same types may have been produced by hammering into the matrices, or by stamps. A minor technique of interest, particularly notable in material of the Shaft Graves phase, is the use of the compass to produce complex decorative patterns on bone and gold items (Dickinson 1977: 76, 85) and in the manufacture of metal vessels (Davis, E.N. 1977, *passim*).

In the later stages of this period some of the more elaborate techniques seem to lose popularity and fine metalwork becomes less common, to be replaced by furniture and other items inlaid in different materials, especially ivory. But faience vessels and inlaid stone vessels have been found in thirteenth-century contexts at Mycenae that seem to represent local production (the more elaborate faience vessels may be imports), and inlaid metal vessels may have continued to be produced, to judge from stray finds at Mycenae and the cup from the Pylos palace. In the Postpalatial Period, however, there is little trace of elaborate work, and craft traditions had generally declined markedly or totally disappeared by its end.

Some final comment should be made on the few iron items found in BA contexts, almost entirely LB. Mostly these are simply hammered rings, but iron appears to have been used in the multi-metal seal-rings, and one point is reported from a Thebes jewellery workshop (Symeonoglou 1973: 170), a so far unique example of practical use before the Postpalatial Period. These hardly represent any real tradition of iron-working, which on present evidence begins with the appearance of iron daggers at the end of the period; iron daggers with bronze rivets, found earlier, appear to be Cypriot imports.

(ii) Pottery

Among the crafts pottery deserves pride of place, for potsherds are by far the commonest artefacts to be found at almost all types of site. Throughout the BA clay was the principal material for vessels used for preparing, serving and consuming food and drink, ritual offering and libation, storage, and a variety of other purposes (e.g. braziers, lamps, crucibles, potter's wheels). Vessels large and small were also used in various periods to hold the remains of the dead, and suitable fragments might be used for grave-covers, pot-lids, rubbers and, once pierced, spindle whorls, or be cut into near-circular 'counters'. Here it will only be possible to survey BA pottery development in outline and give some consideration to the nature of the pottery industry; more detailed studies are cited in the chapter bibliography.

The earliest BA pottery can be seen to have links with that of the 'Final Neolithic', but from an early date characteristics that were to become typical of the whole BA appear. In almost all phases it is possible to distinguish a truly fine ware, normally of light-coloured, thin and well-levigated fabric and often decorated, from a much larger category of plain ware that is also normally light-coloured, but varies in quality from near fine to a thick fabric, only roughly smoothed; overall, such material may make up as much as seventy per cent of the total, while the truly fine ware constitutes more like five per cent. A third category, usually described as coarse, is normally dark brown or red in colour and often rough-surfaced, though sometimes burnished or painted. But while some coarse ware is of poorly prepared clay, the quality of much Minoan and Mycenaean coarse ware is very high, coarse only because of its gritted fabric. Finally, there are the large storage jars known as pithoi, whose fabric is very thick and contains much tempering material but whose surface is generally light-coloured and smoothed, often decorated with applied clay bands, which may have incised patterns, or even with paint.

All these wares are very homogeneous in appearance over wide regions, a feature that becomes increasingly marked until, in the later LBA, standard types dominate production through the Aegean and there are only two distinguishable though related traditions, the Minoan and the Mycenaean. How this homogeneity was maintained and stylistic changes were transmitted obviously has a crucial bearing on general questions of production and distribution methods, but primary data relating to this are scanty, for until recently there has been little study specifically on these topics and no explicit models have been offered. Peacock's models of Mediterranean pottery production, developed from ethnographic evidence (1982: 8–9, and ch. 3, very similar to Van der Leeuw's models cited in Davis and Lewis 1985: 81), provide valuable analogies, but in all modern cases beyond the simplest level production is for direct profit by sale or barter, there being no parallel to the socially embedded contractual system already mentioned (p. 96) as operating in Indian villages. For this reason, modern production tends to concentrate on a narrow range of forms, mainly cooking pots and storage jars, whereas in the Aegean BA a full range of shapes and wares was always produced.

Only Peacock's three simplest models, household production, household industry and workshop industry, are clearly relevant to the Aegean; signs of workshop nucleation are hard to identify, although rural nucleation in the manner of the Romano-British industries might be suggested by evidence from Crete, especially for storage jars (Day 1988). Household production, already mentioned in connection with Neolithic pottery, involves the production of domestic pottery when needed by the women of the household, with a minimum of equipment. Household industry is still part-time work, mainly in the hands of women, but because it is for profit it is more professional and may involve the use of a turntable and kiln. A frequent feature in the ethnographic evidence, that it is undertaken to supplement a meagre living from poor land, is unlikely to be characteristic of the Aegean. The line between household industry and workshop industry is not clearcut, and the products of both may be distributed by simple forms of marketing; but in a workshop industry potting should be the most important source of livelihood, even if combined with farming or other work, and hence, according to Peacock, it is normally in the hands of men. It will be carried out for as much of the year as possible and will frequently involve the use of the wheel, a kiln, and assistants. It will be easiest to search for analogies with any of these models while surveying development through the BA.

The most striking innovation of the beginning of the BA is the development of a much wider and more elaborate range of shapes, particularly forms of drinking vessel and jug, but also small 'luxury' storage vessels like pyxides. The revival of painted decoration in Crete may be associated with this development, since it was applied particularly to jugs, pyxides and animal-imitating shapes, although the 'Pyrgos chalices', evidently an important form of drinking vessel, were decorated with pattern burnish in a Neolithic manner; but these did not outlast EM I, though later goblet shapes seem to derive from them. There was in fact a much wider range of shapes and wares in Crete at this time than elsewhere in the Aegean, where heavy plain and burnished wares, now often light surfaced, continued to dominate and the main domestic shapes were forms of bowl (e.g. Fig. 5.2: 2) and jar, although jugs and cups have been reported from mainland

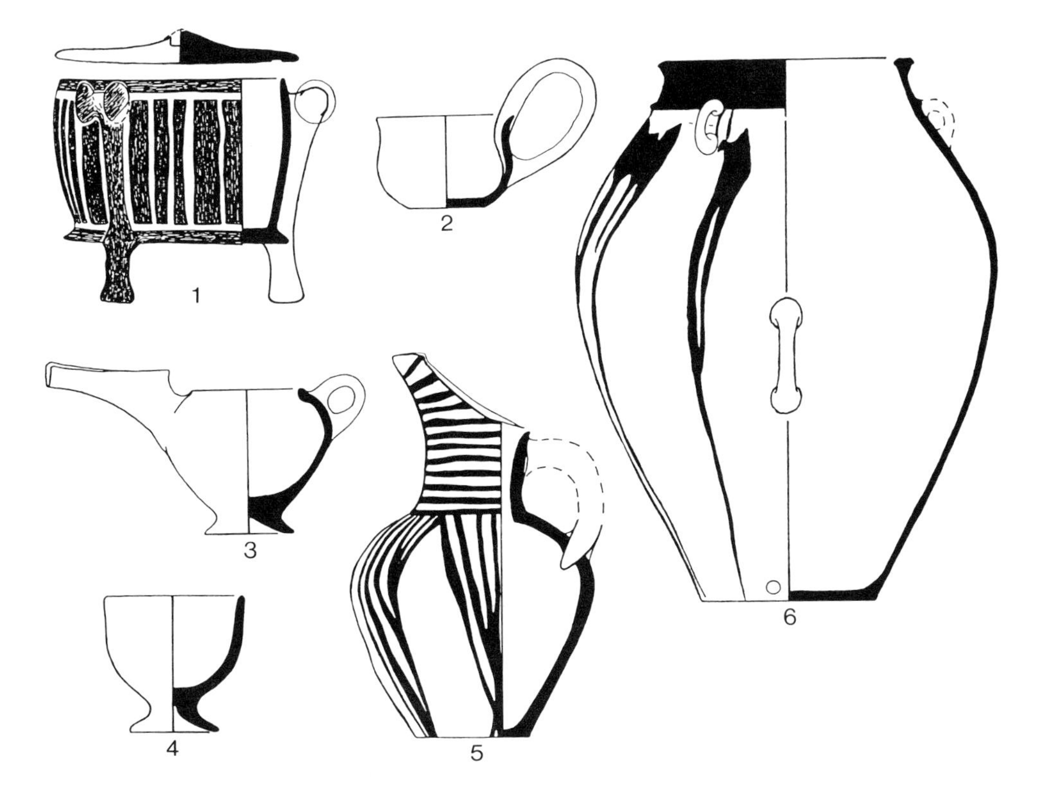

Fig. 5.1 EM II pottery types.
1 White-on-dark footed bowl with lid. 2 cup. 3 teapot. 4 goblet. 5 'Myrtos ware' jug. 6 large amphora. Scale 1:5, except 6 (1:10).

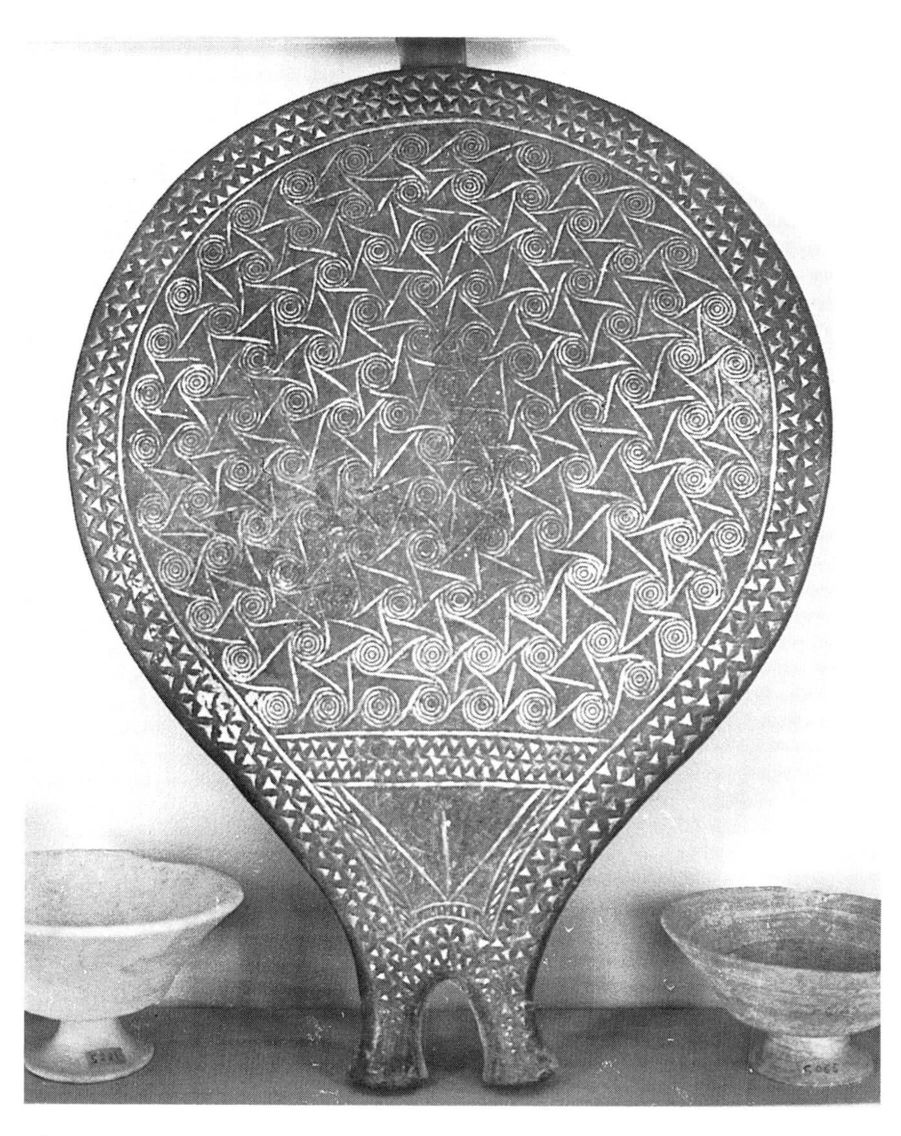

Pl. 5.2 A 'Syros' frying pan, Chalandriani T. 307. Peter Clayton.

sites, and the Peloponnesian 'Talioti' assemblage includes a fruit-stand shape and much use of incision (Weisshaar 1990). The Cycladic potters developed an interesting range of shapes in dark burnished ware, including several types of jar, pyxides, 'bottles', and the first 'frying pans', often decorated with incised and stamped motifs (Fig. 5.2: 1, 3, 5; Pl. 5.2), some of which were imitated in Crete and the mainland (Warren and Hankey 1989: 22–3). But such elaborate pieces may have been made primarily for the grave.

In the next stage, covering the middle of the EBA, Cretan pottery improved still further. The early EM IIA material from the West Court House at Knossos

(Wilson 1985: 293–359) provides a notable range, including some very fine painted jugs. But the 704 catalogued pots from Myrtos, in nine different fabrics with eleven varieties of surface treatment, may offer the best sample for the period, demonstrating the quality that could be achieved even at a relatively unimportant settlement. The pottery includes new shapes (Fig. 5.1), notably the 'teapot', small goblet, and large storage amphora and pithos, and new fine wares, especially Vasiliki Ware, characteristic of EM IIB, on which the painted surface is deliberately mottled, an effect probably produced in a variety of ways (Pl. 5.3; Betancourt 1979, 1985: 46–8). Yet this ware and most other Myrtos pottery was still fired at quite low temperatures.

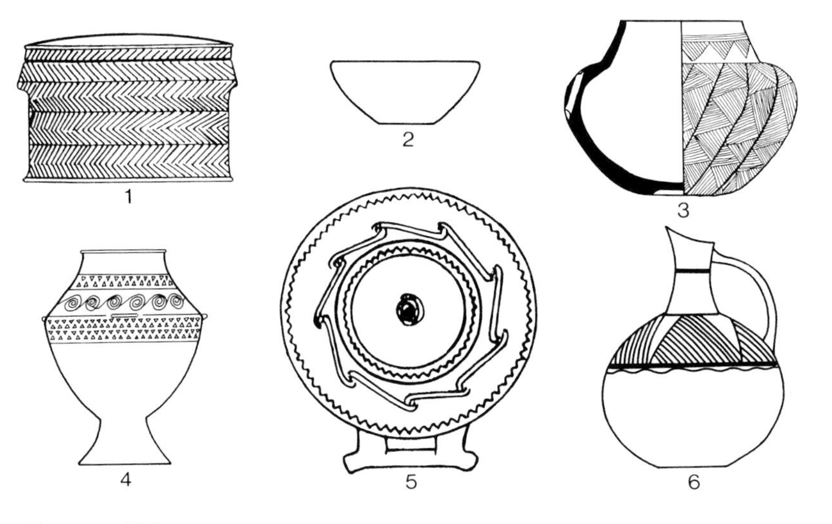

Fig. 5.2 EC pottery types.
1 'Pelos' pyxis. 2 'Kampos' bowl. 3 'Pelos' incised jar. 4 'Syros' pedestalled jare. 5 'Kampos' frying pan. 6 'Syros' painted jug. Scale 1:4.

Much Cycladic pottery continued to be rather coarse and poorly fired with a dark burnished surface, including the 'frying pans', pyxides, and jars with elaborate incised and stamped decoration (Fig. 5.2: 4). But a class of fine light ware coated or decorated with slightly glossy dark paint, often comparable in style and shapes with the contemporary Helladic 'Urfirnis', is also found, though it remains unclear how much was locally produced; a class with simple patterns in dark paint is certainly Cycladic (Fig. 5.2: 6), so some of the coated ware may be. On the mainland the fine wares might be 'Urfirnis' coated or plain and light-slipped (Fig. 5.3:1–3); a very high level of quality was achieved, especially for the characteristic footed saucer and sauceboat shapes, and they are hard enough to have been kiln-fired. Fine sauceboats can be traced to the earliest 'Lerna III' (EH II) phase yet found, at Tiryns (Catling 1982: 22), so the shape may well be Helladic in origin. Further evidence of specialised potting is

Pl. 5.3 EM II teapot in Vasiliki ware. Courtesy of the Trustees of the British Museum.

provided by the large clay hearths with decorated rims, which can be paralleled in the Cyclades, and the relief-decorated pithoi of the Argolid (Wiencke 1970): examples decorated with the same cylinder have been identified at Lerna, Tiryns and Zygouries, indicating either an itinerant group or distribution from a single centre.

Yet despite its range and quality, it is not clear that much of this material was produced in specialist workshops. It remains possible that most material continued to be produced by an advanced form of household production or household industry, especially in the small and scattered Cycladic communities, and it seems possible to interpret the Myrtos evidence thought to indicate a workshop in this light. Here remains of twenty-seven potter's 'mats', many fragmentary or reused, were found (Evely 1988a: 88, 96–7), eight of them together in Room 49 of Period I. But this room seems too small (just over 2 × 1 m) for a workroom; it seems more plausible that it was a storeroom in a communal potting area (pithoi full of potters' clay were found in the adjacent Room 50), to which the potters of the community's households would come in order to do their potting (cf. Betancourt 1985: 35). The wide scattering of other remains of 'mats' in Periods I and II is also hard to square with the idea of a single workshop, and Whitelaw has argued for household production on the basis of the distribution of distinctive forms of decoration (1983: 333–4). The existence of a class of well-fired amphorae (Fig. 5.1: 6) could indicate that one household was moving closer to specialisation of a workshop industry type; the same household might have used

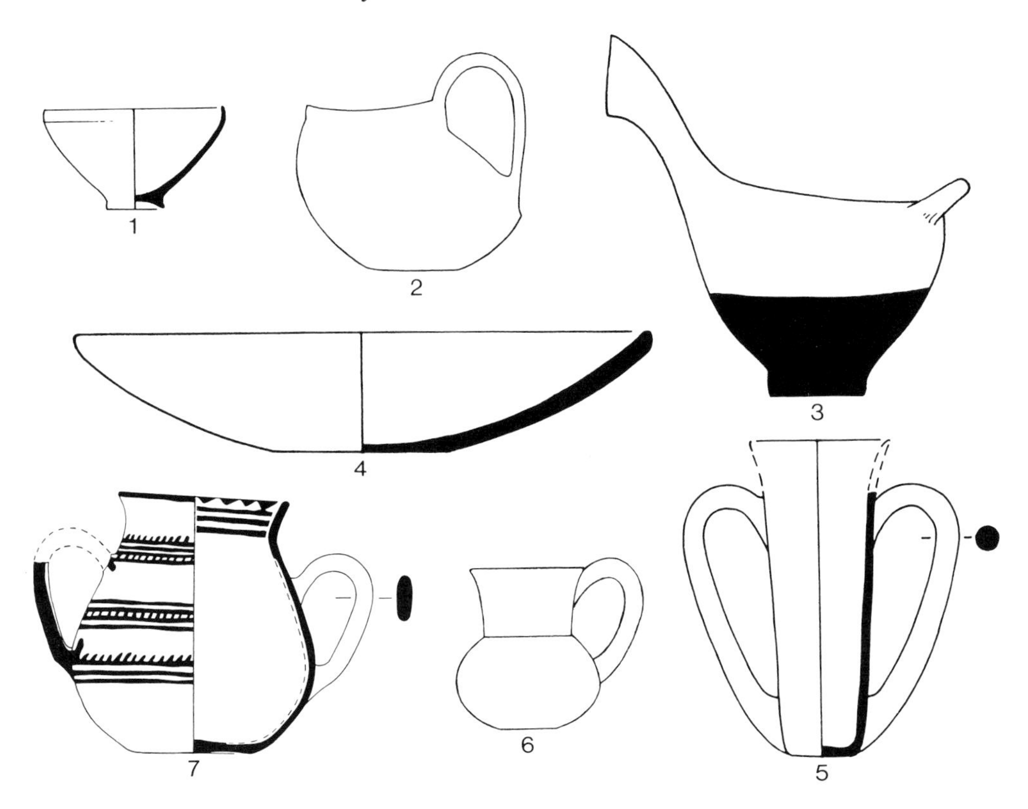

Fig. 5.3 EH pottery types.
1–3 'Lerna III' saucer, askos, sauceboat. 4–6 'Lefkandi I' plate, *depas*, jug. 7 'Lerna IV' Patterned Ware tankard. Scale 1:4.

the unique 'mat' with a socket, perhaps a first step on the way to the development of a wheel (Evely 1988a: 97). Deductions drawn about Myrtos need not, of course, apply to larger centres, but the rarity of evidence for kilns and for truly well-fired fabrics does not suggest widespread specialisation.

The final stage of the EBA has been thought to produce evidence for the arrival of the potter's wheel in the Aegean, in the 'Lefkandi I' pottery style (Fig. 5.3: 4–6), whose strongly Anatolian flavour has suggested that it was introduced by migrant potter families, if not whole population groups. Use of the wheel has been claimed as common at Lefkandi itself (D.H. French in Popham and Sackett 1968: 8), and Rutter has assembled evidence for its frequent use for fine pottery at Lerna IV and contemporary sites (1983: 335–43), particularly the grey burnished ware evidently ancestral to MH Grey Minyan; his argument that 'Lerna IV' shapes result from a fusion of 'Lefkandi I' and 'Lerna III' types (1979a) would provide a background for the spread of the technique. Yet the early Grey Minyan of Lefkandi II is described as mostly handmade (Howell in Popham and Sackett 1968: 9), and Zerner (1986: 60, 63) and Nordquist (1987:

48–9) consider the bulk of MH Grey Minyan and related wares handmade, until the late MBA. Rutter has pointed out (1983: 335 n. 18) that wheel marks can be removed by surface treatment on open vessels, so that early use of the wheel may have been underestimated; but the evidence he cites for the composition of vases from wheelmade and handmade pieces, and the use of both techniques to produce the same shapes at the same sites, suggest that the skill was still rather rudimentary. The importance of workshop tradition certainly should not be underestimated (cf. Davis and Lewis 1985: 91 on potters' conservatism): the Aegina 'gold mica' wares were consistently handmade throughout their long history, and the 'lustrous painted' workshop identified at Lerna seems to have used the wheel for its fine Minoanising open shapes, but not the coarser vessels (Zerner 1986: 65, 67).

The Knossian phase identified as MM IA by Momigliano has similarly produced no evidence for throwing vases on the wheel, though there is some indication of the use of a rotating device on two types of goblet (1991: 264–5). Clear evidence for the wheel appears in the First Palace Period, to which actual wheel-discs from Phaistos, Mallia, Ayia Irini and Kolonna, of imported fabric, may be dated (Evely 1988a: 89–90, 123). Palace patronage may have given a great stimulus to the development of wheel-throwing skill, and its spread elsewhere in the Aegean may be a sign of Minoan influence; the finely carinated Minoan cup type could in fact have influenced the development of the classic Minyan shapes, which are more widely believed to be wheel-thrown (e.g. Zerner 1986: 62), although angularity of body was a common Minyan feature earlier. As the MBA drew to a close finer wares were more commonly wheelmade, but in Ayia Irini V some fine local vases as well as the larger imported Minoan vessels are still handmade (Lewis in Davis, J.L. 1986: 108–9).

The spread of the 'Lefkandi I' assemblage reinforced the popularity of dark-surfaced burnished wares in the Cyclades and revived it in the mainland, and this tradition continued in strength in the MBA, represented by the Minyan wares, which are generally grey or black (Fig. 5.6: 1–4), and the Cycladic red or dark wares (Fig. 5.4: 3, 4), which unlike Minyan include a substantial quantity of closed shapes and are generally of rather coarse fabric. Painted wares of various kinds were also found. On the mainland 'Lerna IV' Patterned Ware (Fig. 5.3: 7) and its light-on-dark counterpart, 'Ayia Marina ware' (Rutter 1988), were succeeded by MH wares decorated in lustrous and matt dark paints on a light ground (Fig. 5.5: 1–3, 6). Comparable matt-painted wares are characteristic in the Cyclades from 'Phylakopi I' onwards (Fig. 5.4: 1, 2), and may have provided the inspiration for the classic Matt-Painted ware, now identified as one of the Aeginetan 'gold mica' wares, for several shapes are shared though the decorative schemes can differ. As already noted, Minoanising wares, both fine and coarse (Fig. 5.5: 4, 5), were produced at Lerna by the same workshop that produced other lustrous painted ware (cf. Jones 1986: 420–4); these wares have also been identified at Ayios Stephanos, and it is an unresolved problem whether there was

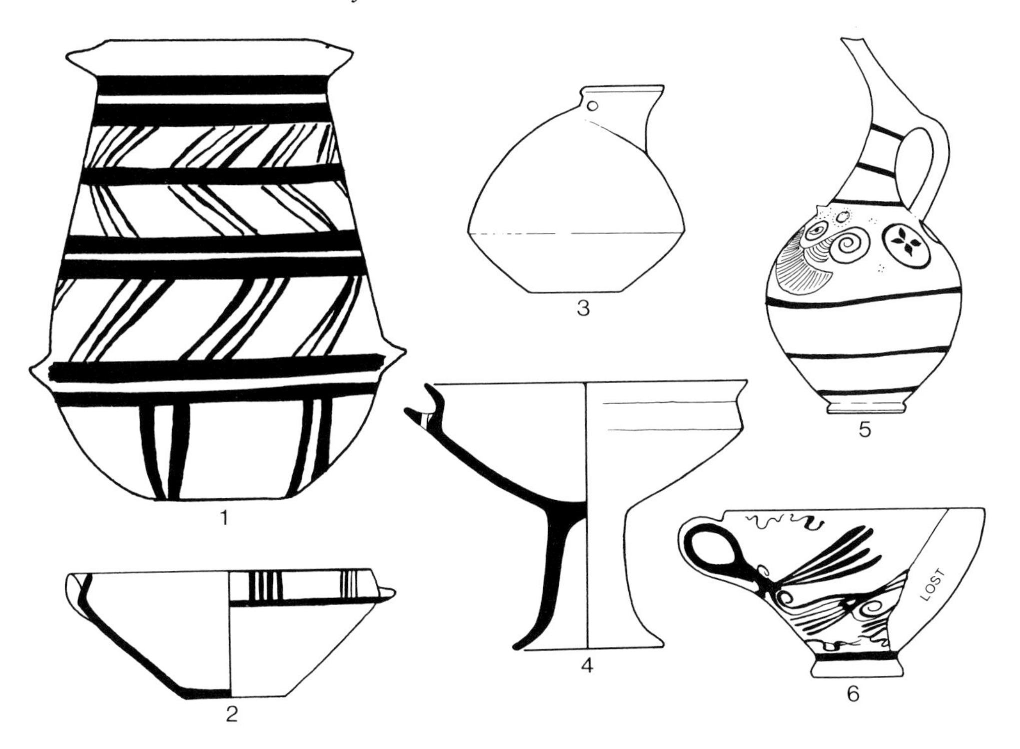

Fig. 5.4 'Phylakopi I' and MC pottery types.
1, 2 Matt-Painted barrel jar, bowl. 3 'duck vase'. 4 Red Polished goblet. 5 'Melian White' jug. 6 Matt-Painted 'panelled cup'. Scale 1:4.

a single workshop or two. Ultimately, Minoanising wares were also produced on Aegina and Kea, where plain and coarse Minoan types became increasingly popular in the later MBA.

All painting styles were used particularly on jugs and jars and other vessels; the most interesting shapes and decoration are found in Cycladic White, probably a largely Melian product (Fig. 5.4: 5). A great deal of rough plain and coarse ware was also produced, especially in the remoter parts of the mainland where standards were generally lower. Overall, the Helladic and Cycladic wares of this period are not remarkable artistically: but the best Grey Minyan and Cycladic red burnished are technically fine (cf. Davis and Lewis 1985: 83 on the latter), and the identification of several MH kilns (Davaras 1980: 125) and of very distinctive workshop traditions probably reflects an increase in specialisation.

The Cretan developments after EM II show the Cretan potters to have been the most imaginative, with or without the wheel. Pottery decorated in a light-on-dark style, which had been a minority ware since the beginning of EM (Fig. 5.1: 1), now became increasingly common, especially in east Crete where the most influential style was developed. Cups, goblets, jugs and teapots were particularly favoured, and motifs include curvilinear forms such as spirals (Figs 5.7: 1–3, 5.8:

Fig. 5.5 MH painted pottery types.
1 'Aegina Matt-Painted' jar. 2 'lustrous painted' jar. 3 'Thick style' Matt-Painted jug. 4, 5 Minoanising jug, cup. 6 Matt-Painted kantharos. Scale 1:5, except 1 (1:8).

1, 2). In the centre, the 'barbotine' style of decoration, in which the surface was worked while still wet into warts and ridges, and further knobs and prickles might be applied, began to appear, especially on jugs (Pl. 5.4). Further advances that may have taken place before the end of the Prepalatial Period include improvements in the quality of the paint, so that the dark coat took on a lustrous sheen, and the first attempts at polychromy, using red in addition to white.

But developments clearly reached their fruition in the Kamares pottery of the First Palace Period. This term in fact includes a range of fine wares, that are mainly decorated with painted patterns in polychrome light-on-dark style, but also with the barbotine technique, especially at Phaistos, and applied ornaments. The most elaborate types have been found at Knossos and Phaistos, but there are comparable styles in eastern Crete and simpler provincial wares that imitate the commoner shapes and use polychrome decoration. Although Kamares pottery has largely been found in the palaces, it is now being suggested that it was produced in rural centres (MacGillivray 1987). There is a very wide range of motifs on the finest ware, but batches with the same patterns were evidently produced (MacGillivray 1987: 274), and some generalisation is possible.

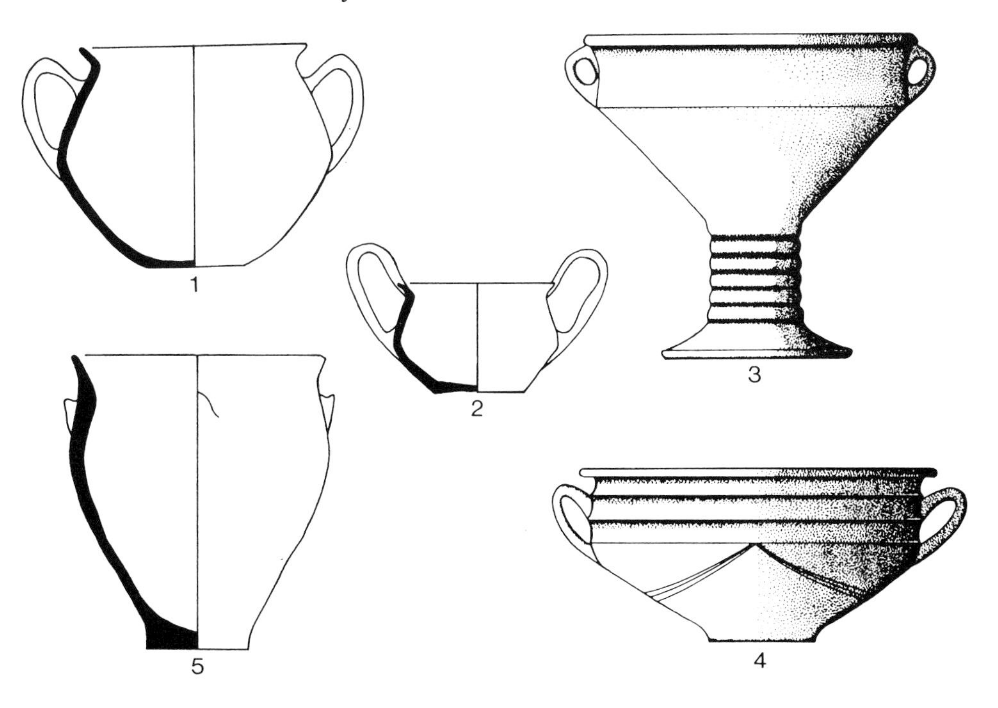

Fig. 5.6 MH Minyan and coarse pottery types.
1 carinated bowl. 2 kantharos. 3 ring-stemmed goblet. 4 'Argive Minyan' bowl. 5 coarse domestic jar. Scale 1:6.

Pl. 5.4 A barbotine jug, Ayia Triada T. 1. Courtesy of the Heraklion Archaeological Museum.

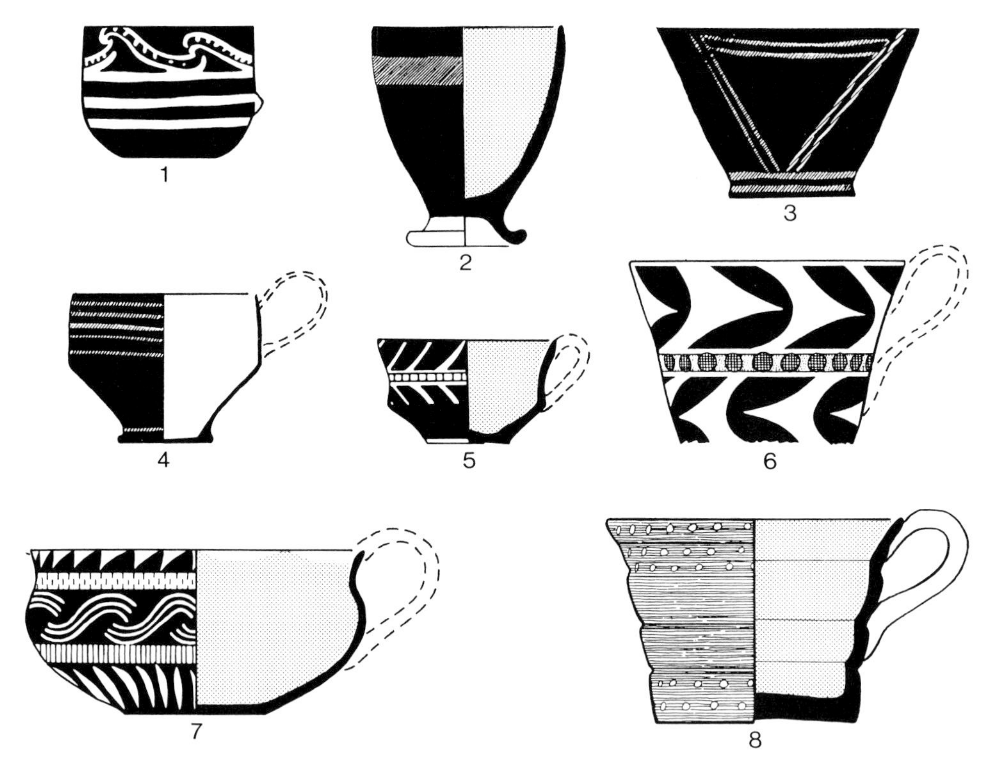

Fig. 5.7 EM III–MM small pottery types.
1 East Cretan EM III cup. 2 MM IA goblet. 3 MM IA cup, ?East Cretan. 4, 6 MM IIA carinated cup, Vapheio cup. 5, 7, 8 MM IIIA carinated cup, semiglobular cup, Vapheio cup. Scale 1:3.

Cups, holemouth jars with bridged spouts and various forms of jug seem the most favoured shapes, and painted motifs are largely abstract, making much use of spiral- and plant-derived forms (Figs 5.7: 4–7, 5.8: 3–6; Pl. 5.5). The pot surface may be divided into zones, but frequently is covered in rich polychrome patterns, employing red, orange and sometimes yellow, as well as white, on a dark-coated, light-slipped or plain background. The patterns may whirl or twist or flow in different directions. Specialities include the attachment of plant, animal and marine forms in high relief, produced particularly at Mallia (Detournay *et al.* 1980: 116–31), and the extraordinarily thin 'eggshell ware' cups, some with stamped decoration that may imitate the effect of metal plate with repoussé ornament. Influences from work in metal and stone can certainly be detected, such as the various types of crinkly rim (Fig. 5.8: 5), but these are better seen as imitating features of metal vessels rather than whole shapes. Such rims must have been shaped by hand, though the potter's wheel does appear to have been widely used for other open shapes; but some types, including 'eggshell ware', were probably produced in moulds (Cadogan 1976: 26, 1988: 97). The

Fig. 5.8 EM III–MM large pottery types.
1 East Cretan EM III jug. 2 MM IA jug. 3 MM IIA holemouth jar. 4, 6 MM IIIA jug, holemouth jar. 5 Gournia kantharos, equivalent to MM II. Scale 1:5.

wheel also appears to have been used increasingly for plain domestic wares, of which the palaces would have needed great quantities: many of the standard Minoan domestic shapes (Fig. 5.11) can be traced to this time.

Everything about Kamares and related wares suggests that they were produced by potters who were not only professionals working in specialised workshops but, at their best, creative artists. Their work can be as aesthetically pleasing as any ancient pottery, and was clearly highly prized in its time; examples have been found widely in the Aegean and there is a scatter in the east Mediterranean, especially Egypt, where there is evidence for local imitations (Kemp and Merrillees 1980: 70–5). But inventiveness on the scale that the best Kamares displays might be hard to maintain over a long period; by the end of the First Palace Period there are signs of diminishing vitality, and although the white-on-dark manner continued to dominate for a further stage, Kamares proper had essentially died by then, whether because of loss of inspiration, changes in taste, or, perhaps most likely, the increasing availability of luxury vessels in more precious materials like metal and faience.

Pl. 5.5 A Kamares jug, Phaistos. Courtesy of the Heraklion Archaeological Museum.

By the end of the MBA the Cretan deposits are marked by large quantities of often rather roughly produced but clearly wheelmade pots (for a fine cup see Fig. 5.7: 8), especially the conical cups which were produced in countless thousands in Crete and, by the early LBA, the Cyclades also (Wiener 1984). By this time, use of the wheel is so generally assumed for Late Minoan and Mycenaean pottery that details of manufacture have rarely been recorded until recently, but on the mainland, at least, there are notable exceptions. In remoter provinces such as Messenia and Thessaly plain wares continued to be commonly produced by hand (cf. the 'milk bowls' of Pylos, as late as LH IIIB, Blegen and Rawson 1966: 352), and a class of handmade closed vessels has been traced well into the LBA at the Menelaion (Catling 1981b: 74). In the Argolid a distinctive class of decorated miniature vases (Mountjoy 1986: 101) was also handmade. Nevertheless, use of the wheel seems to have predominated in the central Mycenaean regions, even for cooking ware, to the extent that the appearance of a class of clearly handmade burnished ware in later LB contexts has occasioned much discussion. This would suggest that workshop production was dominant, and this is supported not only by references to potters in the Linear B texts but by the highly standardised appearance of LB pottery; nevertheless, kilns are rarely found.

The seeds of standardisation in decoration are detectable in developments in the earlier part of the Second Palace Period, although superficially this was a time of much innovation, not only in Crete but more strikingly elsewhere, as the contents of the Mycenae Shaft Graves and Akrotiri houses show clearly. Different Cycladic centres produced elaborate types such as panelled cups (Fig. 5.4: 6), jugs with bird and plant decoration that can be in bichrome style and, at Akrotiri, hybrid wares drawing on Cycladic and Minoan sources (Marthari 1987; but cf. Davis and Lewis 1985: 83 on standardisation in Ayia Irini V). On the mainland Cycladic and Minoan shapes and motifs were incorporated into the new fine wares being developed in different mainland regions, which included a variety of small shapes as well as large jars and jugs; light-coloured surfaces also became favoured, even in the burnished plain ware (Fig. 5.9). The finest of these developments was 'Mainland Polychrome' (Fig. 5.12: 4), apparently based in central Greece.

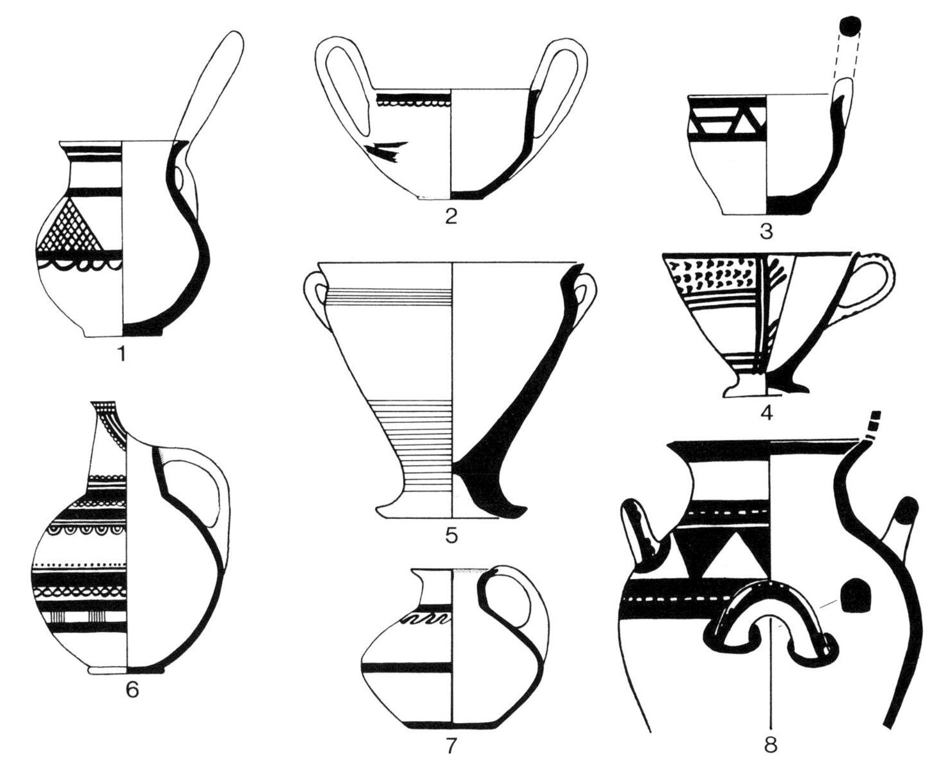

Fig. 5.9 Late MH pottery types.
1–4 Matt-Painted loop-handled jar, kantharos, loop-handled cup, 'panelled cup'. 5 late Minyan goblet. 6–8 Matt-Painted beaked jug, small jug, large jar. Scale 1:4, except 5, 6 (1:6).

But the most significant development of the period was in Crete, where a dark-on-light style first returned to popularity with the ripple-pattern at the end of the First Palace Period, and subsequently expanded to include a standardised range of motifs, especially spirals and plant-derived patterns like reed sprays and foliate bands, usually arranged in horizontal registers on fine ware shapes of all kinds (Fig. 5.10). This was the LM IA style, which was the main inspiration for dark-on-light styles developed in the Cyclades (Fig. 5.10: 5) and on the mainland, the latter being the first stage, LH I, of the Mycenaean style (Fig. 5.12: 1–3). These made their appearance among many competing styles (cf. Davis 1979; Rutter 1990), LH I in particular being largely confined to small vases, but by the time of LM IB the Minoan-derived styles had become dominant in the mainland and Cyclades. Improvements in production technique, paint quality and firing, found in LM IA (Betancourt 1985: 113–14), were certainly adopted for Mycenaean ware from an early stage, and may account for the popularity of these styles; their standardised decoration may also have lent itself to ease of production. Minoan domestic shapes (Fig. 5.11) were almost equally dominant at the major Cycladic sites (Georgiou 1983, 1986), but only the conical cup and tripod cooking pot are commonly found at mainland sites.

Fig. 5.10 MM IIIB–LM IA and related pottery types. 1, 2 MM IIIB/LM IA semiglobular cup, Vapheio cup. 3, 4 LM IA pedestalled cup, semiglobular cup. 5 Theran LC I jug. 6 East Cretan LM IA conical rhyton. Scale 1:4.

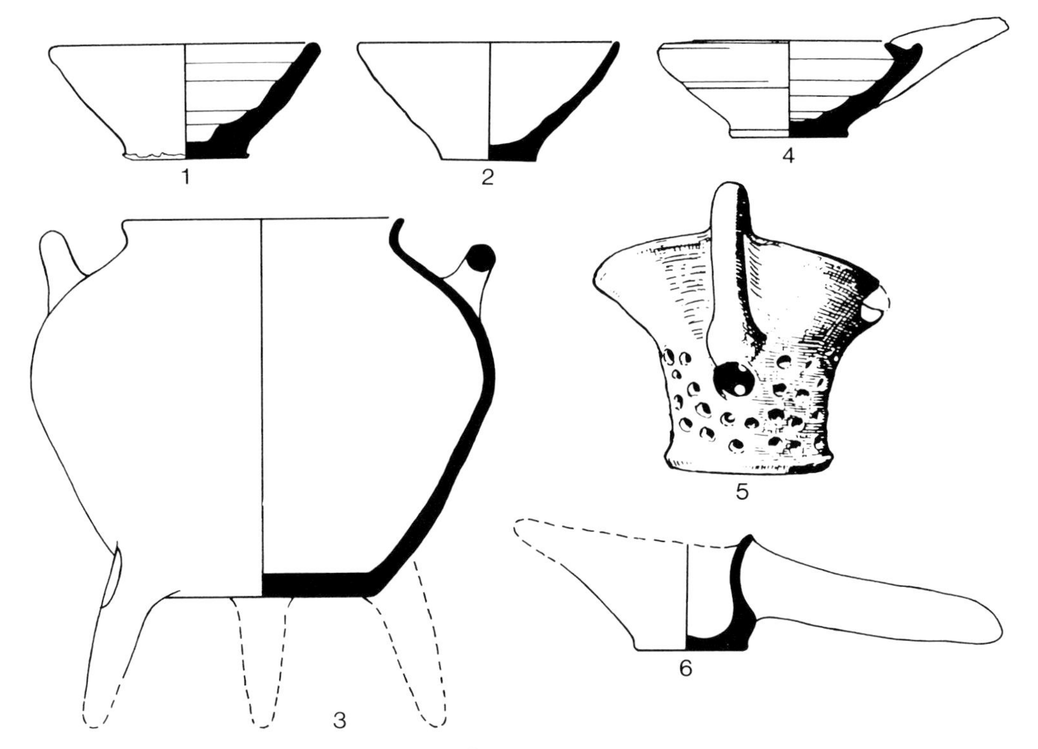

Fig. 5.11 Domestic Minoan shapes.
1 'MM III' conical cup. 2 LM IIIA1 conical cup. 3 tripod cooking pot. 4 lamp. 5, 6 braziers. Scale 1:3, except 3 (1:6), 5 (1:4).

Fig. 5.12 LH I–IIA and contemporary pottery types. 1–3 LH I Vapheio cup, semiglobular cup, squat jug. 4 Mainland Polychrome 'bird jug'. 5–8 LH IIA deep semiglobular cup, squat jug, shallow semiglobular cup, alabastron. Scale 1:4, except 4 (1:6).

LM IB in Crete and its mainland contemporary, LH IIA, are remarkable for the development of classes of very elaborate pottery, to which the term 'palatial' may reasonably be applied (Betancourt 1985: 140–48). It is possible to relate the plant, marine and elaborate geometric motifs of these classes to fresco painting, while features of the shapes, particularly the handles, clearly imitate the effect of metalwork. The shapes are principally closed vessels of varying but generally substantial size, especially forms of jug and spouted jar, including the first fine ware stirrup jars, also imitations of Egyptian stone alabastra and various types of rhyton (Fig. 5.13: 1–6). Cups and other small shapes, which had been prominent in Kamares ware, were rarely produced in this class, except in the late LM IB 'Alternating Style' and imitations of it, and were generally decorated with continuations of the LM IA style. On the mainland, the majority of the 'domestic' LH IIA pottery was produced in standard combinations of shape and motif (e.g. Fig. 5.12: 5–8); two such types, the rounded cup decorated with spirals and Vapheio cup decorated with foliate band, dominated in the early material from Berbati, along with plain goblets (Åkerström 1968, pl. II:4 and pers. commun.).

The fine LM IB classes were probably created in specialised workshops at or near Knossos, but, although exported all over Crete and the Aegean, they were only reproduced to any great extent on the mainland and Aegina, as investigations of Marine Style suggest (Mountjoy *et al.* 1978, Mountjoy 1984). The mainland workshops also specialised in pithoid jars decorated with plant patterns that have few LM IB parallels but are clearly Minoan in manner (Fig. 5.13: 7) and seem to have been created on the mainland. In either case the development depended effectively on the inspiration of a few specialists at a few centres.

The artistic dominance of Knossos in Crete continued in the succeeding stage, which saw the last flowering of the elaborate manner in the Palace Style jars (Niemeier 1985) (Pl. 5.6). The liking for such monumental jars may be a Mycenaean influence, as the adoption of the goblet shape, found in quantity in both decorated and plain wares in LM II, surely was; the decorated examples frequently resemble the LH IIB 'Ephyraean' goblets, but show a wider range of motifs and other differences (Popham 1984: 166–7; Figs 5.14:2, 5.15:3). But LM II has few other connections with the Mycenaean tradition, which had still not established a standard repertoire in LH IIB (Fig. 5.15:1–4), although some types like the 'Ephyraean' goblets are widely found. In Crete LM II saw the establishment of a very distinctive range of highly stylised geometric and plant motifs (Fig. 5.14) that continued, increasingly attenuated, to LM IIIB (cf. Popham 1984: 159–85). LM IIIA1 was extremely homogeneous throughout Crete (Watrous 1984b), but after this phase local schools developed (Kanta 1980, Ch. 5), and Knossos's loss of influence is underlined by the presence there of pottery imported from Khania (e.g. Popham 1984: 186).

Mycenaean pottery followed a somewhat similar pattern (Figs 5.15–18). The LH IIIA1 style was extremely homogeneous throughout the Mycenaean region, though minor local variations are detectable, and applied the same limited range

Fig. 5.13 'Palatial' LM IB and LH IIA pottery types.
1–5 LM IB ewer, hole-mouth jar, stirrup jar, conical rhyton, piriform rhyton. 6, 7 LH IIA bridge-spouted jug, pithoid jar. Scale 1:5, except 7 (approx. 1:11).

Pl. 5.6 A Palace Style jar, Knossos. Peter Clayton.

of motifs to all decorated shapes, large and small. The quality and homogeneity of LH IIIA1 is such that some have suggested that it was only produced in one or a few centres; certainly there must have been a single centre of stylistic influence, which was probably the Mycenae region itself, and the LH IIIA1 found on the Aegean islands was evidently imported, but this is not so clear on the mainland. The situation in LH IIIA2 and IIIB1 is similar, but there is increasing evidence for local variation, which indicates local production, and only part of the Mycenaean region adopted the LH IIIB2 innovations (Sherratt, E.S. 1980); in their absence, however, there was little local development, but rather stagnation

Fig. 5.14 LM II–IIIA1 pottery types.
1–4 LM II cup, goblet, jug, ogival bowl. 5–7 LM IIIA1 goblet, cups. Scale 1:4.

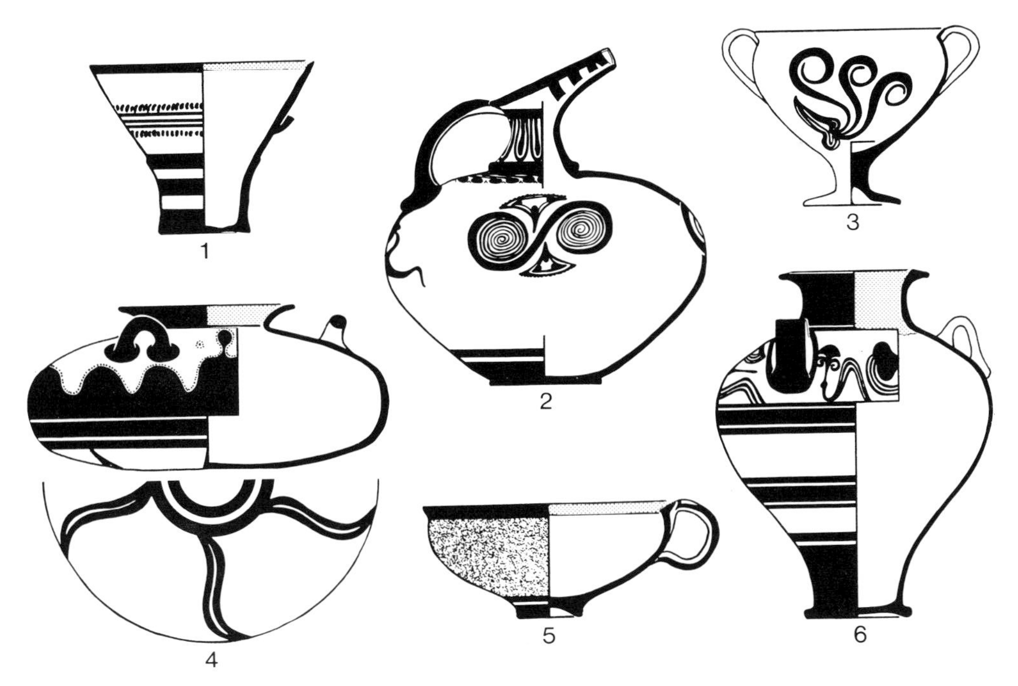

Fig. 5.15 LH IIB–IIIA1 pottery types.
1–4 LH IIB Vapheio cup, ewer, 'Ephyraean goblet', alabastron. 5, 6 IIIA1 semiglobular cup, piriform jar. Scale 1:6, except 1, 5 (1:4).

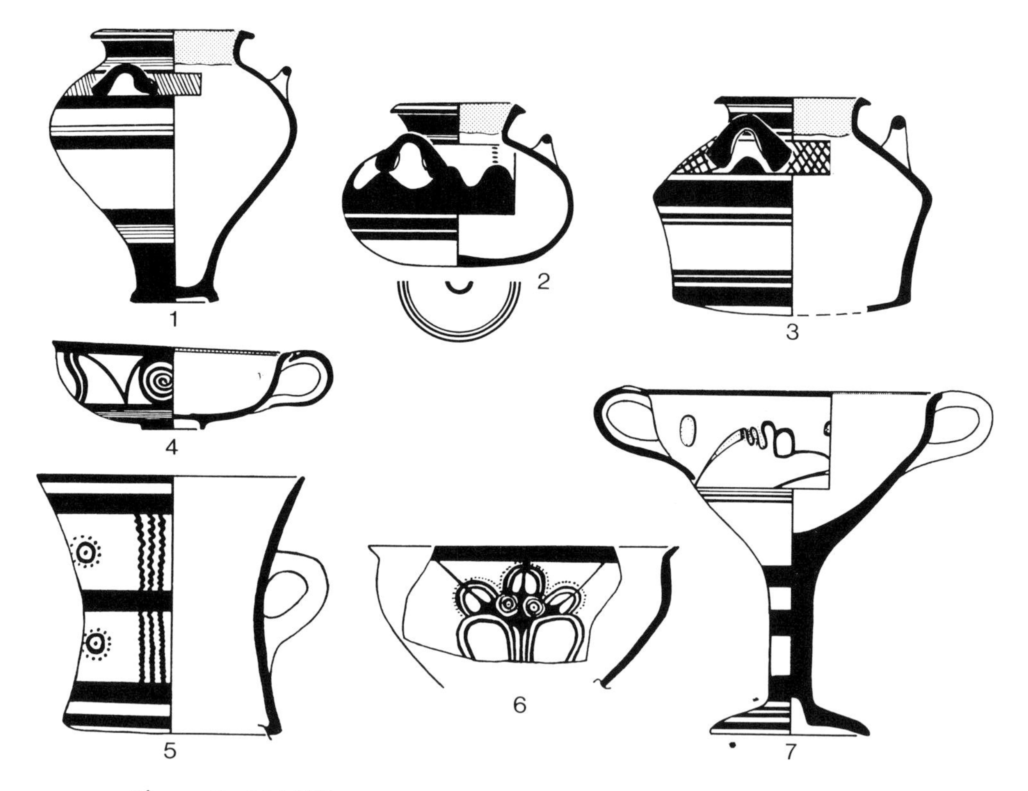

Fig. 5.16 LH IIIA2 pottery types.
1 piriform jar. 2 alabastron. 3 pyxis. 4 semiglobular cup. 5 mug. 6, 7 kylikes. Scale 1:4.

and frequently decline in quality. Thereafter, although there was recovery and, in the developed stages of LH IIIC, considerable innovation, there was no single stylistic centre; a complex pattern of cross-influences and interconnections can be detected (Sherratt, E.S. 1985). As these connections broke down, the different areas began to go their own way, most frequently lapsing into stagnation and continuing a limited range of very simply decorated shapes from the LB repertoire at a mediocre level of quality. Crete and Cyprus retained more of the LB heritage, however, and Cypriot influences were to play a part in the development of Attic Protogeometric.

Throughout these phases the Minoan and Mycenaean styles remained distinct, although they shared many shapes and motifs. They normally arranged decoration in a similar way, in horizontal registers bounded by groups of fine bands; there was a recurrent fashion for isolating motifs in the field, often to considerable effect (Fig. 5.17: 2), but this never became common. In general the best work shows a concern to fit decoration to shape, both in its positioning and in the size of individual motifs, in a balanced manner; the band groups were often

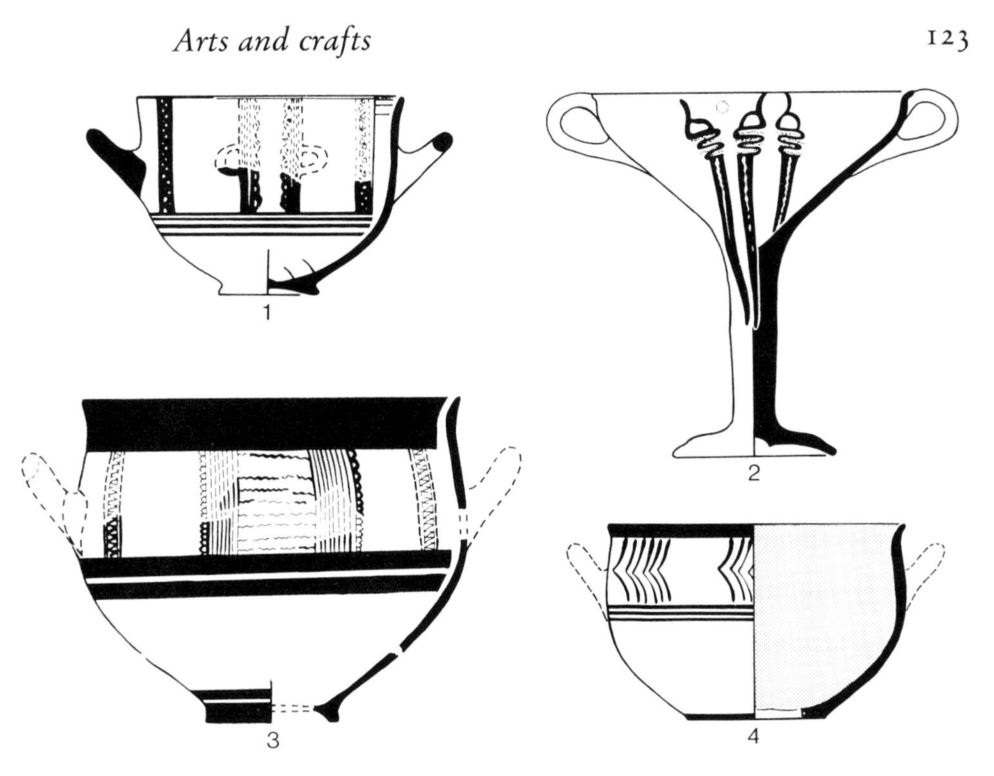

Fig. 5.17 LHIIIB and LM IIIB open pottery types.
1, 2 LH IIIB1 deep bowl, 'Zygouries kylix'. 3 LH IIIB2 Type B deep bowl. 4 LM IIIB deep bowl. Scale 1:4.

painted with extreme care while the pot was still revolving on the wheel. The neat, disciplined results evidently had considerable appeal despite their stereotyped quality. Motifs were almost entirely geometric or highly stylised floral and marine types, but a definite Mycenaean pictorial class appeared in LH IIIA; this consisted mainly of kraters, usually decorated with chariot processions or scenes involving bulls, but including other human and animal scenes (Pl. 5.7). There is not such a well-established class in LM III pottery, although some vases may be decorated with birds, fish or octopuses, and similar themes, together with enlarged versions of pottery motifs and a variety of scenes involving human and animal figures, probably symbolic, appear on the LM III clay larnakes (effectively coffins, see Ch. 6), which were probably decorated by vase-painters (Watrous 1991: 303–4). Decorated larnakes, most often showing mourning figures and other apparently ritual themes, were also produced by a local painting school at Tanagra in Boeotia (Pl. 6.2), but Mycenaean painted larnakes are otherwise very rare.

In general the range of later LB shapes continued already developed forms. Open shapes, kylikes, cups and bowls, are particularly common in domestic deposits; closed shapes, especially jugs, jars, alabastra, pyxides and stirrup jars, are more often placed in graves, and are also prominent among the pottery

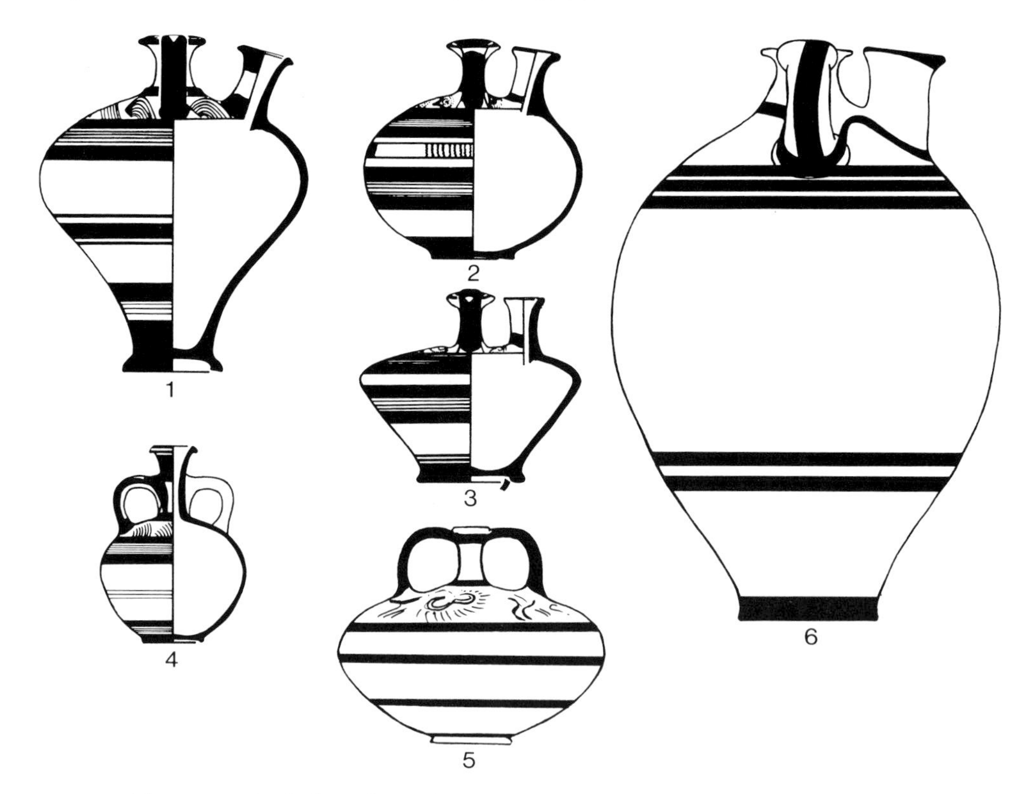

Fig. 5.18 Probable olive oil container types.
1, 2 LH IIIA2 piriform and globular stirrup jars. 3 LH IIIB1 squat stirrup jar. 4 LH IIIA2 flask. 5 LM IIIB stirrup jar. 6 LM IIIA2–B storage stirrup jar. Scale 1:4, except 6 (1:6).

exported in large quantities to the east Mediterranean. One major innovation at the end of LH IIIA, the deep bowl, became so popular as to be a 'type-fossil' in both LH and LM IIIB–C (Figs 5.17; 20:5–6); otherwise the changes in the decorated repertoire are largely changes in detail, and although some shapes disappeared early in LH III many lasted until the end of the BA. There are indications that some shapes local to the east Mediterranean were produced in Mycenaean style as an 'export ware', as to a great extent the pictorial class may have been; production in both cases may have been centred in the Argolid, especially at Berbati (Åkerström 1987), although there is evidence for occasional pictorial experiments elsewhere and for production on some scale near Thebes (Demakopoulou and Crouwel 1984).

Great quantities of plain ware were produced alongside the decorated for most of the period, in many of the same shapes: cups, bowls and stemmed drinking vessels like the kylix and Minoan 'champagne cup' were particularly common (Fig. 5.19). At Mycenae three different qualities of plain fabric can be distinguished (Wardle 1969: 280–1; Mountjoy 1976: 94–102), a notable indication

Pl. 5.7 A Mycenaean 'pictorial krater', Maroni, Cyprus. Courtesy of the Trustees of the British Museum.

of the degree to which pottery production had become standardised. Three distinct fabrics were identified in the Pylos palace (Blegen and Rawson 1966: 352), and it is probable that a comparable variation was widespread; certainly there was evidence for 'rough' and 'standard' production at Nichoria. The cooking wares, consisting mainly of tripod pots, trays, basins, jars, braziers and ladles, were also produced in standard qualities to a great extent. Storage pithoi

Fig. 5.19 Plain LH III and LM III pottery types.
1–4, 6 LHIIIB1 carinated kylix, cup, kylix, strap-handled bowl, tripod cooking pot. 5 LM IIIB 'champagne cup'. Scale 1:4.

are also common, though rarely found in quantity outside palaces and other major buildings, in contrast with their modern parallels (cf. Kanta 1983: 157–60); they vary in details but are basically similar, and must have continued to be made in the already established manner, whether by workshop potters or by specialists in pithos-production.

To a great extent the pottery of the Postpalatial Period (Fig. 5.20) continued these categories and many of their characteristic types, but the decline in quality already visible before the end of LH IIIB continued. There was a progressive narrowing of the range of shapes and motifs, monochrome coating and banding became increasingly dominant (the plain category in fact disappeared), and standards of production declined. The finest pottery of the period was highly elaborate, decorated with registers of intricate geometric patterning and often also in pictorial style: deep bowls, kraters and stirrup jars were the most favoured shapes, and the commonest motifs were birds and warrior scenes on the mainland, and octopuses, often combined with other creatures, in the Aegean, reflecting renewed Minoan influences (Pl. 5.8). But such elaborate pottery constituted a small proportion of the decorated ware and largely disappeared after the LH IIIC Middle phase, although occasional pictorial pieces occur in Dark

Fig. 5.20 LH IIIC Middle pottery types.
1 jug. 2 conical kylix. 3 stirrup jar. 4 krater. 5 monochrome deep bowl. 6 'Close Style' deep bowl. Scale 1:6.

Age contexts. In general, the Dark Age inherited a very shrunken repertoire of shapes and motifs and mediocre standards of quality, although recent finds have shown that the Attic material originally used to define Submycenaean is stylistically impoverished compared with material from the Argolid, and Subminoan also preserved more of the BA tradition.

The questions of how homogeneity was established and maintained, and how within it change took place, may now be considered. In the pre-LB periods, we are dealing with a commonplace of prehistory, the existence of common potting traditions over wide areas; most of the shapes are functional and so will not need to vary much from site to site, but preferences for certain surface colours and treatments are established, and sometimes very unusual shapes like the sauceboat become widespread. If there is a painted style, it will generally involve a limited range of simple geometric motifs on which the potter can draw at will, guided by personal perceptions of what is appropriate that will probably be shaped by tradition; thus, pottery in the style will have a general similarity without necessarily including much strict repetition. Obvious exceptions such as Kamares could not be reproduced; rather, their general appearance and simpler motifs could be imitated. The case was similar with wares like Vasiliki Ware and classic Grey Minyan, whose production involved a degree of specialised knowledge of

Pl. 5.8 A LH IIIC stirrup jar with octopus decoration, Attica. Courtesy of the National Museum of Denmark, Copenhagen, and Dr S. Dietz.

firing and, in the case of Minyan, use of the wheel; thus, the Minyan ring-stemmed goblet was not imitated in much of the mainland, although the appearance of Grey Minyan and the basic angularity of its classic shapes were. There are no clear centres for these common potting traditions, though a richer range might be produced at the larger and more developed settlements, and one can only surmise that new ideas were passed on through a network of contacts between the potters of neighbouring settlements; but only really distinctive forms like the sauceboat, and wares like Vasiliki Ware, would be widely disseminated, while minor variations such as the 'Myrtos ware' painted style would remain local.

The homogeneity of the LB styles, however, involved much more, the mass-production of a series of standard forms which were created at major centres and disseminated from them; such centres would continue to initiate changes in style, followed more or less faithfully throughout the region that shared the style. This was not fully established at the beginning of the LBA, but it is possible to define a short list of standard LM IA motifs and shapes, and LH I consists of a very specific group of shapes and motifs handled in a distinctive manner; despite the appearance of special classes like Marine Style and, later, pictorial vases, these features were to be characteristic of the ordinary decorated pottery from then on, and standardisation of the plain and coarse wares, established from the beginning in the Minoan sphere, developed fairly rapidly in the Mycenaean. The fact that these wares were so standardised made it relatively easy for provincial potters to learn their essentials, to excerpt a more limited range, suited to local preferences, from what was produced at the centre, and to pick up innovations, which frequently involved no more than minor variations on what had already been established. Since the stylistic phases seem to have lasted a minimum of a generation, often more, there will not have been a constant need to keep up with changes, and it should not be forgotten that what survives in the deposits represents the results that potters were satisfied with, not their first experiments. The ability of some potters outside the main stylistic centre to reproduce quite complex types successfully is demonstrated by the wide spread of apparently locally made pots in the fine LM IB and LH IIA styles; but this was not to be the case later with pictorial pottery, although the effect of the fine banding on neat closed LH IIIA2–B shapes was quite well imitated at provincial level.

The precise mechanisms by which knowledge of changes in style was spread remain somewhat unclear. While knowledge of a new style like LH I is most likely to have been spread by the actual movement of potters familiar with the style, the most obvious way for changes to be transmitted thereafter would be by export of examples of new types from the centre. But evidence for exports from centres to provincial sites within a cultural region is scanty, compared with that for exports across cultural boundaries or at times when there were many local centres, as in the Postpalatial Period. They are hard to identify partly because of the homogeneity of style, which extends to appearance: Mycenaean fine pottery from many parts of the Mycenaean region appears much the same, and it would be begging the question always to identify pieces of exceptional quality as from the Argolid, particularly since Argive deposits can show a range of qualities and surface appearances. It may well be that movements of fine pottery in such circumstances were more common than at present suspected; thin-section analysis of coarse wares has suggested a lot of movement in the Aegean and the Mycenaean world (Riley 1983: 288–90). But this was probably because certain clays had valued qualities, and it is quite possible that clay or tempering material rather than pottery was being moved. The main explanation may be that, as already suggested, it was particularly easy to pass what were often minor developments in motifs along the network of interconnections between potters that I have suggested.

The standardisation and very widespread use of the wheel are, as already noted, the best indications of the degree to which pottery production had become a specialised craft, surely practised in workshops. The production of specific export wares that can be plausibly associated with the Argolid is the kind of development that might be expected of a nucleated workshop industry, but no suitable site has yet been identified: even at Berbati the remains do not seem to suggest more than one workshop at any period. The fact that much decorated pottery, particularly in LH IIIA2–B, consisted of containers which obviously held some valued substance, since they were so prominent among the pottery exported to the east Mediterranean, is an indication of the close ties between pottery production and other 'industries', especially the manufacture of perfumed oil, probably the substance contained in small stirrup jars and similar shapes (Fig. 5.18). But already before the end of LH IIIB there seems to be a decline in standards, and mass exports seem to stop; the position that pottery production had achieved was quickly lost, not to be regained again in the Aegean until the seventh century.

A final word needs to be said about the sources of potters' inspiration. Probable links with fresco-painting, metalwork and stone vessels have been mentioned; but just as vase decoration was not reproducing frescoes on a smaller scale, so it seems unlikely that pottery ever imitated metal vessels to a marked degree. Given the general rarity of metal vessels, especially in the earlier periods, it is surely more plausible that where there are parallel ceramic and metal forms the former were the originals, and the occurrence of evidently metallic features is best explained by E.N. Davis, 'The potters are probably not strictly copying metallic prototypes, but more likely quoting metallic features which they have absorbed into their vocabulary of ceramic forms' (1977: 94). The major influences within pottery manufacture and decoration, then, were contained within the craft, but, particularly when a special, 'luxury', ware was intended, potters were ready to draw on non-ceramic sources of inspiration.

(iii) Non-ceramic vessels and furniture

(For the sake of simplicity, vessels which might be of copper or bronze are referred to as 'bronze' throughout.)

Vessels in wood and stone were produced alongside pottery in the early

Neolithic of the Near East, but as pottery was improved and clay shapes began to be developed for most purposes, they became less common. Similarly, although stone vessels, especially bowls, were well represented in the earlier Neolithic of the mainland, no continuous tradition can be traced from then to the BA, and when non-ceramic vessels reappear in the Aegean, it is evident that the major motivating force behind their production was display. Hence they were made of attractive materials, often difficult to work, and were shaped and sometimes decorated with increasing elaboration.

Despite their importance as display items, all had some kind of function. Drinking and pouring vessels are among the earliest types to appear and were always popular, highlighting the ceremonial connections of drinking alcohol, and another large class was connected with the preparation and serving of food. Stone mortars and bronze pans could not easily be duplicated in clay, because their materials were essential to their functions, and bronze cauldrons and the like often reached sizes not easily achieved in clay; but all remain rare, reflecting a style of cooking not to be found in every household. Some functional stone vessels, basins, trays, troughs, lamps and lids, are too roughly worked to be display items but are nevertheless found normally in high-status contexts, while other bronze forms are clearly display versions of types produced in clay, tripod vessels, dippers, braziers and lamps, but no doubt were put to use on occasion.

A further large class may be generically described as containers for luxury items like jewellery and cosmetics, or, in the case of large chests, special textiles. Boxes and chests were evidently of wood, and their appearance can generally only be guessed at from representations and the survival of decorative inlays (chests may well be reflected in the clay LB burial larnakes). Many miniature stone containers from Crete are thought to have been made as grave-goods, but they still could have held some offering, as similarly small jugs and cups could have been used in funerary rituals. Other classes include the clearly ritual 'libation tables' and rhytons, which are unlikely to have had a secular function if in special materials, and items of furniture such as tables, chairs and footstools, which were clearly luxury objects in many cases, made of or inlaid with fine materials.

The close association of all these items with display and status is borne out by the contexts in which the great majority have been found, palaces and other large buildings, religious sites, and the graves of important persons or groups. Even where stone vessels are relatively common, as in the Prepalatial graves of Crete and the Cyclades, there are grounds for arguing that they accompanied the burials of higher-ranking members of society. Burials are in fact the principal source of non-ceramic vessels in this period, though the existence of boxes and chests is demonstrated by the sealings originally attached to them from Lerna. The palaces and major settlements of Crete begin to be productive in the First Palace Period, and these, with the 'villas' and some religious sites, are the source of almost all the Cretan material in the Second Palace Period, while Cycladic material of this time also comes almost entirely from the town sites. But the mainland, hitherto of little significance, begins to be represented by rich grave-finds in this period, and in the later LBA graves again become the source of most of the material in the Aegean, although there is a fair amount from the palatial centres and the Linear B texts document the existence of precious vessels and furniture in palace stores. By the Postpalatial Period, however, production of most classes had virtually ceased, though Aegean-style bronze vessels were produced in Cyprus, and perhaps a few in the Aegean.

On present evidence the earliest non-ceramic BA vessels are those of the Cyclades, in stone; there is a gap at present between the pieces from Kephala and those of a late 'Pelos' stage, but a continuous tradition seems very likely, and the earliest of Crete seem definitely later. In general, the Cycladic vessels are close to contemporary pottery types of bowl, jar and pyxis (Fig. 5.21: 1–3), and there are even stone versions of the 'frying pan'. Most are of white marble, decorated if at all with simple incised patterns, but the softer green chlorite was used for some elaborate vessels, which can have relief spiral decoration also, and veined marbles and other local stones occur.

The earliest stone vessels of Crete, from early EM II contexts, which include bowls, ladles and pyxides, have links with the green chlorite class, but the superficial similarities mask many differences in detail. It seems most likely that Cretan development was essentially local, though accepting stimuli from the Cyclades and perhaps Egypt, since Egyptian stone vessels were reaching Knossos at this time. Egyptian influence is not strongly evident in the early shapes, although it may well be seen in the adoption of the drill to shape vessels (which could, however, also have come from the Cyclades) and the concentration on small shapes for funerary use.

In the later part of the Prepalatial Period the Cretan industry developed quickly. A wide range of local stones was exploited, though the softer forms like chlorite and serpentine were preferred; experimentation was probably encouraged by the great variety available and the close proximity of sources of different types (cf. Warren 1969, Ch. III). Cretan taste evidently preferred coloured and variegated stones to plain white, and the natural banding of some forms was exploited to great effect. The use of local materials, such as the banded marble of Mochlos, and variations in the distribution of some shapes indicate the existence of different local traditions; the main centres may have been in the east and south, but the products are widely distributed within Crete, although hardly any have been found elsewhere. The shape range included many forms of bowl and small container as well as larger types (Fig. 5.21: 4–11; Pl. 5.9), and is largely self-contained, only rarely reflecting pottery shapes like the 'teapot' or Cycladic or Egyptian stone shapes.

At the same time the first certain metal vessels were appearing in the Aegean. Most are of silver, including bowls and goblets from Amorgos (Fig. 5.22: 1), a jug from Naxos, two cups from Mochlos T. VI, and a vase of uncertain shape

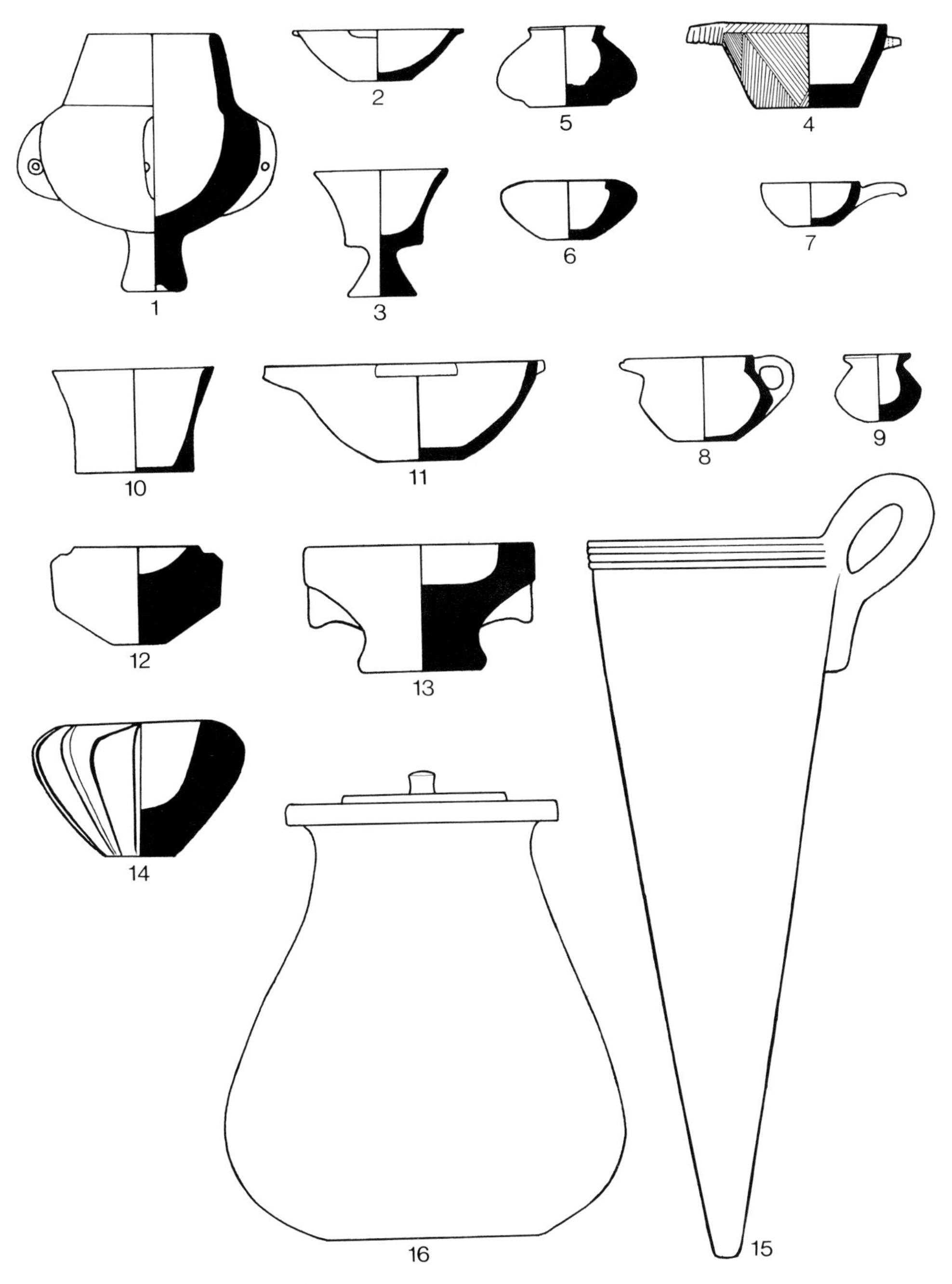

Fig. 5.21 Examples of stone vessels.
1 'Pelos' *kandila*. 2, 3 'Syros' lugged bowl, goblet. 4 EM II incised bowl. 5–11 Prepalatial and First Palace Period: alabastron, shallow bowl, handled bowl, spouted jug, small carinated jar, straight-sided cup, spouted bowl. 12–15 Second Palace Period: libation table, lamp, blossom bowl, conical rhyton. 16 LH IIIB1 jar. Scale 1:4.

Pl. 5.9 Stone jug, Mochlos T. VI. Courtesy of the Faculty Board of Classics, University of Cambridge and Prof. P.M. Warren.

from Voidhokoilia in Messenia (G.S. Korres, pers. commun.). A gold sauceboat in the Louvre is surely genuine (it was acquired in 1887, before the clay shape was familiar) and probably from the Peloponnese, but another, now in Israel, is suspiciously close to it, and there are problems in accepting as genuine, or if so as Aegean, some gold and silver bowls reputed to be from Euboea (Davis, E.N. 1977 (hereafter Davis): 64–5). The dates of a lead bowl from the Trapeza cave and bronze bowl from Mochlos T. VII are not clear, and the latter might fall within the First Palace Period, which is otherwise represented only by a silver kantharos from Gournia T. I (Fig. 5.22: 2) and a small group of functional bronze bowls and tripod vessels from Quartier Mu at Mallia and other Cretan sources (summarised in Matthäus 1980: 310). There is a continuing controversy

Fig. 5.22 Examples of gold and silver vessels.
1 'Syros' silver bowl. 2 silver kantharos, Gournia T. II. 3 gold kantharos, Shaft Grave IV. 4, 5 silver and gold Vapheio cups, Shaft Grave V. 6 gold goblet, Shaft Grave IV. 7 silver shallow cup, Vapheio tholos. 8 gold shallow cup, Marathon tholos. 9 inlaid silver bowl, Dendra tholos. 10 silver jug, Shaft Grave V. Scale 1:4.

over the Minoan origin of many other silver vessels, some from Byblos but most from the Tôd Treasure in Egypt; the case for the latter being Minoan has been vigorously restated in Warren and Hankey (1989: 131–4; but see above, Ch. 1, p. 20). But the fact that pottery vessels undoubtedly imitate metal forms in some respects does not make the forms imitated themselves necessarily Minoan; the possibility of an Anatolian link cannot be ruled out, especially since the kantharos types found in silver and clay have clear Anatolian connections (Davis, 88–94). The knowledge of how to produce metal vessels could well have been introduced from Anatolia.

The range in type and distribution of these early metal vessels is wide, but their rarity in actual Aegean material, including from sites where there were a lot of other finds, such as Zygouries, suggests that they were occasional products by specialists in other metalwork such as jewellers, working to order. It is often presumed, on the basis of supposedly metallic features in pottery, that they existed in significant quantity (for a judicious survey see Walberg 1976: 34–9). I do not find many of the arguments compelling, for features such as thin walls, straight lips and angular shapes appeared in pottery long before any reasonable date for possible metal originals. Angular shapes are in fact conspicuously rare among the earliest extant metal vessels, both in the Aegean and elsewhere, and are not natural to metalwork, since they will strain the fabric (cf. Davis, 123–4, also 175 on NM 392); it might well be argued that when they appear in metal they are imitating work in clay or stone, in which carinated shapes, decorative fluting, ribbing and grooving, and lobed or crinkly rims can be more easily produced. Even rivet-imitations are often not in functional positions (Davis, 86, 94), so that the effect of metalwork rather than a specific shape is probably being imitated. Such imitations may well reflect the rarity and prestige of metalwork in these periods, in fact.

In all probability, then, non-ceramic vessels continued to be mainly of stone in the First Palace Period; a small faience and gold jar from Knossos, dated to the end of the period, is probably local, but unique (Foster 1979: 60–1; a faience bowl reported from Mochlos was probably a Near Eastern import). The production of stone vessels of quality continued in Crete alone, on present evidence, and may increasingly have centred at the major settlements, especially those with palaces; there are some close links with the palatial Kamares pottery, and exotic imported stones now coming into use are found at Knossos and Mallia alone. The craft was undergoing considerable changes during this time: the range of small funerary pots was disappearing, and functional domestic forms were being introduced, almost entirely in the easily worked serpentine that was favoured for all common forms. Bowls, containers and lamps are found in the palaces and houses at major centres; Phaistos has also produced decorated 'libation tables' and small jars, apparently wrapped in gold leaf, which are probably ritual vessels. A few vessels reached sites outside Crete, notably in the Cyclades, Argolid and Egypt, probably accompanying MM pottery.

Pl. 5.10 Gold cup, probably Minoan work, Vapheio tholos. Peter Clayton.

The real explosion in the quantity and range of evidence comes in the Second Palace Period. It is so great as to suggest that more development had been taking place, especially in metalwork, than the evidence at present suggests, but it might also represent a response to a great expansion in wealth and much easier access to raw materials; there seems little doubt that these factors are reflected in the mainland evidence. Metal vessels become much more common and were evidently the most favoured prestige items of all on the mainland; they include both plain and elaborately decorated drinking and pouring vessels, and varieties of rhyton, mostly in gold or silver (Fig. 5.22: 3–7, 10; Pl. 5.10), and functional vessels in bronze (Fig. 5.23: 1–5, 7–9), which are well represented in high-status Cretan domestic contexts as well as mainland graves. The major mainland source, the Shaft Graves, has also produced some unique types; one gets a strong impression that metal was favoured above all other precious materials, and in fact most vessels in other materials from the Shaft Graves and other early Mycenaean sources are likely to be imports from Crete.

Cretan contexts are still very productive of stone vessels, which continue to cover a full range of shapes (Fig. 5.21: 12–15), and the quality of the best examples is such that they might well have been thought the finest form of non-ceramic vessel; certainly, notably few metal vessels have been found in the

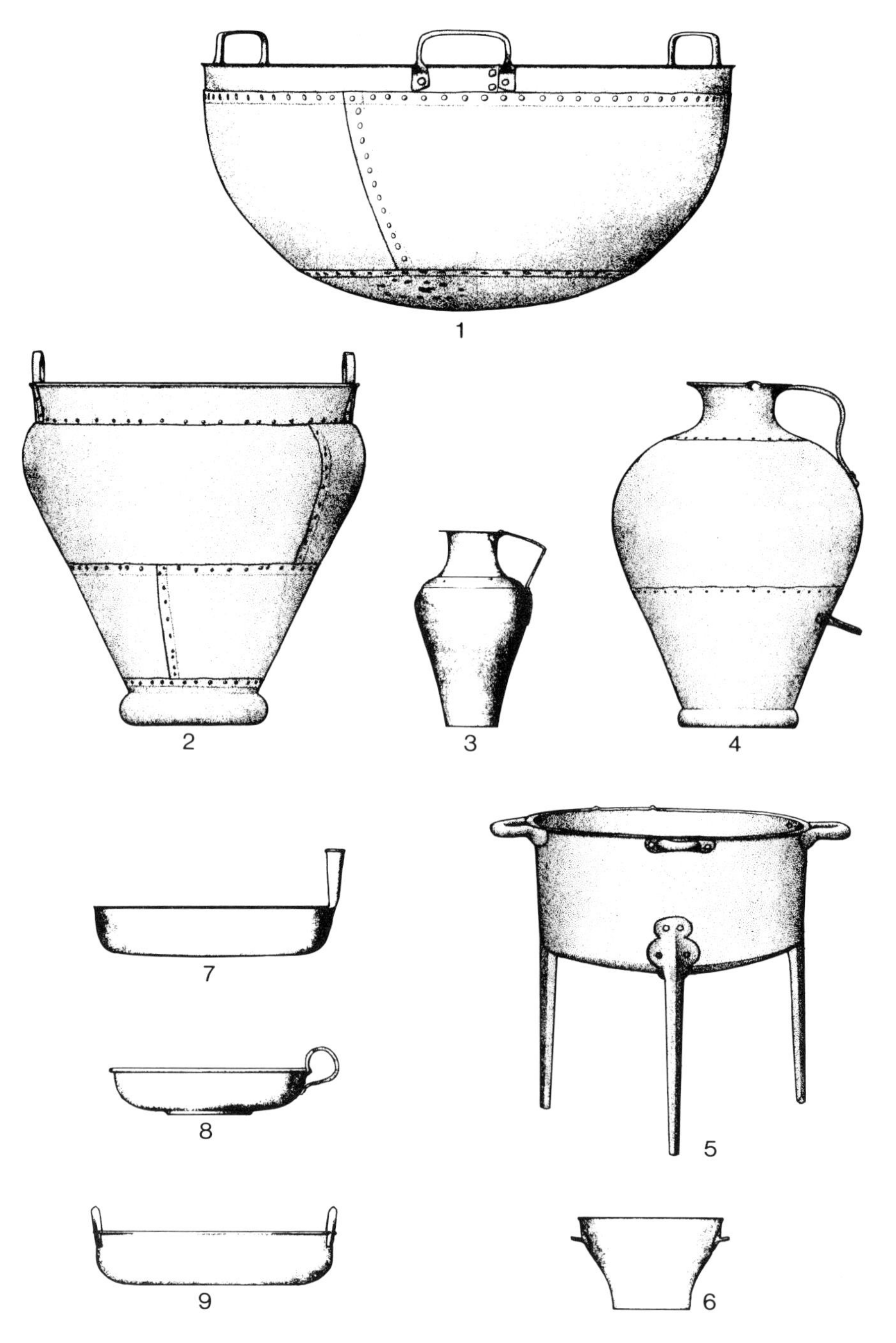

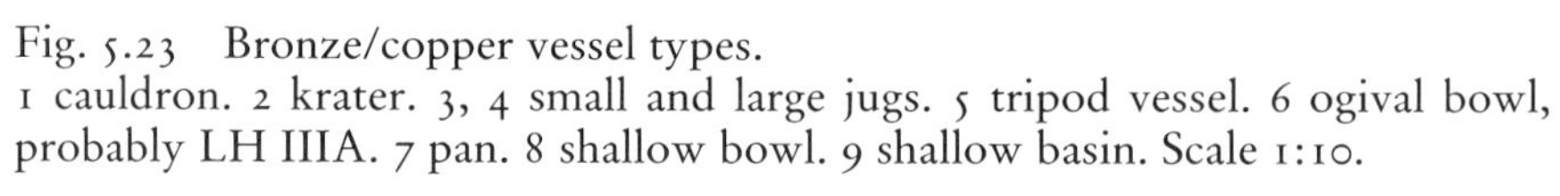

Fig. 5.23 Bronze/copper vessel types.
1 cauldron. 2 krater. 3, 4 small and large jugs. 5 tripod vessel. 6 ogival bowl, probably LH IIIA. 7 pan. 8 shallow bowl. 9 shallow basin. Scale 1:10.

Pl. 5.11 Closeup of the 'Harvester Vase', Ayia Triada. Peter Clayton.

palaces and 'villas'. Although serpentine was the commonest material by far, many other stones were used, not only Cretan limestones and gabbro, but Egyptian alabaster, Laconian *antico rosso* and *lapis lacedaemonius*, obsidian from Giali and Anatolia, and rock crystal which may be imported (Warren 1969: 135–7). Many of these were extremely hard, and though relatively few vessels were made from them they include many of the *tours de force* of Cretan stone-working. A whole class, mostly rhytons in soft stones, was decorated with relief scenes of human and marine themes, which were probably products of a single Knossian workshop (Pl. 5.11). Some were apparently covered in gold leaf, and other vessels have gold or bronze attachments, perhaps reflecting a Cretan liking for mixing materials; but stone vessels remain a self-contained group, rarely imitating shapes in other materials.

These vases were extremely popular in the Aegean at this time, so much so that local schools producing Cretan shapes in local and imported stones were established on Kea, Melos and Thera (Warren 1979), where there was also a considerable industry in more functional domestic shapes; popular shapes were also imitated in clay at Kastri on Kythera and Ayios Stephanos (Rutter 1979b). A massive pithos of local lava from Thera is particularly notable, as the largest stone vessel in the Aegean and a very demanding piece technically (Warren 1979: 87–8); tripod mortars produced in Theran dacite (originally thought

Syro-Palestinian) were exported to Crete (Warren 1979: 86–7, 108). The general popularity of the stone vessels of this period is demonstrated by their frequent survival in later contexts, such as the lamps used in the Pylos palace and the rhytons of the Rhyton Well at Mycenae (Wace 1921: 204–5).

Besides metal and stone vessels there are now other groups. Quite a number of faience vessels are known, but from relatively few contexts, principally the palaces of Knossos and Zakro and the Shaft Graves. These are so individual that few even share the same shape; many are miniatures, and most if not all may have had ritual functions. Faience was also used to provide mouth-pieces and other attachments from ostrich egg rhytons, found in Thera and the Argolid, and for inlays that were attached to boxes, gaming boards and the like. Knossos seems to have been the principal centre of production of these and a range of other items, with a remarkable variety of colouring, some of which suggests continuing influence from the faience crafts of Egypt and the Near East.

Ivory was also used as an inlay material, as on wooden boxes (of which examples have actually survived in Shaft Grave V), and to make boxes, usually the cylindrical lidded pyxides which were a natural form to make from elephant tusks. Although these mostly occur on the mainland, they may well represent work in the Minoan tradition (Krzyszkowska 1988: 231); but ivory working does seem to have become established on the mainland in the early Mycenaean period (Pl. 5.12). However, there is no reason to believe that the faience and stone vessels are anything but imports, as is a single glass bowl from Kakovatos T. A, which may well be Near Eastern. But there is good reason to suppose that metal vessels were made on the mainland, especially at or near Mycenae, and it has been argued that a 'Mycenaean' craft tradition can be distinguished in gold and silver work (Davis, *passim*); in bronze work, the similarities with material from Crete would imply the transplantation of technique (although the krater form, Fig. 5.23: 2, is so far known only from the mainland, Matthäus 1980: 150–7).

impressive, but it is questionable whether it is best explained in this manner. Though it also involves details such as the treatment of handles and rivet-types, it depends largely upon identifying as 'Minoan' all the most complex techniques; nevertheless, many works identified in this way as Minoan are thought to have been made on the mainland, and are often without Cretan parallel in extant work. It is not explained how a 'Mycenaean' tradition could develop so swiftly on the mainland or persist side by side with the often superior 'Minoan' techniques, particularly when these were apparently known on the mainland from the start (cf. Davis, 133–4 on the Grave Iota cup). Nor is the possibility of other metalworking traditions in the Aegean allowed for, although the 'Aegina Treasure' gold cup might well derive from one.

An alternative interpretation might be that the 'Mycenaean' techniques are often the older, more basic tradition of the Aegean, perhaps deriving from Anatolian sources; the 'Minoan' techniques would represent the level of skill

Pl. 5.12 Ivory pyxis, Routsi T. 2. Hirmer Verlag, Munich.

attained by the best specialists, who not only drew on other traditions, as apparently on the Syrian use of niello, but who also innovated. In the Aegean of the period, such persons are most likely to have been trained in the Cretan palaces, but they could have become established elsewhere, as at Mycenae, and have developed further under the stimulus of new patrons with different tastes. The continuance of 'Mycenaean' techniqes would then represent the coexistence of workshops of differing levels of skill, perhaps conservative and preferring to continue traditionally reliable methods.

It will, then, remain difficult to distinguish between imports and local manufacture on the mainland (see further relevant comments in Hurwit 1979 and Younger 1985: 54–5). In general, the shapes of the gold and silver vessels are Minoan, resembling shapes found in clay, bronze, and sometimes stone and faience; but some, like the kantharos and the Vapheio cup with midrib, relate more closely to mainland shapes, or seem responses to mainland taste, like the stemmed goblets, and several are unique creations like 'Nestor's Cup', the gold toilet pots and the 'Battle Krater'. Such a variety of types is not found elsewhere on the mainland and probably did not outlive the Shaft Grave phase; as with other Shaft Grave material, it represents a burst of exuberant innovation which failed to establish a stable range of types. Given the extreme rarity of precious metal vessels in Crete, it may well be that major developments in this class took place at Mycenae, as has been argued for metal inlay work.

In most respects the rest of the LBA presents a picture of relative decline, though this must partly reflect the increasing rarity of the rich contexts that previously produced the evidence. Except in ivory work, there is no evidence of significant development. Stone vessel production seems to have gone into abrupt decline following the end of the Second Palace Period: although gypsum is newly brought into use, this may itself be a symptom of decline, since it is very easily worked, and there are only a few innovations which, as in the pottery, may reflect the influence of mainlanders' taste, the production of LH II-type alabastra, large jars, and pithoi. But all finds after the early Third Palace period in Crete can be interpreted as earlier survivals; only on the mainland, particularly at Mycenae, did stone vessels continue to be made. Quite elaborate jars and rhytons have been found in the LH IIIB1 House of Shields (Fig. 5.21: 16), most being of serpentine but some of other stones; inlays, mostly trefoil-shaped and in rock crystal, were used on some. There is probably a link to the inlaid stone tables listed on texts from Pylos (Ventris and Chadwick 1973: 339–41), of which one example was partly preserved in the palace debris. But this material may be the product of only one or two workshops, as the faience vessels from the House of Shields surely are. The most recent interpretation sees these as products in an essentially Near Eastern tradition, using foreign techniques, even if made in a Mycenae-based workshop (Tournavitou 1990a: 416–17).

In contrast, metal vessels, especially bronze, are well represented in rich tombs of the early Third Palace Period; the range in this material may have reached its widest extent at this time, including drinking vessels and elaborately decorated small bowls as well as the larger and more functional types. Relief work on rims, handles and shoulder plates is a common feature. But gold and silver seem to have been used mainly for drinking vessels (silver conical cups are known from the Kokla tholos), most of which are close to pottery shapes; some are elaborately decorated with relief work or inlay, but many are plain (Fig. 5.22: 8, 9). Tin-coated clay vessels of a wide range of open shapes are also popular, and continue into later stages, when in general the evidence becomes much poorer. Groups of bronze vessels from the Mycenae chamber tombs may be of Third Palace Period date, since they include shapes paralleled in pottery of that time (cf. Matthäus 1980: 261–74 on the 'lekane', Fig. 5.23: 6). Fragments from the Pylos palace and hoards of bronze buried around the end of the period, and the Pylos texts, demonstrate the continued survival, and probably production, of vessels in gold, silver, bronze and lead (the last well represented in the Argolid), but there is not much evidence of development, although some details changed, and it is not impossible that most or all of the precious metal examples were treasured survivals.

In the Postpalatial Period, some bronze vessels can be identified, in tombs and domestic contexts; one large group, the 'Tiryns Treasure', includes several types hard to parallel earlier, which might well be products of the period, but symptomatically the most elaborate, a tripod-stand, is a Cypriot product, as metal vessels from later Dark Age contexts also are. An odd little mug from Perati T. 104, whose decoration relates to late LH IIIB/early LH IIIC pottery, is very crude in comparison, and it seems that metal vase production declined almost if not quite to vanishing point in the last stages of the BA.

Creativity in the Third Palace Period may be identified in the ivorywork, although this drew heavily on the earlier traditions. A number of relief-decorated pyxides fall in this period, but inlays which must have been attached to chests, boxes and furniture are much more common. The partly intelligible descriptions of such furniture in a group of Pylos texts (Ventris and Chadwick 1973: 341–5) suggest extraordinarily elaborate work, using gold, silver, rock crystal and kyanos (blue glass?) as well as ivory inlays; a workshop at Thebes has produced inlays in several of these materials (Symeonoglou 1973, Ch. 5), and ivory chair-legs were found there in a palace storeroom, but it is not really possible to reconstruct the appearance of this material. Such pieces may well be in the direct line of descent from the elaborate gaming boards of the Second Palace Period, and undoubtedly they were the products of palace workshops at a few centres. To judge from the quantities of inlays in the tombs of Mycenae, Menidi and Spata, such items became favoured grave-goods for the elite in the Third Palace Period, but little of this nature survived the destruction of the palaces. What sound like hoarded antiques have been reported from Koukounaries and simple ivory inlays from Perati, but the wealth to buy the materials and the skill to make the items were gone.

(iv) Architecture

This section will concentrate on the more monumental structures of the BA. Although, as seen in Chapter 4, it is possible to identify local traditions in house-types and even to suggest the principles behind the layout of some towns, the plans and internal arrangements of both ordinary houses and settlements are still poorly documented for many phases. Nor is covering the known material in all its variations likely to yield much useful information. For while the majority of buildings can be seen to be constructed in the tradition established in the Neolithic period, mainly of mud-brick on a stone foundation, only rarely are there traces of unusual expertise that would suggest the practice of a specialised craft, and it is surprisingly difficult even to establish what a room's function was in many cases, let alone to identify recurrent patterns.

(a) Buildings

The earliest unusually elaborate buildings, on present evidence, are those of 'Lerna III' (EH II) date, especially the 'corridor houses', examples of which have been found from Boeotia to Messenia, including Aegina (cf. Felten 1986; Pullen 1986) (Fig. 5.24). 'Corridor houses' have a basically rectilinear plan, often neatly

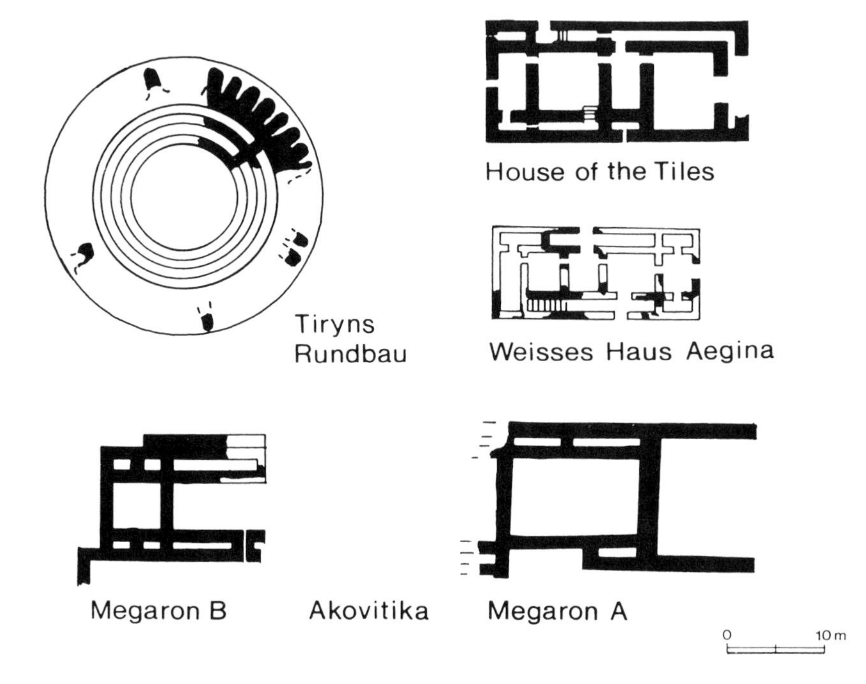

Fig. 5.24 Plans of monumental 'Lerna III' structures. Courtesy of Profs D.J. Pullen and R. Hägg.

rectangular, in which a series of large rooms is laid out axially, flanked by narrow corridors which sometimes contained stairs to an upper storey and could have supported open galleries; a standard unit of measurement may have been used in planning them. The main material of the walls was mud-brick, on a substantial stone foundation; the large rooms would have required substantial timbers for their ceilings, especially as they contain no evidence for internal supports. The House of the Tiles at Lerna, one of the largest examples at 25 × 12 m, includes other refinements such as wood-sheathed door jambs and stucco plastered walls in important rooms, and in both this and the 'Weisses Haus' of Kolonna on Aegina a narrow ground-floor room between two large ones may be a light-well. These and others clearly had roofs of fired clay tiles, presumably slightly pitched; schist tiles, probably placed where the effects of weathering would be greatest, are also found sometimes. Such tiles are in fact being increasingly widely identified at 'Lerna III' sites, especially in the Argolid (Hägg and Konsola 1986, fig. 3, to which add Ayios Dhimitrios in Triphylia, *op. cit.* 30), and were used on the roof of the Tiryns 'Rundbau', which displays even more remarkable expertise (Kilian 1986). It was of massive proportions (diameter about 28 m, outer wall 1.8 m thick), with a bastion-studded exterior, and was divided by concentric ring walls and cross-walls on two storeys, to form a series of small compartments surrounding an inner core. Fortifications were also found at several sites of this period, although only those of Lerna display much sophistication (see further section (b)).

At present these are without close parallel in the Aegean, although large and complex rectilinear structures of similar date have been identified at several sites in Crete, those of Vasiliki being the best preserved, and at Troy (Easton 1990: 435, fig. 4, 441). But the characteristic large rooms flanked by corridors are missing from these, and the monumental buildings of the Near East do not provide especially good parallels either; it seems best to view them as an indigenous development, whose history remains to be elucidated. But in the upheavals of the late EBA this architectural tradition disappeared; even on Aegina, the 'Weisses Haus' had no successor, and the art of tile-making was generally lost. For later monumental buildings it is necessary to turn to Crete.

Here the tradition which was later to dominate in the Aegean can be traced back into the Prepalatial Period. The EM II Vasiliki buildings have structural features which anticipate those of the later palaces, notably the use of timbers to strengthen the walls and a stepped plinth in the foundations; a paved courtyard was also associated with the later of the two sections now distinguished in the 'House on the Hill' (Zois 1976). The existence of substantial EM II structures at Knossos may also be deduced from the identification of a courtyard under part of the later West Court at Knossos, which itself postdates a rectilinear complex identified as the basement storerooms of a building (Wilson 1985), and a massive ramp further north (Catling 1988: 69). This ramp was in turn partly overlaid by a wall of fine construction along the north-west of the palace site. This and the

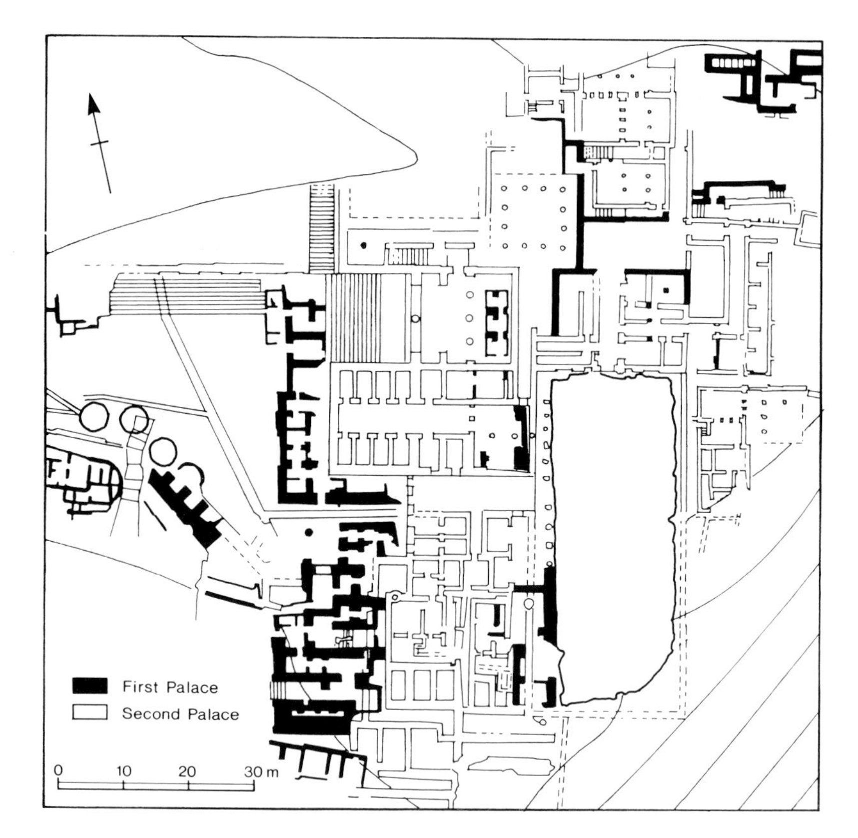

Fig. 5.25 Plan of the remains of the first palace at Phaistos. Drawn by J. Blécon, courtesy of Presses universitaires de France.

'Keep', a massive construction on the north containing deep shafts, are the only structures of those which have in the past been attributed to an 'MM IA palace' that seem securely datable so early; others, such as the Monolithic Pillar Basement are better dated to MM IIA (Momigliano 1991: 163–6). At Mallia too there seem to be traces of a major structure of late Prepalatial date; but the earliest structure that clearly prefigures the later palaces is at Phaistos, dated to MM IB (= MM IIA).

Here two blocks fronting onto a west court were constructed in succession, forming a unified and clearly monumental facade (Fig. 5.25); Levi has argued for the existence of a central court beyond, reached by the broad way between them, but this remains controversial (Warren 1987a: 47–8), though there are clearly structures beyond the west facade. They exemplify a style of architecture that is essentially that of the later palace complexes at Knossos, Phaistos, Mallia and Zakro as well as many other monumental buildings in the First and Second Palace Periods. Elements of this style were certainly transmitted to other parts of the Aegean in the Second Palace Period, even if local building traditions were followed (as in House A at Ayia Irini, largely built in slabs of local schist, cf. Cummer and Schofield 1984: 40–1), and it deserves extended consideration.

Cretan architects evidently did not adhere to any very precise set of rules, such as was developed for Greek temples later. They probably used a standard unit of measurement, and certainly did not build without plan, but they often economised on effort. Foundations were not originally deep or massive, even for the tallest structures. Fine masonry was reserved for the most public and visible areas, and even here courses were not even in height, and blocks were shaped to fit at the edges only, their backs being quite irregular, so that a wall had to be filled out with rubble and coated with plaster to present an even surface. A lack of standardisation is evident in the variations between the mud-bricks in use at different sites.

The basic materials of construction were the same as in ordinary buildings, but differently deployed. Ground-floor walls were built of rubble embedded in a mud mortar and strengthened with timbers laid vertically, horizontally and transversely; this system was at first used rather randomly at Phaistos, and seems to have been designed to give greater strength generally rather than specific protection against earthquakes. Upper storeys were normally of mud-brick, similarly strengthened with timber, and this could be used in sections of the ground floor, particularly at Mallia, and more generally for interior walls and partitions and as an auxiliary material. Important facades were faced with larger stones, often dressed. In the First Palace Period the use of orthostats, slabs set upright on a long side, was common at ground level, but walls of coursed rectangular blocks, laid on a stepped foundation and separated by thin layers of mud mortar, were more favoured later; some might have two masonry faces with a fill between, others might be filled out at the back with rubble in the manner described above. Timber was used less often within these walls, but surviving dowel holes show that this could occur; mostly such holes seem to be for fitting beams to stone, but at Knossos there is evidence for the use of wood clamps to tie the stone blocks together. (Cf. Pl. 5.13 for fine walling, with the original timber slots filled in).

Timber and stone were used for many other structural features, timber for door and window frames, vertical props within walls, and ceilings, which would form the basis for upper-storey floors, stone for thresholds, floor paving, staircase treads, benches and sometimes door jambs. The columns which were one of the major innovations of palace architecture were of wood, set on stone bases and further supported sometimes by stone foundations sunk in the ground beneath them; they helped to distribute the weight of the superstructure, together with stone piers, set within or against walls, and square stone pillars, usually of several blocks but sometimes monolithic.

Timber and stone could also be used purely decoratively: the dado course of walls may have been decorated with timber or stone veneers, to judge from apparent imitations in frescoes, and at a late stage in Knossos stone slabs sculp-

Pl. 5.13 The light-well in the Hall of the Double Axes, Knossos, showing slots for timbers and ashlar masonry. Courtesy of the Visitors of the Ashmolean Museum, University of Oxford, and Mrs A. Brown.

tured in relief were sometimes used, presumably in the upper part of walls. But the commonest decorative material was plaster, laid on walls and floors and painted with a colour wash, geometric patterns and ultimately figured scenes, the well-known frescoes; painted plaster reliefs, both patterns and figures, were used in some rooms, which often seem to have had important ceremonial functions. To judge from the frescoes, paint was also used on the columns and other wood features. The placing of 'horns of consecration' in stone and perhaps wood at various points surmounting the facade should also be mentioned.

The stones used were those most easy to shape with hammer and chisel (the saw was only used occasionally) and were often chosen for their fine light colour, such as poros limestone, which was particularly favoured for coursed masonry and floor slabs. Coloured and variegated stones were used for features like column bases and occasionally floor slabs, often arranged to provide deliberate contrasts; the sculptured friezes of Knossos were of such stones, and dado veneers may sometimes have been, although recovered examples are normally of gypsum. Local supply was evidently an important factor, although stone could be transported over quite long distances, as much of the timber is likely to have been: thus gypsum was particularly favoured at Knossos, sandstone at Mallia and Zakro.

The three greatest complexes of the Second Palace Period show many common features, but there are also divergences in detail, which are more marked when these are compared with Zakro. Here the Second Palace Period complex appears to have been built to a premeditated plan, whose orientation diverges from that of earlier buildings, but which repeats only some features of the 'standard plan', having, for example, no west court and little evidence of a second storey; it was also separated from the town to a great extent by enclosure walls (Chryssoulaki and Platon 1987: 80; cf. Chryssoulaki in Hägg and Marinatos 1987: 99). Yet in details it shows many similarities to Mallia (Cadogan 1976: 126–8), and overall the palaces show more similarity to each other than might have been expected if development had been totally independent at each site. What looks like a miniature palace on a very similar plan can be identified at Gournia (Soles 1991), and as now reported Building J/T at Kommos was part of a complex surrounding a court, though it lacks many palatial features (Shaw 1986: 262–3, 1990: 426).

The basic plan (Figs 5.26, 5.27) consisted of a continuous range of buildings around a central court, oriented more or less due N–S at the three great sites but more NE–SW at Zakro. But although the central court served in many ways as a focus, the western facade, overlooking a western court, may have been most significant; the western court may have served as a place of popular assembly, and while access to the palaces was through narrow and oblique entrances on this side, access to the courts was unrestricted. At ground floor level the plan largely consists of groups of narrow rooms, which most often seem to be storage magazines and work areas, but there were also suites of ceremonial rooms, although more magnificent examples of these are restored on the upper storeys, where the rooms could be larger because of the multitude of supporting walls, pillars and columns below. In some places there were basements, and the east side of Knossos was built into a great cutting, so that there were two levels below the court as well as that on ground level and the upper storey, a striking example of the scale on which Cretan architects sometimes worked.

A complete account of the refinements of palace architecture would take too much space, but it is worth noting some of the most characteristic features, which are without good parallel elsewhere (cf. Graham 1987: 233). These include the multiple pier-and-door partition, or polythyron, and the 'Minoan Hall' of which it is a feature, the sunken chamber or 'lustral basin', monumental stair-ways, the common use of columns, especially in porticoes and propylons, and the light-well. The provision of drainage by stone-lined channels and clay piping is also a remarkable feature, traceable back to the first palaces at Knossos (Mac-donald and Driessen 1988) and Phaistos. The majority of these features are most characteristic of the second palaces and contemporary buildings; but there may be an EM II light-well at Vasiliki, there is certainly a 'lustral basin' complex in the MM II Quartier Mu at Mallia and that of the Throne Room complex at

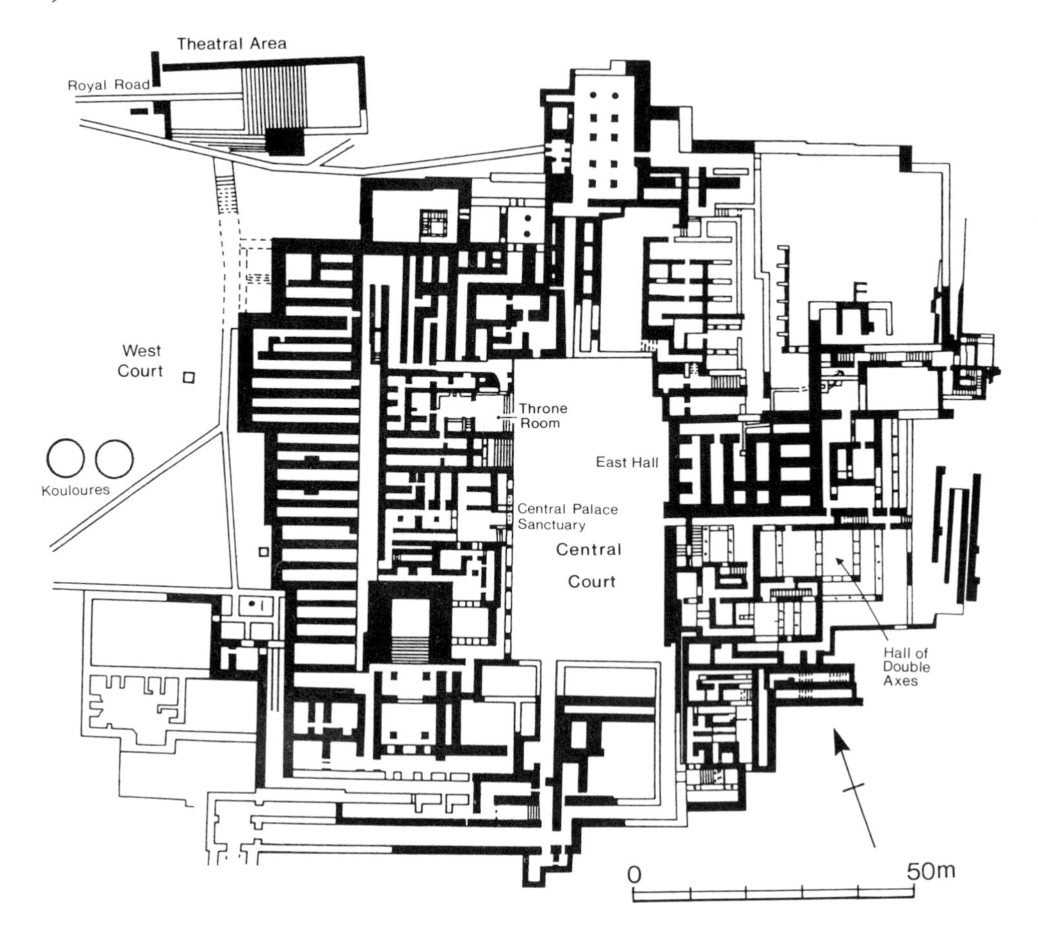

Fig. 5.26 Plan of the later palace(s) at Knossos.

Knossos has been similarly dated, and the use of columns can be traced back to the earliest palace building at Phaistos. The development of such features is a demonstration of the originality and strength of the native architectural tradition, underlining the point that the similarities with Near Eastern palaces sometimes cited relate only to certain techniques of construction, notably the use of timbering and orthostats, and to very general resemblances of arrangement (Graham 1987: 231–2); at Mari there is not even much evidence for an upper storey, in stark contrast with Minoan palaces (Dalley 1984: 12).

Some of the most distinctive features may have close connections with religion or ceremonial. It has been argued that the 'residential quarters' identified by Graham and others, in which these features are prominent, were ceremonial suites (Nordfeldt 1987), and that the polythyron was not simply a device for supporting the ceilings of large rooms, or for controlling access and circulation generally (Palyvou 1987), but was used specifically for regulating the approach to

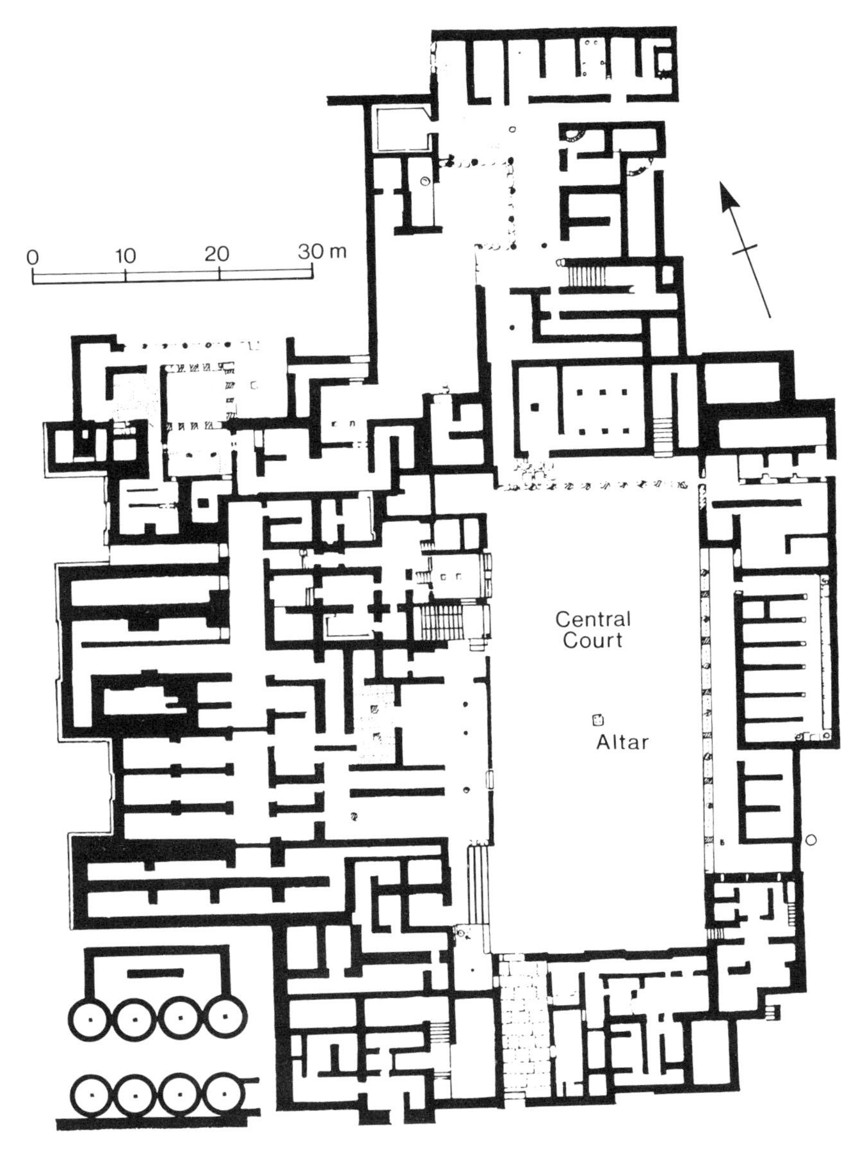

Fig. 5.27 Plan of the second palace at Mallia. After *The Archaeology of Minoan Crete*, p. 67, courtesy of the late Dr R.A. Higgins and the Bodley Head.

religious features, especially 'lustral basins' (Marinatos and Hägg 1986). This will be discussed further in Ch. 8, but certainly, the 'residential quarter' interpretation depends more on a perceived need to identify appropriately private and impressive living quarters for a royal family than on any features of the rooms or their contents, and their magnificence seems more appropriate to a public function. A ruling family or group may well have lived within the palace, but their rooms should probably be sought elsewhere.

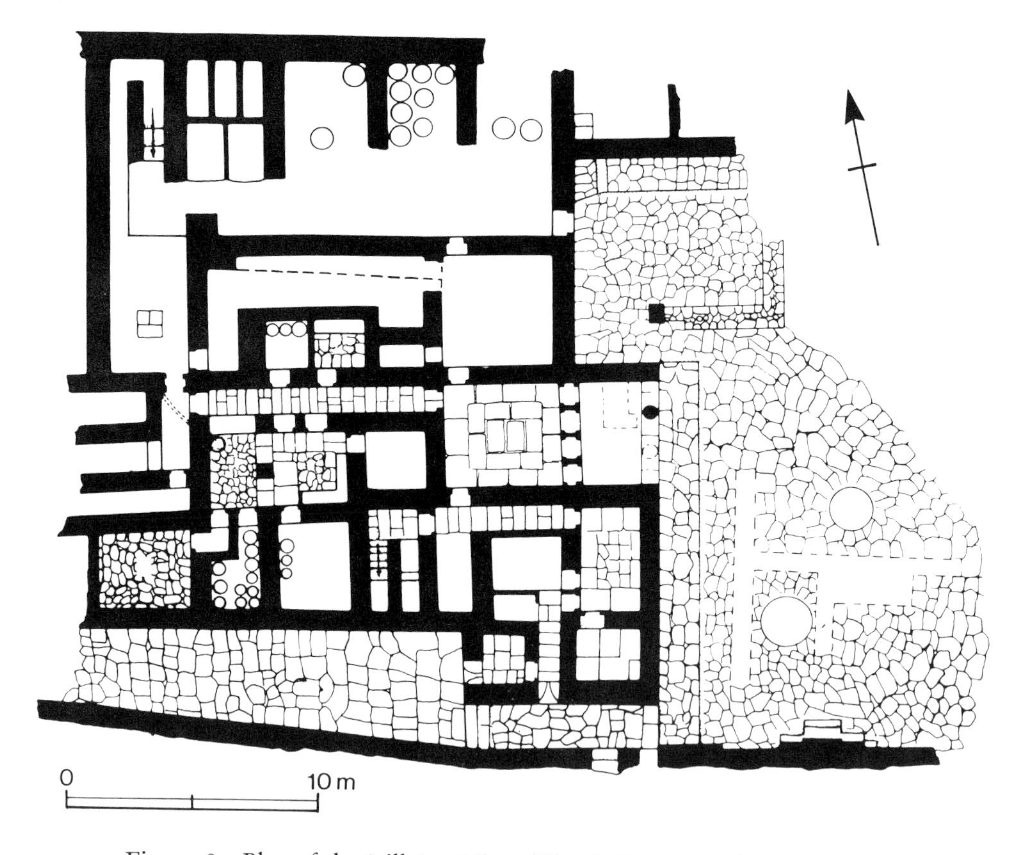

Fig. 5.28 Plan of the 'villa' at Nirou Khani. Courtesy of Mr G. Cadogan.

In varying degrees the features found in palace architecture are reproduced in other Cretan buildings of the Second Palace Period. These range from elaborate structures like the Little Palace at Knossos and the 'villas' (e.g. Fig. 5.28) to more ordinary houses whose architecture has less sophistication but which still make use of features like the polythyron (cf. McEnroe 1982 (Types 1 and 2); Hood 1983; Tzedakis and Chryssoulaki 1987). Outside Crete, examples of such features are particularly evident on Thera: timbering was used in the walls, masons' marks, ashlar facades and polythyra are quite common, and a light-well has been found by a central staircase in the House of the Ladies (Sali-Axioti 1990). But other characteristic features such as colonnades and courtyards have not been identified so far, and in many details the architecture has a different feel (Shaw 1978). Ashlar facades and a polythyron have also been reported from Trianda on Rhodes (Marketou 1988: 30), but elsewhere Minoan architectural features occur only sporadically, such as the 'pillar crypts' of Phylakopi and features of the 'domestic quarter' (in fact ceremonial/ritual?) of Ayia Irini House A, including a light-well (Cummer and Schofield 1984: 41). Only the use of frescoes is truly widespread, extending to Tiryns and Mycenae (below, p. 166).

That monumental structures, often of new forms, continued to be built in Crete after the Second Palace Period is demonstrated particularly by the LM IIIA1 Building P at Kommos and the remains dated to LM IIIA at Ayia Triada. The former, which made extensive use of timbering, consisted of a row of great galleries, tentatively interpreted as ship sheds (Shaw 1986: 263–8, 1990: 426); the latter include a stoa-like structure, consisting of a row of rooms behind a colonnade, and what has been interpreted as a Mycenaean-style 'megaron', built over part of the 'villa', though it has Minoan features, as does a later building at Plati (Hayden 1987: 218; other buildings, including a second 'megaron', are referred to by La Rosa in Shaw and Shaw 1985: 51–2). But at Knossos itself significant new building, as opposed to repair and rearrangement of the palace and other existing buildings, has not been identified as yet, and during LM III the old types of building seem to have become generally obsolescent in Crete, replaced by types that incorporate mainland features (Hayden 1987: 216–17).

Information is still scanty about the earliest important buildings of Mycenaean date at mainland sites, and there is little trace of the adoption of Minoan architectural techniques before the end of the Second Palace Period. The use of small blocks of poros seems to be common in early contexts at Pylos (e.g. Blegen *et al.* 1973: 12–13, 39), but there is no clear report of timber framing. However, this was certainly used in Mansion I at the Menelaion (H.W. Catling, pers. commun.), although the standard of masonry was not remarkable here or at LH IIIA1 Tiryns (Catling 1985: 21), and thereafter timber framing came into common use not only for palaces, but at Mycenae for other buildings on and off the acropolis, although it has not been reported from all major Mycenaean buildings (exceptions include those of Gla and the 'Potter's Shop' at Zygouries).

Information is equally scanty on the plan of the earliest buildings. Kilian's attempt (1987b, fig. 12) to reconstruct a building of Minoan type as the first phase of palatial building at Pylos must seem very doubtful, given that the interrelationships and dates of the various stretches of wall involved are quite uncertain; that beneath Court 63, which might represent Minoan-style rows of magazines, and others of similar alignment (most clearly shown in Blegen *et al.* 1973, Fig. 306) could be argued from the stratigraphy to represent a stage not much earlier than that of the main palace. When plans of major buildings become available in the early Third Palace Period, as for Mansions I–II at the Menelaion, the LH IIIA1 parts of the palace complex at Tiryns, Nichoria Building IV-4 and the Phylakopi 'megaron', they already show the characteristic features of the later palaces, and it is reasonable to suppose that the earliest Mycenaean buildings of importance were comparable but simpler still.

The Mycenaean palaces that are best preserved, at Mycenae, Tiryns and Pylos (Figs 5.29–31) are clearly arranged on quite different principles from those of Crete. The focus of the complex is a 'megaron' suite, a long hall approached through a porch, often with an intervening anteroom, which may be flanked on one or both sides by corridors off which subsidiary rooms open. Its central

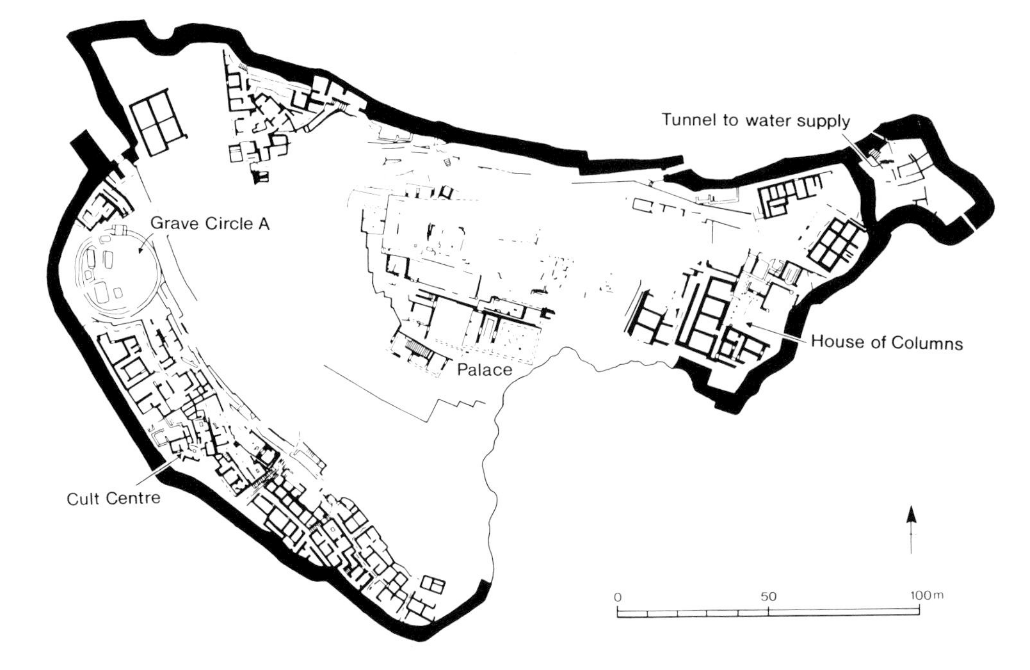

Fig. 5.29 Plan of the acropolis at Mycenae. Courtesy of Prof. S. Iakovidis.

position argues that the megaron suite had important, probably ceremonial functions. There may be other rooms behind the megaron, and there are many indications of an upper storey, but the megaron room itself, to judge from the evidence of Pylos, was not roofed over but had a gallery at the upper level around the sides and a chimney in the roof over the great central hearth. Kilian has presented an argument for identifying a 'double palace' plan, based on the occurrence of main and subsidiary megaron suites, and for associating the two suites with the two most powerful functionaries mentioned in the Linear B texts, the *wanax* and *lawagetas* (1987a). But, though attractive, this theory has difficulties, apart from the question of whether the *wanax–lawagetas* duality was a feature of all the Mycenaean palace societies. At Mycenae the poorly preserved main block has no such duplication, and the 'lesser megaron' must be sought in the separate House of Columns (which may however be a replacement for the abandoned West House group, Tournavitou 1989); and at Pylos there are not only the Throne Room and Halls 64–5 suites, but a third group of rooms, centring on Room 46, which have features linking them to the Throne Room suite. But it is generally agreed that the palaces contained rooms for ceremony, administration (Pylos has a proper archive room), storage of agricultural products and goods, including luxury items, and, to some extent at least, for manufacture and production, thus reproducing on a smaller scale the main functions identified in the Cretan palaces.

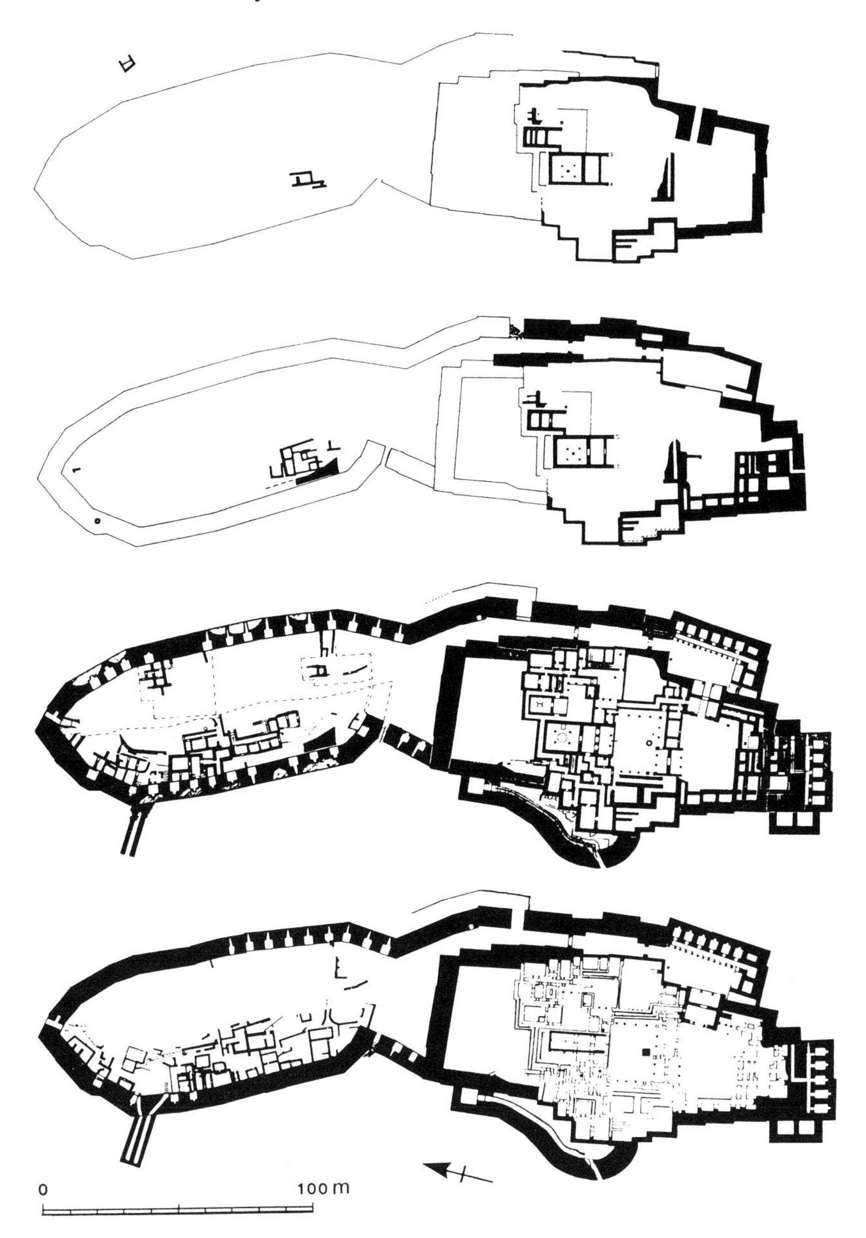

Fig. 5.30 Successive LH III phases of the acropolis at Tiryns. Courtesy of Prof. Dr K. Fittschen, Director of the German Archaeological Institute in Athens.

The clearest picture of a palace is given by Pylos (Fig. 5.31), which shows how much of the Minoan architectural tradition was continued in this different setting (Blegen and Rawson 1966: 34–42). The original structure had a facade of shaped blocks, filled out with rubble plastered on the interior, that has been reconstructed

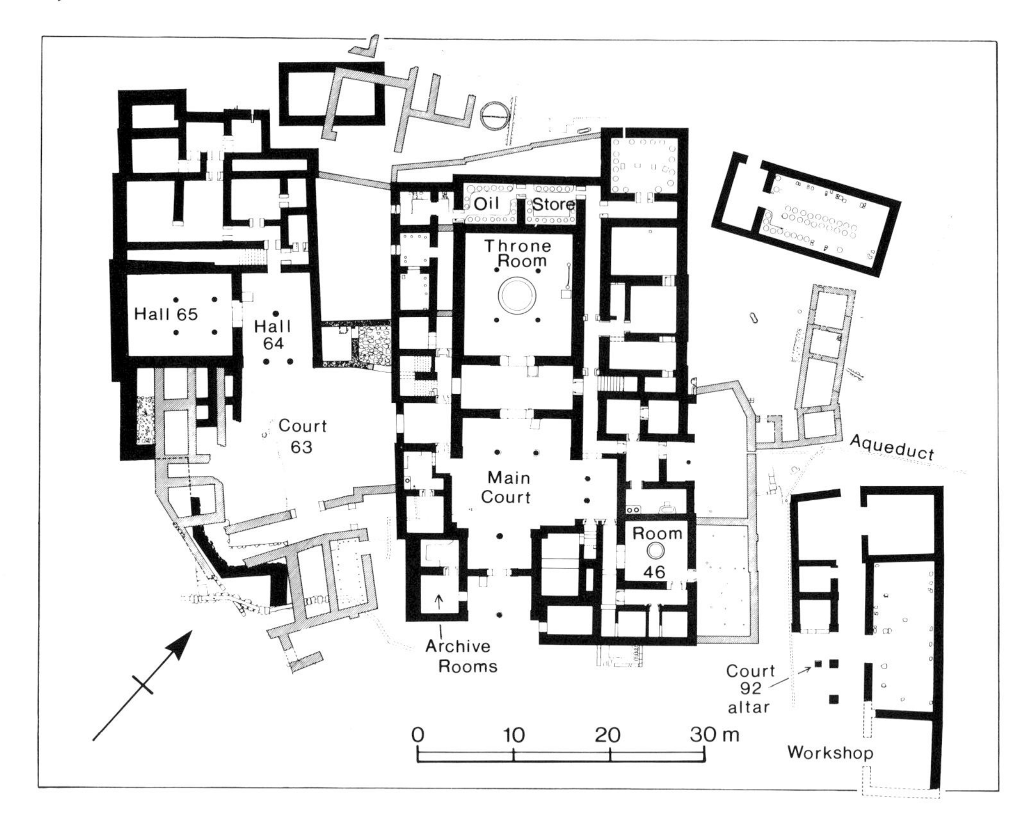

Fig. 5.31 Plan of the palace at Pylos.
Hatched walls are late additions to or adaptations of the earlier plan.

as set within a timber frame; evidence for horizontal beams was also detected on the exterior. The upper storey seems to have been of mud-brick, and later repairs and additions were in progressively simpler style, down to ordinary mud-brick walls (Shelmerdine 1987). There are indications of windows, one or two light-wells, and a drainage system. Fine plaster was used very extensively, in the exterior courts as well as on walls and floors. But columns were used sparingly, in gateways and porches and the main megaron rooms, and have features found only rarely in Crete (fluting) or not at all (painted plaster rings around the bases). Stone and wood, and perhaps bronze, were sometimes used for decorative purposes, but the main decorative medium was fresco, used even on exterior walls in sheltered porches.

Pylos was probably not the most elaborate of the palaces. Fragments of sculptured stone reliefs have been found at several, and other evidence for the decorative use of stone is known from Mycenae, including small stone capitals with leaf decoration (Sakellarakis 1976: 185–6) that might have surmounted columns. Fine threshold and dado slabs and other features of stone are also reported elsewhere on the site. Columns are used much more at Tiryns, where the great court has colonnades on three sides (cf. also the House of Columns at Mycenae). But there is no evidence for significant development beyond the Minoan tradition except the terracotta tiles reported from various sites and frequently taken for roof-tiles (most recently Iakovidis 1990); but their small numbers leave a doubt and the nature of Mycenaean roofs remains problematic, on large buildings and small (Hiesel 1990: 221–5).

Overall, one suspects that the Mycenaean palaces would not have made such an impression of magnificence as the Minoan, although their position and approach would have helped to make them imposing. Other buildings share something of the same character, notably the West House group at Mycenae (Fig. 5.32), which has been interpreted as an administrative and storage centre attached to a major official's residence (Tournavitou 1989), and may be placed on terraces walled in monumental style (cf. the 'Cyclopean Terrace Building' at Mycenae). But the links between lesser buildings of this kind and the palaces are less clear than between the Cretan palaces and 'villas'; the main connecting features are the basic techniques of construction and the use of frescoes. Traces of frescoed buildings have in fact been identified at quite a number of sites of lesser status, e.g. Zygouries, Eleusis and Nichoria, but little can be said of the buildings themselves for the most part, except that they are likely to have functioned as the bases of local administrators as suggested for the Cretan 'villas'.

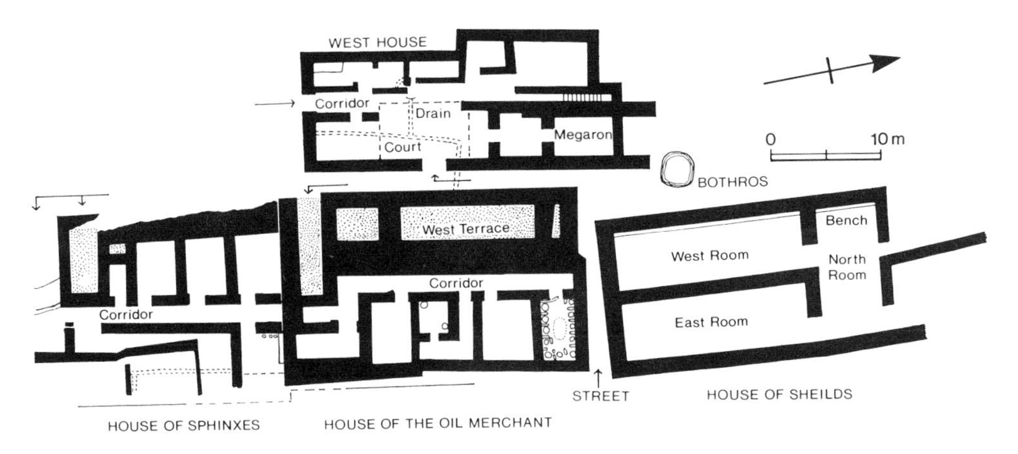

Fig. 5.32 Plan of the West House group of buildings at Mycenae. Courtesy of the Managing Committee of the British School at Athens.

With the destruction of the Mycenaean palaces and abandonment of many sites real monumentality disappears from Aegean architecture, although substantial buildings can still be found at surviving sites. These may have two storeys and make some use of columns; but fine stone masonry and timber framing have largely disappeared. The castle-like structure at Koukounaries on Paros is reported to have ashlar masonry, also a drainage system (Schilardi 1984: 201), but this seems an isolated survival. Even this level of architecture did not survive into the Dark Age, when buildings were mainly very simple structures of mud-brick on stone foundations; the most substantial pre-800 building, the Lefkandi heroön, makes considerable use of substantial timbers, but not of good masonry.

(b) Other structures

Impressive architectural or engineering skill is not to be found in buildings alone. To varying extents it appears in many tombs, which it will be more convenient to discuss in Chapter 6, and in fortifications, ramps, enclosure and terrace walls, roadway systems (including bridges and viaducts), drainage systems and aqueducts, and unusual structures like the Knossos Theatral Area and Mallia 'Agora'. A common factor is the use of stone as the sole or major building material, often in masonry of impressive quality, but there are many variations in detail. In general, such structures increase in number and variety in the later stages of the BA, and further evidence is accruing, particularly from Crete, but they still seem relatively rare in most periods; for example, a town wall is not a normal feature of major sites, in contrast with many parts of the Near East. This may well reflect the availability of skilled personnel, as well as of the resources and will to undertake major expenditure on construction; it is not surprising that they are best attested in the territories of the most important sites at the height of their development.

The history of such public architecture begins with terrace, enclosure, and fortification walls, categories that are not always readily distinguishable. Following the Neolithic examples from Thessaly, the earliest identifiable enclosure/fortification wall seems to be that of Markiani in Amorgos, assigned to the 'Pelos' (EC I) stage (French 1990: 69), but the majority of early fortifications in the mainland and islands are of 'Lerna III' (EH II) and equivalent contexts. Some are no more than rather thin constructions of field stones, without any special features, a type which continues to occur in later phases, but several share the use of semicircular or horseshoe-shaped bastions; entrances, essentially simple gaps in the wall, tend to be near or through these (cf. Fig. 4.5). The tradition may begin in EB I, if the Markiani example belongs to the original structure, but most are later EB (Lerna, Kolonna, Kastri on Syros, and the fortified farmstead at Panormos on Naxos), and comparable bastions occur in the MB walls of Ayia Irini IV and around the Ayia Photia (Kouphota) building, the only example in Crete. In other respects these walls differ considerably, including in materials – the Lerna and Kolonna walls were largely of mud-brick – and this is not the only kind of bastion attested; at best it suggest links rather than a common tradition. There seems no reason to doubt that these walls had a defensive function (except possibly at Ayia Photia), and they have comparable successors, sometimes at the same sites; the concentration of fortified sites on Aegean coasts and islands is very striking, in fact.

At Kolonna fortifications continued to be built and expanded in mudbrick on a stone foundation, and ultimately became extremely complex, incorporating bastion-like protrusions, insets, outworks, and gateways that are characteristically angled and flanked by walling, so that they resemble long passages (Walter and Felten 1981; cf. Hiller 1989, pl. 31). But the majority of fortifications of the later BA were built in stone, often with an inner and outer face, and incorporated fewer refinements. Those of Ayia Irini (late MB) and Phylakopi (probably LB I) make use of large blocks, the latter having a particularly 'Cyclopean' appearance (see Davis, J.L. 1986: 104–5 for comment on these and others), but at Kiapha Thiti in Attica smaller stones were used, with an 'orthostat' facade of flat stones at foundation level (Lauter 1989). The exceptional character of this wall compared with others of likely early Mycenaean date like that of Pylos, a very simple structure of smallish stones, may well owe something to the site's proximity to Aegina and the Aegean generally.

Evidently, although there was still little uniformity, quite sophisticated techniques of fortification were developed in the Aegean islands during the MBA. There is little closely comparable evidence from Crete, but it is becoming increasingly clear that a tradition of utilitarian architecture was being established as early as the First Palace Period. Evidence for a widespread system of Minoan roads and associated 'guard posts' was gathered by Evans even before he began work at Knossos, but has attracted little interest until recently, when a systematic campaign of survey has been begun in the far east of Crete (Tzedakis *et al.* 1989; 1990). This has gathered evidence for a system of basically ungraded trackways, lined by low walls and supported by small cross-walls and terraces where appropriate, and for several types of associated structure, ranging from small 'watchtowers' through remarkably uniform, basically rectangular structures, the 'guard posts' proper, to the largest and finest buildings which have walls of shaped blocks and could have served as centres of administration or as caravanserais. Enclosure walls attached to many of these might be corrals for livestock, and an interpretation as way-stations for those moving livestock, agricultural produce and other goods around Crete might be preferable to one that emphasised a 'military' role of defence or control, but considerably more data are needed. Although MM material has been found at some, it is not clear whether the system is essentially a product of the First or Second Palace Periods, though it does not seem that the buildings were generally in use any later.

The style of the majority of the buildings makes use of large irregular blocks, and may be compared with that of major walls at several sites, including the enclosure wall at Juktas, dated MM IA, a massive terrace wall at Knossos, which may be of First Palace Period date (Hood and Smyth 1981: 53, no. 240), a wall apparently enclosing the Mallia palace, terrace and dam walls on Pseira (French 1991: 76), long stretches of walling, which may be defensive, at Palaikastro (MacGillivray and Sackett 1984: 137) and Katsounaki (a harbour town site apparently forming the southern terminus of the eastern road system), and what looks like a true town wall at Petras near Siteia. It may reasonably be seen as part of a growing preference for building with large blocks, whose result was the true 'Cyclopean' style. Another link with later work is provided by some evidence for viaducts, but there is no good evidence for bridges except at Knossos, where four piers of massive masonry may have supported one, of First Palace Period date (Shaw 1971: 105; for date, Hood and Smyth 1981: 255, no. 282).

Other forms of public architecture can be identified in Crete during the palace periods. Oldest is the Mallia 'Agora', a carefully laid out rectangular space bounded by a substantial wall faced with orthostats, which has four impressive entrances providing access to other important areas (Van Effenterre 1969). Its impressive nature suggests that it had important public functions, but no close analogy has been found, although a 'town square' has been identified at Pseira onto which important buildings face (Fig. 4.19, the Plateia) (Soles 1991 associates the 'public' square at Gournia, Fig. 4.12, with the palace). Another site of public ceremony can be plausibly identified in the Theatral Area at Knossos, which is flanked by ranges of steps and the rectangular base of a structure. The circular platforms to the west of the palace, along an extension of the Royal Road, are of a later phase, LM IIIA, and may have been the site of ritual dancing, such as could have taken place also in the Theatral Area and the palace courts (Warren 1984b).

The true 'Cyclopean' style seems very much a feature of utilitarian architecture in the Third Palace Period, although it is identifiable in a less massive form at Mycenae as early as the Grave Circle B enclosure wall. The term 'Cyclopean' has been widely applied, as by Evans to the Cretan 'guard posts', and is difficult to define with complete precision, but essentially walls in this style should consist of one or two faces of massive, flat-surfaced but irregular blocks. These are set together without mortar, but with smaller stones fitted into the gaps; when there are two faces, there is an enclosed fill of rubble and earth. If the local stone splits naturally into rectangular blocks, the effect will be somewhat different, as at Mouriatadha, where most of the blocks are small, and Teikhos Dymaion. In some respects the style might seem more economical of effort, in that the use of large blocks would allow the construction of stretches of wall to some height more rapidly, but transport of the blocks would be correspondingly more difficult.

At all events, the decision to build fortifications in this style seems to have been taken in the Argolid first. That of Tiryns is now dated in its earliest phase to LH IIIA1 (Kilian 1988a: 134; Fig. 5.30, top), and there is no intrinsic reason why that of Mycenae should not be of this date, although it is conventionally dated to LH IIIA2 (E. French, pers. commun.). Their erection may be linked with the establishment of major palatial complexes and may reflect a consolidation of control and expression of power more than any perceived need for defence; certainly, they encircle only the uppermost parts of the acropolises. The adoption of the style elsewhere may reflect influence from the Argolid, since it is

Pl. 5.14 The Lion Gate, Mycenae. Peter Clayton.

largely found in neighbouring provinces, but the earliest dated example apart from Mycenae and Tiryns is the extremely extensive wall of Gla, now dated to the IIIA2–IIIB transition (Iakovidis 1983: 105); otherwise Cyclopean fortifications, where dated, fall in LH IIIB. The style was not invariably used for late Mycenaean fortifications: at Thebes a wall dated LH IIIA had a mud-brick superstructure, as did the original Lower Citadel wall at Tiryns, while at Grotta on Naxos the main material is reported as baked brick (Kilian 1988a: 133, 134, and on Grotta also Catling 1986: 75). The resources to build such great walls may not have been available everywhere, and it has been suggested that the Mycenaean economies were overstrained by these massive public works; their absence, as at Pylos, may reflect prudence or recognition of limits to their resources on the part of local rulers.

The main Cyclopean fortifications were laid out with considerable care, and incorporated refinements like sally-ports and bastions to protect gateways, but rarely towers. Regular insets may have been a method of changing line, but also, perhaps, a deliberate attempt to enhance visual effect. Gateways were certainly made impressive by the use of much more massive blocks or, as at Mycenae, coursed walling in dressed rectangular blocks of conglomerate, and gates themselves are post-and-lintel constructions of massive slabs (Pl. 5.14). Usually these give direct entrance to the interior through a single or double gateway, but

Tiryns was ultimately provided with a very complex entrance system. Only at Mycenae has a sculptured relief been found surmounting the gateway, which incorporated lost attachments, perhaps in bronze; it may always have been unique.

Walls of this type enclosed large citadels, small forts (e.g. Katsingri near Tiryns, Kilian 1988a: 133) and whole settlements as well as large empty spaces, at Krisa and Eutresis. Gla is in a category of its own, since the structures within it are clearly laid out to a prior plan (Fig. 5.33). It seems to be an artificially created site, which may have served as a centre of administration and storage, and perhaps also as a fortress to control the system of Cyclopean-walled dykes and canals in the Lake Copais region. These are still being studied, but seem likely to represent a drainage system (Hope Simpson 1981: 66–9; cf. also Kilian 1988a: 133). The style has also been identified in a dam near Tiryns, a road system radiating from Mycenae, including bridges and culverts (Hope Simpson 1981: 15–17, 21–3; Fig. 5.34), and a wall at Isthmia in which the two faces are bonded together, most plausibly interpreted as a defensive wall (unfinished?), facing north (see most recently *Hesperia* 61 (1992) 6). Dating evidence is still scanty for many of these structures, but it may reasonably be argued that this is the only period in which a road system centring on Mycenae, or a dam protecting Tiryns, would or could be built, or in which the resources would have been available to drain parts of Lake Copais.

The construction of many new fortifications in LH IIIB and the extension of the Mycenae and Tiryns circuits may reasonably be interpreted to reflect increasing preoccupation with defence, as may the Mycenae road system (perhaps built primarily for chariots, Crouwel 1981: 150) and refinements like the incorpora-

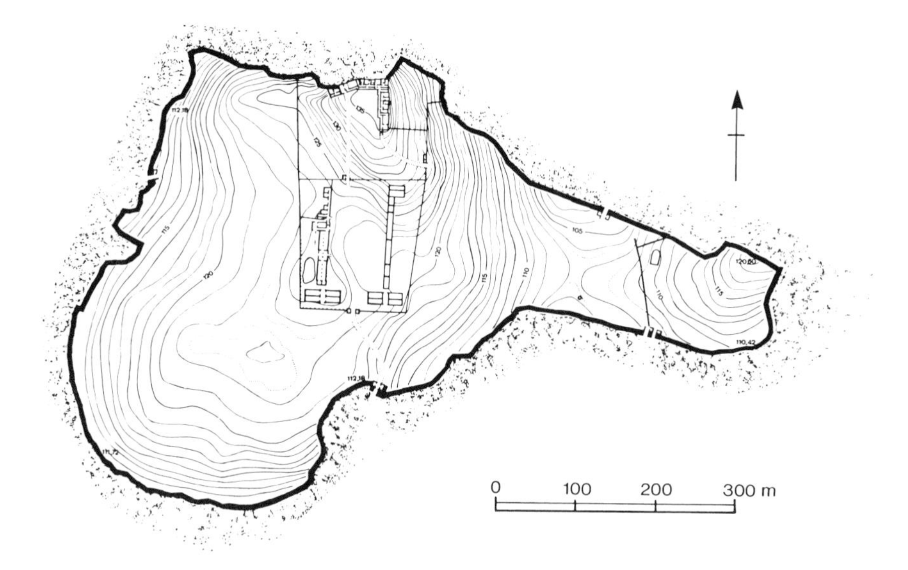

Fig. 5.33 Plan of Gla. Courtesy of Prof. S. Iakovidis.

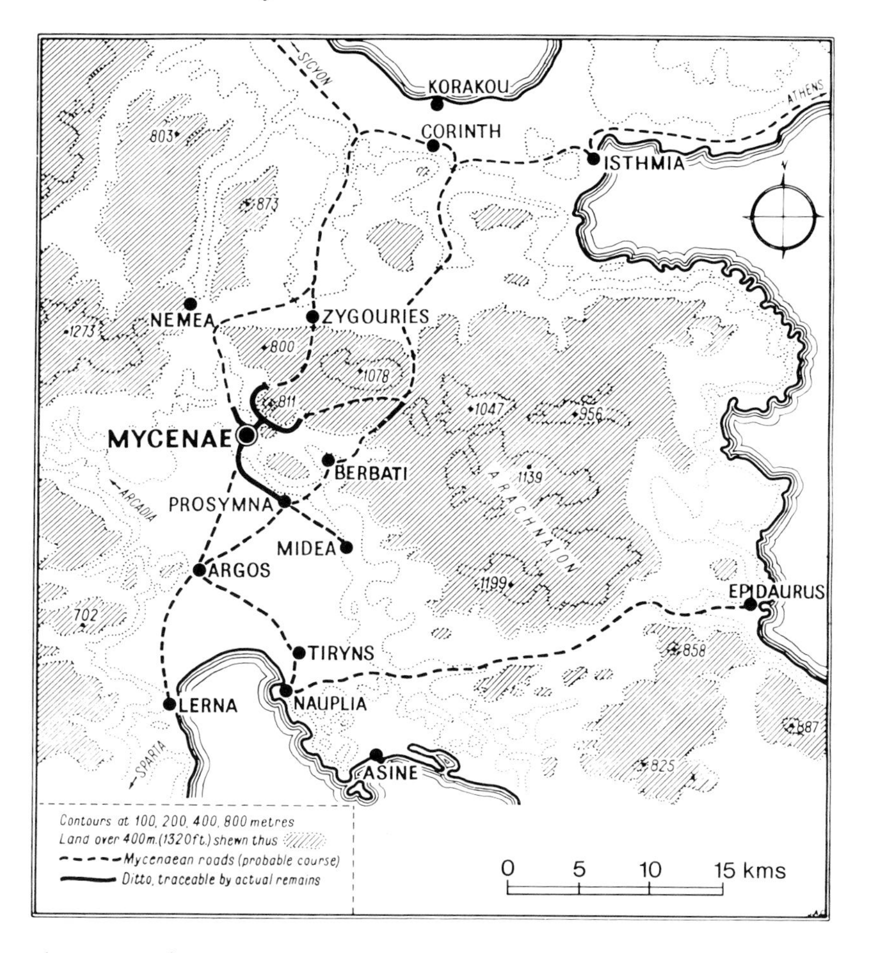

Fig. 5.34 The suggested Mycenaean road system in the north-east Peloponnese. Courtesy of Macmillan Publishers Ltd.

tion of chambers within the final wall of the Lower Citadel at Tiryns and the corbelled chambers built onto the southern sides of the Upper Citadel, and the tunnels cut through the rock to water sources at Mycenae, Tiryns and Athens. These demonstrate a striking degree of practical knowledge about water sources and of engineering skill in reaching them, and may fairly be seen as a 'Mycenaean' development in utilitarian architecture, like the Cyclopean style in its final form; the only earlier Aegean parallel is the spring chamber associated with the great fortification wall at Ayia Irini (Davis 1986: 9–10). But the aqueducts at Pylos and Thebes (Blegen and Rawson 1966: 332–6; Symeonoglou 1985: 50–2), like the drains at Mycenae and Tiryns (Iakovidis 1983: 15–17, 67–8) and unlike the Cretan drainage systems, made little or no use of clay piping but were essentially ditches covered and generally lined with slabs.

After the collapse of the palace economies nothing comparable was undertaken. The Tiryns and Athens water-supply systems rapidly became rubbish dumps, and the only example of apparently new work is the castle-like structure with outworks at Koukounaries on Paros, which may be seen as the last gasp of a dying tradition.

(v) Frescoes

There seems no doubt that, in the Aegean, the continuous history of wall painting begins in Crete, where painted plaster has been found in contexts from Late Neolithic onwards: most early material is red-coated (black is also found), but one example of a pattern in red on white from Phaistos has been attributed to Final Neolithic. The nature of the technique has not been fully agreed; but it has most in common with later fresco-painting, in that paint was applied to lime plaster which was wet, at least initially, and in this respect was quite distinct from Egypt and anywhere else in the Near East (Immerwahr 1990 (hereafter referred to as Immerwahr): 14–15).

There had been many improvements in technique by the First Palace Period, especially in the preparation of the plaster base and of pigments, which now included blue, grey, yellow and white at Knossos. But the material is still very fragmentary and, where there is enough to give some idea of decoration, shows only geometric patterns on a light ground, on walls and floors (Immerwahr, 22, cf. Cameron *et al.* 1977: 159, n. 71 for Phaistos and Mallia material). Knossos material from Royal Road contexts dated to MM IIIA produces examples of dark backgrounds, new pigments (orange and green), and some evidence of floral compositions (Cameron *et al.* 1977: 176–8), but there is no real hint of the assured style to be seen in the Saffron Gatherer, which may well be the earliest surviving figured fresco (dated MM IIIA by Hood, 1978: 48–9, but MM IIIB/LM IA by Immerwahr, 170). However, the Minoan-style frescoes, including floral compositions, identified at Alalakh and Tell Kabri should date in the seventeenth century (Niemeier 1991), and those of Avaris (Tell ed-Dabʿa; Bietak 1992), which are both full-size and miniature and have many links with Minoan themes, including bull-leaping scenes (Pl. 7.1), suggest that the figured style could have been established before LM I. A general trend in Minoan art towards naturalistic themes in the later First Palace Period shows some Egyptian links, and artistic exchanges with Egypt could lie behind the birth of figured painting (Immerwahr, 35–6, 62, also 1985); but at present the origins of Minoan figured frescoes remain unclear.

The amount of material from Second Palace Period contexts is considerable, though dominated by the finds from Knossos and Akrotiri; in fact, Knossos has produced so much compared with the other palatial centres, although mostly in very fragmentary condition, that it must surely be considered the birthplace of figured frescoes and centre of the art generally. Walls, floors and even ceilings might now be decorated in important rooms, not only with flat-surfaced frescoes, whose figures can range from miniature (6–10 cm) to lifesize, but with painted plaster reliefs, both geometrically patterned and figured. The most significant frescoes were those on the walls, which were usually divided into three horizontally, with the main zone in the centre, flanked by zones of pattern or coloured bands, but rarely divided vertically except where features such as doors, windows or wall-beams intervened and made the creation of panels natural. Miniature frescoes generally ran in narrow bands over features that would otherwise have interrupted them (cf. Cameron 1987: 327, fig. 11).

The zones flanking the main fresco might be decorated with stylised representations of veined stone or wood, especially in the dado, and similarly floor frescoes can include imitations of animal-hide coverings, although geometric patterns are commoner (the Dolphin Fresco from Knossos is thought by some to have decorated a floor). The walls may be coloured or left in plain light plaster, upon which a very wide range of themes may be painted, including representations of plants on a large scale, as at Amnisos (Pl. 5.15), and scenes of animal life, as in the monkeys and birds fresco from the House of the Frescoes at Knossos; but more often such natural themes and settings formed a background only, for scenes involving human and/or divine figures. It is worth commenting at this point that the apparent naturalism of many frescoes is deceptive; often features of different species of plant or animal are combined, and the highly characteristic convention of showing landscape features surrounding a figure, as if seen from above, which is found as early as the Saffron Gatherer fresco, is obviously non-naturalistic. Nevertheless, as has often been noted, the Minoan painters were more skilled at conveying an appearance of life and movement than the more accurate Egyptian painters.

There are strong indications that many if not all scenes involving human figures had a ritual, ceremonial or symbolic significance, depicting rites and festivals or activities in preparation for them, even sometimes including representations of deities (Televantou 1990 argues for an essentially historical, narrative interpretation for the miniature frescoes of the West House at Akrotiri, Pls 4.1, 2, but this is controversial). Such paintings could be arranged in planned programmes (cf. Hägg 1985a): Cameron has argued for thematic unity in both east and west wings of the Knossos palace, centring on a festival of birth and regeneration (1987), and N. Marinatos has analysed those of Xeste 3 at Akrotiri in terms of initiation ritual (1984a, Ch. VI). Relief frescoes, which seem to have an association with important ceremonial rooms, include what may be divine figures (e.g. the 'Lily Prince' as interpreted in Niemeier 1988; Fig. 8.9: 5), clearly symbolic representations such as tethered griffins, and ritual sports (Immerwahr, 53, 171). The frescoes of the last palace at Knossos continue this approach: ritual/ceremonial interpretations can be given to such famous works as the Campstool Fresco (incorporating 'La Parisienne') and the miniature bull-leaping scenes.

The spread of frescoes not merely to islands of Minoan culture like Rhodes

Pl. 5.15 Fresco of lilies, Amnisos 'villa'. Peter Clayton.

and the Minoanised Cycladic towns, but to the mainland, or at least Mycenae and Tiryns (Wace 1923: 159; Kilian 1987b: 213, 1988a: 134), is a notable feature of the Second Palace Period. Frescoes are in fact far commoner at Akrotiri than at any Cretan site apart from Knossos; Morgan has recently argued that Akrotiri was itself the main source of influence for both Ayia Irini and Phylakopi, although these have subsidiary Cretan links also, and that a distinct Cycladic school with its own themes developed (1990). This seems very likely; but how knowledge of themes and their treatment was transmitted remains unclear, as does the origin of Mycenaean fresco-painting generally. The many thematic links of Mycenaean frescoes with those of the last palace at Knossos suggest that the early Third Palace Period, rather than earlier, was the time when the art became fully established on the mainland.

The frescoes of the last palace from Knossos can show a coarsening of technique, such as the use of heavy outlines, which is found in many mainland frescoes. But there seems no reason to interpret this as mainland influence; rather, as might be argued for its appearance on the mainland, it is attributable to inferior training and skill, and those Mycenaean frescoes which do not show it are not necessarily earlier, but simply by painters of higher training and skill. But this is not to deny that some of the latest frescoes do show a conspicuous deterioration in quality: misunderstandings of earlier painting conventions can be identified, and in one famous example from Tiryns a bull's tail has been mispainted twice and the errors left visible.

The fact that this was part of a bull-leaping scene emphasises the degree of continuity from Minoan painting; in fact, since this art largely disappeared from Crete after the destruction of the last palace at Knossos (but Immerwahr, 98–9, notes possible evidence for 'postpalatial' frescoes at Knossos), surviving painters may have migrated to the mainland to work in the palaces there. Apart from the basic techniques and systems of wall division and the use of both miniature and lifesize figures, Minoan themes such as processions of women in Minoan-style dress, bull-leaping scenes, and architectural facades were taken over (cf. also the 'Minoan genii' on Pl. 5.16). But there is a strong impression that wall-paintings were used because this was 'traditional'; it is highly unlikely that bull-leaping was ever actually practised on the mainland, and one may wonder whether high-ranking Mycenaean women were actually so 'Minoan' in appearance, even on ritual occasions. At Pylos 'wallpaper friezes' seem to use traditional themes for pure decoration, and the thematic links in the Throne Room's decoration are hard to see (Immerwahr, 133–4), although here and elsewhere ritual/ceremonial themes still occur in appropriate places. Deity representations, which may well include the helmeted female griffin-carrier of Mycenae (Morgan 1988: pl. 157), often appear un-Minoan in character also. There is a recognisable degree of conventionalisation and loss of naturalism, though lively elements can still be discerned in the narrative scenes of hunting and war, which are difficult to parallel in earlier material and may, like their counterparts in other arts, reflect something of the ethos of the Mycenaean ruling elite. There is a detectable fondness for zones of pattern or rows of animals, and floor frescoes, which were popular in major rooms and approaches to them, always seem to be laid out as a grid pattern of squares or rectangles, filled with conventional patterns.

Pl. 5.16 Fresco showing 'Minoan genii' carrying a palanquin, Tsountas House, Mycenae. Courtesy of the National Archaeological Museum, Athens, and Dr K. Demakopoulou.

Although all the palace complexes have produced evidence of frescoes, the evidence from the major palace sites and others is very scrappy and rarely suggests elaborate themes except at Mycenae; but finds of fragments at sites like Zygouries, Eleusis, the Menelaion and Nichoria indicate that important local buildings might contain simply decorated rooms. The art was also used for decorating other features, as it had sometimes been in Crete (notably the Ayia Triada sarcophagus), including the great ceremonial hearths in the palaces, what may be a banister or balustrade at Tiryns, and likely altars at Pylos (Court 92) and Mycenae (Room 31). But it was too closely tied to the palaces to survive their final destruction: a female representation from a LH IIIC context at Mycenae may not be of this date (Immerwahr, 119–20), and the only certain Postpalatial occurrence is in vase-painting style, attributed to the painter of the Warrior Vase, on the T. 70 stele at Mycenae (Immerwahr, 149–51).

(vi) Figures

Figures of some sort are a common feature of the Neolithic period, although found with more frequency in some phases than others, but for long periods of the BA they are rare or totally absent in large parts of the Aegean area, and the

BA material consists largely of distinct groups which have no obvious relationship with each other. Any theory presupposing that all had identical or very similar functions, reflecting constant religious or social requirements, must therefore be automatically suspect. It seems reasonable to suppose that most had some symbolic function in the related spheres of religion, magic and ceremony; some could have been toys, but their context and, in many cases, materials often argue against such an interpretation. There seems little point in discussing them without some consideration of function, so that where this is thought to be religious Chapter 8 will be partly anticipated; but the primary purpose of this section is to set out the features of the main groups.

Undoubtedly the most impressive EB series is the Cycladic (Fig. 5.35). Its antecedents are not completely clear, but there are plausible links with Neolithic material from Saliagos, Kephala and the mainland, and the schematic class has general parallels in contemporary western Anatolia and Crete. It is in many respects a distinctive group. The figures are almost exclusively anthropomorphic and made of white marble, and the majority have been found in graves, but the existence of repaired examples and the large numbers found as offerings on Keros demonstrate that they were not made purely for the grave. Barber has suggested that they were so significant a feature of Cycladic society that every adult, at least, would have had one, supposing that for the bulk of the population they were of wood or clay; but there is no evidence for their production in clay, apart from some fragmentary heads from Mikre Vigla on Naxos which show similarities to the EC type but are otherwise undatable, and an interpretation dependent on the argument that the bulk of a class has not survived is inherently risky.

The earliest figurines associated with EC material are of a schematic type that at best gives an impression of head and arms by projections from a body, but more naturalistic types which add legs, clearly distinguish the head, and make some attempt to suggest bodily features, were already being developed in the period of the 'Pelos' group. These are named the Plastiras and Louros types after cemeteries in Paros and Naxos respectively; these two islands, the sources of the best Cycladic marble, may well have been the major centres of development. The Plastiras type, in particular, shows facial features, and includes both females and males, clearly represented as standing, while the Louros type has a more simplified and schematic form that may well be a stage in the development towards the classic type.

This, the folded-arm figurine (hereafter abbreviated as FAF), is the dominant type of the 'Syros' group, and not only reached as far as Asia Minor and western Greece, but was locally imitated in Crete and Attica. The type has several variants, which seem to form a chronological sequence, but all are characterised by an upturned face, beaky nose, long neck, and stylised, rather flat body whose proportions are rather spare but often elegant. Facial detail can be shown by incision or paint, also used to represent hair, body divisions, even jewellery, but the mouth is only rarely shown in any way. The FAF type is normally female,

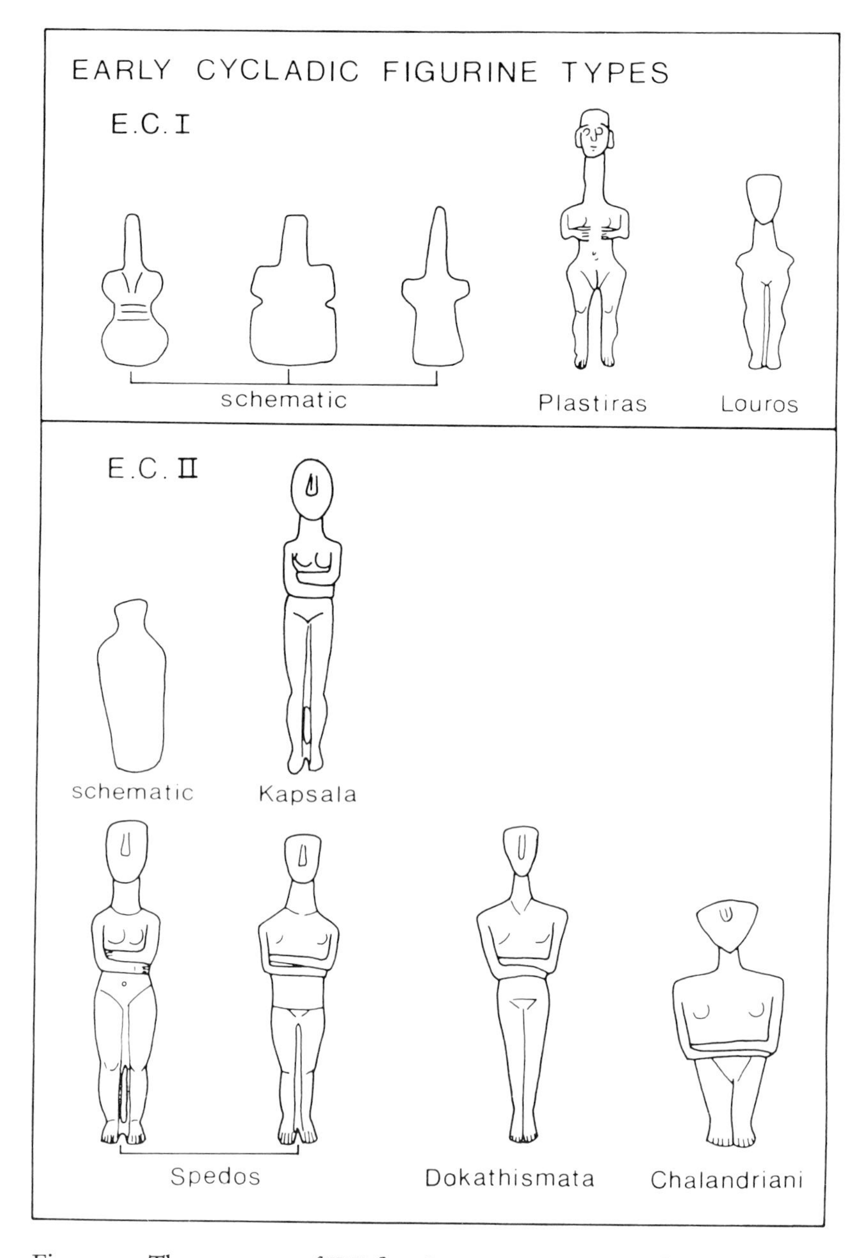

Fig. 5.35 The sequence of EC figurine types. Courtesy of Mrs J.L. Fitton.

sometimes evidently pregnant, but represented with pulled-up knees and down-sloping feet that would be more appropriate to a lying position; complete examples range from less than 20 cm to 1.5 m in height, and even larger ones may have existed. The widest range in size is found in the Spedos grouping, to which many of the more elaborate forms, musicians, seated figures (Pl. 5.17), and multiple

Pl. 5.17 Seated Cycladic figurine. Courtesy of the N.P. Goulandris Foundation and Dr I. Lemos.

figures, also belong. At a late stage standing figures return, especially males defined as the 'hunter-warrior' type, and the canons of proportion and pose that seem to have been rigorously adhered to earlier seem to be breaking down. Before the end of the EBA they ceased to be made, but schematic forms in marble occur rarely in MC–LC contexts.

Figurines occur in a minority of graves, which are generally rich in grave-goods, but not in all rich graves, on settlement sites, as at Ayia Irini and

Phylakopi, and as dedications at the ritual site of Dhaskaleio Kavos on Keros; some repaired examples show that they could be used for a considerable period. There seems much to be said for the view that they were associated with a single individual or household in life, perhaps as an attribute of social or religious status (Renfrew speculates on their use in 'household shrines', 1991: 99), although this does not explain their occurrence in groups in some graves. They might also have been used for ceremonial exchanges, which might explain some distant find-spots, for displays at ceremonies, especially the more complex examples and, in the case of the unusually large examples, as cult images (Renfrew 1986: 138–41, 1991: 99–100, 102–4). The production of imitations in Crete and Attica suggests that they could have some similar functions in the local societies; indeed, the Cretan imitations may have lasted longer than the originals, but here too they ultimately disappeared without posterity.

The contemporary mainland material is considerably less striking, and apart from a scatter of imported FAFs and local imitations is entirely of clay and includes few anthropomorphic pieces. It is quite possible that most reported finds are Neolithic strays, as seems even more likely for two stone pendants representing the lower half of a seated female body in a Neolithic-looking style, that have been argued to be MH (Diamant 1974); but a painted female torso from Lerna IV and a standing female from Zygouries, where there is no Neolithic phase of occupation, are probably EH. The rest are animals, mostly cattle and rams, and generally from rather unspecific settlement contexts, though at Lithares they may be offerings. Clay cones with projections from 'Lerna III' contexts in the north-east Peloponnese have been interpreted as schematic figurines, but this remains uncertain.

In Crete, however, a vigorous local tradition can be traced in the EBA, which may have its antecedents in the Neolithic. It includes several varieties of schematic figure made in various stones, ivory and bone (Branigan 1971; Fig. 5.36: 1), clay human and animal figures, and anthropomorphic vessels interpreted as goddess representations as well as imported and local FAFs and derivative types. In general, figures much over 20 cm in height/length are rare before the LBA, although a schematic stone example from Samba (Touchais 1985: 847, figs 190–1) is 67.5 cm high, and exceptionally large clay examples which may well be MM rather than LM have been found at some peak sanctuaries; they may even have existed in bronze, to judge from the context of a mould fragment for an apparently life-sized hand from the Phaistos palace (Laviosa 1968). Few are remarkable as examples of modelling before the peak sanctuary types, although a stone figurine from Porti is worth noting (Warren 1989: 68).

The majority of early figures come from collective tombs, which makes it difficult to be clear when their types became obsolete, but they evidently did, for the peak sanctuary range is rather different and at first made entirely of clay; some metal examples thought to antedate the end of the First Palace Period have been reported. There is also a probable change in function, for the peak sanctuary figures and comparable pieces from elsewhere seem to be almost entirely dedications. These later figures are generally modelled more in the round, articulate the body more, and show more details of dress and gear than previously; many were painted (e.g. Fig. 5.36: 2 and 4 are decorated in white on black, with red also on 4's ears, and 3 is red-coated). Most human figures are shown standing in attitudes of worship (Fig. 5.36: 2–4), but seated figures and small groups are also known; there is also a wide range of wild and domestic creatures (Fig. 5.36: 6, 7). These figures continued to be made and dedicated in the LBA, both at peak sanctuaries and in other contexts; an exceptional series of models from Kamilari T. 1, which probably falls in the Second Palace Period, shows a group of dancers and a much-discussed offering scene, among others (Branigan 1970b: 116–18, pls 14–15).

Cast figures in bronze, occasionally silver or lead, became increasingly prominent as dedications in the Second Palace Period; most are worshipper figures or animals (Fig. 5.36: 5, 8), but unusual types such as a baby and a bull-leaping group are recorded (Hood 1978: 112–13 figs 96–9). Once established, this tradition lasted into the Postpalatial Period and beyond in Crete, but they are very rare elsewhere. Many, especially later examples, are rather roughly produced, but some are very fine, though lacking the surface finish of Greek bronzes. The finest examples were made in other materials: the Temple Repositories 'snake goddesses' in faience (Pl. 5.18) appear to be unique, for examples of the same type in ivory and stone are generally thought forgeries, but other types of ivory figure are becoming well-known. These have often appeared in important buildings or settings, such as the Knossos palace, Arkhanes and Nirou Khani 'villas', and most recently the Plateia complex at Palaikastro.

The last, the 'kouros' (Pl. 5.19), is particularly remarkable, being composed of a serpentine head, inlaid with rock crystal eyes, on an ivory body made up of parts fitted together with wooden dowels, provided with gold leaf accoutrements, and originally set on a base (most recently, Moak in MacGillivray *et al.* 1991: 143–4). Others have preserved traces of similarly mixed technique, which can be paralleled in the Near East (MacGillivray *et al.* 1989: 426–7); but stylistically there is nothing Near Eastern about most of them (two babies from Palaikastro have been compared to Egyptian work). The modelling is of very high quality: muscles, veins and nails are faithfully rendered on figures that seem mostly to be 30–40 cm high (the Palaikastro 'kouros' is close to 50 cm). Many have been interpreted as bull-leapers, and might have been set up in representations of this probably ritual sport, but associated remains of bulls are lacking apart from a faience head from the Knossos palace deposit, which might have been attached to a wooden body.

The famous group of two women with a boy across their knees from Mycenae (Higgins 1981: 131, fig. 159) has stylistic links with these and might therefore be a survival, although no comparable pieces are known; it is considerably smaller (7.8 cm), perhaps forming the top of a staff or sceptre, and may well represent a

Fig. 5.36 Some Minoan figurine types. 1 schematic figure, probably Prepalatial, Porti. 2, 3 male worshippers, Petsopha. 4 female worshipper, Petsopha. 5 bronze male worshipper, Second Palace Period, Tylissos. 6, 7 bovid and bird offerings, Petsopha. 8 bronze goat offering, Second Palace Period, Ayia Triada Room 17. Scale 1:2.

divine group. But other ivories from the Third Palace Period at Mycenae, the male head and lion from the Room of the Ivories (Taylour 1983: 57, figs 36–7), have a good claim to be local products, given their context and the copious evidence for ivory working in this period. Such finds remain rare, however, and the bulk of figures of all kinds in the LBA were of clay.

Pl. 5.18 Faience figure, the Temple Repositories, Knossos. Peter Clayton.

Undoubtedly the most impressive are the large figures, ranging from about 70 cm to 1.35 m high, from the 'temple' at Ayia Irini (Caskey, M.E. 1986). All represent women dressed in Minoan ceremonial style, wearing either garlands or necklaces, at least some apparently dancing, and their manufacture must have required considerable skill, but comparable work elsewhere is hard to identify. They are suggested to have been arranged in a permanent display, which was added to throughout the Second Palace Period, reaching a total of over fifty.

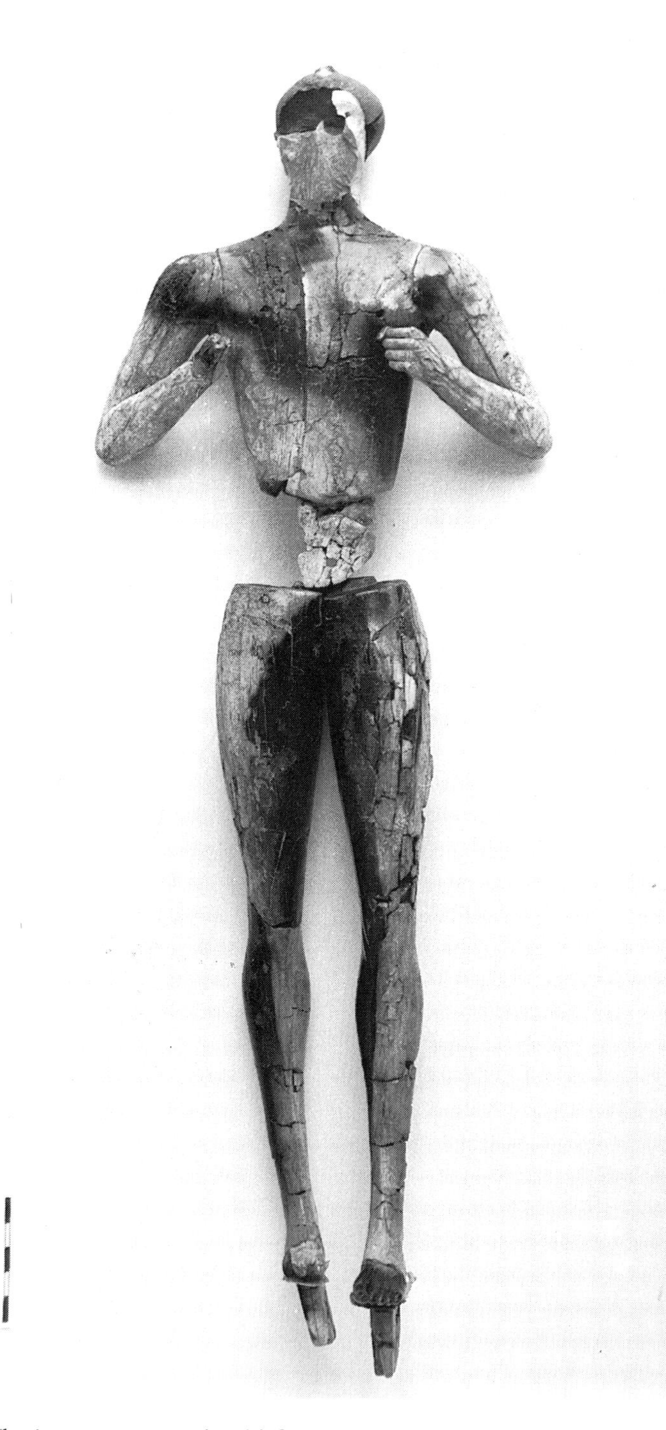

Pl. 5.19 The ivory, stone and gold figure, Building 5, Palaikastro. Courtesy of the Managing Committee of the British School at Athens and Prof. J.A. MacGillivray.

They were valued enough to be repaired and repainted on occasion, but were not recovered following the Second Palace Period destruction, and only one made in a similar style was recovered from a later context.

Clay figures on this scale are hard to identify in Crete itself; the few examples indicated by fragments are most often suggested to be dedications. More elaborate types of clay figurine that probably represent goddesses rather than worshippers have been found in contexts from LM II onwards, the majority displaying the 'upraised arms' gesture and many having attached attributes, including snakes, birds, poppy heads and 'horns of consecration'. These vary considerably in size (up to 85 cm) and quality: some are quite well-proportioned, with carefully shaped features; others, although decorated, are frankly rather grotesque (Fig. 8.13: 1, 2). Many come from contexts identifiable as shrines or sacred deposits, but ordinary clay figurines are relatively rare in any Cretan context.

In contrast, a major Mycenaean tradition of figurine production can be identified. Its early development is not well documented, but it was evidently influenced by Minoan types and was well established by LH IIIA1. More than any other group it can be described as mass-produced, since it consists very largely of standard forms, but these were generally carefully made and painted. The dominant human form is the standing female, with arms variously arranged: early examples have arms crossed like some Cretan worshipper figures, or carry children, while the Psi type characteristic of LH IIIB–C has upraised arms like the Cretan goddess figures (Fig. 5.37). Equally common are the indeterminate cattle figurines (Fig. 5.38), while seated figures, chariot groups, driven oxen, other types of animal and furniture models appear. As French has noted (1971: 106), there are striking Cypriot parallels for some of the rarer forms. None is very large, 1–11 cm being average height for the females. They have a varied range of contexts and appear in most of the Mycenaean world, though lacking until a late stage in the Dodecanese and rare outside the area of Mycenaean culture, occurring mainly at places where contacts were frequent. Their contexts include several that clearly involve ritual deposition, and further discussion will be reserved to Ch. 8.

Larger figures with coil-made or wheel-thrown bodies are becoming better known (Fig. 8.13: 3, 4). Some are probably cult images, like the 'Lady of Phylakopi', for which a parallel is now reported from Tsoungiza (Wright *et al.* 1990: 636), the smaller figure from Room 32 in the Room of the Fresco complex at Mycenae, and others of similar quality, but the group associated with the Room of the Idols at Mycenae is plausibly interpreted by Moore (1988) as intended to represent participants in a ceremony. Large animals, usually cattle, with hollow wheelmade bodies are being found more commonly also; they may have been developed at Kato Symi, where many have been found, and spread as an offering type in the thirteenth century and thereafter (Fig. 8.6: 9). Separate large plaster heads, which may have been fitted to wooden bodies that could have

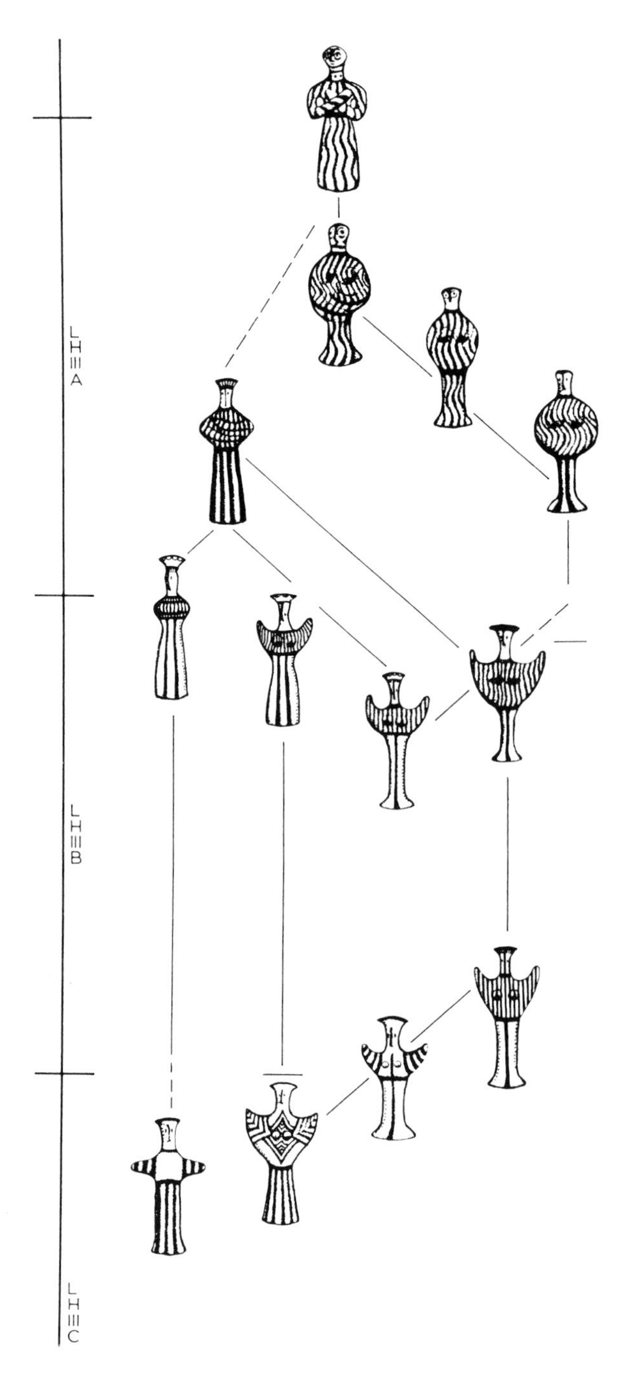

Fig. 5.37 The sequence of LH female figurine types. Courtesy of Dr E.B. French, drawn by T. McNicol.

Fig. 5.38 The sequence of LH animal figurine types. Courtesy of Dr E.B. French, drawn by T. McNicol.

been of sphinx type rather than wholly anthropomorphic and as such may have represented supernatural guardians of holy sites, occur at Mycenae (Hood 1978: 102, fig. 83), Asine and Athens. Coiled snakes are a unique find from Mycenae (Taylour 1983: 52, fig. 28).

The main survivals into the Postpalatial Period are the late forms of Psi figurine and wheelmade cattle figurines, although others are known, for example from the Perati tombs and the Ayia Triada Piazzale dei Sacelli deposits, which have a wide and impressive range, including male figures. The male figures and figurines found at Phylakopi (Fig. 8.13: 5) may be largely an innovation of this period; some unusually large female figurines from Tiryns show that the ability to produce fine work persisted (Fig. 8.13: 6). But the bronze 'smiting god' figures of Near Eastern origin (Fig. 8.13: 7), which may have reached their Aegean findspots before 1200, inspired no local imitations, and the whole Mycenaean figurine tradition disappeared eventually; only Crete and Cyprus preserved BA types to any extent, and for a period figurines of any kind are barely found in the Aegean outside Crete.

(vii) Jewellery and ornaments

Personal ornamentation can be traced back in Greece to the Palaeolithic through finds of perforated shells and animal teeth and of red ochre, but little that is very impressive is reported from Neolithic contexts and it is not until the middle of the EBA that a considerable variety begins to be documented. In all regions of the Aegean tombs are a major source, and where they are scarce or absent, as in the post-EB Cyclades or Second Palace Period Crete, information is limited; though frescoes can provide useful supplementary evidence, there are problems in correlating their evidence with the finds. For example, headbands, common in tombs, never seem to appear in representations; the suggestion that they are purely funerary must therefore have attractions, although some show evidence of repair and many seem far more solid than would be required for purely funerary use. It would be unwise to treat the evidence of representations as wholly realistic.

Because so much of the material comes from graves that either held multiple burials, or have unstudied skeletal material, it is not easy to be certain about who wore the ornaments. In earlier BA contexts there is often a marked negative correlation between finds of weapons and jewellery, suggesting that the former were grave-goods of men, the latter of women and (female?) children. But representations of the Second and Third Palace Periods make clear that jewellery could be worn by both sexes as a sign of status: men are shown particularly with necklaces, armlets, and wrist-ornaments incorporating sealstones (Kilian-Dirlmeier 1988), while in the 'Boxing Boys' fresco from Akrotiri one wears a necklace, armlet, and anklet of beads, and gold earrings. If this was originally a Minoan custom, it was certainly adopted in other parts of the Aegean. Overall, the wearing of jewellery is a likely indication of relative wealth and status, even in its simplest forms, as frequently emphasised by the value of its materials, and hence it is only ever found with a proportion of burials.

From the EBA onwards most of the prominent forms are of metal, partly reflecting its perceived value but also perhaps its capacity to be shaped into complex forms. At first there are considerable variations in the distribution of metals and other materials, which may reflect patterns of contact. But in later phases most materials seem to have been widely available, and access to them was probably limited largely by wealth. Thus, that the elaborate pins of Lerna IV–V were carved of bone (Fig. 5.39: 6) surely reflects the relative impoverishment of Helladic culture at the time. The profuseness of gold in early Mycenaean contexts, as opposed to its contemporary rarity in Crete, has been thought to indicate a real difference in access to supplies, but may have other explanations; the rarity of amber outside the mainland throughout the LBA, however, probably does reflect privileged access to its European sources. Some of the most striking stones used were imported from the Near East, notably carnelian, amethyst and lapis lazuli (cf. Younger 1979b; Higgins 1980: 36, 38), and it may well be that ideas of their magical potency, based on their colour, were transmitted with them (cf. David 1982: 103).

A considerable variety of forms can be identified, most appearing already in the EBA to join the beads and small pendants which seem the only common

Neolithic forms (Hood 1978, fig. 184). Headbands and other items were worn on the head; twists of wire and pins were probably most often ornaments for the hair, although the former might also be used as earrings, the latter to pin cloaks. Strings of beads were most commonly worn as necklaces, tight around the neck or more loosely, down to the chest, but there is good representational evidence for their being worn in the hair and on arms, wrists and ankles, and sometimes they formed headbands. Elaborate earrings, pendent from simple wire circlets, can be found, and even more massive pendants that must have been worn as pectorals; the former appear in the representational record, but not apparently the latter, although they are even harder to accept as wholly funerary items than the headbands. Wire and sheet armlets and bracelets can also be identified. Items that adorned dress include a variety of cutouts from metal sheet and more rarely what appear to be buttons; many of the common LB conoid 'whorls' may also have functioned as clothing weights, designed to maintain complex arrangements of folds, and dress ornaments (Iakovidis 1977). Some large plate ornaments in the Shaft Graves may have been ornaments for robes or shrouds (Dickinson 1977: 50, 75).

Almost certainly the appearance of many types of metal ornament in the EBA represents one facet of the strong Near Eastern influence in metalwork at this time, which extended to the adoption of ultimately Mesopotamian types and techniques: much may have been learned through Anatolia, but some types may have come directly from Syria to Crete (Higgins 1980: 47–8, 53–4). But Aegean jewellery was not simply a reflection of Near Eastern fashion; it had distinctive characteristics. There is in fact a striking degree of local variability, even between individual sites, not merely in the materials used, but in the types favoured. Thus, the Cyclades have rare silver headbands and armlets, and fine pins of silver, bronze and bone (Fig. 5.39: 1, 2). Zygouries has produced similar metal pins and likely fragments of headbands, also some probable earrings; but the Leukas graves contain no headbands or pins, being notable rather for gold bead necklaces, also some earrings, and silver bracelets (Fig. 5.39: 3–5). The Cretan material, largely gold, is dominated by headbands and bead necklaces, but also includes clothing attachments, probable hair ornaments in the form of leaf sprays, and armlets (Fig. 5.40: 1, 2); the Mochlos graves are rich in these, but lack the ivory or bone pendants of the Arkhanes and Mesara tombs. Finally, the Thyreatis treasure's main piece is a gold necklace of concentric wire hoops interspersed with pendants on chains (Higgins 1980, pl. 2); neither its date nor its context seem certain, but there is no obvious reason why it should not be from a mainland source. The elaborate gold beads with spiral and floral attachments from the Ampheion at Thebes also deserve mention: parallels indicate a 'Lerna III' (EH II) date (cf. Higgins 1980: 48–9).

This confused picture hardly suggests a common Aegean tradition, but rather selection from a repertoire, mostly paralleled in the much richer jewellery of the Troad and north Aegean, as local skill and fancy allowed. No part of the Aegean

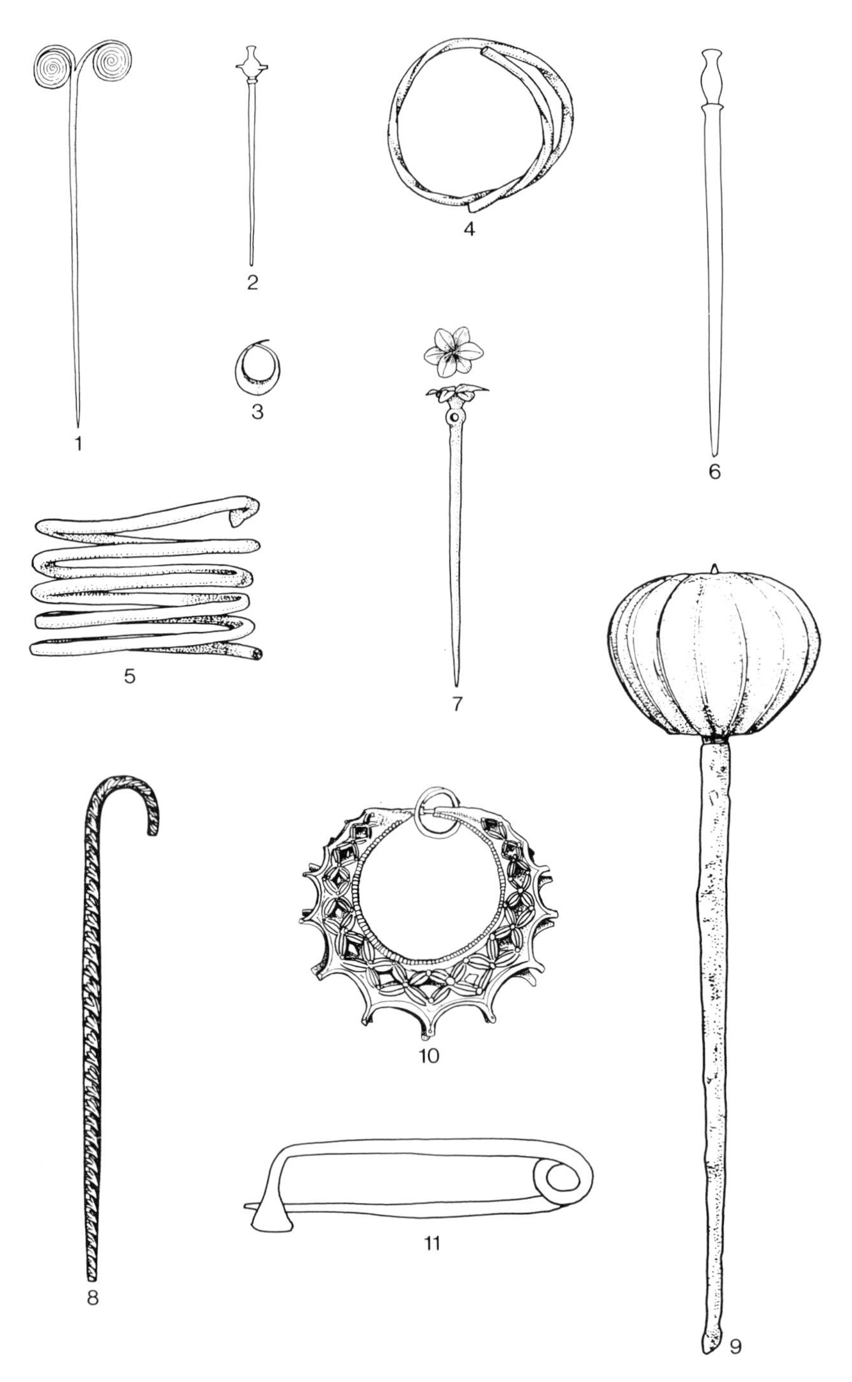

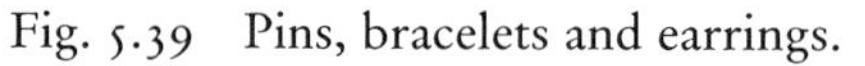

Fig. 5.39 Pins, bracelets and earrings.
1–5 Prepalatial: bronze pin, Syros; silver pin, Naxos; gold earring, silver bracelets, Leukas. 6 MH bone pin, Lerna. 7 gold toggle-pin, Mallia. 8 silver crook pin, Knossos. 9 rock-crystal headed bronze pin, Shaft Grave III. 10 gold earring, Shaft Grave III. 11 bronze violin-bow fibula, Mycenae T. 3. Scale 1:2.

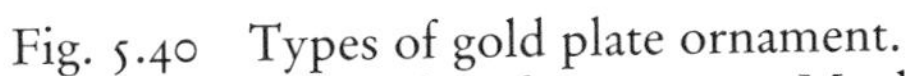

Fig. 5.40 Types of gold plate ornament.
1, 2 headband and leaf-ornament, Mochlos. 3 pendant, 'Aegina Treasure'. 4 headband, Shaft Grave IV. 5 'star' ornament, Shaft Grave Xi. 6 disc clothing-attachment, Shaft Grave III. 7, 8 cutout clothing attachments, Shaft Graves IV, III. 9 bead made from cutouts, Shaft Grave V. Scale 1:2, except 1, 4 and 5 (1:4).

can be seen as the clear leader, although there are cross-connections; for example, the headbands of the Cyclades and Zygouries resemble those of Crete, but the two groups vary considerably in decoration and even in Crete the antenna-like attachments that may originally have decorated all the Mochlos headbands (Davaras 1975: 109–10) may be a purely local feature.

The much poorer documentation of the MBA makes it difficult to observe trends. In Crete it seems likely that types similar to those current in the EBA continued to be produced, although there might be greater elaboration: pieces decorated in the granulation and filigree techniques, most notable of which is the insect-pendant from Chrysolakkos at Mallia, are probably of MM date (Higgins 1981, fig. 39). The dating of the Chrysolakkos material, which also includes fragments of headbands, clothing attachments, leaf pendants, and beads of gold, is a vexed question, and much may be Prepalatial; but a fine toggle-pin with flower head (Fig. 5.39: 7) does seem to belong to the later building (Pierpont 1987: 84–5), and the sheer quality of the insect-pendant suggests a date later than the Prepalatial phase. At all events, such finery seems likely to be that of a small elite, and may not have been paralleled in other parts of Crete. More widespread, and reflecting a more modest level of prosperity and status, are types found in some Mesara tombs and the rock-cut tombs of the Knossos region, which began to be used in the later First Palace Period; these include earrings, bracelets, short pins, and finger-rings with bezels, mostly of bronze, as well as stone beads, occasional sealstones, and rare gold ornaments.

On the mainland, metal items were clearly rare and the burial of any sort of jewellery rarer still for the bulk of the late EH and MH phases; thus, settlement strata, not graves, provide the bulk of the evidence from Lerna. There are some signs of continuity from the EBA: simple bronze pins and stone beads occur throughout Lerna III–V, and wire circlets and earrings essentially similar to EB types are found in the relatively early MH burial tumuli of Drachmani, Aphidna, and Voidhokoilia. A steatite pendant and two bronze toggle-pins from Lerna may be direct Cretan imports, as may the stone and faience or glass paste beads of the late MH graves and a quite exceptional gold pendant on a chain from Argos, also from a later context (Touchais 1980: 698). But it is not until the late MH graves that a range of ornaments similar to that current in Crete can be identified.

The most distinctive feature of this material is the increasing variety of metal types, not only wire circlets, spirals and bracelets, but pins and sheet metal ornaments, mostly gold headbands. These seem to represent an increasingly vigorous development of a tradition that was now obsolescent in Crete but still strong in the Aegean, to judge from the headbands from Aegina (Higgins 1987) and Kea (Ayia Irini T. 16). The mainland examples are also distinctive in their decoration; repoussé dot patterns had been used on such items since the EBA, but the symmetrical circled boss and dot patterns so popular on the mainland (Fig. 5.40: 4, 5) are a wholly local phenomenon, on present evidence. The earlier

Shaft Graves, which are probably contemporary with many of the late MH graves elsewhere, have good examples of these and the other types mentioned.

Various stylistic links place the 'Aegina Treasure' in the period around the end of the MBA and beginning of the LBA; this is best interpreted as the result of ancient tomb robbery in Aegina (Higgins 1979), but there is no reason to suppose that it is all contemporary, let alone from a single grave. Its dominant types are elaborate pendants (Fig. 5.40: 3) and earrings, which have few parallels, especially in the Shaft Graves material; technically they are also far more elaborate than most of this, relating rather to fine Cretan work like the Chrysolakkos pendant. But there are no examples of granulation and only one of filigree, although the inlay technique is well represented, especially by some ornate rings, and the generally high level of skill is indicated by the apparently mechanical reproduction of some of the pendants and the remarkable openwork disks. Gates has identified some interesting iconographic links with Near Eastern material (1989), but erroneously, in my belief, relates these to early Mycenaean developments. They fit more plausibly in the Minoan tradition; but the group may represent a very localised and unrepeated outburst of creativity.

Even at their richest, in fact, the Shaft Graves offer little more than an expansion of the established traditions of metal sheet and wire ornament detected in the late MH graves. Headbands and other ornaments in plate that include probable headdresses and dress-ornaments dominate the material (Fig. 5.40: 4, 5). Armlets, elaborate pins (Fig. 5.39: 9), and earrings (Fig. 5.39: 10) are also quite common, and in the richest graves, III, IV and V, cutout dress attachments of gold sheet or foil and a few relief beads of related types (Fig. 5.40: 6–9), and gold-covered bone discs, roundels and lozenges decorated in intricate geometric styles on disc-shaped cutouts, are prominent. The wearing of necklaces, bracelets and earrings can all be paralleled in the Akrotiri frescoes, which also show at least one hair-pin (Marinatos 1984a: 79, fig. 56), and individual items, notably in the women's graves Omicron and III, can be paralleled in the Minoan and Theran representations and occasionally by actual examples, but the closest parallels for this range of jewellery come from other early Mycenaean sites, especially in Messenia (cf. Dickinson 1977: 72–9).

This suggests that the Shaft Graves material represents and may even partly have inspired a mainland tradition of ornament. But much of it had a short life: finds from Messenia indicate that similarities were sometimes only general (cutout dress-attachments are found, but the types are different), and the Shaft Graves animal art that some have thought 'nomadic' (Vermeule 1975: 22–6) has no parallels here. In point of fact, the fauna of this art are Aegean, whether real or fantastic, and it is best understood in an Aegean context. In Messenia, it may be noted, beads with pendant attachments like those found in the 'Aegina Treasure' and in Crete can be identified, but there is no other indication of closeness to Minoan or other Aegean traditions.

The shortage of material from Crete in the Second Palace Period is particularly

Fig. 5.41 Some common types of relief beads. Courtesy of the late Dr R.A. Higgins and Methuen & Co. Over lifesize.

frustrating; the metal crook pin is one of the few distinctive types (Fig. 5.39: 8). As a result it is impossible to trace with any precision the development of the relief bead, the most significant innovation of the LBA (Fig. 5.41). A few examples from the Shaft Graves and contemporary contexts in Crete are not paralleled in the rich tombs of the succeeding phase such as the Vapheio and Kakovatos tholoi, although other Cretan forms are found in these, and the type only becomes prominent in the rich graves of the early Third Palace Period. Quite possibly the standard repertory of forms was only established then, in Knossos workshops. The forms are motifs well-known in Minoan art, mainly stylised florals but some marine and other types. The classic beads have a flat underside and relief surface and are perforated through the edges, often with two or three sets of holes; at first they were of gold, and so may have been formed by working gold sheet into a matrix, and could be embellished with granulation and enamelling. But blue glass was increasingly used as a material, allowing them to be cast in steatite moulds; examples have been found not only at Mycenae and Knossos but also Palaikastro and Nichoria (McDonald 1975: 121). This was not necessarily a cheaper material, as has tended to be suggested in the past, since it was almost certainly imported in ingot form, to judge from the Ulu Burun shipwreck, and it may even have been valued and thought magical for its colour (above, p. 180). But glass beads may have been less laborious to produce: the moulds have matrices for several types, allowing the casting of different forms simultaneously (Pl. 5.20).

Necklaces of these beads are most prominent in the material for the Third Palace Period generally, making up the bulk of the finds with other, simpler forms of bead. Clothing attachments, often of the same type as the relief beads or

Pl. 5.20 A steatite jewellery mould, Mycenae. Courtesy of Drs E.B. French and K.A. Wardle.

of flat gold sheet stamped with or cut out in the same types, are the only other prominent form of ornament, although wristlets holding sealstones were probably often worn. The elaborate metal seal-rings, usually decorated on the bezels with complex scenes or inlaid cloisonné patterns, were probably worn on the finger (Popham and Catling 1974: 223). Simpler rings and circlets and short pins, mostly of bronze or bone, occur sporadically, as do a variety of objects identified as pendants; but the more elaborate forms of ornament like headbands and earrings seem to have largely disappeared. But there are at least two cases of relief bead necklaces being worn as headbands (gold in Arkhanes T. D), and one of the most elaborate relief forms, the bracket or curled leaf, which often has attached discs of gold or glass, may have been worn on the head. Figurines and fresco representations suggest the existence of elaborate forms of headgear that may have been largely of perishable material but have been adorned with beads.

This period has produced several examples of jewellery workshops, particularly at Thebes (Tournavitou 1988 assembles references), though these were also producing inlays for furniture. Gold, faience, glass and semiprecious stones are the main raw materials reported, but remarkably, evidence for the production of relief beads is largely lacking, although there is a fine example of a standard mould from workshop area 34 of the Citadel House at Mycenae. The discovery of many granulated beads in one of the Thebes workshops indicates that this technique was still being practised and demonstrates how the lack of rich and well-dated contexts may affect our perception of the period.

Nevertheless, there seems some truth in the standard view that, after the period of creativity which saw the full development of the relief bead, new inspiration seems to have been lacking. It is probably significant that no new forms of relief bead seem to have been developed. Towards the end of the Third

Palace Period, the first examples of fibulae, safety-pinlike items in bronze (Fig. 5.39: 11), appear singly in tombs and on sites; these must have been dress-fasteners, presumably for cloaks or shawls; most probably these were introduced from elsewhere in Europe, plausibly Italy. The commonest form of ornament, in sheer numbers, was the conoid 'whorl', which could have served as bead, button, tag-end or clothing weight (if most often the latter, this would testify to the wide spread of a fairly elaborate form of women's dress); these were now most often of serpentine or steatite, although generally clay earlier.

The Postpalatial Period undoubtedly saw a massive decline in this field, but the evidence from Perati, the richest and best-published source, suggests that it was gradual. Here many types of ornament are represented still. Rings are particularly prominent, many in silver from the nearby Laurion source, but there are also armlets, wire hair-ornaments, earrings, pendants, and many forms of bead have been identified. But the earrings, many pendants and some bead types are clearly Near Eastern, from Cyprus, Syria or Egypt, and although glass beads are quite common, few are relief beads (these are, however, preserved at other sites, and even occur in metal elsewhere). 'Whorls' remain common, some being in fine materials like rock crystal and ivory. Bronze fibulae, in the original 'violin bow' and more developed arched type, occur singly and in pairs, in a few tombs at Perati and also at other sites in both settlement strata and tombs. A single long bronze pin, and the head ends of two others (one iron on a bronze shaft, one glass on an iron shaft) also occur, evident precursors of a type that was to become standard in the Dark Age as the most elaborate form of ornament.

Like the fibulae, these are best interpreted as dress-fasteners, but they were clearly items of display; the feature of a bead head in a different material is found at other sites, and even before the end of the BA they were reaching over 25 cm in length. Their source is disputed between European and Near Eastern origins; dress-pins are regular in some European cultures but none of the Aegean types finds close parallels there, whereas they do have such parallels in the Near East. But the Aegean dimension should not be overlooked, even though they have changed their function and become more elaborate than the ordinary BA pins. In general, the impression given by the late material is that metal ornaments, though of quite simple types, were increasingly invested in as symbols of wealth and status as other symbols ceased to be available; for a while, pins, fibulae and finger-rings dominate the material to the exclusion of almost anything else, even beads, of which even imported examples seem to fail. Thus, the types of jewellery reflect the general decline at the end of the BA.

(viii) Seals

These have already been mentioned in the previous section, because they evidently could be worn as ornaments and symbols of status, perhaps also as magical amulets. But they deserve more extended consideration, for they are among the most numerous and attractive small artefacts of the Aegean (dimensions rarely exceed 3 cm and are often less than 2 cm), and despite the various indications of Near Eastern influence (Yule 1980: 232) are essentially Aegean in character.

In a recent discussion, Younger draws an important distinction between stamps, used to decorate items and materials, which can be traced back to the Neolithic in the Aegean (Fig. 5.42: 1), and seals, used for administrative purposes (1991: 36), which are not identifiable before the middle of the EBA. By this time seals had been current in the Near East for a considerable period. Their main administrative use was in monitoring the storage and movement of goods, most often by stamping a clay covering that was applied to a container, or over cords fastening boxes or doors. This would ensure that the clay could not be broken undetected and replaced, since the sealing could not be duplicated without possession of the seal. If magical power was thought to reside in the shape or decoration of the seal, the act of sealing would also have provided magical protection for the sealed goods; the decoration might also have incorporated some kind of reference to the goods that were protected, or to their ownership.

Only at Lerna do the collections of sealings associated with the House of the Tiles provide clear evidence of some administrative use in the EBA (perhaps only to indicate the source of stored goods, Wiencke 1989: 505). That none of the seals used to produce them has survived may indicate that they were of wood, or (as suggested by Younger, 1991: 46, who argues for clay) that sealing activity did not take place where the sealings have been found. The seals' designs are exceptionally fine when compared with other mainland and Aegean material of the period, mostly quite intricate, radially symmetrical arrangements of loops and other shapes (Fig. 5.42: 2). They are undoubtedly from a local workshop, which did not survive the destruction of Lerna III, although the appearance of similar motifs on some Cretan seals might represent the survival of this tradition (one Lebena seal has been thought a Helladic product, Rutter and Zerner 1984: 81). But sealings are rare in Lerna IV, and later pre-LB material on the mainland consists of a scatter of conical clay stamps of the old type, decorated with simple linear motifs, and some likely Cretan imports (Younger 1991). The continuous history of Aegean seals began in Crete, probably no earlier than EM II.

Here the material from the Myrtos settlement is particularly significant, indicating not only local manufacture (at least two are unfinished, and all are in local stones), but also, through the occurrence of a sealing, local use at a small site (see Catling 1987: 57 for another of this date from Trypiti); the seals' motifs, simple line groups and a chevroned cross, are typical examples of the early group considered to derive from a Neolithic 'koine' by Younger (1991: 46), which survived for a considerable period (Blasingham 1983: 164–6). Many others come from Prepalatial tombs. Early examples are mostly made of soft stones, bone or boar's tusk, and often poorly worked, but more elaborate seals were also

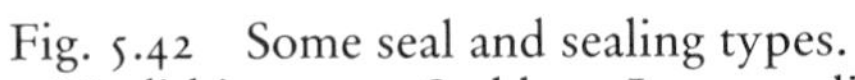

Fig. 5.42 Some seal and sealing types.
1 Neolithic stamp, Sesklo. 2 Lerna sealings, House of the Tiles. 3, 4 Early ivory seals, Koumasa. 5, 6 MM 'Petschaft' and cushion. 7 late MM – LM I 'talismanic' amygdaloid. 8, 9 early LM lentoid and amygdaloid. 10 gold seal-ring, Mycenae T. 84. Scale 3:2.

produced, many in hippopotamus ivory (Krzyszkowska 1988: 215–16); these were evidently valued, as they might be repaired. Most are essentially flat-based stamps with a 'handle' of very varied type, even animal- or bird-shapes; often the shapes reflect the natural forms of bones and tusks (Krzyszkowska 1988: 215; Fig. 5.42: 3, 4). Motifs include not only simple and complex geometric and stylised leaf patterns, but animal and human figures in a primitive outline style; various schemes of arrangement are used, in some of which the principle of rotation is already apparent (Yule 1980: 229). There are resemblances between the geometric motifs and those used to decorate local pottery, Cycladic stone items, and the Lerna seals, but to a great extent the seal-carvers seem to have drawn on their own imaginations or followed the wishes of their patrons in both shapes and motifs.

Despite the natural expectation that these seals were used, Prepalatial sealings are very rare in Crete. The earliest deposits of sealings fall well within the First Palace Period, during which a sealing system seems to have been adopted at the major centres under direct Near Eastern, perhaps specifically Egyptian influence; but there are traces of local adaptations even in the earliest group, from the Phaistos palace, and within the period new forms of sealing which were attached by cords to objects or covered the bindings of documents were developed, together with distinctive Minoan sealing practices (Weingarten 1986b). Marked changes are observable in the types, motifs and techniques, which are likely to be associated with the governing elite's adoption of seals as an administrative tool. But there is considerable variation in practices and products between different workshops: the relatively crude material from the Mallia workshop closely associated with Quartier Mu (Poursat 1983: 278) was evidently more or less contemporary with the much finer work represented by many of the sealings from the Phaistos palace, although this deposit has a wide range and includes old-fashioned types (Yule 1980: 226–9, 231).

At first soft stones continued to be favoured and prisms, especially the triangular type, were particularly common, very often inscribed with groups of signs. But seals began to be made of hard stones, which often had exotic origins and had previously been used to make beads (Younger 1989: 54). Working such stones required a new technique of drilling with the help of the bow-lathe, and led to the popularity of new shapes that provided better surfaces to work on, discs, cushions (flattened cylinders) and the first lentoids, as well as the most elaborate form of handled stamp, the *Petschaft* (Fig. 5.42: 5, 6). Geometric designs still predominated in a great variety of forms, some clearly paralleled by Kamares pottery motifs (Blasingham 1983: 16–17); patterns based on drill-produced circles and elaborate 'architectonic' arrangements were also developed. At Phaistos a group of figured scenes includes some that are very naturalistically rendered, among which are the first examples of the 'flying gallop' depiction of rapid movement; mythical beasts like the griffin also appear, and there are rather stiffly rendered human figures, which may in some cases represent divinities. In the Hieroglyphic Deposit from Knossos, probably from the end of the First Palace Period, animal themes are also common, and there are some examples of the depictions of human heads, which form part of the larger 'Group of the Chanting Priest', all having a likely religious significance (Younger 1989: 58–9). Narrative scenes involving humans or animals were being developed, and it becomes increasingly possible to isolate closely related groupings, the work of individual artists or workshops, within the material.

Seal-engraving reached its height in the Second Palace Period. The number of popular shapes dwindles, the dominant ones being the lentoid, particularly characteristic of the Aegean, and the amygdaloid, which may derive from the prism (Fig. 5.42: 7–9). The metal seal-ring, most often oval-bezelled (Fig. 5.42: 10), also becomes quite common, being favoured by elite administrators, and the value generally attached to seals is demonstrated by the provision of gold caps for the string-holes. The range of scenes and the quality with which they are rendered are very striking; in this miniature field there are achievements fully the equal of larger work on frescoes and precious vessels. Animals are shown with great attention to detail in various poses, resting, wounded in the hunt or attacking one another (most often a lion against a bull); these are very popular themes, but there are also many scenes of human hunting, warfare, ritual and religious symbolism of similar quality. A remarkable group of sealings from Zakro show peculiar combinations of human and animal parts to form various monsters that may well have a special explanation related to administrators' needs (Weingarten 1986a), and there is also the apparently amuletic class of 'talismanic' amygdaloids, which were rarely used to make sealings (Fig. 5.42: 7).

It is at this period that seals returned to the mainland, the earliest in context being those from the Shaft Graves and T. θπ4 at Eleusis. Some are clearly direct Cretan imports, like two 'talismanic' seals from Grave Circle B, but others have been thought local products, for reasons of treatment and content rather than style, which remains essentially Minoan. Many from early Mycenaean contexts are of excellent quality, but collections like that in the Vapheio tholos cist can include much cruder works, which might be by less skilled apprentices of the original masters or by jewellers who had not tried their hands at seals before; some reflect the stylistic tendencies of the more mediocre work in Crete. A class of seals in soft stones, having more stylised and schematic decoration, was certainly becoming increasingly popular in the early and middle stages of the LBA throughout the Aegean.

Greater economy of technique, with limbs portrayed by straight cuts and eyes and joints by drill holes or blobs, is an evident feature of seals of the early Third Palace phase at Knossos, and a Cut Style making no use of the drill at all is identifiable. The lentoid now became the most popular shape by far, and animal figures are often violently distorted to fit the circular field. Animal representations remain much the commonest form of motif except on seal-rings, where ritual-related themes continue popular. But after this period, deterioration is more marked. The softer stones and more schematic styles become increasingly dominant, and motifs like the lion attacking a bull were constantly repeated, often in rather poor style. It is coming to be thought that by the end of the fourteenth century work in hard stones had ceased; Younger (1979a) identifies as perhaps its latest exponent a 'Rhodian Hunt Master', who attempts to capture attention by elaborate crammed compositions on gaudy stones. But work in soft stones and on glass, with increasingly crude and sticklike figures, may well have continued for some time longer, although it is widely believed that seal-cutting was a dead art by the Postpalatial Period. Earlier works continued in use throughout the later LBA, identifiable on a considerable proportion of the Pylos sealings, for instance, and among the relatively few seals from the Perati cemetery; but for whatever reason, there was a decline to extinction in the later LBA.

(ix) Writing

Aegean writing cannot be described as an art, in the way that painting Egyptian hieroglyphics might be, but it was certainly a specialised craft, practised by very few persons, and this seems the best place to present a summary account. Its origins remain mysterious: although there is evidence for the use of signs from the Prepalatial Period, as potters' and masons' marks and on seals, no clear line of development can be traced between these, which are found widely in the Aegean, and the earliest evidence for a true script in First Palace Period Crete, although some signs recur and sealstones inscribed with short groups of them seem to precede written documents.

It is not surprising that a form of writing was developed at this time in Crete, when there would have been an increasing need to record stored commodities and their movement, which seems to be the factor that gave impetus to the development of writing in Mesopotamia much earlier. The idea of using writing for this purpose surely reached Crete through its Near Eastern contacts, but only the idea can have been transmitted, for there are no evident links between Cretan writing and any Near Eastern system. Rather, the system seems to be a local invention: the signs of the earliest script, miscalled 'hieroglyphic', include stylised but recognisable pictures of parts of creatures, plants or artefacts, and some linear symbols (Olivier 1989, fig. 24), and, it is supposed from their small number, were used to represent open syllables, as probably in Linear A and certainly in Linear B. Some signs represent numerals and others, the ideograms, types of livestock and commodities; the ideogram system was considerably expanded in the later scripts and the numeral system changed, and in Linear B earlier fraction signs were used for weights and measures, but these are the only major developments in sign-use identifiable.

From the start the signs were both written on tablets and other shapes of damp clay, with a sharp instrument, and inscribed on a variety of artefacts, especially seals, even painted on pots. In a marked divergence from Near Eastern practice, the clay documents were not baked but merely sun-dried, and so have only been preserved fortuitously when baked by a fire. It is frequently suggested that there were other records in perishable materials like papyrus or parchment, but the positive evidence for this is very slight, and it is quite open to question whether the Aegean civilisations used writing for any purposes but those that are represented in the preserved material. The clay items were clearly records of some kind, concerned with commodities, but the nature of the other inscriptions is not clear; it is of particular interest that over half the sign-groups on seals belong to one of three groups (Olivier 1989: 240), which might suggest that they represent or belong to formulae, like many Linear A sign-groups.

The 'hieroglyphic' script is strongly associated with north Crete, especially Mallia, but there is very little trace of it at Phaistos, where a 'proto-Linear A' can be identified even before the end of the First Palace Period (Fig. 5.43). The relationship between the two scripts is complex, since they share signs and other symbols, and examples of both have been found in an archive at Mallia, of early Second Palace Period date, although there is little trace of the 'hieroglyphic' script thereafter. As Olivier has pointed out, there is nothing to prove that they do not represent two different languages, or at least dialects (1989: 249–50). But whatever its relationship with 'hieroglyphic', Linear A became the script of Second Palace Period Crete: very similar formulae made up of several sign-groups have been found on items from religious sites throughout the island (most recently, Karetsou *et al.* 1985), while the group which clearly signifies 'total' is found on texts from both Ayia Triada and Zakro. These are strong arguments that it was used for a single language; there are few links between the sign-groups of the two classes, but this may simply reflect the different contexts of the material.

Linear A was not only widely used within Crete (Fig. 5.43), but appears elsewhere in the Aegean: tablet-fragments have been found at Phylakopi and Ayia Irini, and other inscribed items at Akrotiri, Kastri on Kythera, and Ayios Stephanos. It also seems to have been the inspiration for the development of a script in Cyprus, and was clearly the main ancestor of Linear B, although the latter shows considerable changes, including better text lay-out, a wider range of pictorial ideograms, and the use of weights and measures symbols, all of which may have enhanced its efficiency as an administrative tool (Fig. 5.45). Despite recurrent attempts to suggest a separate development on the mainland, the argument that Linear B was developed at Knossos during the early Third Palace Period still seems the most likely (Palaima 1988a, b).

The quantity of Linear B writing recovered is massively more than for the earlier scripts (Fig. 5.44). But 99% of the total is made up of tablets and other matter related to administration, including the painted inscriptions on storage stirrup jars, which generally relate to origin or producer; there is no trace of its use for dedicatory inscriptions on offerings, but a few inscriptions on open vases

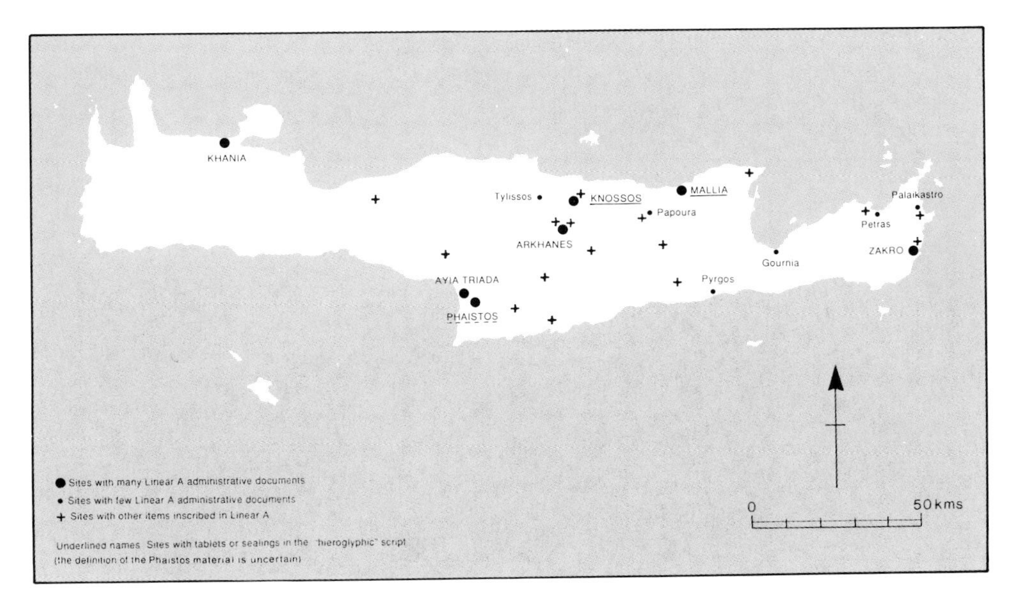

Fig. 5.43 The distribution of items inscribed in the 'hieroglyphic' and Linear A scripts.

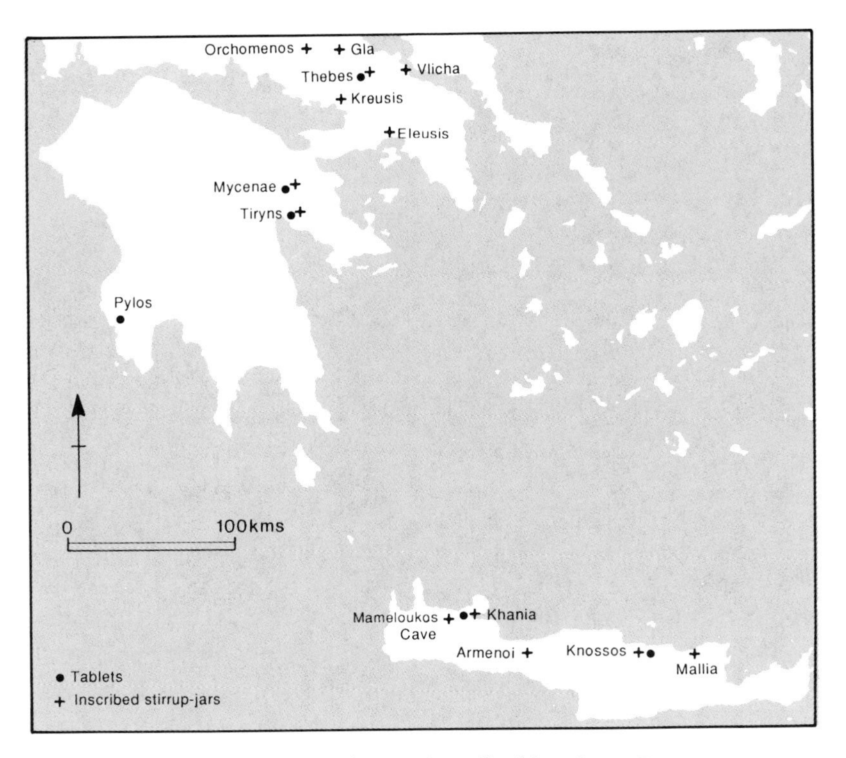

Fig. 5.44 The distribution of items inscribed in Linear B.

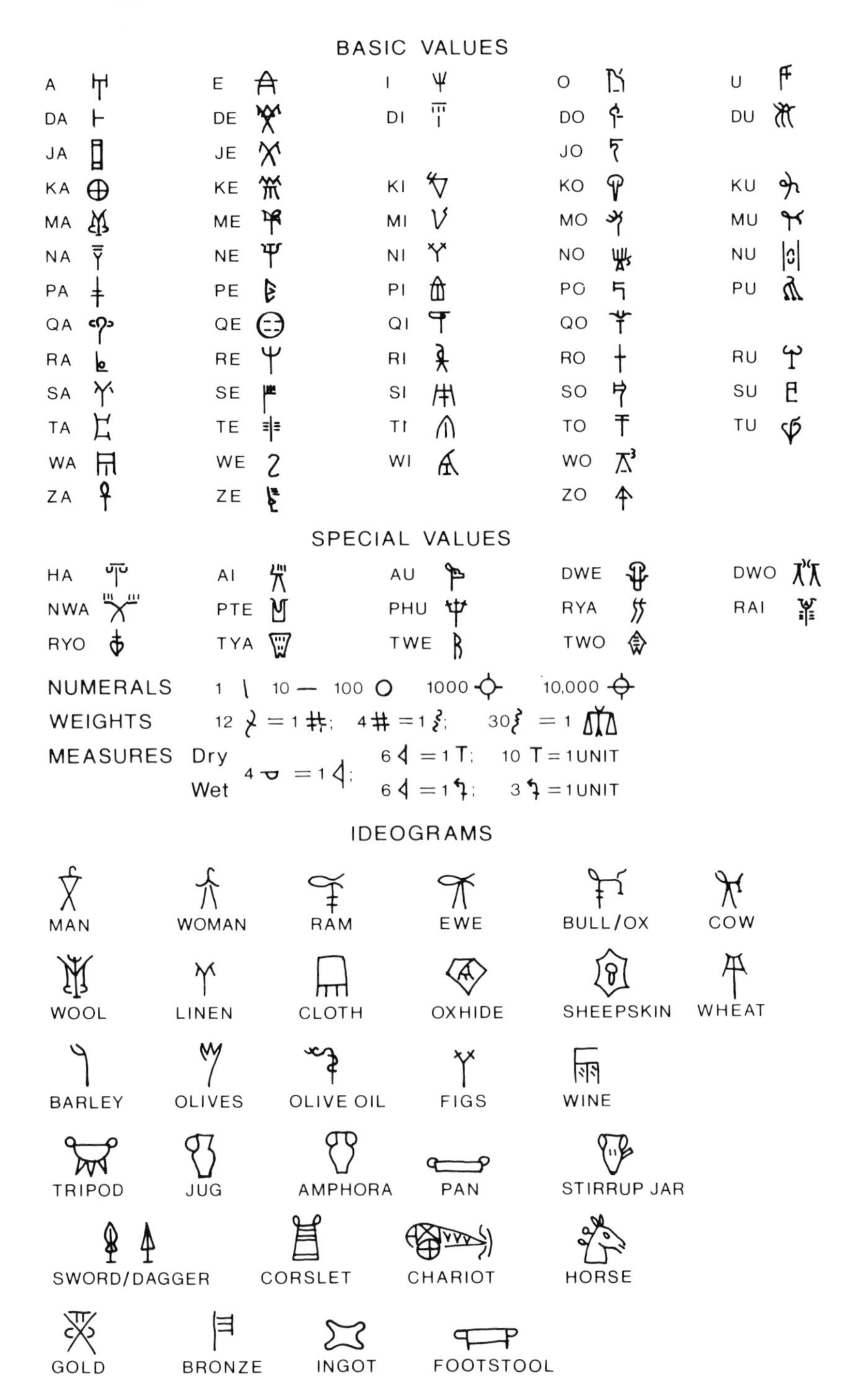

Fig. 5.45 The Linear B syllabary, with a selection of ideograms and other symbols. Courtesy of Dr J. Chadwick.

may be purely personal (Hallager 1983: 72–3). The analysis of scribal hands suggests at least 66 working at Knossos and 33 at Pylos (Olivier 1984: 14), but some of these are 'secondary hands', rarely found, which may belong to officials whose reports and records were organised into larger documents by full-time scribes based at the palaces.

Overall, there is no reason to suppose that literacy was at all widespread or developed in the Aegean. Writing seems to have reached its peak, in terms of variety of uses, in the Second Palace Period; but the inscribed items normally have high-status associations, in their contexts (palaces, 'villas', rich sanctuary sites) and/or materials, and the texts on them are never very long. The only hint of longer texts (ignoring the problematic Phaistos disc, cf. Olivier 1989: 251–2) is provided by the evidence, again from administrative contexts, for sealed packets, wrapped in string, which have been interpreted as documents of leather or parchment; but their nature remains quite uncertain. Later, there is an evident narrowing of use almost entirely to administrative purposes. Indeed, the rules for using Linear B to write Greek are such as to militate against its use for long passages of continuous prose, in which the scope for alternative readings would become too great; it could only work when confined to a narrow vocabulary, so that the reader would be aware of possible alternatives. The very fact that writing disappeared so easily from the Aegean after the collapse of the palaces with which it is so closely associated suggests that it was not deeply rooted.

(x) Weapons and armour

The picture of Aegean weapons and armour that may be developed by combining the evidence of finds and mostly LB representations must be regarded as heavily biased towards the upper end of the social spectrum, and mostly concerned with display of status rather than reality. Hunting and the defence of livestock from predators are likely to have been the main purpose for which most members of the population would own anything classifiable as a weapon, and missile types would probably have been prominent among these, as also in warfare, to judge from the stocks kept at Knossos (Ventris and Chadwick 1973: 361, 513–15). But missiles are rarely shown in representations, which concentrate upon well-equipped warriors or hunters. A similar concern with status can be detected in the burial of weapons with the dead.

The common types of weapon are few, the dagger, spear, sword and (as indicated by finds of arrowheads) the bow. The axe and mace, widely favoured as weapons in the Near East, occur only as ceremonial/ritual items; Branigan identifies some blades as halberds, a type quite common in Europe, but they are so few and varied that one is bound to wonder whether this is correct (1974: 17). The typology of Aegean weapons and armour is in fact largely independent of other regions, after the early stages when spear and dagger forms can often be linked to Anatolian types. The dagger probably began as a multi-functional artefact, since it would have been a more efficient knife than a length of wood set with obsidian blades, and could have been used as a razor, sacrificial weapon, or in warfare (but not in hunting except to administer a *coup de grâce*). Its early popularity is unlikely to be connected with exceptional efficiency as a weapon, since the majority of blades do not exceed 20 cm in length and would have been outranged by any other hafted weapon; rather, it is likely to have attracted prestige primarily for being made of a valuable material, enhanced from an early stage by the decoration of blade or hilt.

A preference for attaching dagger hilts by rivetting to the base of the blade rather than with the help of a tang, as in Anatolia and Cyprus, was quickly established; although this was not always successful, as demonstrated by blades like the Myrtos dagger which required re-rivetting because of fractures at the original holes (Warren 172: 213), it was persisted with, suggesting that the results were reasonably serviceable. At an early stage the important advance of strengthening the blade with a central ridge or midrib was made (Fig. 5.46: 1). This feature is found particularly on longer blades, which were already reaching 35 cm by the middle of the EBA (Fig. 5.46: 2), or more if a 45 cm weapon from Leukas R7 is of or near 'Lerna III' (EH II) in date (longer weapons like Branigan 1974, nos 479–80, 489–91 are probably later). This lengthening of the blade suggests a concern to improve reach, of which the sword is the natural sequel; in fact, flat blades of sword length were being produced in Anatolia before the end of the EBA.

In comparison with daggers, early bronze spearheads are rare (many spears may still have been entirely of wood, as argued in Chapter 3 for the Neolithic period, cf. Morgan 1988: 106–7). The complex arrangements for hafting, involving fitting a tang or flat end into a haft and running binding thongs through slots in the blade (Fig. 5.47a: 1), both features which have Anatolian connections, may have made them difficult to produce. Early examples are very variable, only some having midribs, but the majority are 15–25 cm in length, which has led Höckmann to suggest (1980: 14) that they were used principally as throwing weapons. But it seems unlikely that they would have balanced well; more plausible as javelin-heads, though very rare, are some much smaller flat tanged or socketed forms (most 3–4 cm long, some up to 9 cm), which have normally been classified as arrowheads (Buchholz 1962, Group VIIB; Höckmann 1980: 125–6, M3–6). They could equally well be arrowheads, but in any preserved material these are extraordinarily rare in pre-LB contexts outside the Helladic region. Even here the first common type, the barbed form with basal notch (Buchholz Groups III–IV, Banks 1967 category d; Fig. 5.47b: 1) is not found much before 'Lerna IV' (EH IIIB) and contemporary stages. Production of these in chert and obsidian seems to have been a mainland speciality, establishing a tradition which continued well into the LBA (Fig. 5.47b: 2).

The occurrence of fortifications suggests that warfare was not unknown in the early periods, but for lack of representations nothing can be said of it or of

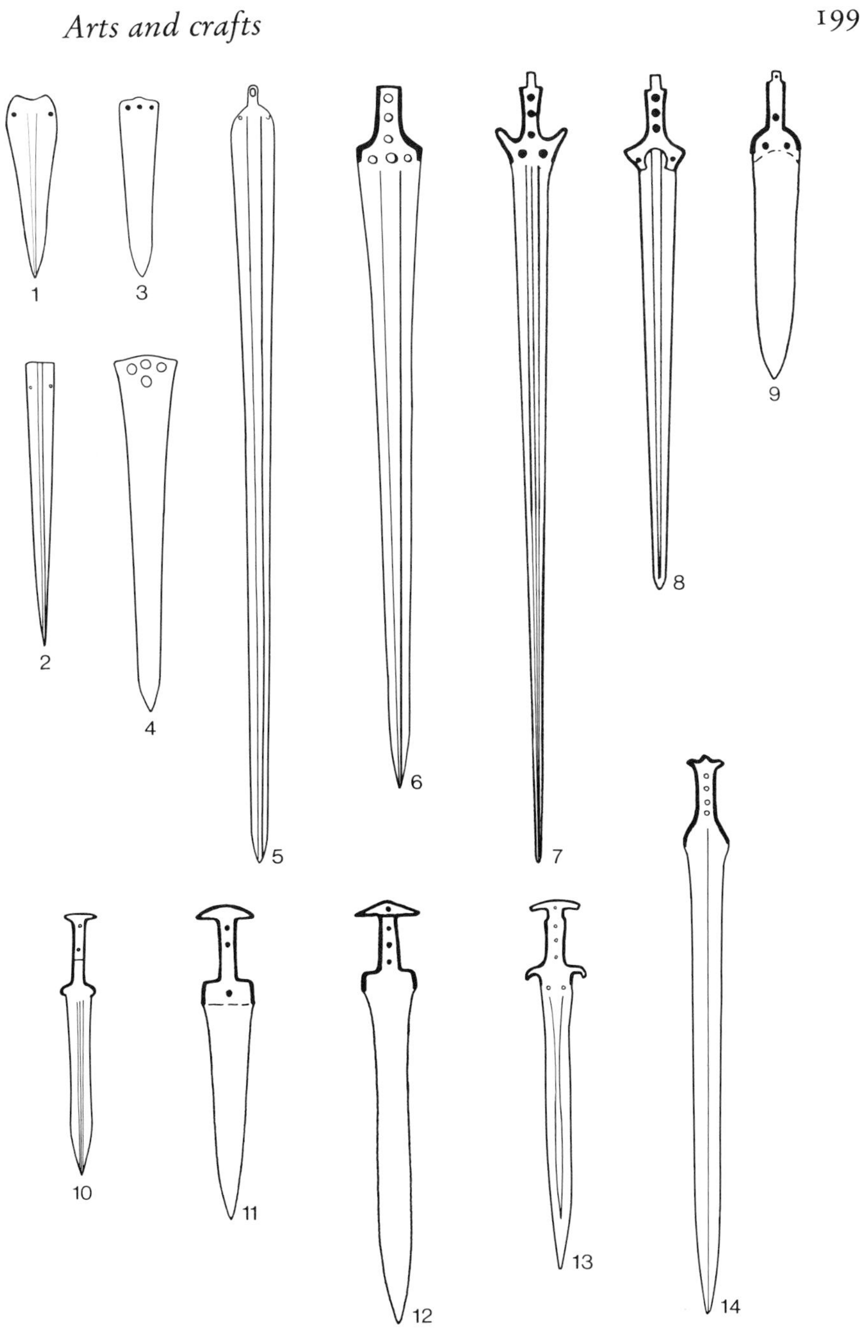

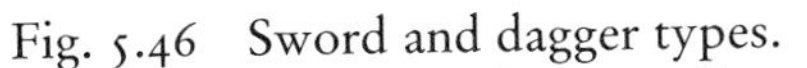

Fig. 5.46 Sword and dagger types.
1 Prepalatial Minoan dagger. 2 'Syros' long dagger. 3 later MM broad dagger. 4 big dagger, Shaft Grave Nu. 5–8 sword types A, B, Ci, Di. 9–11 dagger and short sword types Ei, Dii, Fi. 12–14 sword types Fii, G (late), (Naue) II. 1, 7–9, 11–12 courtesy of Mr M.S.F. Hood and Thames and Hudson Ltd. Scale 1:8.

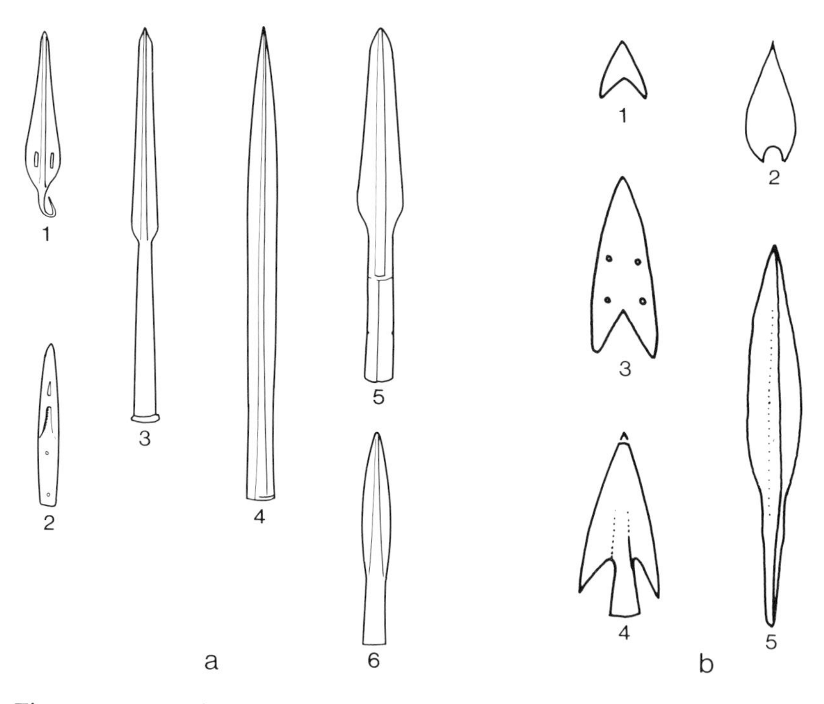

Fig. 5.47a Spearhead types.
1 EC slotted. 2 'shoeslot'. 3 early LB socketed. 4 'one-piece'. 5 later LB socketed. 6 late short-socketed. Scale 1:8.
Fig. 5.47b Arrowhead types.
1, 2 MH and LH stone. 3–5 LH III bronze (last perhaps javelin head). Scale 1:2.

defensive armour, and this continues to be true for the First Palace Period. But it is clear that a period of development must lie behind the fairly homogeneous type of heavy-armed warrior recognisable in the Second Palace Period material. One might expect that the palace societies in Crete would play a major role in this development, but the contribution of other parts of the Aegean should not be underrated. The association of two early-looking long swords with Amorgos (Branigan 1974; nos 480, 491), which is in general a notable source of pre-LB weapons, suggests that Cycladic smiths continued the development towards the long sword already detected in earlier long daggers, and may have influenced the production of the Type A sword (Branigan 1968b: 198–9).

But there is plenty of evidence from Crete for weapon development, especially in daggers (Branigan 1968b, cf. Fig. 5.46: 3 for a common form), and the Type A sword (Fig. 5.46: 5) was being produced at Mallia before the end of the First Palace Period; this appears to be a notable centre of weapon-smithing, since it has also produced some fine daggers, a unique broad blade of sword length, probably ceremonial, and the earliest datable examples of the 'shoeslot' spearhead (Höckmann Group B, Avila Type I; Fig. 5.47a: 2). This was the commonest form of spearhead in the MB Aegean, and was probably made outside Crete also (a mould was found at Sesklo); it may be seen as a final refinement of the split-haft type. Examples with tangs and blade-slots still occur, including the massive (40 cm) blade from the Anemospilia shrine, which may well have been a sacrificial weapon (Sakellarakis 1991: 154), and Höckmann has argued that the socketed spearhead was developed in early MB Crete, but none of the examples that he dates early have good contexts.

The clearest representations of early Second Palace Period warriors are on a miniature fresco in the West House at Akrotiri (Fig. 5.48), most of whose features can be paralleled in other representations, such as the Shaft Grave IV 'Battle Krater'; generic rather than specifically Mycenaean warriors are most probably intended (cf. Morgan 1988: 114–15). Full armament consists of a helmet, a shield that usually covers most of the body, a long spear and a sword. There is no indication of other forms of body armour such as corslet or greaves; the long shields seem to have been thought to give sufficient protection (but see below on possible corslet-attachments in boar's tusk). It seems very plausible

Fig. 5.48 An early LB warrior, from the West House miniature fresco, Akrotiri.

that the large shields were developed to give better protection as weapons' range was extended, but their origins are obscure. Two types can be identified, the 'figure-of-eight' and the 'tower', which seems to come in short and long versions (Morgan 1988: 107–9). Both were evidently made of hide stretched over a wooden framework and were curved to provide some protection at the side; they were suspended from a shoulder-strap, and so both hands could be used to thrust with the spear if so desired (as in several cases on the 'Battle Krater'). Their relative merits are unclear, but the 'tower' type, though carried by all the Akrotiri warriors, is very rarely shown later.

The helmets shown, as Morgan has demonstrated (1988: 109–15), reflect a basically conical form made up of strips of leather fitted together and sometimes plated with boar's tusk in a variety of ways; no two of those shown on the Akrotiri fresco are identical. This was undoubtedly a highly expensive process, since the tusks of many boars would be needed, and remains of such plates are found rarely, generally in evidently wealthy graves. Since boar's tusk is, in fact, quite hard, it is not surprising that plates which may have been attached to a corslet rather than a helmet have sometimes been identified, as in the Aegina warrior burial.

Representations also suggest that helmets were often ornamented with horns, plumes and other attachments, in various materials: some small bronze discs from Shaft Grave IV may have been such attachments.

The long sword and spear dominate both representations and finds from the Second Palace Period. The style of fighting clearly relied mainly on thrusting strokes, for which the spear would have been the most efficient, since it had the longest reach; but it is relatively rarely found, in comparison with swords and daggers, and was not lavishly decorated as they often were. The socketed spear-head (Fig. 5.47a: 3) appears to have been introduced at this time, scarcely before the LBA, from the Near East, where it was well established. At first it may have ben rare, since 'shoeslot' spearheads are placed with several warrior burials; but during the LBA it was the standard type in various forms. The split socket always seems to have been preferred to the cast socket, perhaps, as Höckmann argues (1980: 19–21), because its greater elasticity allowed a haft to bend rather than break; otherwise, it is difficult to see any great significance in the many variations in blade, midrib shape and proportions, which may reflect local smi-thing traditions as much as anything. Most of the early examples were consider-ably longer than earlier spears, ranging from 30 to 60 cm, and had very long sockets; a few much smaller blades may well have belonged to javelins.

The Type A sword was now established as a major weapon; blades well over 90 cm long have been found in the Shaft Graves and the Arkalochori cave, and the majority seem likely to have exceeded 70 cm. How effective they were remains debatable, since there is an obvious point of weakness in the hilt–blade joint, which generally involved a very short tang with only one or two rivet-holes, fitting into hilt plates that were also rivetted to the shoulders. But they are certainly shown being used, and the existence of many plain examples suggests that they were not produced purely for show (which might seem a considerable waste of skill and material, given the numbers that are known). Some mainland blades have longer tangs with three rivets, and the development of the Type B sword (Fig. 5.46: 6), on which this is a regular feature, may be seen in the context of an apparent interest in producing more efficient weapons in some parts of the mainland, particularly the Argolid. The main feature of Type B was the use of flanging, a feature found on earlier, smaller weapons, around the tang and shoulders to strengthen it. The distribution of examples strongly suggests that this refinement was brought to completion by the Mycenae smiths, since the Shaft Graves contain several examples that seem to be experiments on shorter blades, and very few type B long swords have been found at all outside the Argolid, none in Second Palace Period Crete. Examples of Type B are shorter and broader than Type A, although several exceed 60 cm, and could perhaps have been used for a slashing stroke, but the high midrib would have diminished such a stroke's effectiveness. A wide variety of short swords, large daggers (e.g. Fig. 5.46: 4), and increasingly massive knives (Dickinson 1977: 70) has also been found, suggesting that this was a phase of considerable experiment, especially on the mainland, but these forms did not last long.

One further innovation of the period that requires mention is the chariot. Crouwel plausibly argues that it was introduced to the Aegean from Syria, where almost all the features of the earliest representations can be matched, and transmitted to the mainland from Crete with other items of military equipment (1981: 148–9); transmission from central Europe directly to the mainland has been suggested (Sherratt, A.G. 1987a: 65), but the dating of the earliest evidence for chariots in central Europe is not clear and the case for significant Aegean contact with this region remains rather tenuous. As Crouwel's analysis shows, from the beginning the Aegean chariot had individual features, notably a complex system of support for the pole, which may represent an adaptation to the often hilly terrain of Greece; further development in the Aegean was equally independent, producing the 'dual chariot' that was standard in the Third Palace Period. The chariot's main military purpose is likely to have been the transport of heavy-armed warriors, which is in fact the only attested use in the Near East at this time other than as a platform for archers. No doubt it might also be used to frighten foot soldiers unfamiliar with it, but its practical value seems limited, and after the early period the great majority of representations show it in ceremonial contexts. Nevertheless, the numbers maintained by the palaces indicate that it was thought to be worth all the expenditure and skilled personnel that maintaining a chariot force would require.

The succeeding period sees a continuing emphasis on the heavy-armed warrior, who was given better protection through the improvement of body-armour; by the time that the Dendra T. 12 suit of armour (Pl. 5:21) was buried, in the early decades of the fourteenth century, this development was essentially

Pl. 5.21 Suit of armour, Dendra T. 12. Courtesy of Prof. P. Åström.

complete. It was clearly local, since it relies upon shaped pieces of plate rather than the scales characteristic of the Near East, and includes greaves, which are not found in the Near East at all; only the high collar has Near Eastern parallels (Catling 1970: 446). A recent reconstruction of this armour (Wardle, D.E.H. 1988: 474–6) has demonstrated that it is by no means as cumbersome as often suggested, but is a sophisticated piece of smithing, which provides protection from the lower face to the thighs and allows easy movement. However, it would require heavy internal padding, could not be put on singlehanded, and would effectively prevent the wearer standing up again if he had fallen; it would also be difficult to shoot a bow or ride while wearing it. The Dendra material includes evidence for arm-guards and greaves, and was combined with a helmet plated with boar's tusk and having bronze cheek-pieces; a roughly contemporary Knossos grave provides an example of a bronze-faced helmet, and a hand-guard has been identified in a Mycenae chamber tomb (Xenaki-Sakellariou 1985: 76–8).

Other pieces of bronze armour are known, especially from a storeroom in the Thebes palace, but the total number of finds remains small and it is very unlikely that such armour was widespread (cf. Catling 1970: 447 on the rarity of bronze suits of armour in the Near East). The interpretation of the Linear B texts supposed to refer to corslets of this or similar type is implicitly questioned by Catling (1970: 449), and at best may indicate systems of overlapping plates (Chadwick 1976: 160–3). Probably most body-armour was of leather, sometimes reinforced with bronze strips, plates or shaped pieces (the Thebes pieces are shoulder and arm covers, Verdelis in Åström 1977: 37). What kind of shield was carried in the 'warrior grave' phase is unclear, but the development of greaves would surely have rendered the need to cover the legs with a long shield unnecessary.

The weapons current at the time that bronze armour was being developed are directly derived from the earlier ones and represent an essentially similar array. Both the Types C, D and G swords, that derive from Type B but have projections from the shoulder to protect the hand (Fig. 5.46: 7, 8), and the streamlined 'one-piece' spears (Fig. 5.47a: 4) were probably developed at Knossos by a workshop which specialised in fine, often decorated weapons (Macdonald 1987). Höckmann has suggested that the 'one-piece' form was specially designed to puncture a bronze-faced corslet (1980: 58–9), although this may be to attribute more stopping power to such armour than it possessed (the plate is only 1–2 mm thick, McDonald and Wilkie 1992: 276). The early examples are certainly formidable blades, ranging up to 54 cm in length and, to judge from the decoration found on several, were clearly prestigious possessions. The Type E dagger or short sword (Fig. 5.46: 9), which combines a flat daggerlike blade with a flanged hilt and was ancestral to later sword types, may well also have been evolved at Knossos, where it occurs in LM II contexts.

Another development worth noting is the growing popularity of bronze arrowheads (Fig. 5.47b: 3, 4); the recording of quantities of missile heads in the

Knossos Linear B texts suggests that their use was more of a feature of warfare at this time than the rare early LB representations of archers might suggest. As before, some examples are big enough to have been heads for small javelins and darts (cf. Fig. 5.47b: 5), which may also be listed in the texts (Chadwick 1976: 172). In fact, bronze-faced armour may have been developed as much to protect against missiles as against heavy thrusting weapons.

Weapons in the later stages of the Third Palace Period are comparatively unremarkable. Spearheads seldom exceed 25 cm in length (Fig. 5.47a: 5), swords are rarely as much as 40 cm (Fig. 5.46: 10); among the latter the flat-bladed Type F, developed from Type E but with a T-shaped pommel on the flanged hilt, became increasingly common (Fig. 5.46: 11). A general shortening of weapons may reflect a need to stretch bronze supplies further, or simply a wish to arm more warriors; Linear B texts show that the palaces maintained stores of arms, from which levies might have been supplied. Such weapons, and the adoption of smaller forms of shield, would suit fighting in closer formation. Late in the period a tendency to shorten spear sockets (e.g. Fig. 5.47a: 6) may have been intended to make them more suitable for throwing by lightening the head; hunting scenes on frescoes often show a pair of presumed throwing spears being carried. A stripped-down form of the chariot, the 'rail chariot' (Crouwel 1981: 70–2; cf. Catling 1968b: 46–8) also seems to have been developed at this time. These indications of concern with efficient if unspectacular military equipment might suggest that warfare was becoming more prevalent.

Late in the period the first examples of the European Type II sword, perhaps of specifically Italian origin, appear (Fig. 5.46: 14). The size (most are 50–85 cm) and exotic origin suggest that these were the new prestige weapons; they would have been considerably superior to the Type F sword as melee weapons. Longer versions of the Type F and G swords (Fig. 5.46: 12, 13) seem to have been produced to match them by some smiths; but others learned to make the new weapons, and the Type II was the commonest form of Postpalatial sword, appearing in several well-provided warriors' graves. Some Postpalatial swords were decorated with ivory hilt-plates and gold bands, as no extant examples of the later Third Palace Period had been, and this may be taken, with the burial of armour plates of bronze or boar's tusk and, at the very end of the period, of bronze shield bosses, as a sign of renewed emphasis on the status of the warrior. Long and short types of spearhead, some apparently related to European types, also occur in Postpalatial contexts, but evidence for the bow becomes extremely rare.

Representations of warriors are quite frequent on elaborate Postpalatial vessels, though more often in procession, sometimes in chariots, than in conflict. They consistently wear greaves and carry spears, sometimes levelled for a throw, but vary in types of helmet, shield, and presence or absence of corslets and swords (which are never shown in use). The elaboration of some helmets shown suggests that, at the end as at the beginning of the LBA, the representations reflect an ideal of status, only partly matched in the heterogeneous material, whose variety suggests that good weapons were at a premium. It may have been a considerable time before the last bronze weapons went out of use.

Bibliography

Hood 1978 and Higgins 1981 provide useful accounts of most arts, now sometimes dated. On the topic of distinguishing Mycenaean from Minoan art, see recently Hurwit 1979: 414–16 and Younger 1985: 54–5, with which I am in full agreement.

What follows is not intended to be exhaustive, but a guide to detailed surveys, which are still lacking for some large groups of material, e.g. EH and Cycladic pottery, EC stone vessels.

Architecture: Sinos 1971 (house-plans); Themelis 1984, Hägg and Konsola 1986, Shaw 1987 (EH, especially monumental); Shaw 1971, Cadogan 1976, Graham 1987 (Minoan, especially palatial); Iakovidis 1983 (major LH citadels), Kilian 1987a, 1987b (LH palaces), 1988c (LH generally), Hiesel 1990 (LH house-plans). On individual sites see references for Ch. 4.

Figures and figurines: (a) Cycladic: several relevant papers in Fitton 1984 (summarised in Barber 1987: 119–32), Getz-Preziosi 1985, Fitton 1989, Renfrew 1991.

(b) Mycenaean: French 1971, updated in 1981b, cf. also Renfrew 1985: 413–29.

(c) Minoan metal: Verlinden 1984.

(d) on Minoan peak sanctuary types see Rutkowski 1991, which centres on a large group from Petsopha.

Frescoes: Immerwahr 1990 (on dating see Warren in *Antiquity* 65 (1991) 173); Hood 1978, Ch. 3 is also a useful discussion. On Thera see now Doumas 1992.

Jewellery: Higgins 1980.

Non-ceramic vessels: Davis, E.N. 1977 (gold and silver); Matthäus 1980 (bronze and copper); Warren 1969 (Minoan stone); Sakellarakis 1976 (Mycenaean stone); Foster 1979 (faience).

Pottery: Betancourt 1985 (Minoan); Zerner 1986, 1988 (MH and LH I); Mountjoy 1986 (Mycenaean).

Seals: Boardman 1970, Ch. II, updated by Younger 1973 (itself updated by articles in *Kadmos* 1982–8), 1989, 1991, Yule 1980.

Weapons and armour: Sandars 1961, 1963 (swords); Catling 1968a: 95–107 (swords, especially Type II, and spears); Höckmann 1980, Avila 1983 (spears, arrowheads); Buchholz 1962, Banks 1967: 59–77 (arrowheads); Catling 1970, Verdelis in Åström 1977: 29–65 (armour); Catling 1968b, Littauer 1972, Crouwel 1981, Chs V–VI (chariots).

Workshops and processes: Evely 1988b, Tournavitou 1988; a full-scale discussion of the Minoan material by Evely is forthcoming. Dalley 1984, Ch. 3 is interesting for Mesopotamian parallels.

Writing: Palaima 1988a, 1988b; Olivier 1989.

CHAPTER 6

BURIAL CUSTOMS

Introduction

Tombs provide a large proportion of the evidence for every phase of the BA, but the material is unevenly distributed geographically and chronologically. Full publications or even detailed preliminary reports are only available for a minority of cemeteries, and information about the human remains of any phase is particularly scanty. Not a single multiple-burial cemetery has been fully reported in this way, and the largest published sample, covering over two hundred burials, mostly MH, from Lerna (Angel 1971), comes from the tombs found in the excavated area, perhaps a fifth of the whole site.

The shortage of such information makes analysis of burial practice hazardous. Any attempt to detect consistent patterns of associations that might reflect the use of different customs for groups of different sex, age or marital status, for example, is scarcely possible. Unsurprisingly, there has been a general unwillingness to consider the social dimension of burial customs except in the simplest terms, although Tsountas long ago drew attention to marked disparities of wealth between different groups of chamber tombs at Mycenae and presented evidence suggesting distinctions of various kinds in the EC cemeteries. Accounts of practice have tended to be normative, minimising variations observable within cemeteries, and to focus on features of tomb construction and types of object found, but have rarely related these to ritual/ceremonial considerations; a rather pragmatic picture has been the result. Systematic studies of social and ritual dimensions of burial customs are at last beginning to be undertaken, but few studies have been published so far.

Where figures of the numbers of dead are available, they are frequently low compared with what might be expected. This has sometimes been explained in terms of post-depositional factors, for example that cemeteries have been destroyed, or covered by deep soil accumulation, in later periods. Another possibility is that many of the dead were disposed of in ways that lack recognisable features or dating material, or did not involve a tomb at all, such as exposure. The notable variations between periods and regions in the quantities of burial evidence identified make offering any universal explanation hazardous, but it is certainly tempting to suppose that in many periods the recognisable burials are those of a group defined in some way by status and that others were excluded from this type of rite, although no doubt receiving some kind of funeral (cf. the model recently proposed for the Dark Age in Morris 1987, especially Ch. 6). Indeed, children's burials are so generally under-represented that it is highly likely that most were excluded in this way, and it is certainly possible that this was true for some classes of adult dead also.

There is a high degree of variability in burial form in the Aegean, but underlying this variability are many elements of uniformity in custom. Most obviously, until the Postpalatial Period virtually all burials were inhumed; cremations are so rare as to invite special explanations. The body may be laid out on its side in a contracted position, or extended on its back; since the contracted position is commonly reported from early contexts, even where there is plenty of space, it may well have had some ritual significance, though its later occurrences could reflect nothing more than a wish to limit the effort expended on preparing the grave. Often items were placed in association with the body, although the burials of infants and small children, where identifiable, are rarely so accompanied. The beliefs inherent in this provision of grave goods may not have been identical in every phase, and since they were not always provided this does not seem to have been an essential part of the ritual; in many cases they may be the remains of a ritual consumption of food or drink on the occasion of burial.

Burial itself may sometimes have been a two-stage process, involving a secondary ritual once the bones were bare of flesh (cf. Soles 1973: 399–400, Cavanagh 1978). Plausible evidence for this has been detected in multiple-burial tombs, where earlier remains were often moved into repositories of some kind or heaped against a wall, but it cannot be documented as regular. Frequently, fires were lit on such occasions, whether to fumigate the tomb, clean off the last remnants of flesh from bones, or in some ritual. On such occasions of rearrangement within the tomb grave-goods may often have been removed; it has been speculated that the dead were thought powerless to avenge this once their bones were bare.

Apart from such post-funerary activities, there are reasons to suppose that ceremonies took place in some cemeteries. That these reflect true worship of the dead is now generally thought unlikely, but they might well reflect ceremonies conducted in honour of the dead collectively, or even more general cult practice. This topic will be discussed further in Chapter 8: as will be seen, the evidence has various special features, which must make it a weak base from which to reconstruct a generally held belief in the rebirth of the dead, as suggested by Goodison (1989: 20–30). It is nevertheless possible that such a belief was developed by some groups, perhaps as part of the process by which status and ranking were becoming defined; certainly, there is a strong association between evidence for ceremonies conducted at tombs and cemeteries, and other indications of the special status of the burials in them.

Many of the practices found in the EBA can be linked to the scanty evidence for Neolithic customs, as might be expected if there was substantial continuity of population. The use of caves and rock shelters in Crete continued from Neolithic times, and the 'Final Neolithic' cemetery of Kephala on Kea, of stone cists and built tombs, also seems a natural precursor of the typical EC cemeteries. From the beginning of the EBA cemetery sites are identifiable in increasing numbers in the Cyclades and Crete, though the mainland has produced nothing for the first stages of the EBA and generally small amounts of evidence, if from many sites, for the 'Lerna III' (EH II) stage. Many of the Cretan tombs can be described as in some sense communal and were used for many generations in succession. But elsewhere in the Aegean, although tombs and repositories are found which contain several burials, none were on a remotely comparable scale; it is rare for more than a dozen burials to be reported from the same source, and often these belong to only one major pottery phase. The distinction must reflect an important difference between the societies of Crete and the other Aegean regions, and the long-continued use of many Cretan tombs is a significant index of the stability of Cretan society.

The Cyclades

The EC cemeteries show the greatest consistency among EB burial forms of the Aegean (Fig. 6.1). Most commonly the tombs are cists, built of upright slabs in a rectangular or trapezoidal shape, with further slabs used for the roof and sometimes the floor; a rough stone wall may replace one side slab, and sometimes an 'upper storey' is constructed on the original roof. In the later

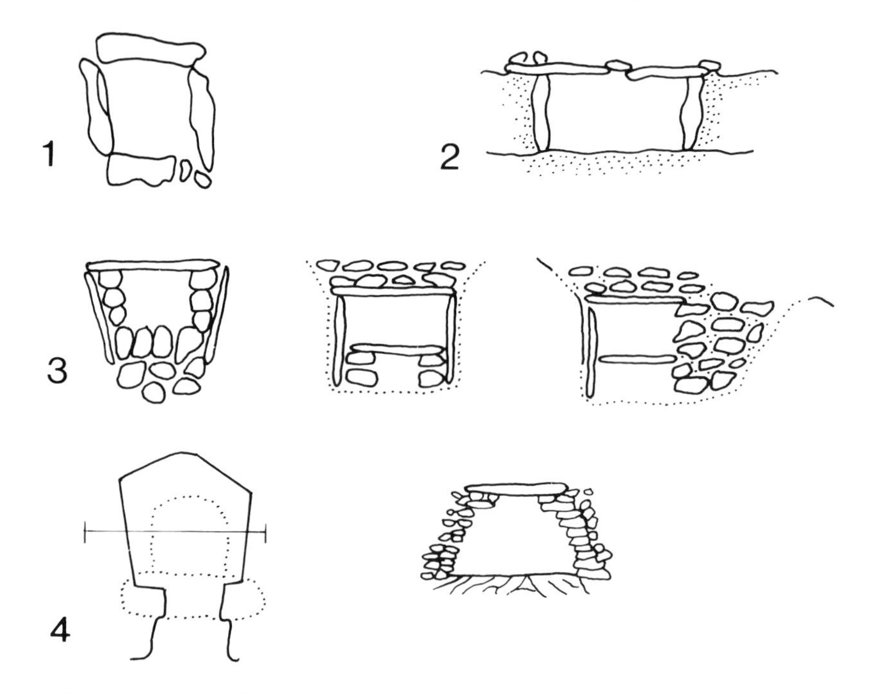

Fig. 6.1 EC tomb types. 1–3 slab and/or built cists. 4 corbelled cist. Courtesy of Dr R.L.N. Barber.

'Kampos' (EC I/II) and 'Syros' (EC II) groups localised variants occur, most notably on Syros, where small tombs of rectangular or circular shape were built with corbelled walls and slab roof, and an entrance-like extension in front; but the slab cist remained dominant, and was still being used in the MBA on some islands. Such tombs were often used for a single burial, but might be used repeatedly; when identified, burials are normally adult, and children's burials are rare.

Cemeteries were usually small. Even where it seems that a complete group has been recovered, there are rarely more than thirty and sometimes fewer than twenty tombs. Much larger cemeteries of between fifty and a hundred or more have been found, particularly in the 'Syros' (EC II) group, but often these show evidence of use from an earlier period. The cemetery of Chalandriani, a type site for the 'Syros' group, is quite exceptional in size: more than 650 tombs are now preserved (there may originally have been a thousand or more), divided into two separate groups, of which one subdivides into four variously sized clusters that are individually larger than most other Cycladic cemeteries. The Chalandriani cemetery must represent an exceptional concentration of population, or a decision by many communities to use a common burial ground (but there are two other cemeteries of this group on Syros, one of 94 graves), whereas most cemeteries can hardly represent more than the burials of a single family or hamlet over a few generations (cf. Broodbank 1989).

Recent excavations, especially by Doumas (1977), have found evidence for features not much reported before, the grouping of burials (by families?) and apparent distancing of richer from poorer, the construction of grave-markers, retaining or enclosure walls, and platforms that may be ritual sites, but these may only have been features of more important cemeteries, like Ayioi Anargyroi on Naxos, where all occur. Stones decorated with various patterns have also been found in association with cemeteries, especially on Naxos (Marangou 1990: 158). Otherwise, practices were simple enough: the dead were placed in a contracted position, perhaps arranged so that they could 'look' to the front of the grave (Goodison 1989: 24), and often provided with goods, ranging from a single pot to whole collections of stone and metal items, including vessels, jewellery, figurines, and occasionally weapons. Such distinctions must surely relate to ranking within the population, but for lack of good skeletal data study of this aspect has barely begun.

Cemeteries elsewhere in the Aegean have been linked to the Cyclades through their tomb-type or the presence of characteristic EC pottery or stone forms, to the extent that Cycladic colonies or a Cycladic element in the population have been postulated (Sapouna-Sakellaraki 1987: 262-3). But the Cycladic items are mixed with other types and never dominant, and both tomb types and burial customs frequently differ from Cycladic norms: thus, at Ayia Photia and Manika the tombs are rock-cut chambers, and multiple burial seems to be much commoner in such cemeteries than in the Cyclades. Moreover, where identified, the associated settlement does not have strong Cycladic features (Sampson 1988). Some other explanation for the occurrence of Cycladic forms must be sought.

Remains of burials post-dating the 'Kastri' (EC IIIA) group in the Cyclades are rare. Occasional examples of the traditional cist can be dated to the MBA or later on Kea, Syros, Naxos, Ios and probably Amorgos, and at Ayia Irini and Phylakopi there are infant jar-burials, which at the former are part of a small extramural cemetery of various forms but at the latter are scattered and intramural. The Ayia Irini cemetery also includes examples of more elaborate built graves of MB and early LB date, and evidence of rock-cut tombs can be identified on Melos and Thera. Those from Phylakopi include both shafts and chamber tombs of varied shapes (Fig. 6.8: 2–4), which seem to have been used from 'Phylakop I' (EC IIIB) into the MBA and perhaps later; unfortunately, they had been almost completely robbed, so that nothing can be said about patterns of use. The provision of grave-goods, including pottery and jewellery, continues to be well-attested; weapons of advanced type, MB or at latest early LB, given an Amorgos provenance probably came from graves. Burials were normally single, but one Kea pithos, enclosed within a built structure, held several, as the larger and more elaborate chamber tombs at Phylakopi probably did. Later graves are of identical types to Mycenaean graves and will be discussed with them.

Crete and the Minoan region to the end of the Second Palace Period

In Crete (Fig. 6.2) the material is so rich and varied that it is difficult to absorb, and understanding is hampered by the prevalence of group burial, as well as the fact that important sites are often only known from preliminary reports. Although two major types of tomb, the predominantly south Cretan circular tombs and the rectilinear 'house tombs' of the north and east, have received extended study, the amount of detail available on individual tombs and cemeteries varies considerably, and even where contents are well published there is more often little but a vague estimate of the number of burials, with no data on age or sex. There is also a major shortage of evidence from Western Crete before LM III.

It is noteworthy how often funerary material is grouped in specific areas which show considerable continuity. The necropolis at Arkhanes (Phourni) is particularly remarkable (Fig. 6.5): here various types of structure have produced evidence covering an EM II–LM IIIA2 range, although there is proportionately much less material after the First Palace Period. The Sphoungaras area close to Gournia seems to have been its main cemetery to the end of the Second Palace Period, and the region to the north of Mallia is similarly filled with material from the Prepalatial and First Palace Periods. At other sites such as Palaikastro and Zakro tombs of various dates cluster around the settlement. The south Cretan circular tombs, which were generally used for considerable periods, can be found

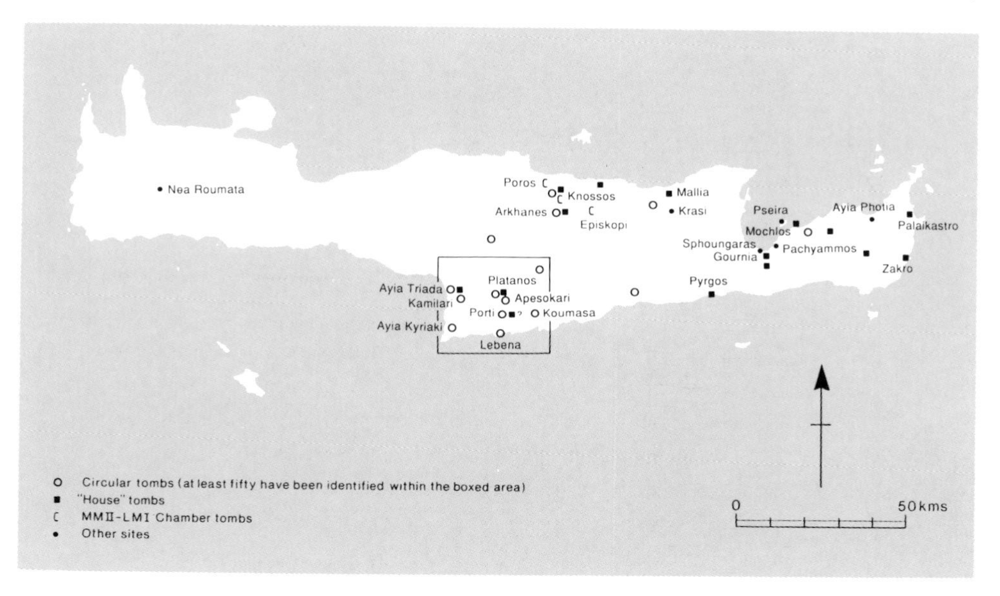

Fig. 6.2 The distribution of some major tomb types in Crete.

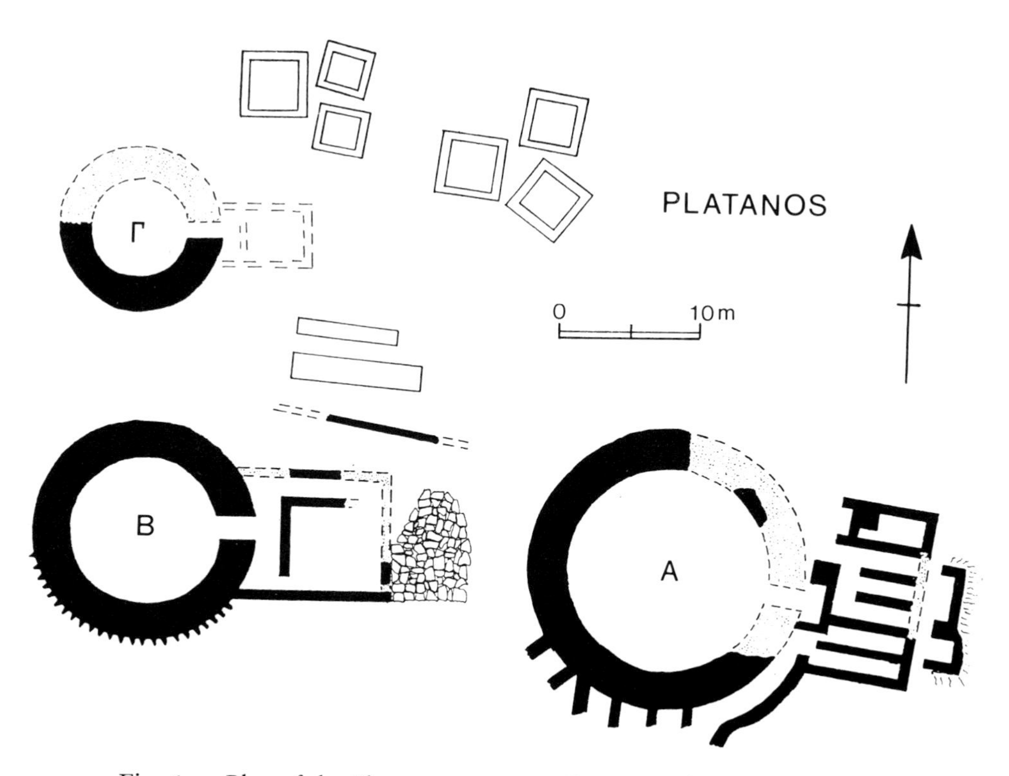

Fig. 6.3 Plan of the Platanos cemetery. Courtesy of Prof. K. Branigan.

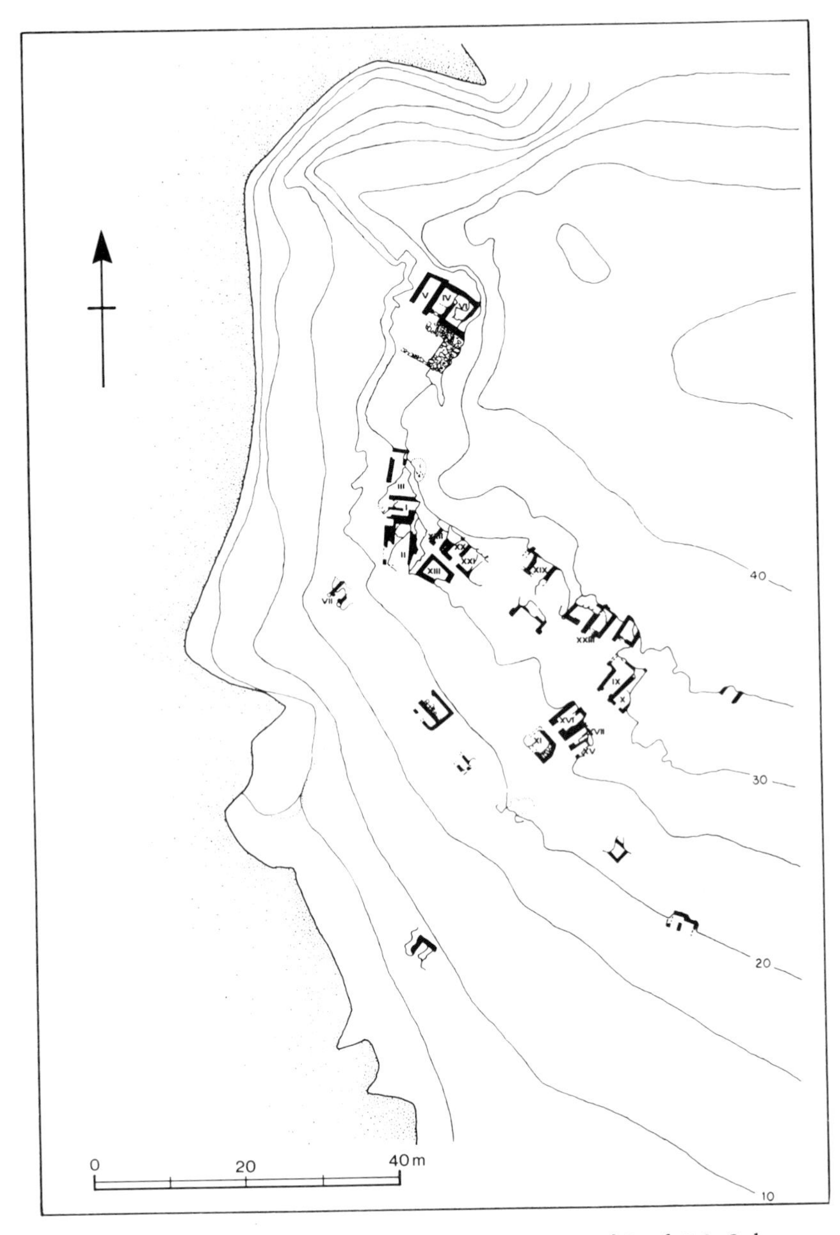

Fig. 6.4 Plan of the Mochlos cemetery. Courtesy of Prof. J.S. Soles.

isolated or in small groups of two or three, but some seem to have become focusses of whole cemeteries of various kinds of burial, contemporary with and succeeding them (Fig. 6.3). But there is a widespread falling-off in use of the old burial areas in the Second Palace Period, and cemeteries of the later LBA are generally in new sites and consist of new types of tomb. Thus, the end of the Second Palace Period forms a natural break.

Apart from the types of tomb already mentioned, many others occur sporadically in the Prepalatial Period. The Neolithic tradition of using caves and rock shelters continued in north and east Crete, and even fissures in the rock might contain burial remains, as at Mallia. Cists, pits and simple interments are sometimes reported; at Ayia Photia they are rare occurrences among the large cemetery of rock-cut chamber tombs, itself a unique type for the period, and may have been used only for children's burials, but on Pseira they are quite common (Catling 1989: 106; French 1990: 76). It seems rare for any type to have been used for only one or a few burials; however, from EM III onwards the custom of placing the skeletal remains of individuals in clay pithoi and larnakes (coffin-like lidded tubs) became increasingly common in all parts of Crete, although these could also hold collected parts of several burials. Such pithos and larnax burials can be found in separate cemeteries, as at Sphoungaras and Pachyammos, or associated with if not inside built tombs, as at some circular tombs and especially among the great structures of Arkhanes. Isolated examples of pithos burials are occasionally reported, and they are also common in some of the First Palace Period rock-cut chamber tombs around Knossos. Since the pithoi and larnakes were not used solely for individuals' burials, it seems more likely that their use signifies a concern to isolate particular burials than a wish to stress individuality as against membership of a group.

Given that the majority of tomb types were used for group burial, the nature of the groups using them must be an important topic. The general impression given by the rather vague reports is that burials in caves, rock shelters and most 'house tombs' can be counted in tens (the 196+ skulls reported from Arkhanes T. 6 seem to represent the clearance of remains from several neighbouring tombs, Sakellarakis 1991: 98), whereas circular tombs generally held hundreds, probably because they were in use for much longer. By estimating the length of the period of use and calculating the likely average rate of burial, various authors have argued that the circular tombs were used by 'clans', by small groups of families, or by only single families, while Soles has suggested that 'house tombs' were normally used by one or two families at most. The calculation that a family will produce five burials to a generation, so twenty to a century, has often been used in this connection. But the descendants of an original pair will sooner or later, perhaps in the next generation, establish more than one family; do all such descendants become entitled to burial in the same tomb? Whatever the contributing group, the contributing population must surely start rising progressively. Other methods of calculation have been based on the grave-goods; the most plausible calculates from the number of vessels likely to be used in a burial ceremony, but even this must involve assumptions. In the absence of accurate data on skeletal remains it cannot ever be assumed that all members of a household, or of several households if these used the same tomb, were buried together; there might have been selectivity against one sex, against non-adults, particularly infants, or in favour of holders of a certain rank or office (which might explain why the rich and elaborate complexes Ts. I–III and IV–VI at Mochlos (Fig. 6.4) held so few burials relative to their long period of use). But the few studies of skeletal material suggest that in several tombs adults of both sexes and all ages were buried together; evidence for sub-adults and children is rarer.

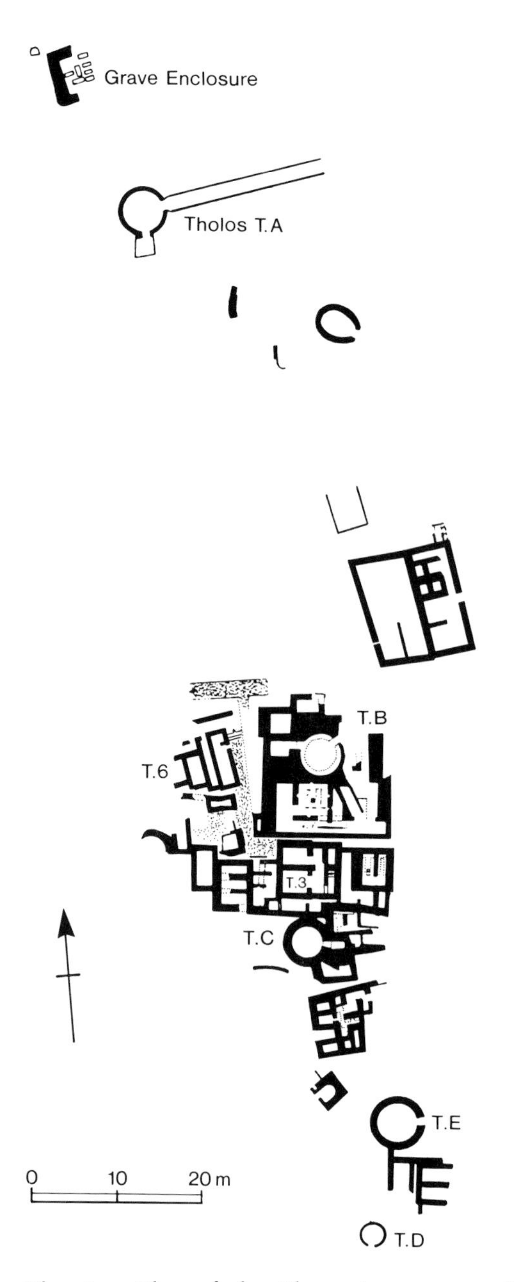

Fig. 6.5 Plan of the Phourni cemetery, Arkhanes. Courtesy of Prof. J.A. Sakellarakis.

A more relevant consideration may be that the circular tombs and 'house tombs' must have required more labour to build than a single pair of parents and their children could supply; at least a group of adult siblings, if not several households, related or not, must be postulated, which would suggest communal use, unless relatives or neighbours cooperated to build tombs which only one household would use. In some cases, as in those of Mochlos just mentioned, tombs can be so large and elaborate as to suggest that they were intended for an elite group; the variety of lesser tombs in the same cemetery suggests gradations of rank, though the relatively insignificant T. XIX was as rich as the greatest complexes. In general, both 'house tombs' and circular tombs vary widely in their size and elaboration and the quality of grave-goods, and those which contained valuable goods like gold ornaments, daggers or seals, have produced far too few for it to be likely that such goods were buried with all adults of one sex, let alone both; thus, there may have been recognised differences of status among the individuals of lineages using a particular tomb. Overall, they may represent a social stratum ranking higher than the users of the caves, rock shelters and the like, but this cannot be taken for granted, since such burial places can also contain fine pottery and items like seals and stone vases. Overall, much basic analysis remains to be done in this field.

The 'house tombs', as their name suggests, often resemble a house in plan, consisting of variously grouped rectilinear 'rooms' (cf. Figs 6.4, 6.5), and were constructed in much the same manner, though having much more substantial stone foundations for their walls and evidence for wooden doors. The more elaborate include architectural features that can be paralleled in major buildings, such as corridors, internal pillars, even in one or two cases an upper storey and painted plaster on some walls. But the circular tombs cannot be convincingly related to any form of building in Crete or elsewhere, and their origin remains rather mysterious. Their nearest parallels are an EM I tomb at Krasi which seems transitional to the standard type (Branigan 1970b: 143–5), an even simpler tomb recently reported from Nea Roumata (Catling 1982: 59), and the Ayia Photia rock-cut tombs, which began in EM I and share with the circular tombs a chamber, often roughly round, an antechamber, and the use of a large slab to close the entrance, in front of which there is often paving, as in some circular tombs. But none of these tombs held very many burials (Nea Roumata only one), their sources are equally unclear, since they are apparently earlier than the rather rare Cycladic types with which they have been linked, and are all found well outside the southern region in which the circular tombs are concentrated, although T. E at Arkhanes is as early as many of these (dated EM II in Sakellarakis 1991: 126). It seems best to consider all these local developments whose inspiration is still unclear.

Since none has survived intact, it remains unclear precisely what the circular tombs looked like. That they were largely built in stone and that their walls were corbelled inwards up to quite a height seems beyond dispute, but the arguments against the largest having full stone vaults is strong (see most recently Cavanagh and Laxton 1981: 131–2 in addition to Branigan 1970b, Ch. 3); but this may have been a feature of smaller tombs (cf. Blackman and Branigan 1982: 44–5 on Ayia Kyriaki). The largest examples may have been closed at the top with a roof of light timbers supporting brush or reeds (as perhaps at Kamilari T. 1), or with mud-brick. They are rarely particularly accomplished in style, although often care was taken to use heavy blocks in the lower courses, to support the weight, and sometimes walls were thickened or buttressed and sunk slightly into the ground for the purpose; always, it seems, the original chamber and antechamber were founded on rock. Doorways often but not always faced in an eastward direction and were low, under 1 m, in the earlier examples, although raised to human height or more in some later ones. An antechamber before the entrance seems a common if not standard feature, plausibly interpreted by Branigan as for the laying out of the newly dead before the burial rite. In several cases, further groups of rooms were built onto the eastern side, either at an early stage in the tomb's history or, more frequently, later. These rooms often bear some resemblance to the more complex 'house tombs', but this may be fortuitous, for it does not seem that their primary purpose was to hold the remains of burials and their goods (although ultimately many were used in this way), but rather to provide space for the performance of rituals once the tomb itself had become congested. congested.

The nature of such rituals can be at least tentatively suggested. There are good indications that in both circular tombs and 'house tombs' the newly dead was placed in a contracted position, frequently with the head to the east, accompanied by grave goods. Most often these consisted of pottery, much of which may have been used during the funeral ceremony, but frequently some form of personal adornment, stone vessels, weapons or implements, and more rarely items that may symbolise rank or authority such as gold ornaments and seals of various materials were provided. Figurines and other items of plausibly ritual purpose are quite common in the circular tombs, but rare in 'house tombs' and comparable structures, though they do occur at Arkhanes. There are other indications of local variations in custom: daggers were popular in the circular tombs but not elsewhere, seals are rare in eastern Crete, and gold ornaments have only been found in certain circular tombs, at Mochlos and occasionally at Arkhanes. After the body had decomposed, if not before, the remains would be removed to another part of the tomb, and ultimately skulls and principal bones might be stored, but the rest thrown out. There is good evidence, from the circular tombs especially, for periodic clearances and fires, which may have been ritual or fumigatory, and for the removal on these occasions, if not at each funeral, of more valuable offerings. The contrast between finds in the lower and upper layers of Platanos T. A, separated by an episode of clearance and burning, is particularly striking (Xanthoudides 1924: 89, Branigan 1970b: 109–10).

The quantities of often miniature vases and stone vessels found may, as noted above, have been largely used for various rituals. Branigan has suggested not only libation during the burial and perhaps food offering but a 'toasting' ritual, involving a few persons close to the dead, for which many of the cups and jugs, including those of stone, would have been used. There is no clear trace of this from 'house tombs', though the pottery from these has rarely been fully published, but the 'Pyrgos chalices' commonly found in the antechambers of the Ayia Photia tombs could reflect something similar. Arguments for more general religious ceremonies at both circular tombs and 'house tombs' have been put forward by Branigan and Soles, but discussion of this must be reserved to Chapter 8, although it may be noted here that very little if any of the evidence is clearly inconsistent with collective ceremonies in honour of the dead, comparable with those practised by the later Greeks.

There is no indication of any essential changes in customs during the Prepalatial and First Palace Periods, apart from the introduction of pithoi and larnakes to hold the dead and sometimes some grave-goods also. Towards the end of the First Palace Period the use of large, generally irregular rock-cut chambers became an established custom in and around Knossos (Fig. 6.8: 5), and grave-goods were placed with the dead much as before, although gold ornaments and ritual items seem to be lacking. In the same period a very late example of the circular tomb and a small 'house tomb' were constructed on Gypsades hill near Knossos; at first they were separate, later combined into a single complex (Soles 1973: 257–9). But by this time most of the known tombs of these types elsewhere seem to have gone out of use, although occasional finds of Second Palace Period type have been made in some, and some Mochlos tombs either continued in use, as Kamilari T. 1 certainly did, or were reused after a gap.

A structure of the First Palace Period that deserves special mention in this context is the Chrysolakkos complex at Mallia. Often considered a 'royal ossuary', its function and history have recently been subjected to critical re-examination (Pierpont 1987; cf. Baurain 1987, especially 69–71). As Pierpont, and Soles before him (1973: 132–9, 242–52, and especially 256) have made clear, this structure in fact consisted of two successive buildings, the later reusing part of the earlier, whose features are generally confused on published plans (the supposedly ritual features are particularly associated with the first phase). The evidence for funerary use is remarkably slight, and the best indication for a link with burial, apart from the presence of some human bones, is the structure's position in the middle of the Mallia cemetery area. It is also evident from Soles's analysis of artefacts (1973: 348–55 especially) that many types found at Chrysolakkos which have ritual associations occur in undoubted tomb-contexts, and many of its features can be paralleled in the more elaborate 'house tombs' such as Arkhanes T. B. It may well be that the complex was used for rituals connected with burial rather than as a final resting-place for the dead, but the last word has not yet been said.

Evidence for burials in the Second Palace Period is surprisingly thin apart from the chamber tombs around Knossos previously mentioned, which now include examples at Poros, particularly notable for their elaboration and wealth of goods (cf. Catling 1987: 53), and probably Episkopi Pediadhas (Kanta 1980: 63–4). The pithos cemeteries of Pachyammos and Sphoungaras continued in use and isolated examples have been reported elsewhere. As noted above, some Mochlos tombs and Kamilari T. 1 were still in use, and so were several others in the 'house tomb' tradition, Arkhanes Ts. B and 3 and the Pyrgos tomb, thought by Soles an unusually elaborate variant of the class (see Cadogan 1978: 71–4, Hankey 1988 for this tomb). Soles also assigns Ayia Triada T. 5, thought a 'house tomb', to this period (1973: 259–69), and analyses the 'Temple Tomb' at Knossos as a two-storeyed 'house tomb' with entrances on both levels and a rock-cut chamber at the further end (269–75). From its elaborate features this has also been supposed to be a 'royal tomb', though the finds belonging to this period are not very rich; but the suggestion that it is a shrine (Popham 1970: 74–5) does not explain the skeletal remains within the 'pillar crypt' and chamber. Evidence for funerary use is certainly more copious than at Chrysolakkos, but use of the term 'royal' begs questions that must be reserved for later discussion of the nature of Cretan society at this time.

In the wider zone of Minoan culture outside Crete, burial evidence has only been reported from Kythera so far, consisting of two isolated pithos burials (one MM IA) and a number of chamber tombs of the Second Palace Period. These are evidently related to the type found in central north Crete, but in several cases have more regularly shaped chambers, either single or forming the centre of a series of radiating sidechambers (Fig. 6.8: 7), both types hard to parallel in Crete, and, as in some of the later Cretan tombs, contain no evidence for the use of pithoi or larnakes to hold the dead. Quantities of pottery and occasionally other items were provided as grave-goods.

The Helladic region before the Mycenaean period

Evidence of burial customs from the mainland, almost all apparently relating to 'Lerna III' (EH II), is startlingly varied. Various forms of rock-cut chamber tomb have been reported increasingly widely, the most notable being those of the enormous cemetery at Manika in Euboea, which are finely cut in a variety of different chamber shapes (Fig. 6.8: 1) and contain from one to seven burials and a relative wealth of grave-goods, with some evidence of differentiation of goods according to gender and frequent cut marks on the bones, which may have been intended to facilitate placing the body in the desired contracted position. Other such tombs have been found, particularly in central Greece, but also elsewhere (Sapouna-Sakellaraki 1987: 256–9). Built tombs like those of Syros are found, along with cists, at Ayios Kosmas, usually used for several burials, and elsewhere in Attica, large pits that served as ossuaries at Perachora, and pit and cist burials are widely reported (e.g. Thebes, Tiryns, Elis, Ayios Stephanos).

Most remarkable of all are the graves of the R cemetery on Leukas, which include 'Lerna III' types among their goods as well as other items of roughly similar date and some that may be rather later but still in the Prepalatial Period. These were stone-filled circular platforms, which may have supported low tumuli and contained cist and jar burials, the latter sometimes within built chambers; similar burials were sometimes made in subsidiary attached structures. In many cases a burnt area containing bone and fine goods was associated with the platforms, which was interpreted by Dörpfeld, in his determination to relate the finds to Homeric descriptions, as evidence of partial cremation of the dead, but more probably represents part of the ritual of depositing goods. Many of the graves contained exceptionally rich collections of metal goods, including gold, and must represent the richer members of a prosperous community if not a dynastic group (Branigan 1975). But nothing similar has been found on the mainland, although these tombs have been claimed as the ancestors of the MH tumuli.

However, there are indications of comparably rich burials which would reflect the development of a ranked society. The monumental Ampheion grave at Thebes, a massive cist covered by a mound of mud-brick and set on top of a hill, is surely of this period (Hope Simpson and Dickinson 1979: 246; see Müller 1989: 18–19 for further details); it had been robbed, but among the surviving finds were some very elaborate gold beads with EB parallels. The gold sauceboat in the Louvre, the only certainly genuine precious vessel of Helladic type (above, p. 134) and the Thyreatis treasure of gold jewellery in Berlin should have come from graves, that might have rivalled those of Leukas. But most burial contexts have produced at best a few minor items of finery; even metal is rare except at Manika, where the range of goods and some of the types have Cycladic parallels. The remains suggest both primary and secondary burials and a general use of the contracted position, but no trace of the cut bones reported from Manika has been identified elsewhere (e.g. among the Ayios Kosmas material, carefully studied by Angel).

Hardly any of the cemeteries and graves mentioned are known to have lasted beyond 'Lerna III' (EH II): there is 'Lefkandi I' (EH IIIA) material from some Manika graves, and a few children's pit graves, at Lerna and Tiryns, fall in 'Lerna IV' (EH IIIB). But the MBA is very well represented by burials on the mainland, although they are scattered, and only from Lerna and Asine are there really large samples which appear to cover the bulk of the period (Blackburn 1970; Nordquist 1987, Ch. 8). The great majority of MH burials were made intramurally, in pits, cists, or, if small children, sometimes in pots or under pithos-fragments; they tend to be found in small groups, presumably associated with particular houses but sometimes in apparently derelict parts of the settlement. Normally burials were made singly, in a contracted position, without any fixed orientation and lacking detectable grave-goods (which would not rule out items of perishable materials like cloth and wood). When found grave-goods consist most often of pottery, sometimes also simple ornaments, very rarely anything else; they are not a common feature. The high proportion of infant and child burials, as exemplified at Lerna and Asine, suggests that, exceptionally, the complete membership of at least some families was being accorded similar burial rites, though it remains unclear whether the whole population was receiving this treatment. Careful study has suggested that some of the Lerna graves had markers; traces of such a custom have rarely been noticed elsewhere, but the general impression is that, like the provision of grave-goods and the reuse of a grave (hardly ever more than once), it was rare. Along with variations in the size and quality of graves and other details of burials, these features may represent distinctions in status being made between different individuals, but much more data are needed (see the thoughtful discussion in Nordquist 1987: 103–6).

Burial tumuli are also found; their incidence is still too sporadic for them to be considered a standard feature, and not all examples are well substantiated (for reasons outlined in Dickinson 1977: 51 I cannot accept that tumuli covered the Mycenae grave circles), but their numbers are increasing, although most have been reported from Messenia, Attica and the Argolid. Their origins are uncertain: there is no clear evidence for a link with the burial tumuli of the northern Balkans and central Europe, regions with which other contact is difficult to demonstrate, and the suggestion that they derive from the Leukas R graves also has difficulties (Dickinson 1983: 59). Only a few are clearly early; the majority belong to the mature and late phases of MH. The amount of labour required to build them suggests that they held the burial of persons of special status. Normally they contained several burials, the remains being often placed in big pithoi (Fig. 6.6) but also in pits or cists; sometimes relatively rich grave-goods such as metal jewellery were provided, and pithoi that might have served for libations and other possible ritual features are sometimes associated.

In the later stages of MH there are foreshadowings of Mycenaean practice at some sites, including the establishment of extramural cemeteries, the elaboration of graves and their more frequent reuse, and the provision of richer grave-goods, all features which may be associated with increasing differentiation of status and the emergence of an elite class. The Shaft Graves of Mycenae provide the best example of such developments, covering as they do a period of a century or more, but it is becoming increasingly clear that they are only the best-documented and richest example of a widespread phenomenon, which takes a variety of forms at different sites (Fig. 6.7; Dickinson 1989: 133–4).

The development and spread of Mycenaean burial customs

Mycenaean burial customs are at present attracting renewed attention, which may elucidate many features. Various types of tomb with a chamber were adopted, and in these and other types which survived from later MH, such as the Eleusis stone-built tombs which derive from the cist (Mylonas 1975–6), the

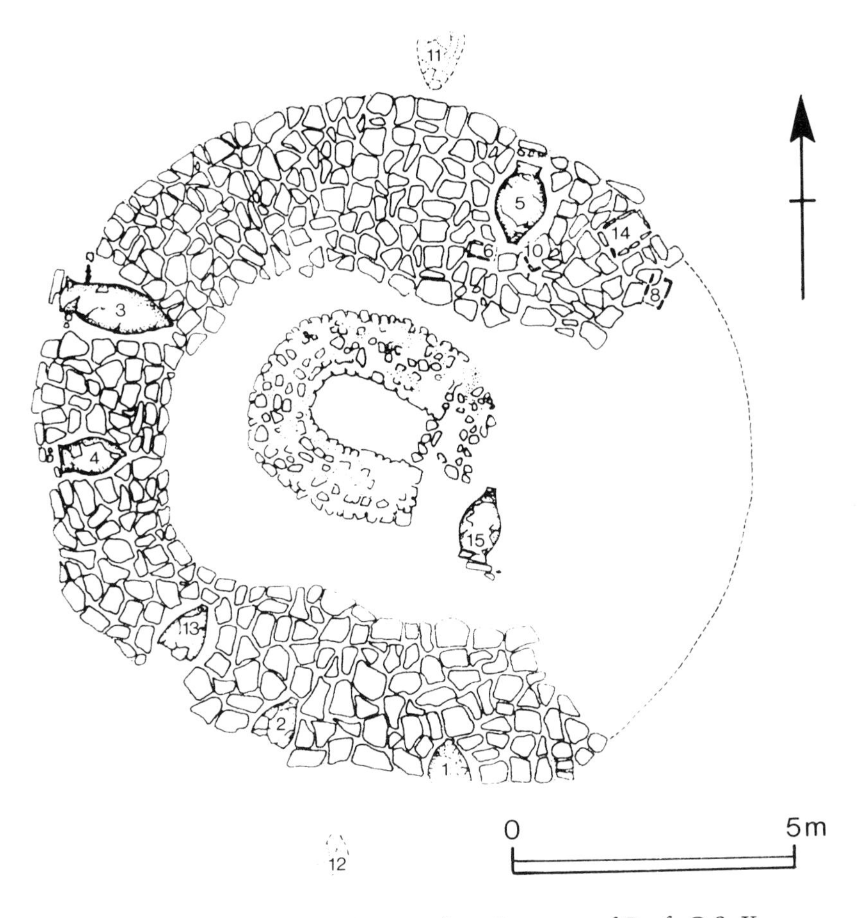

Fig. 6.6 Plan of the Pappoulia tumulus. Courtesy of Prof. G.S. Korres.

practice of using a tomb several times was normal. The types include the stone-built tholos (Fig. 6.10), reserved for elite burials, smaller stone-built tombs, of which many imitate the tholos in some degree, and rock-cut chamber tombs (Figs 6.8: 9; 6.9), some of which can be large and elaborate and contain as richly provided burials as many tholoi but which generally seem to hold burials of more ordinary status. All share the features of an open dromos and underground roofed chamber, very often linked by a narrow, roofed-over stomion.

The precise origin of the basic chamber tomb type is not clear, since only a few of the north Cretan and Kytheran chamber tombs are close in form (Fig. 6.8: 6, 8), but those of Kythera, like the mainland tombs, lack the pithos burials common in Crete, and there may well be a link. The careful cutting of many of the early tombs, such as Prosymna Ts. 25 and 26 and the tholos-shaped examples at Volimidia, argues that they are the work of specialists, who would surely have come from somewhere in the Aegean if not from Crete itself. The differences in

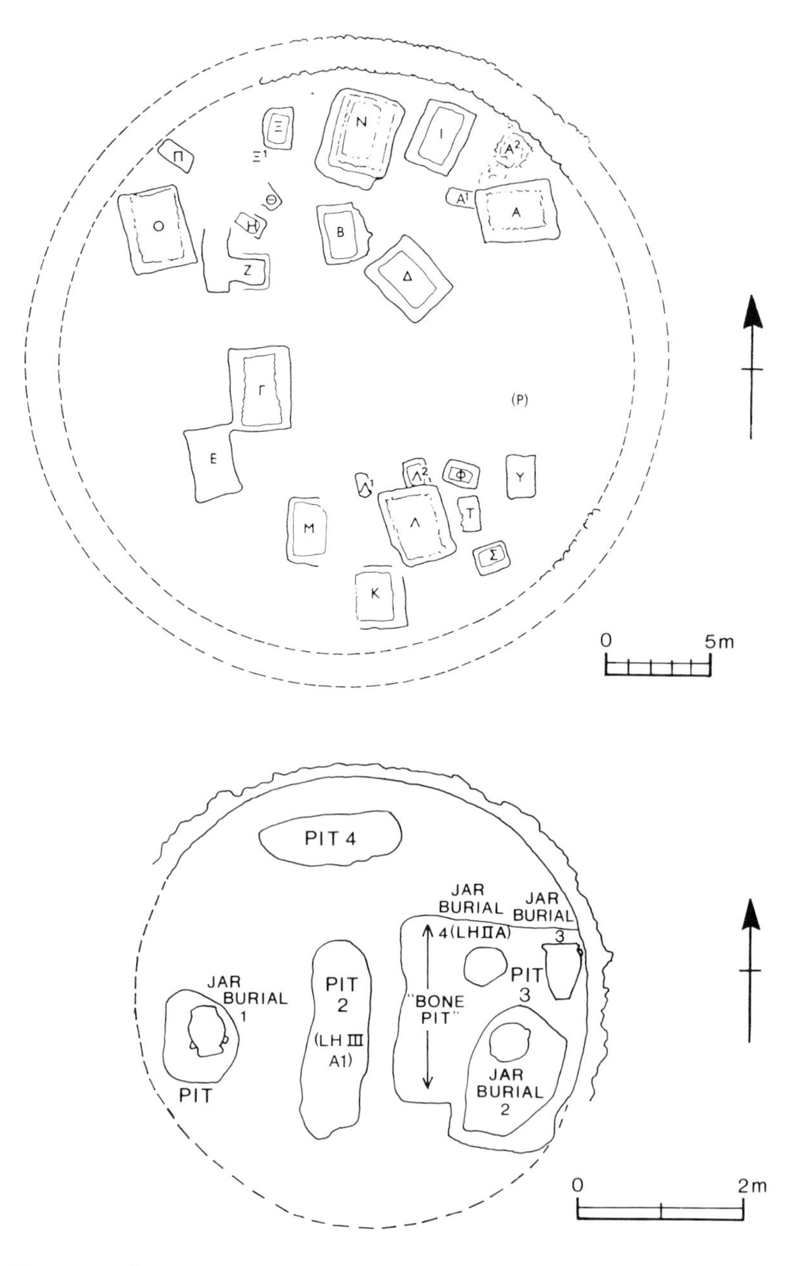

Fig. 6.7 Plans of Grave Circle B, Mycenae, and the Pylos 'Grave Circle'.

form would then reflect the different requirements of their users, which also show up in the patterns of use.

There is much to be said for the view that the tholos tomb is essentially a superior version of the chamber tomb, although the relative chronology of the earliest examples known at present suggests that if anything the tholos was

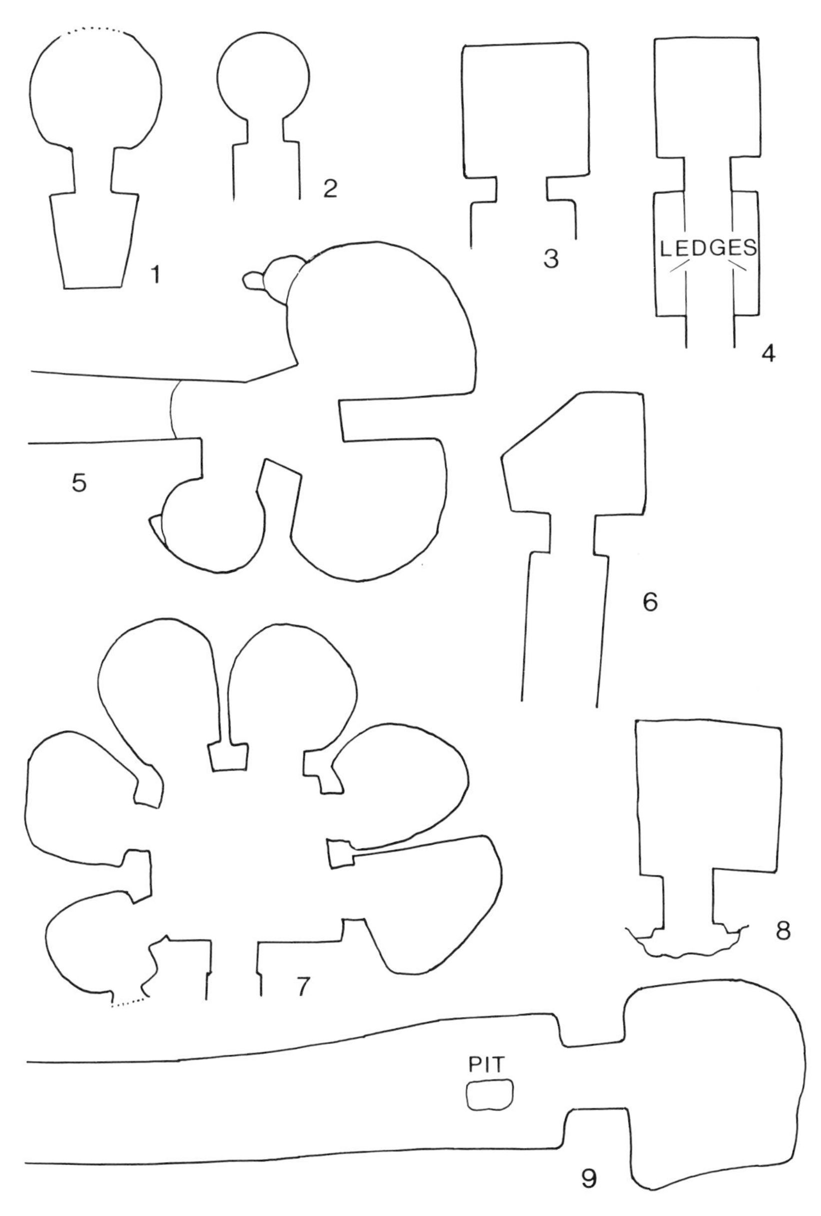

Fig. 6.8 Plans of various types of rock-cut chamber tomb.
1 Manika. 2–4 Phylakopi. 5, 6 Ts. V, I from Mavrospelio, Knossos. 7, 8 Ts. E, G, Kythera. 9 T. 530, Mycenae. Scale 1:10.

developed earlier; moreover, all indications point to Messenia as the region where it was developed, but chamber tombs are very rare here apart from the early Volimidia cemeteries. Certainly, the tholos tomb shares the basic features of the chamber tomb, and there are smaller stone-built tombs which look more like stone versions of chamber tomb shapes than anything else. The direct

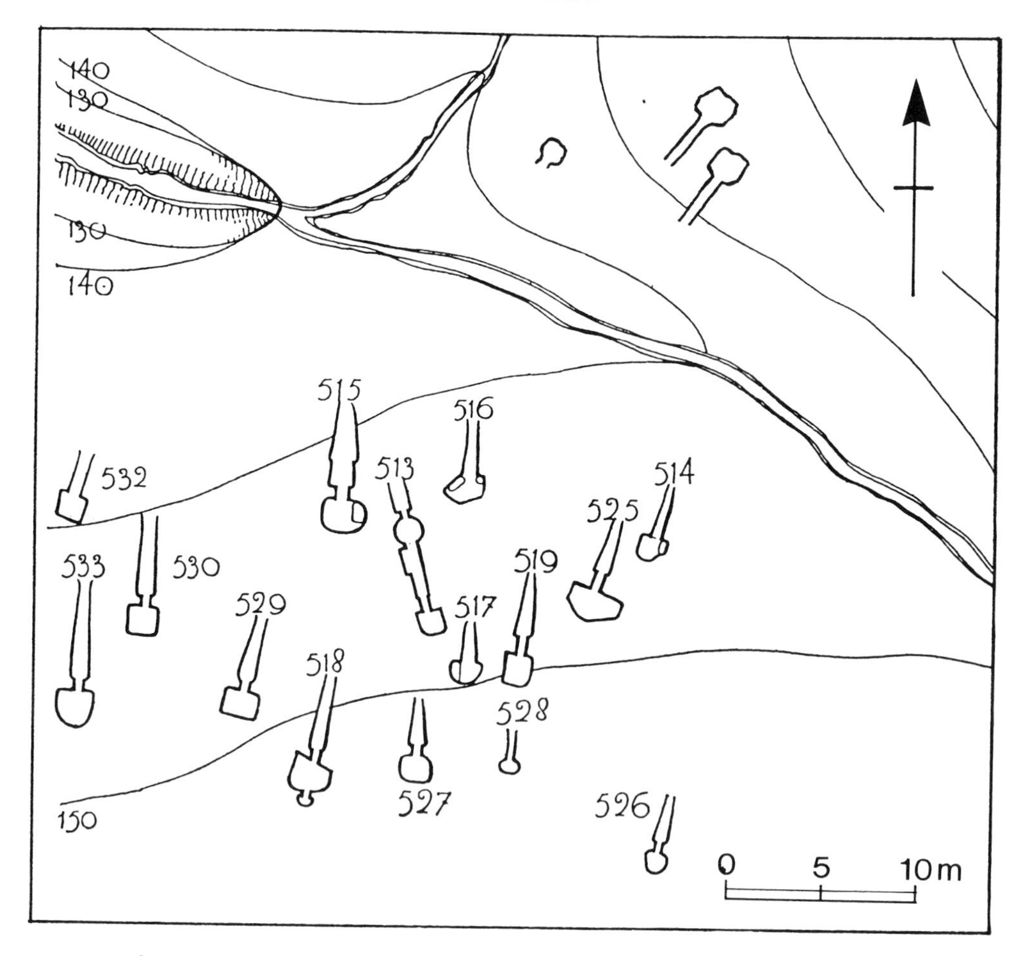

Fig. 6.9 Part of the Kalkani chamber tomb cemetery, Mycenae.

derivation of the tholos from the Cretan circular tombs, as argued by Branigan and other Minoan specialists, is fraught with difficulties: none of these can be proved to have been vaulted or built underground, none has a dromos, and most have attached complexes of chambers, which are not found in any early tholoi. The nearest parallel is Arkhanes T. B, which was apparently vaulted and had a dromos; but it also had a side-chamber, part of the original plan, and was at the centre of a monumental, partly two-storeyed structure (see Sakellarakis 1991: 90–6). To derive a widespread mainland form from such a unique structure is surely faulty methodology. Finally, although tholos tombs seem normally to have been used for a series of burials (at least 16–17 in Pylos Ts. III and IV), the patterns of use detectable in the Cretan circular tombs and the somewhat comparable Pyrgos tomb seem to be lacking.

If, then, the tholos is simply a superior chamber tomb, the vaulted roof may be a natural consequence of its combination of circular shape with a largely

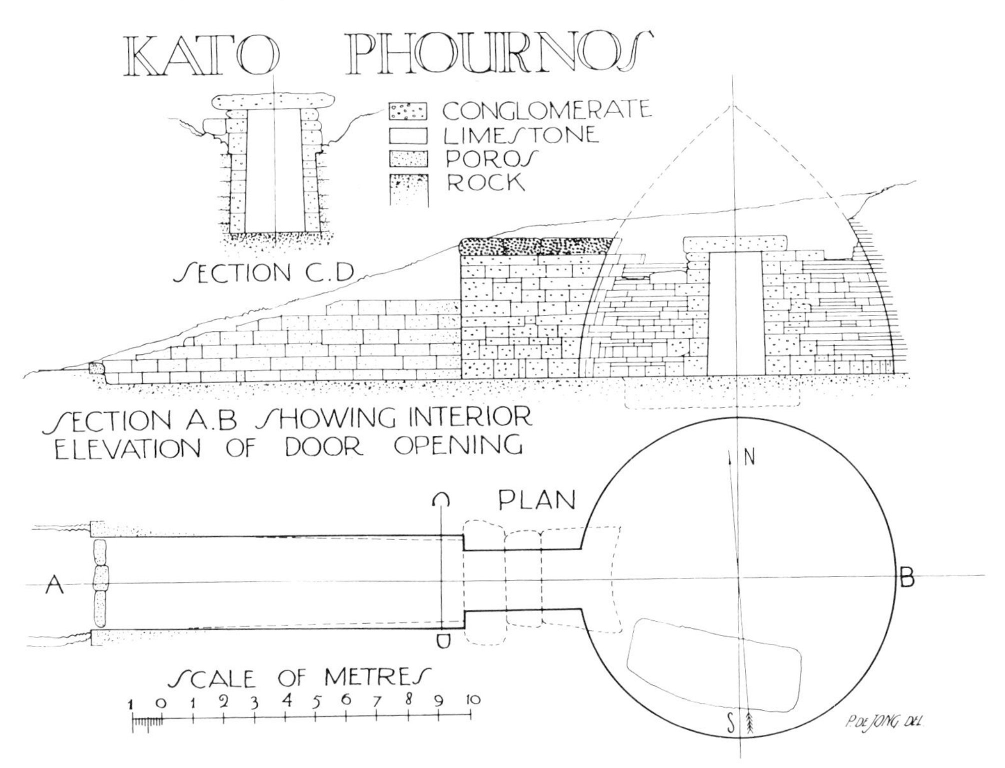

Fig. 6.10 Plan and section of the Kato Phournos tholos tomb, Mycenae. Courtesy of the Managing Committee of the British School at Athens.

underground structure (in most cases the roof seems to have projected to some extent), as the most functional form available; the covering mound would contain the structure's outward thrust. A circular shape may well have been chosen because the burial tumulus was normally circular in plan; there are indications of links between the two forms in Messenia (cf. Dickinson 1977: 60, 1984: 117, 118; Korres 1984: 147–9; the Pylos 'grave circle' (Fig. 6.7) seems too thin to have supported a tholos dome, but may represent an intermediate form). At all events, the tholos became the most characteristic form of 'princely' tomb in the Mycenaean world, although it has not been found at some major sites, such as Thebes. The majority of examples were built in the Second Palace Period and used for a few generations, though a minority, including some of the most magnificent (Pl. 6.1), were built or continued in use in the Third Palace Period, to which all examples found outside the mainland, mostly in Crete, also belong.

Apart from the tholos, chamber tomb and related stone-built tombs, other types of tomb can be found on the mainland, especially in the early Mycenaean period, when relatively many burials in pits and cists, and some in tumuli, can be identified. But these become fewer as the Mycenaean period develops, although local traditions persisted in some regions, notably Messenia, and even at

Pl. 6.1 The facade of the Treasury of Atreus, Mycenae, with restored half-columns flanking doorway. Courtesy of the Trustees of the British Museum.

individual sites like Eleusis; chamber tombs became increasingly common in many regions, and must have been used by a significant proportion of the population at some sites. Whatever the type of tomb, burial customs seem much the same; there is no warrant for assuming that cist-users are a poorer class, let alone that there were separate cemeteries of cists and pits for such a class. Indeed, some relatively rich burials could be placed in cists down to LH IIIA1 at least, as at Athens and Iolkos. The choice of tomb-type must reflect a combination of regional or family tradition, availability of skilled tomb constructors and comparable considerations.

The poorest identifiable burials in any kind of tomb were generally provided with one or more pots and sometimes other small items as grave-goods. In many tombs various forms of ornament, sealstones, metal items (including some weapons) and, in the LH III phases, figurines, are commonly found with one or more of the burials. The richest tombs are notable for gold jewellery and seal-rings, also, in the case of early male burials, weapons, quite often elaborately decorated; at Mycenae relatively many are rich in precious vessels and later in ivory work, especially inlays of various kinds, both of which only occur rarely in most other cemeteries (Dendra includes several comparably rich graves). Some chamber tombs have frescoed doorways, and one at Thebes, of exceptional size and provided with two dromoi, has a frescoed interior (Immerwahr 1990: 201),

Pl. 6.2 Larnax, Tanagra T. 6. Courtesy of Dr T.G. Spyropoulos.

but these are uncommon, as are the stone markers found in dromoi, reported particularly from some Rhodian tombs. The construction of benches, pits and built graves within chamber tombs and tholoi is quite common. These might be intended for primary burials or for those removed from the tomb floor, which might otherwise be transferred to a pit in the dromos, or simply swept into heaps, with some of their goods, at the side of the chamber. Such practices were recurrent in tombs that were used for long periods, and also common in cases where an old tomb was opened for reuse after a gap, presumably by a different group.

There is evidence for rites associated with the funeral, although none is as well documented as one would like. Normally a burial would be laid out on the tomb floor or placed drectly in a pit or built grave, with goods arranged about it. The occurrence of drinking vessel fragments in association with tombs, especially in dromoi, has often been interpreted as indicating some kind of libation or toasting ceremony to the dead. The scenes on the Tanagra larnakes (Pl. 6.2) suggest a procession to the grave, with ritual lamenting by female mourners, very much as on the monumental Athenian vases of the eighth century, and given the requirement for mourning by kinswomen in Classical Greek practice it seems likely that this was a very old and widely observed custom. But there are no traces of any general cult of the dead, and the position even in special cases like Grave Circle A at Mycenae remains unclear: the so-called 'altar' certainly seems from the stratigraphical data to be a feature of the original use of the circle in the sixteenth century, not a constant site of cult activity through into later Mycenaean times (Dickinson 1977: 47).

The major Mycenaean types of tomb and the burial customs associated with them can be seen to spread throughout the Aegean in the course of the LBA. The chamber tomb is particularly widespread; it was to become characteristic on Crete and Rhodes and occurs on many other Aegean islands, including Aegina, Naxos, Melos, Kos, Karpathos and Skyros, also at Miletus and Müsgebi in south-west Anatolia. Similar tombs built in stone, often resembling tholoi but small, occur more rarely, but have been found on Tenos (Catling 1981a: 37–8), Delos, Samos, at Colophon and, containing multiple cremations, at Panaztepe near Smyrna (Mitchell 1990: 95). In the neighbourhood of Knossos two other forms that have clear links with the mainland, particularly the Argolid, the shaft grave and pit-cave, are found mingled with chamber tombs in new cemeteries established in LM II–IIIA. The earliest mainland-style tholos in Crete, on the Kephala ridge near Knossos, most probably dates to LM II, and other vaulted stone tombs with a rectangular chamber at Isopata further north are not much later; the latter type was to become quite popular for high-status burials throughout LM III Crete, along with fewer true tholoi, and there were stone-built tombs of poorer quality such as Arkhanes T. D, which held a very rich LM IIIA2 female burial.

The Isopata group also includes rock-cut tombs of considerable size and unusual features, especially the 'Tomb of the Double Axes', whose central pier recalls a feature of some earlier north Cretan chamber tombs. These seem to have been used for the burial of a single high-ranking individual, like some on the mainland (especially Dendra T. 12), and in general the new types of tomb in Crete were not used for many burials. This may be because burials were very frequently placed in larnakes, thus limiting the space available, but it is also characteristic of the Dodecanesian chamber tombs, which normally held only one to three burials before the Postpalatial Period. Thus, the group or 'family' element in the use of chamber tombs was diluted in these regions, and they were not used for long periods. But the burial customs associated with these new types of tomb are very close to the Mycenaean, and many richly provided burials are known from Crete, especially from the Knossos region in LM II–IIIA.

The old types in Crete also survived or, like some circular tombs, were apparently reused for LM III larnax burials (Kanta 1980: 85, 87 (perhaps MM?), 95); Kamilari T. 1 and Arkhanes T. B were certainly in use in the early Third Palace Period. The famous Tomb of the Painted Sarcophagus at Ayia Triada, dated to LM IIIA, is considered a survival of the 'house tomb' tradition by Soles (1973: 275–7). The scenes on the sarcophagus are often believed to show funerary rites, including animal sacrifice (Pl. 8.3) and libation (Long 1974), but probably for a very special burial; actual evidence for animal sacrifice is found within the roughly contemporary Tholos T. A at Arkhanes, whose preserved female burial was extremely richly provided and clearly of high rank. The pithos burial tradition survived in some east Cretan sites, as at Olous (Kanta 1980: 129–32), where they often contained cremated remains. This is an unusually early occurrence of this rite, which also was used for some of the LH IIIA–B burials in chamber tombs at Müsgebi, and so may derive from native Anatolian practice. The unique 'grave enclosure' at Arkhanes, in which rock-cut pits within a rectilinear enclosure held larnax burials of apparently LM IIIA date, three marked with rough stone stelae, should not go unmentioned; the association of precious vessels and other fine goods, and indications of a ritual pit nearby, where funerary or post-funerary libations might have been made, suggest that these burials had special status (Sakellarakis 1991: 67–72).

In all the variations of Cretan practice the use of the larnax, now most often shaped like a footed rectangular chest, is prominent; several are decorated with remarkable scenes that surely have a ritual content, while others have decoration closer to that of vases, which may still have some symbolic reference (Watrous 1991). This preference for larnax-burial is a major distinguishing feature of LM III Crete, setting it off from the rest of the Aegean, although such larnakes have occasionally been found at some mainland sites, usually as isolated instances. Their frequent occurrence in two cemeteries near Tanagra in Boeotia (Pl. 6.2) remains an unexplained phenomenon (there is no other reason to suggest a Cretan element in the population, as proposed by Kanta 1980: 297).

To a great extent the Postpalatial Period in the Aegean saw the continuation of the older customs. Cremation became a minority rite at several centres, but normally such cremations are represented by pots containing ash, found alongside inhumations within tombs of the traditional types; only a tumulus recently found at Khania near Mycenae (Catling 1985: 21), which held pot-cremations exclusively, seems a new type of tomb, though its contents are purely Mycenaean. The rite is commonest on Aegean islands and coasts, as at Perati (where the ashes within pots often seem to belong to two or more persons, Musgrave 1990: 285), on Rhodes and on Crete, but isolated examples can occur in chamber tombs as far away as Elis (Agrapidochori) and Achaea (Kallithea). The chamber tomb remained the dominant form of tomb: examples are newly constructed at several sites, although generally smaller and less impressive than before, and older ones are reused, as happened to some tholos tombs. But no new tholoi were built in this period, although vaulted rectangular tombs continued to be constructed in Crete and in the Dark Age small tombs of tholos type can be found in Messenia and Thessaly. Variations of the old types, like the pits provided with miniature dromoi at Perati and the 'cave dormitories' of Kephallenia, which held many pits cut in the floor, all apparently used for repeated burials, can occur; tholos-shaped chamber tombs are found in Kephallenia also, as at Pellanes and Palaiokastro in the Peloponnese, continuing a rare tradition.

A notable feature of the period is the return of cist and pit graves to popularity. These are frequently found in new cemeteries, and most often contain single burials only. The significance of this has been widely debated, but both the move to a new site and abandonment of chamber tombs may have more to do with convenience than any deliberate abandonment of socially important customs or the arrival of new population groups (cf. Dickinson 1983: 66–7). But ultimately the old cemetery areas and old types of tomb were abandoned, even when, as at Argos, the site continued to be inhabited, and this is very likely to have significance for the history of the community concerned. Apart from the introduction of cremation, customs remained much as before, although the range and value of goods placed with the dead continually decreased and many types eventually disappeared. As in other fields, Crete preserved more of its BA traditions into the Dark Age than other areas of Greece, although group burial also continued to be practised in the small stone-built tombs of Thessaly and Messenia. But the association of particular types of tomb with 'ethnic' or tribal groups remains hazardous, and other explanations need to be sought for the changes. In Cyprus, however, the appearance of chamber tombs of Aegean type and of cremations, generally in tombs of this type and contained in amphorae, at the very end of the BA may plausibly be associated with the immigration of Greek-speakers, though, as earlier in the Dodecanese and Crete, they rarely contained more than two burials (Vandenabeele 1987).

Bibliography

Morris 1987, Ch. 2 provides a good discussion of modern approaches to interpretation of funerary material. Laffineur 1987 includes papers covering many aspects of Aegean burial customs. Other surveys considering the significance of practices and interrelationships of types are Doumas 1977, 1987 (EC); Branigan 1987b (practices in circular tombs); Pelon 1976 (circular tombs, MH tumuli, grave circles, and tholoi); Cavanagh and Laxton 1981, 1982 (the construction of tholoi); Cavanagh and Mee 1978, 1990, Mee and Cavanagh 1984, 1990 (aspects of MH and LH practice); Kilian-Dirlmeier 1985, 1986, 1988 (Minoan 'warrior graves' and links with Mycenaean practice).

Minoan For general discussion of tomb-types see Pini 1968, for Prepalatial cemeteries Soles 1988, for circular tombs Xanthoudides 1924 and Branigan 1970b, for 'house tombs' Soles 1973, 1992, for the Mallia cemeteries generally Baurain 1987. The Knossos cemetery evidence is summarised in Driessen and Macdonald 1984: 65–6, see also Hood and Smyth 1981: 11, 12–14; particularly significant cemetery publications are Evans 1905, Forsdyke 1927, Hood and de Jong 1952, Popham and Catling 1974. The fullest account of the Arkhanes cemetery is Sakellarakis 1991: 66–134. Kanta 1980 gives much data on LM III cemeteries, excluding Knossos; for those of the Arkhanes region see also Sapouna-Sakellaraki 1990: 77–83. On LM III larnakes see Watrous 1991.

Cycladic See the relevant sections in Barber 1987.

Helladic Hope Simpson and Dickinson 1979: 427–9 provides references for almost all tombs known to 1977; see also Sapouna-Sakellaraki 1987: 256–9 (EH rock-cut tombs), Sampson 1987 (the Manika cemetery), Pullen 1990 (EH intramural burials), Müller 1989 (tumuli), Dickinson 1983 (MH and LH tomb-types), Hägg and Nordquist 1990 (many papers, relating mainly to the Argolid; note in addition to others cited elsewhere Protonotariou-Deilaki 1990a, 1990b for valuable accounts of data).

On the Shaft Graves see Karo 1933 and Mylonas 1973 (the basic publications), Kilian-Dirlmeier 1986, Graziadio 1988, 1991, Laffineur 1989b, 1990, Dietz 1991. On the early Messenian material see especially Korres 1984. For tholos tombs with well-preserved contents see particularly Persson 1931 (Dendra), Marinatos, S. 1957 (Routsi T. 2), Demakopoulou 1990 (Kokla). The most extensive and useful publications of LH chamber tomb cemeteries concern Mycenae (Wace 1932, Xenaki-Sakellariou 1985), Prosymna (Blegen 1937), Dendra (Persson 1931, 1942, Åström 1977), and Perati (Iakovidis 1969, 1980).

CHAPTER 7

TRADE, EXCHANGE AND FOREIGN CONTACT

Introduction

Discussion of Aegean contacts with the outside world has until recently been dominated by three tendencies: to interpret all such evidence in terms of trade; to envisage trade as a commercial, wealth-creating activity, so that it may be used to explain the growth of wealth without elaboration; and to view the evidence from an Aegeocentric angle, in which the Aegean societies are treated as the prime movers in any trading activity or connection, even as controlling sea trade in much of the Mediterranean (Fig. 7.1).

It has become increasingly clear how simplistic and question-begging such approaches are. An enormous literature has grown up on the topic of ancient trade, or exchange, and many different types have been distinguished. There is not space to discuss them in detail here (for a helpful account see Harding 1984, Ch. 2), but it is worth drawing attention to the degree to which commodities of considerable value could move as 'gifts' or dowries for princesses between Near Eastern kings and other persons of high status, and also worth noting how goods might be exchanged for something intangible such as good government, protection, loyalty or, in the case of offerings to a god, benefits in the future. Some evidence cited in the context of 'trade' in the Aegean, such as the quantities of valuable materials in the Shaft Graves of Mycenae, might well be partly interpretable in such terms.

Theoretical models of ancient trade tend to take one of two positions, the formalist and the substantivist (usefully discussed by Earle in Knapp and Stech 1985, especially 106–7). Both can overstate their case, the formalists appearing to place an unrealistic emphasis on choices made by individuals and the profit motive, the substantivists to place the provision of goods and services entirely within a system of social obligations or, in the more advanced societies, of collection and redistribution systems organised by a central authority. Certainly, the latter view is too extreme, for even in the apparently state-dominated economy of Egypt there is evidence of private buying and selling by the second millennium, according to an agreed system of value in terms of metal, at least among the town-dwelling class and substantial farmers (Kemp 1989, Ch. 6), and elsewhere professional merchants are identifiable, some apparently acting for or closely tied to a palace, but others largely independent, like the 'family firms' of Assur and Kültepe. Admittedly, these are phenomena of fully urbanised

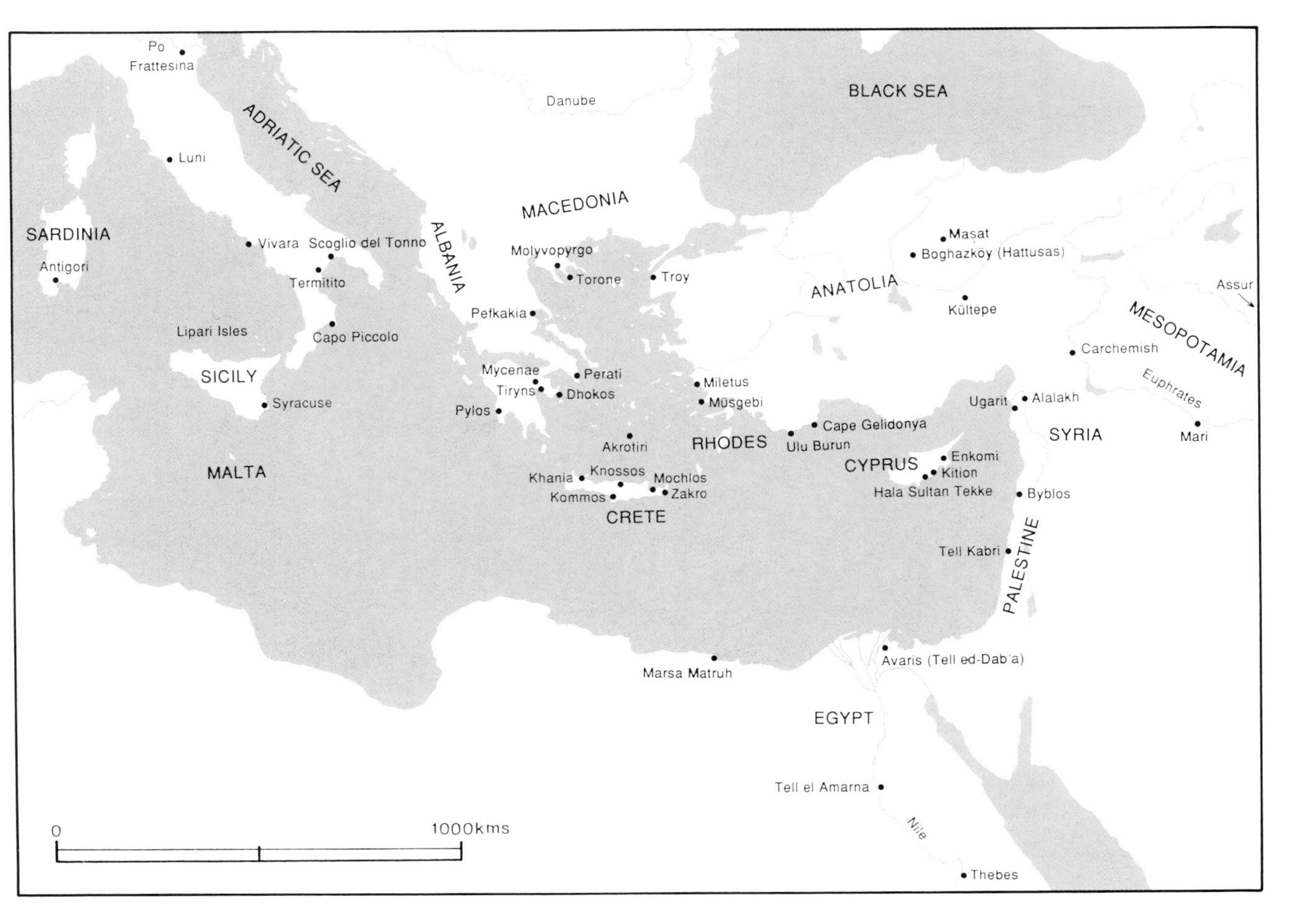

Fig. 7.1 The zone of Aegean overseas contacts in the Near East and Mediterranean.

societies; it remains questionable how far the motivation of spending to gain social prestige, let alone to make a commercial profit, would have operated in the Neolithic and EBA anywhere, let alone the Aegean.

It was suggested in Chapter 3 that networks of contacts between communities were part of the natural behaviour of human groups, in the Aegean as elsewhere, for purposes of obtaining marriage partners and useful materials, learning new skills and ideas, and providing some insurance against local failure of food supplies or other trouble. It would have been easier for such networks to develop once communities became settled, but it might also become more necessary to depend on them, to satisfy needs for commodities not available within a reasonable distance. But though raw materials might travel along the networks, it is very hard to believe that this reflects profit-seeking trade. Undoubtedly, obsidian was being collected from Melos and circulated around the Aegean long before there was any population on the island. It is in fact the earliest example of the widespread distribution of a useful commodity in the Aegean, and its usefulness would have given it intrinsic value, though it was by no means essential, as used to be assumed; good workable chert (generally called flint in older sources) is widely available (Blitzer reports a dozen sources within an hour's walk of Nichoria, in Keller and Rupp 1983: 112). In the course of time, exchanges of this and other commodities (cf. Runnels 1985 for millstones of andesite, probably from Aegina) might have taken on a more economic aspect, in that they were depended upon; but this could have remained concealed within an ostensibly social and perhaps ceremonial system of exchanges. As has already been shown in Chapter 3, such exchanges might take goods over remarkable distances by the Late Neolithic period, from Bulgaria to the central Aegean, but this example clearly involves prestige items that could have had little utilitarian value.

The expectations generated over the many centuries of the Neolithic period by the circulation of obsidian and other goods according to accepted social conventions would surely make it inconceivable that when Melos was finally settled its inhabitants should take it into their heads to announce that the obsidian was 'theirs', and would in future have to be 'bought'. Even if they had, their likely distribution in tiny settlements around the island would surely make it impossible to enforce such a claim. Rather, these social conventions might lead any group wishing to collect obsidian to feel obliged to conciliate the local population by bringing useful or valued items and materials, which they might need to do anyway to obtain supplies of food and water. Thus, a form of exchange could develop, from which the inhabitants of Melos might benefit, without necessarily bartering obsidian directly for other goods. Certainly, no evidence that might indicate systematic exploitation of the obsidian sources by the Melians can be identified; rather, the evidence suggests that it continued to be collected casually, sometimes by people who were unskilled in its working, even after a substantial settlement had become established at Phylakopi (Torrence 1986, not satisfactorily answered by Barber 1987: 118–19). By this time, in fact, the demand for obsidian was probably slackening; contrary to what is suggested by Barber, it is not as common on the mainland in MH contexts as earlier (cf. Nordquist 1987: 43, 64).

The development of metallurgy introduced a factor that might have influenced exchange in a more commercial direction, for a whole new range of specialised skills was needed to recognise and work metal sources and to manufacture metal items. These factors combined with metals' intrinsic attractiveness to put metal objects at or near the top of the hierarchy of prestige goods, in the Aegean as elsewhere, and thus to make them desirable to emerging elites. Indeed, the usefulness of bronze to the style of civilisation developing, not only for weapons, but for tools to be used in building monumental structures and substantial ships, meant that its constituent metals would come to be perceived not merely as desirable but very probably as necessary. One might therefore expect the elites of the Aegean societies to take active steps to ensure supplies, as of the precious metals used to display prestige, and thus to develop the concept of trading for them.

It remains a question how extensive these steps were. Organised production of trade goods or of commodity surpluses, and the extension of political control over trade routes or strategically placed points along them, have been suggested or implied in discussions, and the need for metals has been considered the mainspring of all trading activity, driving the leaders of the Aegean cultures to sponsor and control trading and to promote searches for new sources of supply. But there is an obvious danger here of falling into the Aegeocentric trap. There is a case for arguing that Aegean contacts with neighbouring regions in the later stages of the BA formed part of much broader patterns of exchange, which may have been directed from Near Eastern centres, and it remains questionable whether any actions leading to contact were actually initiated in the Aegean. This does not, of course, prove that the same was true earlier, but the question of the direction from which contact with the Near East was initiated is highly relevant. For in the Neolithic period Aegean connections with any part of the Near East beyond western Anatolia are hard to demonstrate, and one might well expect the more organised societies of the Near East to have taken the initiative in establishing contact through exploring westwards.

However the connection with the Near East was originally established, it endured and strengthened, which implies that it was felt to be of value on both sides. Assuming that metals and luxuries like ivory were the main Aegean requirements, one is bound to wonder what the Aegean had to offer that seemed valuable to the Near East. At present it does not seem that Aegean metals or stones made their way to the Near East in any quantity, nor is there evidence for the bulk movement of any artefact except pottery at any stage; indeed, pottery is generally found in such small quantities that it hardly seems likely to represent a significant trade item, though some forms were clearly prized. Assuming that exchange over these distances did involve goods in quantity, one must of necessity consider perishable commodities, which Near Eastern records show to have played a very considerable role in trade. These could include foodstuffs, liquids, textiles, hides and skins, timber, livestock and slaves, all of which the Aegean could potentially provide. It has been perceived as a difficulty that many regions in the Near East could have produced such commodities and so, it is assumed, would have no need to import; but this takes no account of factors such as relative quality and cost, perceived convenience, local specialities, and the prestige value attaching to the exotic. The trade between Assur and central Anatolia in the early second millennium, documented by the Kültepe texts (for a useful summary see Larsen 1976: 86–92), provides interesting evidence. Textiles were one of the two major commodities taken to Anatolia, including some of 'Akkadian', i.e. south Mesopotamian, origin; obviously they were thought superior to local textiles, but this superiority may have derived from their foreign source as much as from quality. In the case of the Aegean, it may be that from the Near Eastern standpoint local commodities were often low-priced and could therefore offer scope for profit to Near Eastern traders; some, such as textiles, might very well have commanded special prices for their quality (cf. Barber 1991, section 15).

The Assur–Anatolia trade is unusual in involving only a few commodities: tin and textiles went from Assur to be exchanged mainly for Anatolian silver, and though the Assyrian traders based in Anatolia dealt locally in copper and wool, these were hardly ever sent back to Assur. But more often, to judge from other Near Eastern documentary evidence, the contents of the wrecks at Dhokos off Hydra and Cape Gelidonya and Ulu Burun off south Anatolia (see below), and later Roman and mediaeval analogies from the Mediterranean (cf. Knapp 1990: 147–8; Braudel 1972: 107), traders handled a variety of commodities, and they may, as later, have planned to 'tramp' around a circuit, dealing in whatever was needed or available (cf. Cherry and Davis 1982: 339–40, citing Braudel). Certainly, the extraordinary range of commodities carried in the Ulu Burun ship fits Braudel's concept of 'travelling bazaars' very well: the quantities of copper, tin, glass and resin carried surely exceed what any single state of the Aegean or western Anatolia could require. If they were intended for a single destination, this would probably have been an 'emporium' site, the centre of supply for a whole region, and as such of a complicated network of collection and distribution involving many communities. The fact that metals and obsidian could reach quite remote sites, in the absence of other tangible signs of external links, is sufficient indication of the existence of such local networks, through which goods might feed into larger systems that might ultimately extend beyond the Aegean. In fact, one might expect much exchange to be carried out through short trips, involving small cargoes, as has been typical in the Aegean more recently (Braudel 1972: 109).

The main purpose of the following sections is to review the evidence; discussion of questions raised above may be postponed to Chapter 9.

The Prepalatial Period

The settlement of the Cyclades must surely have influenced the patterns of contact and exchange in the Aegean. Although, as already indicated, it seems unlikely that they were settled purely for motives of trade, an interest in metals might well have influenced both settlement and the development of exchange. Certainly, despite the small and scattered nature of their communities, the evidence for their influence in the Aegean, in the form of Cycladic artefacts and local imitation of Cycladic types, is impressive. Melian obsidian is found universally, often in great quantities at individual sites, and metal from Cycladic sources was certainly reaching Crete. An interpretation of this evidence as indicating 'colonies' has been discounted above (pp. 211–12); it is better interpreted in terms of exchange, in which the evidence of longboat representations has been thought significant, and the islanders have been seen as important actors (e.g. Renfrew 1967, 1972: 454–5, 472, and Runnels 1985: 42–3). The wide distribution of Cycladic items and influences is one of the major elements helping to create Renfrew's picture of an 'international spirit' in the Aegean of the middle EBA, although it also entails the recognition of Helladic, Minoan, north Aegean, Anatolian, Egyptian and ultimately Mesopotamian types or connections.

Not every element in this picture has stood up to closer examination. Broodbank has effectively cast doubt on the significance of the longboat, pointing out that most if not all representations can be associated with Syros only, and questioning its interpretation as a trading vessel (1989). Nor does the occurrence of Cycladic items and materials everywhere necessarily demonstrate solely Cycladic activity; after all, obsidian was being fetched from Melos long before there was any population in the Cyclades, and there is no reason to suppose that this stopped, or that supplies of metal or Cycladic items could not be fetched by expeditions from elsewhere. When Cycladic items do occur, moreover, it is not clear that they reflect 'trade', certainly not in the form of exchange of manufactured artefacts for food, as suggested by Runnels (1985). It is hard to believe that any communities could or would rely on producing goods to exchange for their basic food supply, or that there was sufficient demand within the Aegean to enable them to do so.

It is relevant, in this connection, to draw attention to the remarkable differences in the distribution of Cycladic types. Thus, 'frying pans' occur, mostly in local forms, quite widely in the Helladic region, but only two examples are known from Crete (Coleman 1985: 202), although other Cycladic pottery types occur here (Zapheiropoulou 1984). Cycladic figurines and their local imitations are quite rare in the Helladic region outside Attica and Euboea, but well distributed in central Crete, including the Mesara; however, they scarcely ccur in east Crete, being notably absent from the cemetery of Ayia Photia, whose Cycladic links are often stressed. Cycladic influence, equally, has been detected in the development of Cretan stone vessel manufacture; but comparable influence cannot be seen in the Helladic region, although Helladic metal types can nearly all be found a Cycladic parallel.

The whole picture of exchanges and influences in this period is marked by such peculiarities of distribution. Although there are many links in metal types, the different regions have strongly individual characters, not only in preferred forms but also in materials. Hippopotamus ivory and Egyptian stone vessels reached Crete (Krzyszkowska 1988: 228; Warren 1980: 493–4), but they are found no further into the Aegean. Only a handful of potential Minoan items have been found outside Crete, except at the probable 'colony' of Kastri on Kythera, and, equally, few Helladic items appear in Crete, where sauceboat fragments, whether Helladic or Cycladic, occur only at Knossos (where there is certain Cycladic material) and a few western sites (Rutter and Zerner 1984: 81; Wilson 1985: 358–9). This is the more remarkable, in that they are massively popular in both Helladic and Cycladic regions, and can occur as apparent 'exports' as far away as Servia and Troy (Jones 1986: 381–2, 409 n. 24).

It is not easy, then, to produce a coherent interpretation of material that may reflect several varieties of exchange. Occurrences of fine stone items like Cycladic figurines and vessels seem more likely to reflect ceremonial exchanges than anything commercial; but the quantities of fine 'Urfirnis' pottery found in the Cyclades may, if they are actually of mainland manufacture, represent a precursor of the considerable trade in pottery detectable in the MBA in the same region. In this connection, the evidence of the Dhokos wreck, which is reported to contain over a thousand pots, including many fine ware types but also storage vessels (Koutsouflakis 1990: 35–6), will prove very interesting; that the same wreck also contained many andesite millstones is a strong argument that this is a local trading vessel, dealing in a variety of commodities, which might include agricultural produce carried in container vessels. But exchange, whether it involved useful materials like metals and obsidian or not, still seems rather haphazard, disorganised and small-scale, probably linking individual communities rather than whole regions.

However, exchange was evidently increasing in scale and importance, and in the case of Crete the range of connections was extending beyond Anatolia to the Near East. Here one might suspect Near Eastern enterprise, for which the motivation remains obscure, unless some Aegean silver was being channelled eastwards (cf. Stos-Gale in Hägg and Marinatos 1984: 87; but this should relate to a later period). The argument for Aegean trading links to the west, via Leukas, deserves mention, but depends to a large extent on questionable assumptions about the sources of Aegean metal and a commercial interpretation of the occurrences of items like Cycladic figurines in Elis and the bossed bone plaques found at Troy, Lerna and sites in the central Mediterranean, which need re-examination (Branigan 1975: 41–2; note Rutter and Zerner 1984: 76–7 n. 10, against the Minoan attribution of Leukas items). Certainly, there is nothing to indicate any such connection later, until the Second Palace Period; the Leukas R cemetery is very unlikely to have lasted beyond the Prepalatial Period.

Cretan contact with the Near East probably continued unbroken from this time, but the contexts for Helladic and Cycladic items in Crete are EM IIA, when clear, and only the continued appearance of obsidian demonstrates Cretan contact with the Aegean for some time thereafter. The 'Lefkandi I' types of pottery, so widespread further north, make no appearance in Crete, and the apparent collapse of traditional Cycladic society may have broken many connections, including that with Leukas. Cycladic sources of metal were superseded by Laurion (perhaps because known ore sources had petered out?), but this development is not closely dated and it is not clear that it has any connection with the Cycladic collapse, plausible though this might seem. The continuing existence of an exchange system in the central and northern Aegean is demonstrable particularly in the pottery from Pefkakia, where Helladic and 'Trojan' types are reported, and Lerna IV, where there is evidence for contacts with the Corinthia, Euboea, Aegina, the northeast Aegean and probably the Cyclades (Rutter 1988: 86).

The First Palace Period

Previous assessments of Aegean exchange in the earlier MBA (e.g. Rutter and Zerner 1984: 77–9) are bound to be affected by the proposed reclassification of what has been termed MM IA. In fact, much of the relevant material, including contexts at Knossos in which imported Helladic and Cycladic pieces have been found (MacGillivray 1984b: 73), should be placed later, and while much pottery at Lerna still seems classifiable as MM IA, it probably derives from Kythera and western Crete. Contact between the most important Cretan regions and the rest of the Aegean may thus have been limited and indirect for the first period of the MBA, and only have begun to expand after the First Palaces had been established.

But there is much evidence for exchange patterns involving the Cyclades, Aegina and the central parts of the mainland throughout the MBA. Pottery is the main indicator of these, but it is extremely likely that materials such as metals and obsidian were distributed through them, and that the pottery often served as containers for produce of some kind. The patterns are to some extent independent of each other, but meet at certain settlements that appear to be key points, 'emporium' sites that may have acted as conduits for commodities from wide areas. Kolonna on Aegina is pre-eminent among these; as well as millstones of probably Aeginetan andesite, fine vases and cooking pots occur in increasing quantities at central mainland sites; they were clearly an article of trade in their own right, probably because of their quality, for even the cooking pots were wheelmade. In fact, the Kolonna township on Aegina may have played a dominant role in contacts between the central mainland and the Aegean, and Aeginetan traders may have distributed the probably Cycladic 'duck vases' and other vessels found at central mainland sites (Rutter 1985), and perhaps many of the so-called 'Balkan' flasks first identified at Lerna, if these are Cycladic, as Zerner believes (1978: 180–6; some analytical evidence suggests more than one origin, Mee in Jones 1986: 424).

But the characteristic Aeginetan wares are hardly reported outside this region, except from Ayia Irini. Cycladic centres may have developed their own contacts with the mainland; although Cycladic material is only reported from a few mainland sites, Grey Minyan of the mature phases was very popular in the Cyclades. The distribution of 'duck vases' and various types of pyxis and other container which seem likely to be Cycladic in origin (Rutter 1985) introduces further complications, since these appear not only in the Cyclades, Aegina and at eastern mainland sites, but also, in the case of 'duck vases', on Samos, Rhodes, Kalymnos and at Troy; they are even locally produced in Anatolia and Cyprus, but totally absent so far from Crete. It now appears that the very Cycladic-looking incised pyxides and lids found in some quantity at Knossos and occasionally elsewhere in Crete are of local manufacture, so at best inspired by Cycladic forms (MacGillivray *et al.* 1988). Rutter's suggestion that these containers held specialised products seems very plausible; different forms may even have been used to differentiate between products or producing centres, but their sources and date-range have yet to be firmly defined. Many examples should date within the late Prepalatial Period, but it is worth stressing that a group found at Eutresis belong to a mature MH context at earliest, and may well be later. Evidence for internal exchanges in the Cyclades is not so easy to find because of the rarity of good sites, but the fine Cycladic White ware, of which most was probably produced on Melos, was very popular within the Cyclades, though only occurring rarely elsewhere, as at Lerna and Knossos.

A largely separate web of connections may have centred on Lerna, where large quantities of Minoan and Minoanising pottery have been found that suggest a special link with Kythera. This pottery is identical in fabric not only to the Minoanising ware of Ayios Stephanos, but to the 'lustrous painted' ware of apparently mainland style, first identified at Lerna but now known at many east Peloponnesian sites; they may well have been manufactured in the same workshop, somewhere in the east Peloponnese, but the possibility of two workshops, at Lerna and Ayios Stephanos, does not seem ruled out. The rarity of Minoanising pottery at other sites, even as close to Lerna as Asine (Nordquist 1987: 50), suggests that this was a highly directional trade, which did not involve the movement of pottery beyond the mainland, to judge from the material from Kythera; it may have involved indirect links with central and eastern Crete, since pots of this origin reached Lerna, but they may date later than the early MBA.

The existence of local networks linking the central mainland to remoter parts is indicated by the distribution of 'Balkan' flasks, which reached Ayios Stephanos and Kirrha, and of Grey Minyan, which has been rarely reported from west Peloponnesian sites and more copiously from central Thessaly (where the source may be workshops no further away than Iolkos or Pefkakia). Presumably materials like metals and obsidian were spread through such contacts. A single central Greek Matt-Painted jug fragment has been identified in Lerna VA material, of the same ware as one from Eutresis (Zerner 1978: 178–9). Grey Minyan may have been spread in the Cyclades by the activity of ships originating from mainland ports, which, to judge from the appearance of the characteristic Minyan ring-stemmed goblet shape at Molyvopyrgo and Troy, extended to the north Aegean, where there is little trace of Cycladic or Minoan activity (see now French 1990: 53 for 'imported Minyan' at Torone); but the source(s) of this Minyan have not been precisely located within the Minyan-producing area.

Cretan interest in other parts of the Aegean may be detected in the occurrence of First Palace Period pottery and, rarely, of other Minoan artefacts at Cycladic and Helladic sites; the distribution extends as far as coastal Thessaly and is balanced by the occurrence of Cycladic pottery at Knossos (MacGillivray 1984b: 73–4). While it would be a mistake to underrate this material, it is not conspicuous enough to suggest that Crete played a very strong role in Aegean exchange. Although it seems likely that Laurion was the main if not the only source of Crete's silver, lead and copper, there is no indication that the re-foundation of Ayia Irini, surely associated with the exploitation of the Laurion ores, was a Cretan enterprise, for Minoan pottery is not conspicuous there in the first stages, compared with Melian and Helladic wares, although it steadily increased in quantity later; thus, the metals may have passed through the hands of Cycladic middlemen, perhaps to be picked up at Akrotiri.

The main direction of Minoan interests at this time may be indicated by the expansion of the Minoan culture-sphere to take in the Dodecanese and the adjacent Anatolian coast. This process was already taking place in the First Palace Period (Benzi 1984; Laviosa 1984), and may plausibly be linked with increasing exchange with the civilisations of the Near East, though it could also reflect a 'forward policy' designed to check possible aggression from Anatolia (cf. Melas 1988a: 59). As in the Prepalatial Period, only Crete has produced examples of Near Eastern artefacts, and only Minoan artefacts have been clearly identified in Near Eastern regions. One of the most remarkable early finds in Crete is an Early Cypriot III jar-fragment from Knossos (Catling and MacGillivray 1983; but the context may be as late as MM IIA, Momigliano 1991: 166); but certifiably Near Eastern finds such as pottery, Egyptian scarabs and stone vessels, and Syrian daggers are rare. The total of Minoan artefacts, mainly pots of Kamares ware, from Near Eastern sources is likewise unimpressive, although Kamares was popular enough in Egypt to be imitated.

But here it is possible to call on documentary evidence to fill out the picture somewhat. Documents of the eighteenth century BC from Mari mention goods from 'Kaptara', apparently 'gifts' to the king from the king of Ugarit, where a group of Kaptaran merchants was based (most recently, Heltzer 1989, especially 13–14). The context is the distribution of tin, which seems to have come through Mari from further east, and was distributed both as 'gifts' and commercially in a wide region of Syria and upper Mesopotamia. Assuming the equation Kaptara (also transliterated Caphtor) = Crete is correct, this not only provides an important context for Minoan activity in the Near East but a whole list of Minoan exports, including weapons, textiles, pottery and even sandals. That these were thought worth sending as 'gifts' probably indicates their superior quality (one weapon was certainly very ornate). From the viewpoint of Mari, the Kaptarans at Ugarit may have seemed marginal figures and their homeland remote; no gifts were sent to its rulers. But the Kaptarans were clearly well-established at Ugarit and could act without any intermediary other than an interpreter.

Gold, ivory and other materials, like the exotic stones occasionally used for beads, seals and inlays (cf. Younger 1979b, 1989: 54 on their sources), may also have been acquired at Ugarit or elsewhere in the Near East, for example from Egypt. But there is no reason to believe that copper was being acquired from Cyprus; indeed, it is now thought that copper was not being produced there on a large scale before the seventeenth century, a view that may be reinforced by the rarity of references to Alasiya, generally taken to be Cyprus, in the Mari documents. The rarity of Minoan items in Cyprus may then reflect the reality, of casual exchanges in a trade whose focus was Ugarit.

If the Mari documents give a representative picture, it would seem that on the Minoan side exchange involved mostly small quantities of potentially high-value items, which might reflect the scale of the Minoan need for tin and other valuable materials in this period. But it must be emphasised that contacts may have been considerably more varied and intense than the evidence for exchange alone would suggest. The indications of Near Eastern influences in many fields of Minoan culture in this period can be balanced by that for the imitation of Kamares pottery in Egypt and for the decoration of important buildings with frescoes showing surely Minoan themes, at Avaris (Tell ed-Dabʿa, Pl. 7.1) and other Near Eastern sites (above, Chapter 5, p. 164), though their dating relative to the Minoan sequence will be disputed (cf. Niemeier 1991, linking with LM IA).

The Second Palace Period

The evidence for exchange in this period is dominated by four factors: the immense growth in Minoan influence of all sorts throughout the Aegean; the involvement of newly wealthy mainland centres in exchange on a considerable scale; the increasing signs of Near Eastern activity in the Aegean; and the evidence for contacts with Europe. These factors were surely interconnected: the new wealth of the mainland should not be considered in isolation from the evidence for greater wealth in the Aegean as a whole, and this may well be linked to the Near Eastern interest. Cause and effect are particularly difficult to sort out in this field, but it is hard to believe that the growth in wealth and in the intensity of exchange were not interconnected. The widespread occurrence of lead weights, which can even appear in early Mycenaean princely tombs with scale-pans, and at Vapheio with a set of balances (Dickinson 1977: 84), may indicate the importance attributed to exchange, which such evidence would suggest to be of a commercial type; but as noted above precious items and materials could sometimes have reached their findspots as some kind of diplomatic gift. Wiener has argued that the driving force behind the 'Minoan thalassocracy' was the need to safeguard the trade-routes upon which Crete had to rely for supplies of the constituents of bronze; in his view 'the security, economy, and hierarchy of Crete depended significantly on bronze' (1990: 146), and although his arguments are not conclusive they deserve to be taken seriously.

Here the primary purpose is to summarise the evidence and to try to identify its basic patterns. As before, a considerable amount of pottery moved about the Aegean. In the latest stages of the MBA Cycladic wares continued to be quite widely distributed: they are conspicuous at Knossos, where Melian, Theran and possibly Naxian jugs and jars have been identified (MacGillivray 1984a), while others occur in MM III contexts at Pseira and Kommos, and were influential enough in the eastern mainland for shapes and motifs to be imitated in late MH fine wares although few actual imports have been identified outside Grave Circle B (see Nordquist 1987: 50 for Keian ware at Asine). Aeginetan wares also continue to occur widely in the eastern mainland, and Minyan in the Cyclades; but they are less common than before at Ayia Irini, while Minoan fine wares are becoming increasingly common and types of Minoan domestic pottery are beginning to be adopted (Davis 1986: 5–6, 105–6).

A Minoanisation of the local pottery industries can in differing degrees be detected in the Cycladic towns and on the mainland, where, as with Cycladic influence, it is first identifiable in the imitation of shapes and motifs (actual imports are surprisingly hard to identify), then in the more thorough-going Minoanisation represented by the LH I style. Not only this style, but other decorated wares of mainland origin, especially 'Mainland Polychrome', which is evidently not Peloponnesian (Jones 1986: 433), began to be distributed both within the mainland and beyond: they are notable particularly in the Cycladic towns, but examples reached the east Aegean and probably Troy, where LH IIA certainly appears (Dickinson 1986b: 271–2, to which add French 1990: 53 for LH I–II at Torone). Minoan-style pottery of the east Aegean and a little Giali obsidian reached Ayia Irini (Davis *et al.* 1983). But very little pottery from other Aegean sources has been reported in Cretan contexts until LM IB, when LH IIA vases are occasionally found; in contrast, LM IA and IB fine pottery of Cretan

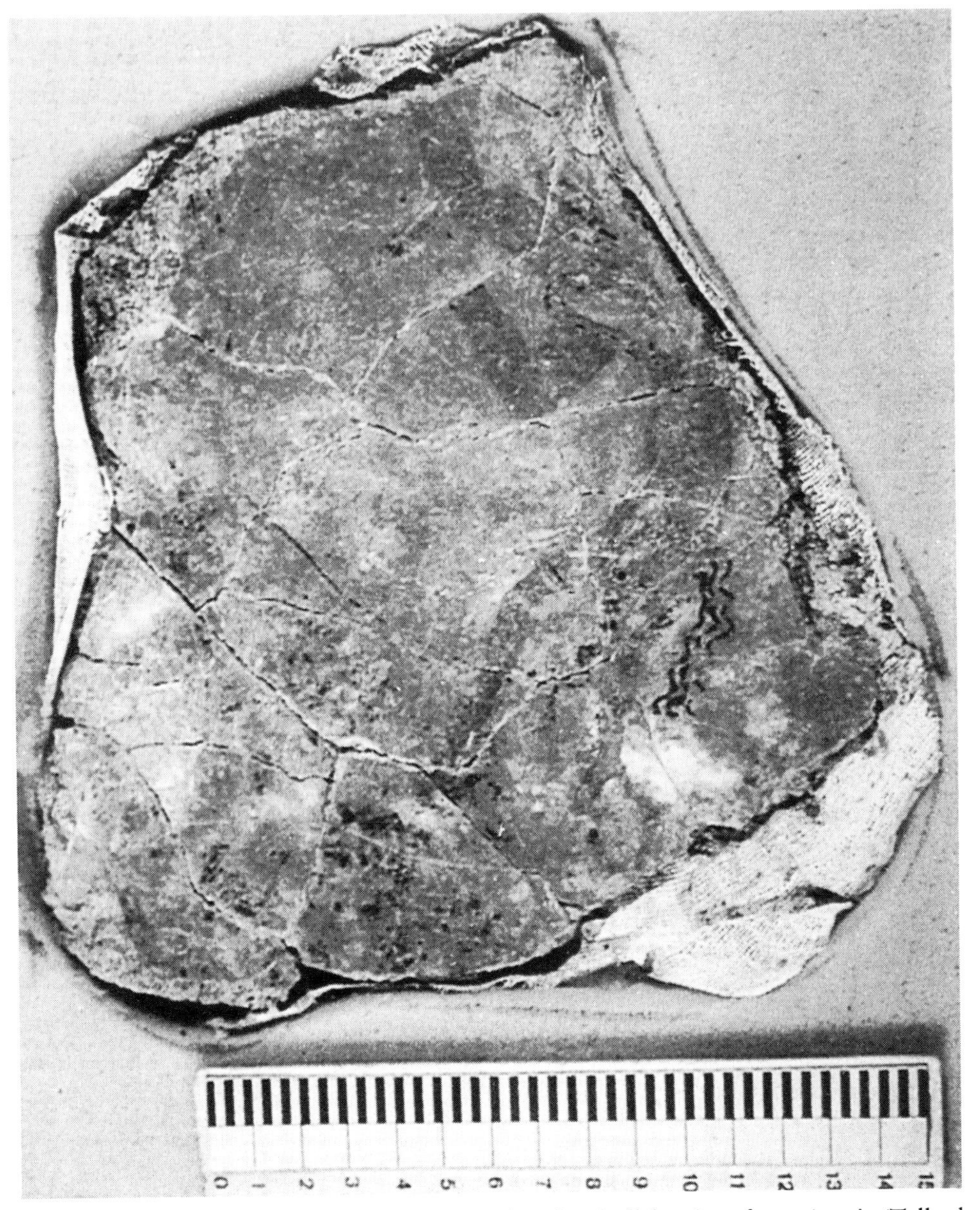

Pl. 7.1 Miniature fresco fragment showing bull-leaping, from Avaris (Tell ed-Dab'a), with tracing to show figures. Courtesy of Prof. M. Bietak, the Austrian Archaeological Institute, and the Egypt Exploration Society.

origin has frequently been identified at all Aegean island sites, and although certifiable imports are curiously rare on the mainland the fine LM IB styles were imitated and adapted.

The popularity of Minoan pottery and local production of Minoan types is of course only one facet of a general Minoanisation of the Aegean in this period.

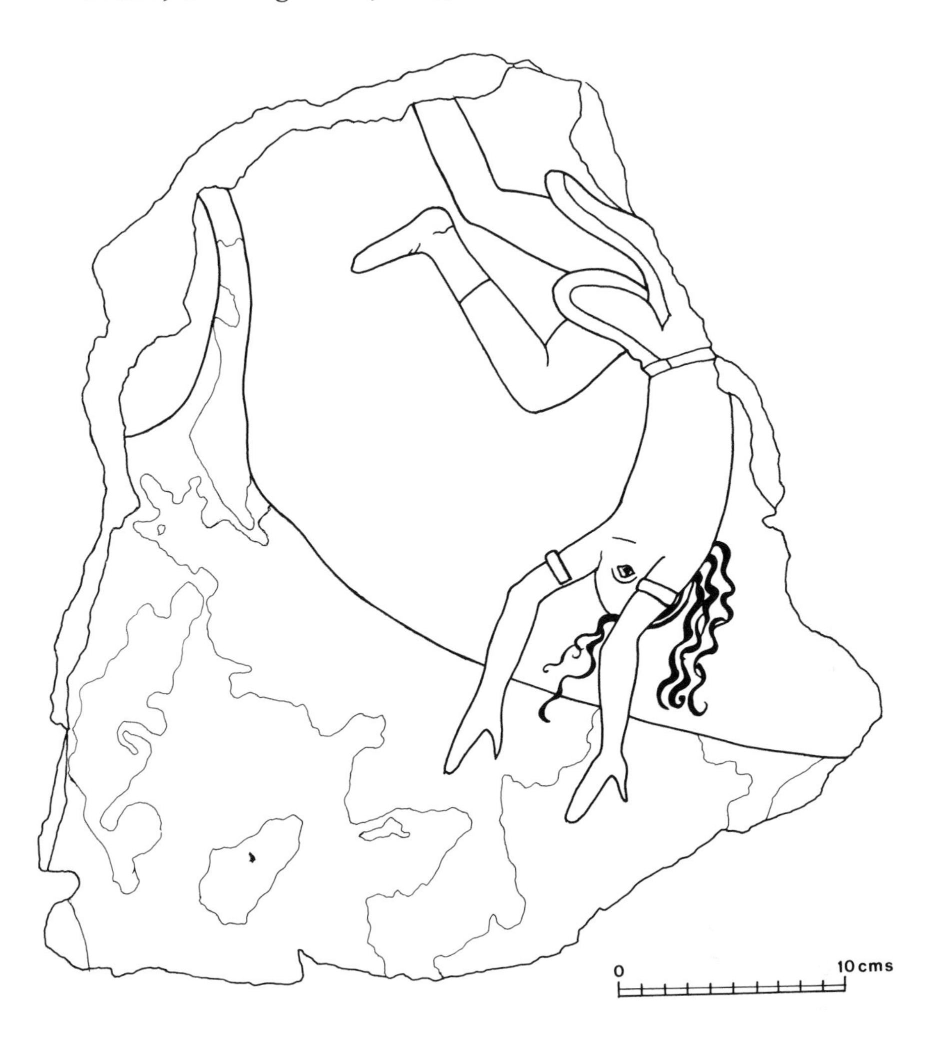

The evidence is strongest in the field of arts and crafts, where it is almost overwhelming; although there continued to be local traditions, ultimately no stylistic idiom separate from the Minoan survived. In the Cyclades this Minoanisation extended to the apparent adoption of the Minoan type of loom, the use of a Minoan weight system (though not exclusively) and the Linear A script, and features that may well reflect the adoption or adaptation of elements of Minoan social life and religion such as the incorporation of Minoan elements into local architecture, the extraordinary popularity of the conical cup, and the use of a variety of ritually-linked items and themes that have Minoan parallels. On the mainland such features are at first hard to trace outside the Argolid, and in general the level of Minoanisation was much more superficial (Dickinson 1984, 1989: 135–6); but Mycenaean culture developed increasingly close ties to Minoan civilisation during the Second Palace Period.

The remarkable collections of treasure represented by the contents of the Shaft Graves and other early Mycenaean princely graves are without Aegean parallel in scale, but many items may be or are Cretan products, and it is best to take this as evidence of the general availability of metals and other precious materials in the Aegean at this time, together with the masses of bronze items from Crete and the various groups of precious vessels from Cretan contexts and Akrotiri. Silver, copper and lead from Laurion evidently circulated freely, and some metal, including gold, may conceivably have come from Laconia (above, pp. 28–9), which was certainly a source of fine stones used in Crete. From outside the Aegean came not only luxuries such as gold, ivory, ostrich eggs, exotic stones, including Egyptian alabaster and central Asiatic lapis lazuli and, to the mainland only, European amber, but the essential tin, and now certainly copper also, in the form of 'oxhide' ingots. These have all, when tested, proved to be of non-Aegean metal, some Cypriot but more from unknown, possibly Anatolian, sources; their presence demonstrates increasing involvement with and perhaps dependence on the Near Eastern trading system, since this ingot type is now generally recognised to be a standard Near Eastern form. Near Eastern pottery, including the standard Canaanite amphorae and some Cypriot wares, is now being identified increasingly at Cretan sites, and has been traced as far as Akrotiri and Phylakopi, though not yet to any mainland centre. Indeed, it seems likely that Crete was the main channel for Near Eastern materials and innovations (such as the war-chariot) at this period; other Aegean material is totally lacking from Near Eastern contexts of the sixteenth century and is confined, in the last stage of the Second Palace Period, to a scatter of LH IIA and IIB vases at sites from Cyprus to Egypt, and a Type B short sword that was almost certainly found in Cyprus and is likely to have been a mainland product.

Certain Minoan material is also rare in Near Eastern contexts: some LM IA pottery has been found in Cyprus, LM IB vases at sites from Cyprus to Egypt, and LM I stonework at Amman (Hankey 1974: 168, 175–6). But there is other evidence: the Cypro-Minoan script of Cyprus appears to derive from Linear A, suggesting a significant level of contact between Crete and Cyprus, and there are quite numerous references in Egyptian Eighteenth Dynasty sources to 'Keftiu', which appears to be the Egyptian equivalent of Kaptara/Caphtor and to be associated with Crete and the Aegean, as indicated particularly by the later list of Keftiu places in a text of Amenophis III's reign, which include several Cretan placenames (see most recently Cline 1987: 2–6), and the paintings from the tombs of high officials at Egyptian Thebes, dating from the early fifteenth century onwards, of which those of the reign of Tuthmosis III are most accurate (Wachsmann 1987). On these, persons described as coming from Keftiu and/or 'the Islands in the Midst of the Sea' have a very distinctive dress and appearance that can be closely paralleled in Second Palace Period representations, and bring as 'tribute' various items with good Minoan parallels, especially precious vessel types such as rhytons and Vapheio cups, some bull figurines, and even likely agrimi horns; but there are several clear conflations with other recognisable types of 'tribute-bearer' in the fullest scenes, in the tombs of Menkheperassonb and Rekhmire, which demonstrate that they cannot be taken as absolutely faithful representations of reality.

The most natural interpretation of these pictures is that they reflect Cretan missions that may have combined diplomacy with trade; the apparent value of the goods suggests the importance of the connection, though it does not necessarily indicate the range of trade commodities or even that there was any commercial trade involved. The goods may represent gifts designed to conciliate the power that had established a considerable presence in Syria, in hope of ensuring secure conditions for trade there. That this trade was particularly concerned with the commodities mentioned above, especially copper and tin, seems likely enough; but this evidence does not really give even the limited impression provided by the Mari documents of how these were 'paid for', or what profit Egypt or the Near East in general drew from the connection.

The fourth major development of the period is the clear evidence for links with other parts of Europe, which takes two separate forms, both relating almost exclusively to the mainland (some decorated pottery has been thought LM IA, but this requires re-examination). LH I and contemporary mainland wares have been found in some quantity in the Lipari islands and Vivara, where there is also a considerable amount of coarser domestic ware (Re 1986); a single decorated piece from Capo Piccolo near Croton may be as early, and LH II pieces have been found at other sites in the south Italian region and (a single cup) in Albania (Dickinson 1986b: 271–2; Knapp 1990: 124). The presence of 'Mainland Polychrome' and the analytical data linking some of the Vivara material to the south Peloponnese or Kythera indicate that this pottery has a variety of origins.

The appearance of amber seems to be a separate phenomenon, since it does not appear in these central Mediterranean contexts so early (though some Messenian pieces may be of Sicilian rather than Baltic amber). It occurs first, mainly in the form of elaborate necklaces that have their best parallels in British 'Wessex culture' material, at Mycenae, Pylos and Peristeria, and has a wider distribution in the Peloponnese and central Greece before the end of LH II (Harding 1984: 68–82; for a recent catalogue of finds, Harding and Hughes-Brock 1974). A newly reported find in Switzerland, a gold-cased amber bead of probably 'Wessex' manufacture, strengthens the possibility that the amber necklaces could have travelled across Europe (where similar elaborate beads were used, but to make different forms of necklace) and down the Adriatic (Barfield 1991). They are evidently prestige items, and it is difficult to think in terms of an 'amber trade'; but even prestige items should require some return, which is very difficult to identify. The supposition that it was items of fine metalwork effectively depends upon recurrent attempts to identify the influence of Mycenaean metalworking techniques in elaborate pieces found in central and western Europe, since no finds of Aegean metalwork have been identified in an archaeological context north of Albania; but, as Harding has demonstrated, the claims of such influence can be explained in other ways.

In fact, the context in which such a prestige chain exchange might have been established and the nature of early Mycenaean connections with Europe remain rather mysterious. Theories that Mycenaean and perhaps also Minoan wealth in this period grew through channelling European metals, particularly copper and tin, to the Near East (Dickinson 1977: 55–6 (but cf. 1989: 136); Cadogan 1976: 38; Sherratt, A.G. 1987a) require better support in the actual data, including analytical evidence, before they can be more than speculations (cf. Harding 1984: 280). In particular, Sherratt's arguments for an important link with the metal-rich Carpathian cultures involve nothing as tangible as pottery or amber, but depend upon claimed influences and connections that are often disputable and chronologically vague (cf. Harding 1984: 107–8, 197–200). Leaving aside the amber (whose presence in Greece can hardly be explained by the 'Carpathian' theory), the evidence is increasingly suggesting that the central Mediterranean was the main area of Aegean interest in the LBA; even here, it is not readily explicable, although the distance involved suggests that it was of some importance.

The Third Palace Period and Postpalatial Period

A striking feature of the third Palace Period is the increasingly international flavour of the evidence for trade, which is such that attempting to isolate the contribution of particular cultures, let alone identify one as dominant, is a hazardous and potentially futile process. No better illustration could be provided than the contents of the Ulu Burun shipwreck, which include materials and items from Egyptian, Mesopotamian, Syro-Palestinian, Cypriot, Aegean and more generally European sources (apart from amber beads, see Vagnetti and Lo Schiavo 1989: 222–3 for an Italian sword; Knapp 1990: 120 summarises the finds). The Cape Gelidonya wreck, until recently thought to contain a predominantly Cypriot cargo, though including a few Mycenaean pots, has now produced a Type II sword (Italian?) and Aegean storage stirrup jars (Bass 1991: 69–70). The Marsa Matruh site in western Egypt, where Cypriot material is present in considerable quantities, has also produced Syro-Palestinian, Egyptian and a few Aegean sherds; at Kommos in south Crete a rich range of imported pottery includes Egyptian, Syro-Palestinian, Cypriot, Mycenaean and Anatolian. Cypriot pottery has been identified, though always in small quantities, at Troy, Boghazköy and Maşat in central Anatolia (Åström 1980), Tiryns (with Syro-Palestinian types, Kilian 1988a: 127), and in Sicily and Sardinia, and Anatolian grey wares in Cyprus and the Near East (Allen 1990). The grey and handmade burnished wares being identified increasingly in Aegean and Cypriot contexts, especially at Kommos and Khania, represent a further distinctive element; they may prove to have a variety of origins, but plausible Italian, even

Sardinian parallels have been claimed for many pieces (cf. Kilian 1988a: 127–33; Knapp 1990: 121, 127–8).

Given that in earlier periods similarly small quantities of Minoan and Mycenaean pottery have not been considered to give a true index of the volume and importance of Aegean activity, it is reasonable to argue that the small quantities of Cypriot and Syro-Palestinian material in the Aegean cannot be used to counter the view that the great Cypriot and Syrian centres were the focusses of long-distance Mediterranean trade, although sites like Kommos and Tiryns were clearly important nodes in the network. This is made the more likely by the evidence of the shipwrecks and other underwater finds of ingots, which indicate that a bulk trade in metals which were not of Aegean origin was a major element of this long-distance activity. The 'oxhide' ingot shape in which both copper and tin were often transported is not an Aegean but a Cypriot and/or Syrian form; no fragments tested have proved to be of Laurion or other Aegean metal. That its shape could be used as a Linear B ideogram for 'ingot' (Ventris and Chadwick 1973: 51) and that the weights in which copper was recorded by the Knossos and Pylos palaces would fit such ingots (Zaccagnini 1986, especially 415) are indications of increasing Aegean dependence on Near Eastern sources, although Laurion copper was also in common use.

This is the proper perspective in which to place the undoubtedly impressive evidence for the distribution of Mycenaean pottery. It begins to be found outside the mainland on a large scale in LH IIIA1, in the Cyclades, Dodecanese, Near East and central Mediterranean, now including eastern Sicily. The quantities of LH IIIA2–B1 decorated pottery exported are far greater than ever recorded for Aegean pottery before: it seems particularly common in Cyprus, where the numbers of vessels represented must total many thousands, but there are considerable quantities, from dozens to hundreds, at many other sites, in both the Near East and the central Mediterranean. The main areas of distribution are, in order of apparent significance: (i) Cyprus, the Syro-Palestinian coast, and up the Nile to Thebes; (ii) the central Mediterranean, now including Sardinia; (iii) the Anatolian coast; and (iv) central Macedonia. The range is usefully summarised by Hankey, in the context of the Near East: 'neat containers for small quantities of high quality, perhaps perfumed oil, table ware (more than used to be thought), trivia, cult odds and ends, and ceremonial vases of varying size and importance' (1979: 154). These categories do not all appear everywhere, but examples of 'ceremonial' vases are beginning to turn up in the central Mediterranean (e.g. a pictorial krater fragment at Termitito, a rhyton fragment at Antigori); and while containers make up a considerable proportion of the total, indicating the importance of the trade in their contents, probably perfumed or high quality oil, open vessels were also popular. Some rare shapes that imitate Near Eastern forms and the pictorial class generally may have been deliberately produced for the Near Eastern market, but overall the pottery represents a large selection of what was produced in the Mycenaean region itself.

In contrast, Minoan pottery, widely but thinly spread in LM II–IIIA1, thereafter becomes hard to identify before LM IIIB, when it again becomes widespread in the Aegean and the Near East, especially Cyprus (Hankey 1979; Popham 1979; Kanta 1980; Ch. 6). It includes not only small stirrup jars and elaborate amphoroid kraters, but a range of open vessels, and examples reach as far as Marsa Matruh and Antigori; much is apparently Khaniot, which is widely distributed in Crete itself (most recently Hallager, B. 1985; see also Jones 1986: 461). But the characteristic storage stirrup jars, most of which are Cretan, testify to Cretan export of olive oil and perhaps wine on a considerable scale from LM IIIA2 onwards: west Cretan examples are particularly common on the mainland, but also occur elsewhere in the Mediterranean, and central Cretan examples reached Cyprus and the Near East (Haskell 1990). Nor is there any reason to suppose that Crete ceased to import luxury goods and materials from the Near East, although the quantities may have declined after the collapse of the last palace state at Knossos, where many Egyptian stone vessels have been found in LM II–IIIA contexts (Warren 1969: 112–14).

The occurrence of Mycenaean (and some Minoan) pottery in contexts that seem dominated by non-Aegean material, such as the two shipwrecks and Marsa Matruh, and at sites as remote from its main areas of distribution as Carchemish and Maşat in the Near East and Luni in Etruria, two sites on Malta, and Montoro in eastern Spain (Martín de la Cruz 1990), are best interpreted as indicating that it became so common an item of exchange that it might travel about quite independently of the presence or activity of 'Mycenaeans' or other Aegeans. Its popularity is strikingly demonstrated by the production of imitation wares at various sites in Cyprus, Palestine, Macedonia, Troy and south Italy (where one workshop imitated LM III rather than LH III decoration, Vagnetti and Jones 1988: 337); the globular stirrup jar shape was also imitated in faience and stone in Palestine and Egypt. These imitation wares include a high proportion of open vessels, and could themselves be exported; their popularity may represent a response to a decline in the Mycenaean pottery industry in the later thirteenth century (cf. Sherratt and Crouwel 1987: 344).

No other class of artefact was systematically exported from the Aegean. Bronze weapons and implements of a few well-known types, mainly swords, spears and double axes, concentrate in the Balkans north of the Greek mainland, where local smiths produced versions of them, but only very rarely are they found beyond (e.g. a type F sword from Surbo in Apulia), and arguments for Mycenaean influence on European metalworking beyond the Balkans can point to no *common* European types that clearly reflect Mycenaean originals. Indeed, the lack of evidence for such influences in regions where pottery finds suggest considerable Mycenaean activity must seem a strong argument against identifying them in regions where no pottery is found. Other finds seem to reflect casual or small-scale exchanges: single ivory attachments, which seem to have become separated from their furniture (footstool?) backing, have been identified in

Cyprus and Sardinia (Krzyszkowska 1991), and there are a few occurrences of beads and sealstones, which include examples from graves at Syracuse (Wilson 1988: 122) and Beşik Tepe very close to Troy, the latter almost identical with one from the Ulu Burun wreck (Bass 1986: 283–4). The Syracuse find may be compared with the evidence for other Mycenaean artefacts in and near Sicily, including glass beads and bronze mirrors (Harding 1984: 248–51); but some of the mirrors and many other bronze types, including vessels, found in this region are now thought more probably Cypriot, and datable no earlier than the late thirteenth century (Lo Schiavo *et al.* 1985). The appearances of Mycenaean figurines, mostly in Cyprus and Ugarit, may reflect a Mycenaean presence, but these were hardly trade-items.

Indications of the export of more elaborate items, like those shown being carried by 'Keftiu' people on the Theban tomb-paintings, the latest of which fall early in this period, are few, a Minoan stone vase from Alalakh (Warren 1969: 55–6) and some precious metal vessels, one inlaid, from Cyprus (Catling 1964: 46). But knowledge of high-quality Aegean originals seems implied by the hybrid Aegean–Oriental styles of ivory and faience work (on the latter, Peltenburg 1991) which developed in the Near East in the thirteenth century. The later Keftiu tomb-paintings, occurrence of items with the cartouches of Amenophis II and III and the latter's wife Tiy in the Aegean, and the place-names list and other material relating to Amenophis III, which may reflect an official Egyptian embassy to the Aegean whose intended terminus was Mycenae (Cline 1987, especially 19–23, and 1991, especially 40–2; contrast Wachsmann 1987: 95–7, 113–14), could represent a milieu of diplomatic contacts in which such objects might figure. But references to Keftiu are very rare after the Eighteenth Dynasty, although Mycenaean pottery continued to appear in Egypt, nor can anything comparable be traced in the Ugarit texts, although it has been argued that one of the richest men there owned a ship that was trading with Crete (Heltzer 1988).

The only other claims of diplomatic contacts between a Near Eastern power and the Aegean are founded on the controversial equation of Ahhiyawā, a kingdom with which the Hittite kings had dealings in the fourteenth and thirteenth centuries, with some part of Mycenaean Greece, suggested to be named Akhaiwia, even with the territory of Mycenae itself. Among the many difficulties raised by this theory are the lack of evidence for appropriately significant contacts between the centre of Hittite power in Anatolia and the Mycenaean world (cf. Sherratt and Crouwel 1987: 345), and the absence from the Ugarit documents of any reference to Ahhiyawā (or indeed any name that might refer to the Mycenaeans); the theory also relies heavily on the questionable notion of a Mycenaean 'empire' powerful at sea. The scanty information about Ahhiyawā includes nothing pointing positively to the Mycenaean world, and it seems best to consider this an unproved (and in my view unlikely) theory.

Overall, then, there seems good reason not to overestimate the Mycenaean role in Mediterranean trade, especially in the east Mediterranean. But its importance to the palatial economies and the level of prosperity in Mycenaean Greece as a whole, and the potential importance of the Aegean market to Cyprus and Syria, should not be underrated; indeed, it has been suggested that in the thirteenth century Cypriot attention turned increasingly westwards (Knapp 1990: 135, 146, citing Muhly). Here it is possible to draw on documentary evidence, though indirectly, to fill out the picture on the Aegean side. As stated in Chapter 4, the Linear B texts of Knossos indicate that the palace supervised and supported a large-scale wool and textiles industry and gathered large quantities of agricultural produce; there are also indications of the production of perfumed oil. The quantities involved suggest that part of these commodities was used in exchange, though there is no explicit reference to this in the texts, and that in this as in many other features Knossos set an example followed by the later Mycenaean palaces, which certainly handled wool and organised the production of textiles and perfumed oil on a considerable scale. That these were major commodities in trade between the Aegean and the outside world, especially the Near East, must seem very likely.

It is a remarkable fact that the majority of exported Mycenaean pottery tested by optical emission spectroscopy, including that from the Cyclades and Dodecanese, belongs to Type A, which has a wide range but is centred in the Argolid, although there is some evidence for exchange of pottery within Crete, the Cyclades, and central and northern parts of the mainland. This is not too surprising, given that the Argolid was evidently the centre of stylistic innovation for the Mycenaean style for most of the Third Palace Period, but it would seem to imply Argive dominance of the oil trade with the Near East, if not generally, at least in the period when Mycenaean pottery was so popular; the evidence for production at Pylos may well date after this. The distribution of Cretan oil jars on the mainland complicates the picture, suggesting that Mycenaean centres were processing for export much that they had not produced; but more data are needed in this area.

The apparent decline in eastwards traffic in the later thirteenth century, deduced from the great diminution in imported Mycenaean pottery, may have been compensated for by an increase in activity westwards, in which one significant force may have been a Cypriot response to deteriorating trading conditions in the Near East (Knapp 1990: 152). Contacts with the central Mediterranean, particularly Sardinia, where the earliest identifiable Mycenaean pottery is LH IIIB, may have intensified in the thirteenth century. This is the period when the claimed Italian wares are most prominent at Kommos, and when Cypriot metal types and metalworking influences are identifiable in Sardinia and to a lesser extent elsewhere in Italy, also when European metal types which have their closest parallels in Italy, especially the Type II sword and violin-bow fibula, begin to appear in the Aegean and Cyprus (Harding 1984: 278).

Certainly, in the Postpalatial Period links with the central Mediterranean are still strong; but the general situation had changed. Many important centres had suffered disaster, in both the Aegean and the Near East, and some, like Ugarit and Pylos, never recovered; the systems of which they were significant parts must have collapsed, and would have been hard to rebuild in an age of insecurity. The ability to attract traders and to produce tradable quantities of goods surely declined markedly in the Aegean, although some centres continued to prosper for a while; Perati, one of the most notable, may have controlled the Laurion mines, which were evidently still in production. Because very distinctive types of pottery were being produced in different regions of the Aegean, it is possible to trace complex patterns of interconnection, influence and exchange, although pottery exchanges can only be documented in ones and twos. The era of mass pottery export was gone, but the exchanged pottery includes a large number of elaborate stirrup jars, suggesting that local production of fine oil or other specialised products continued in many different centres on a small scale, a situation reminiscent of the early MBA.

It has been suggested (Sherratt, E.S. 1985) that Cyprus, the Dodecanese and Crete formed an early nexus, which stimulated the revival of the central regions of the mainland, themselves strongly interconnected, to judge from the pottery. This nexus probably conducted much of the continuing trade with the central Mediterranean. From here came further metal types, including developments of the Type II sword which influenced local production, and amber, including beads of a distinctive ribbed form, which has a wide distribution in the central Mediterranean (Harding 1984: 82–7). Contact with the Near East can also be documented through the appearance of a wide range of Near Eastern beads and other small items in the richer tombs of Perati and other major Aegean communities; but these rarely seem to go further west, although at Frattesina in the Po valley Near Eastern materials, ivory and ostrich egg, have been found, with a LH IIIC sherd and evidence of glass-working (Harding 1984: 85, 286). The survival of a degree of international exchange can be documented by the contents of the 'Tiryns Treasure', the bulk of which seems to be datable late in LH IIIC; it includes not only a Cypriot tripod-stand and gold pendant, but the extraordinary 'sun wheels', woven of gold wire in a manner paralleled in Czechoslovakia and strung with ribbed amber beads on bronze spokes.

But more and more the evidence for such links seem to be confined to Crete, although it is possible to trace vestigial links between Cyprus and various sites in the central mainland regions in the Submycenaean phase. It remains unclear whether this was caused by, or contributed to, the decline of sites like Perati, Lefkandi and Tiryns. But these connections do not seem to have produced much of a flow of goods, and before 1000 the Cyprus–Sardinia link seems to have lapsed, although Crete retained contacts with the Near East. By the end of the BA, most of the Aegean was reduced to a state of shortage of materials and at best intermittent contact with the wider world from which it was not to recover for generations. Even contacts between the east and west sides of the Aegean, or between the Aegean and the west coast of Greece, are hard to certify, although the recurrent need for metals would have ensured that no major site could have existed in complete isolation.

Bibliography

The basic data on the spread of types and influences in the Aegean have largely been presented in Chapter 5. For general discussions of the material relating to Aegean trade in the Mediterranean context, largely or entirely concerned with the LBA, see the papers in Marazzi *et al.* 1986 (note especially Niemeier's very useful Aegean distribution maps for many types of item) and Gale 1991, also Knapp 1990 (a most useful survey). Many of the papers in Hägg and Marinatos 1984 are relevant to the topics of this chapter; updated discussions of some appear in Hardy 1990, including Wiener's comprehensive survey of the 'Minoan thalassocracy' topic (cf. also Melas 1988a).

Further useful discussions are: on early Minoan overseas activity Branigan 1989; on the 'Keftiu' question Wachsmann 1987 (cf. also Sakellarakis, E. and J. 1984); on the Ahhiyawā controversy most recently Bryce 1989 (also Macqueen 1986: 39–41); on Mycenaean links with Europe Harding 1984; on Cypriot material in the Aegean Catling 1991; on the Cape Gelidonya shipwreck Bass 1967, on the Ulu Burun shipwreck Bass 1986, Pulak 1988, Bass *et al.* 1989, and on both Bass 1991; and on the Linear B material that may relate to trade Killen 1985, Appendix I.

Jones 1986 summarises relevant analytical work on the provenance of pottery; see Ch. 5 on the MBA, 6 on the LBA in the Aegean and central Mediterranean (note 477–93 on storage stirrup jars, 542–71 and 589–609 on Aegean pottery in the Near East).

CHAPTER 8

RELIGION

Introduction

An enormous amount has been written about Aegean prehistoric religion, which has often included quite detailed pictures of beliefs and practices. Unfortunately, a very large proportion of this depends on accepting highly questionable hypotheses. This is particularly true of the theory which underlies Evans's immensely influential model of Minoan religion, and which largely reflects theories put forward by Frazer in *The Golden Bough*, that the original form of religion over a wide area of the ancient world centred on a dominant goddess of fertility, whose young consort's annual death and rebirth symbolised the decay and regrowth of vegetation. This is aptly characterised by Nilsson as 'a piece of syncretistic theology' (1950: 396), that depended on the completely questionable interpretation of female figurines as 'mother goddesses', and the equally dubious assumption that 'Mother Goddess' cults recorded in Graeco-Roman times from Syria, Anatolia and elsewhere represented an unchanged survival of the original religion in the remote past (cf. Evans 1921: 3–6, 51–2). Similarly, the hypothesis, still accepted by Nilsson, that there were distinctive Indo-European religious ideas and institutions, which would have been introduced to the Aegean by speakers of proto-Greek, can be seriously questioned (cf. Renfrew 1989, Ch. 10), and Burkert has warned against the oversimplifying schematisation that has accompanied attempts to identify these in Greek religion (1985: 18–19, 201). In fact, the whole process of extrapolating earlier forms of religion from later sources is now recognised to be extremely hazardous. The practice of using evidence for the continuous use of individual sites to justify transferring documented Graeco-Roman practices and beliefs back to prehistoric times begs the question completely, for in Renfrew's useful dictum, 'continuity of practice does not mean lack of change in that practice, and certainly cannot be taken to imply constancy of meaning' (1985: 3).

How may the study of prehistoric Aegean religion be approached without these traditional props? In a penetrating analysis of the problems involved in identifying and interpreting prehistoric religious material, Renfrew has offered a preliminary framework of general theory, including a list of questions that 'can in principle be answered from the archaeological material alone, in favourable circumstances' (1985: 25). But, although this is undoubtedly a very valuable approach to the identification of sacred sites, symbols and representations, it cannot go far towards revealing the system of belief and activity within which these had significance, as the traditional accounts appeared able to do. Indeed, to assemble a detailed picture of a system of belief must remain virtually impossible without texts; but some of the likely general characteristics of Aegean religion may be suggested through analogy with the Near East. The justification for this is that the Aegean and Near Eastern societies developed out of similar Neolithic farming cultures and, although their responses to varying geographical settings and social developments certainly differed, many of their basic preoccupations would have remained the same, and should have been reflected by similarities in their religious beliefs.

Thus, the Aegean societies surely shared the belief common not only to the religions of the Near Eastern societies but to those of all recorded farming cultures, that there exist supernatural powers that can control the weather, the productivity of the soil and the fertility of living creatures, and that these powers require to be propitiated, if the natural processes are to continue. One might also expect that the methods of propitiation used would parallel those universally recorded: that is, at public ceremonies these powers were invoked with shows of respect and other acts intended to please, and were given or promised gifts, especially offerings of food, drink and living creatures (cf. Fig. 8.1). Since their function was effectively to secure the survival of the community, the social importance of these ceremonies would be hard to overestimate, and probably they would be recognised as the most important part of religion, but this would also include household rituals and magical practices; observances to do with the

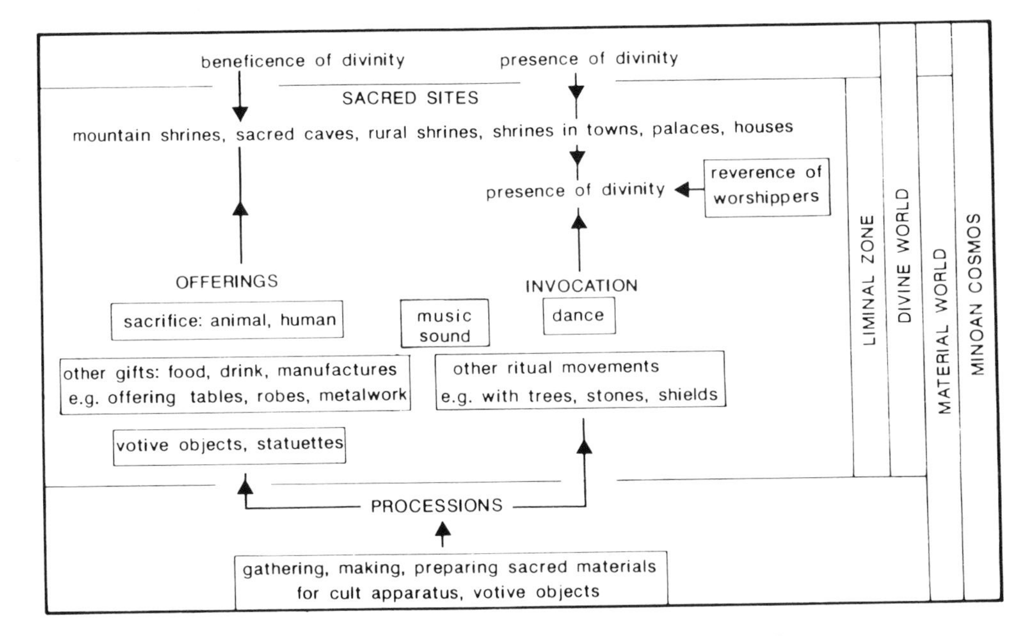

Fig. 8.1 Minoan religion as ritual action. Courtesy of Prof. P.M. Warren.

dead, while involving rituals, should not strictly be classed as religious unless they involve the invocation of gods. The importance of the public ceremonies would surely guarantee the according of special status to those who acted as intermediaries between the community and the supernatural powers.

How these powers were originally envisaged, and how gods of the kind attested from an early date in the Near East developed, are questions not readily answered. But even a superficial survey of the material reveals the great importance of the local associations of these gods, by which they are often better distinguished than by their often similar if not effectively identical functions or nature. As states developed, the more important gods of their constituent communities began to be organised in pantheons, whose membership and hierarchy might change according to political circumstances, for gods tended to grow and decline in importance along with their host communities. The greater gods increasingly acquired individual personalities and functions, and their names might be given to local analogues in a process of priest- or ruler-led harmonisation; but however widely they were acknowledged, their worship nevertheless remained tied to a particular centre more often than not. The importance of these local cults is demonstrated by the attention paid to them by Near Eastern rulers as part of their religious duties, and is underlined by sources like the lists of divine witnesses to Hittite treaties, which carefully distinguish gods of identical function, even name, according to their local cult centre or special title (Pritchard 1974: 200–6).

The Near Eastern analogy should not be pressed to suggest that all these features ought to be mirrored in the Aegean, but one might expect a comparable tendency for communities to recognise local gods, not least because the physical barriers are often more marked than in southern Mesopotamia or the Nile valley, where such local gods are identifiable from the earliest stages. The model of Minoan religion developed by Evans, centring upon a universally recognised great goddess and her consort, who were worshipped, perhaps with one or two other gods, as equally powerful in all spheres of the cosmos, including the underworld, under different 'aspects' (cf. Platon and Levi in Hägg and Marinatos 1981: 210–11, also Gesell 1983: 97, 1985: 1, 64–6 for 'aspects') is such a radical departure from this pattern that it surely requires justification. In particular, the crucial concept of 'aspects', which is used to argue that different features and material reflect the worship of a single god, deserves critical attention; it is hard to parallel in Near Eastern religions, and one is bound to ask what prevents interpreting the same evidence in terms of separate gods. Indeed, the apparent assumption that only a single god was worshipped at any particular cult place runs counter to a lot of evidence (cf. Boulotis 1990).

It is not impossible that Aegean, and particularly Minoan, religion developed in a highly individual fashion; certainly, it has many distinctive features. But the whole topic needs to be examined outside the framework inherited from the past, which is so heavily dependent upon questionable theories and methods. There is not the space here for such an examination, and this discussion will concentrate more upon evidence for ritual sites and activities, on which much useful work is now being done, rather than upon the number or nature of the power(s) with which these are to be associated. The Prepalatial material from the Aegean will be discussed together, because it has been thought to show broad similarities, then the evidence for the development of Minoan religion and its possible influence elsewhere in the Aegean, and finally the evidence for Mycenaean religion.

Religion in the Prepalatial Period

Various general resemblances can be perceived between the potential evidence for religion in the Neolithic and Prepalatial Periods. In both cases it is notably diffuse, in that arguably ritual items are found in a variety of contexts, but sites of ritual activity, particularly repeated activity of the kind that one would associate with communal practice, are very hard to find. Often it has been considered more as a source of the earliest examples of later features or concepts than in its own right. The main recent attempts to discern common strands have focussed on tombs as centres of communal religious activity, especially in Crete (Peatfield 1987: 90, 1990: 124–5; Goodison 1989: 27–9), which Goodison has argued to reflect a belief in the rebirth of the dead, linked with the annual cycle of plant growth and, symbolically, with the rising and setting of the sun (1989: Ch. 1).

Such theories have their attractions, but tend to draw a rather impressionistic picture of the evidence, passing over striking variations in the distribution of features, and do not clearly distinguish between evidence that might relate to ceremonies in honour of the dead, individually or collectively, and more general religious activity. Features that are integral parts of a tomb, such as niches or small chambers, and are thought to have been used for cult, or are closely associated with a tomb, and structures found in a cemetery that were supposedly used for ritual, are surely interpretable in the former light, which could reflect formal rituals of the kind well-known in later Greece rather than true worship of the dead. Occurrences of figurines and other likely ritual items are only relevant if it can be shown that they are not grave-goods (as they evidently were in the Cycladic cemeteries), and have some association with one of these features; but even at Koumasa, where they were unusually common, they are not found in the paved area that has been interpreted as the site of communal rites (Branigan 1970b: 133 fig. 27). Such finds are in any case hardly general in Crete, but are notably lacking from 'house tombs', except at Arkhanes.

The features most likely to be intended for communal use are the enclosed and/or paved areas, sometimes containing an altar-like structure, which were sometimes laid out in association with tombs. But outside the Mesara, where six examples are known, these can only be documented at Mochlos T. IV–VI, plausibly Arkhanes Ts. 6 and 12 (Sakellarakis 1991: 101, 104), and Lakkoudhes on Naxos (for most examples see Goodison 1989: 28–9). This is not a particularly strong basis on which to argue for an essential focus of EB communal religious activity, particularly since in at least two cases (Apesokari and Kamilari) the whole complex is post-EM, and careful analysis at Ayia Kyriaki showed that it was not part of the original plan (Blackman and Branigan 1982: 48). It is possible that these are more formally laid out versions of a widespread feature, but some indication of, for example, flattened earth areas at other sites needs to be adduced. As it stands, the evidence seems compatible with a developing practice of ritual activity at certain tombs, perhaps particularly those containing highly ranked families or individuals, as Soles has suggested (1988: 59–60); the later Pyrgos tomb, which clearly held a selected group, would fit this interpretation well, and if the famous Kamilari model does show cult of the dead, which is by no means certain (Branigan 1970a: 174–5), the seated figures might be ancestors of two families of rank which used the tomb. It might further be speculated that this rank derived from or was associated with importance in communal ritual, which was further indicated by the burial of figurines and other ritual items with the dead, and that this was why ritual significance was sometimes attached to their tombs; if theories of rebirth were current, they may have been attached to these families or individuals only. Some finds, such as the Koumasa and Platanos 'phalloi', could well indicate that rituals conducted at tombs were not concerned solely with honouring the dead, but it does not seem safe to go further than this, on present evidence.

In general there are indications of much local variety in practice, which might reflect different religious concepts. Thus, the EC figurine tradition has a wide Aegean distribution and influence, but it is barely found in the greater part of the Helladic area, where figurines of any kind are very rare, or in eastern Crete. Some types of Cretan figurine are widespread, but most are quite localised (Branigan 1971: 69), and other types of likely ritual item, such as the MM clay 'votive bells' or 'horned masks' (Gesell 1985: 16–17; Fig. 8.6: 1), have restricted distributions. The use of caves for ritual purposes is hard to demonstrate outside Crete, although this is plausible for the Cave of Zas on Naxos. The Keros deposition site and the Myrtos 'shrine' are unique. Such local variability surely militates against Van Leuven's argument for a pan-Aegean tradition of shrine types and lay-out going back to the Neolithic period (1981), which in any case needs much better definition and supporting arguments. It might better suit Goodison's picture of a loosely organised 'animistic' form of religion, largely based in the household (1989: 11), which could provide a suitable setting for the possible use of hearths as focusses of cult activity at some 'Lerna III' (EH II) sites (Caskey, M.E. 1990), and for the occurrence of figurines and other likely ritual items on settlement sites.

But it is hard to believe that there were no larger gatherings to perform rites, and there are in fact a number of open-air sites where this could have happened, apart from those associated with tombs. Notable are paved or otherwise court-like areas, at Lerna III (Wiencke 1989: 502), Vasiliki (the West Court), Knossos

(Wilson 1985: 293), and Mallia (first phase of the 'Agora', Touchais 1989: 688). These might be functional predecessors of the west courts of the later palaces, but the most specific link with ritual is provided by the 'cupule stones' in the Vasiliki paving. Isolated deposits of material, sometimes including figurines and 'votive bells', have been found at north Cretan sites, both within and away from settled areas (Gesell 1985: 16–17), while the earliest use of the Juktas, Petsopha and Atsipadhes peak sanctuaries seems to go back to this period (Peatfield 1990: 125, 1992: 71–2). But the most prominent example of an open-air site for communal ritual is Dhaskaleio Kavos on Keros (Renfrew *et al.* 1989; Renfrew 1991: 100–101).

Here, on a strip of shoreline on the western side of the island, a mass of stone figurines and bowls, apparently deliberately broken, had been deposited, with decorated pottery and other fine goods, all of the 'Syros' group. The site had been very badly disturbed, and no focus for this ritual could be certainly identified (but Doumas, in Marangou 1990: 95, links to a cave). The wealth of finds on this insignificant island suggests that it was a prehistoric analogue to Delos, a ceremonial centre for many neighbouring communities, but the significance of the ritual and its links, if any, with the deposition of figurines in tombs remain unclear. Its abandonment, and the general disappearance of the EC figurine tradition, may be associated with the other indications of a breakdown of EC society, and could reflect a major shift in beliefs. But clay figurines that show some facial similarity to the EC types were among those dedicated at the Mikre Vigla settlement site on Naxos, at the top of the hill, although it is unclear whether this took place in the open air or within a shrine (Barber and Hadjianastasiou 1989: 67–8, 114–32).

Built rooms where rituals took place have also been identified. They are uniformly small (the theory that the large central rooms of the 'corridor houses' had a ritual function is tempting, but lacks supporting evidence), and could therefore only have been used by small groups, at best representatives of the community. The case for a shrine at Myrtos is presented most elaborately by Gesell (1985: 7, 114–16), but there are problems, most notably the lack of a potential place of offering, such as have been identified in the 'hearths' of many MM shrines and the 'Lerna III' (EH II) House L at Eutresis. To require such a feature as proof of a shrine may itself be begging questions, and perhaps this intepretation should be provisionally accepted; but the possibility that it was simply a place of storage for the figure, from which it would be taken for open-air ceremonies, cannot be altogether dismissed.

Whitelaw, who is sceptical of the identification (1983: 342 n. 10), draws attention instead to rooms at Myrtos which contain a 'cupule stone' set in the floor. These stones, sometimes called 'libation tables' or 'kernoi', are distinguishable by a variously shaped arrangement of hollows cut or hammered into their upper surface, often surrounding a central, larger depression (Pl. 8.1); the arguments for their ritual significance are increasingly strong (Soles 1973:

Pl. 8.1 A 'cupule stone', Myrtos. Courtesy of the Managing Committee of the British School at Athens and Prof. P.M. Warren.

327–31, Pelon 1988: 42–3). They are generally found set into areas of paving, very often at entrances or in passageways or streets, and have a largely east Cretan distribution, including EM II examples from Trypiti (Vasilakis 1989: 55), Myrtos (Warren 1972: 230–1), and the Vasiliki West Court (Gesesll 1985: 8), many of MM date from Gournia, including one associated with an altar-like structure built against T. II (Soles 1979: 154–6, 162), and several of exceptional elaboration from Mallia, mostly from the palace or Chrysolakkos (Pelon, *ibid.*). It seems likely that they were used for small offerings of foodstuffs or liquids, but the variations in context and the number and arrangement of the hollows, and their frequent reuse as wall-slabs, remain puzzling, and their relationship to later types of offering table, which normally only have a single central depression, is unclear.

Another item whose ritual use seems clear is the anthropomorphic pottery vessel, of which most examples come from funerary contexts but one from the Myrtos 'shrine' (Warren 1973b) (Fig. 8.9: 1, 2). All apparently represent females, are largely hollow and can be filled through perforations; the contents can then be poured out, often with the aid of a handle at the back, either through a jug held in the crook of the arm or, in two cases, through the breasts. They are surely related to a larger class of zoömorphic and other vessels which could have been used for libations, found particularly in the Mesara tombs (Branigan 1970b: 80–3); but some certainly have attached snakes, a clear ritual symbol in later Minoan religion, which would strengthen an interpretation as representations of goddesses or powerful spirits. Pouring from them might then symbolise a willed act on their part, offering water or general nourishment to their worshippers. But since the jug-holding motif does not appear later and the breast-holding motif is very rare, it seems dangerous to identify them as simply the earliest representations of deities supposedly popular later; rather, they could incorporate concepts which their considerable variety of form suggests were local, if related, and which were to be given more specific form in developed Minoan religion.

This bitty account of the Prepalatial material, largely centred on Crete, inevitably reflects its nature: patterns of association are few, and while many forms of symbolism can be identified (cf. Goodison 1989, Ch. 1.8–10), their significance is rarely obvious. Without making assumptions of the kind that I have questioned it is not possible to impose any overall patterns, although there are clear associations with the natural world, as are surely to be expected in any early form of religion. It is worth stressing that many of the classes of symbolic item, especially the figurines and anthropomorphic and zoömorphic vessels, disappeared during the period or barely survived it, while symbols important in later Minoan religion, the double axe and 'horns of consecration', have barely made an appearance. Change, rather than continuity, might then be the more natural expectation, as already suggested in the case of the Cyclades. But there is very little evidence for religious practice in the Cyclades, and effectively none on the mainland, before the Second Palace Period, so that the natural tendency to concentrate on the abundant Minoan material is in fact forced.

The development of Minoan religion

Already in the Prepalatial Period it is possible to document examples of features that were to be part of the Minoan religious system for a very long time. With the great increase in the quantity of evidence from MM I onwards, types of site and patterns of ritual activity can be widely identified, and the increasing liking for representing ritual activities and religious symbols in various ways, especially in the Second Palace Period, provides scope for much more specific accounts of such features than is usually possible for a textless religion. There are enough links to justify making some general comments that cover both First and Second Palace Periods, but it should be remembered that religious concepts may have developed considerably in sophistication over this long time, and emphasis may have shifted as a result of social changes.

One development is the emergence of a priestly class, clearly identifiable in the representations by dress and other details of appearance, paraphernalia carried (sometimes preserved in archaeological contexts), or activities (e.g. Zeimbekis 1991; Younger 1989, Pl. XII: 62–6 and the central figure on the 'Harvester Vase', Pl. 5.11). Their origins may well be sought in the persons with whom, I have suggested, figurines and other ritual items were buried, and whose tombs may have been the centres of cult, in the Prepalatial Period. The representations and other evidence make clear that they included both men and women, each sex perhaps playing a dominant role in some rituals, though both might participate (Marinatos 1987b). This is a notable contrast with the great Near Eastern religions, in which, although women could hold some important positions, priests were generally male.

The rituals in which this class took the major roles (Fig. 8.1) included types found commonly elsewhere, such as acts of offering and sacrifice, processions and dances; but there was also a class of summoning rituals, designed to produce the epiphany of a god, in which he/she was imagined as coming to inhabit the body of a participant or some natural or constructed feature, or as simply invisibly present. Sites for such rituals have been identified in palaces and other buildings, but one prominent class of representations shows an open-air setting (Pl. 8.2), in which a tree may be clasped or shaken, or a large rock kneeled at and beaten. It is not clear how important epiphany rituals were in the earlier stages of Minoan religion, but they have a good claim to be considered its most individual element. In contrast with the Near East, where a major part of priestly duties was the round of activities centring on cult statues, including dressing, feeding and entertaining them, only in the context of the robing ritual is there any possible evidence of this kind in Crete, and even this might have involved a human representing the god (Warren 1988: 20–2). In fact, whether there were any permanent cult images in Crete at all remains controversial, although temporary representations might have been set up for epiphany rituals (Marinatos and Hägg 1983, Marinatos 1990b: 69; cf. also Sakellarakis 1991: 139–40 on Anemospilia. The mould for a lifesize hand from Phaistos, above, p. 172, might be relevant).

A further highly distinctive feature of Minoan religion is the popularity of natural sites relatively distant from settlements, both open-air sites and caves, in contrast with many parts of the Near East, where cults were generally based in temple complexes or more modest structures standing within settlements; indeed, some have argued for the primacy of such sites, and while this is not universally accepted the importance of many such sites is now undeniable. The separation of the great Near Eastern complexes from the rest of the inhabited area by walls, or through elevation on terraces, is not easy to parallel in the Minoan material, although walls surrounded some open-air sites and narrow entrances and polythyra were used to restrict access to shrines and ceremonial rooms.

For all our capacity to detect these individual features of Minoan religion, it

Pl. 8.2 Gold ring showing epiphany scene, Isopata T. 1, Knossos. Hirmer Verlag, Munich.

remains difficult to have a clear picture of its character, which might in any case have changed over the centuries as those of the Near East can be seen to do. The most explicit theory is offered by Marinatos (1984a: 119–20), that the major festivals celebrated and renewed harmony between human society and the natural world, which might seem a reasonable deduction from the popularity of rural sites and the emphasis on natural settings in many representations. But there is a danger here of succumbing to the recurrent temptation to create an ideal Minoan society in terms that reflect modern preoccupations. Even if the arguments for a human sacrifice at Anemospilia (Sakellarakis 1991: 154) and ritual cannibalism practised on children in a Knossos building (Wall *et al.* 1986) are discounted – though the arguments are quite plausible in both cases – the incontestable evidence for animal sacrifice is a reminder that all was not sweetness and light. Warren's analysis of the purposes of ritual as the 'positive' promotion of fertility and 'negative' minimisation of the potentially destructive (1988: 34–5) fits patterns already suggested as characteristic of farming culture religions, and may be the best that can be achieved without texts.

The evidence for sites of ritual activity can be divided into four broad categories, buildings which are or incorporate shrines, open-air sites (particularly peak sanctuaries), caves and tombs. All four categories are well represented in MM, for this is the period of much of the plausible evidence for ritual activity at tombs (notably Arkhanes T. B, Apesokari T. 1, Kamilari T. 1, Gournia Ts. I–II), for clear shrines and sacred complexes in buildings, and for ritual deposits in at least some caves (notably Kamares, Amnisos and quite probably Psychro). But open-air sites, especially peak sanctuaries, are most numerous of all, although information is still scanty in many cases. Caves are virtually confined to central Crete, but peak sanctuaries are widespread, though not universal; they are notably hard to identify around the Mesara, apart from Kophinas, and in the Gulf of Mirabello region (Fig. 8.2).

Assessing the relative importance of the sites is not easy, but a good case can be made that the peak sanctuaries were the most important communal cult centres, from both their commanding position and the quantities of material found. The arguments for shrines associated with palaces or near-palatial complexes like Quartier Mu are more inferential, depending on a link with large open spaces where sizeable numbers could be gathered, and only one, the Salle β complex at Mallia, has monumental features (Marinatos 1986: 19–20), but these too are likely to have been important. Others, like the independent sanctuary at Mallia (Gesell 1985, no. 75), may be of purely local significance. The caves, though sometimes spacious inside, have produced relatively little material and were often above the snow-line, so only accessible for part of the year. Ritual activity at tombs, as already noted, is less likely to have been of a general nature than to be connected with the burials that they held.

Indications of differences between the cults practised at these different sites can be drawn from features of the material, most obviously that figurines and other models in clay are very common on open-air sites but very rare in caves, where pottery seems to be the standard offering. Yet such models can occur in tombs (Soles 1973: 350–6) and settlements, although the contexts are rarely illuminating: even 'votive limbs', considered by Peatfield the most characteristic peak sanctuary type of all (1990: 120), have been found in Quartier Mu at Mallia (Detournay *et al.* 1980: 107–8). The 'votive bells' referred to above also occur in a variety of MM I–II contexts, including the Juktas peak sanctuary (A. Karetsou, pers. commun.). It seems a natural conclusion that some types could be used as general offerings in different contexts, but the strong association of clay offerings with peak sanctuaries and other open-air rural sites like Piskokephalo (cf. Rutkowski 1986: 115–16) remains notable.

The relationship between the peak sanctuaries and palaces has been seen as complementary, but the argument that the foundation of the sanctuaries was inspired by the palaces (Cherry 1986: 31, cf. Peatfield 1992: 83) not only downplays the evidence that some may have been in use earlier, but ignores the fact that most are remote from the early palace centres and have no obvious connection with them; in fact, none is closely associable with Phaistos or Mallia, and even Juktas might seem to go more naturally with Arkhanes than with Knossos

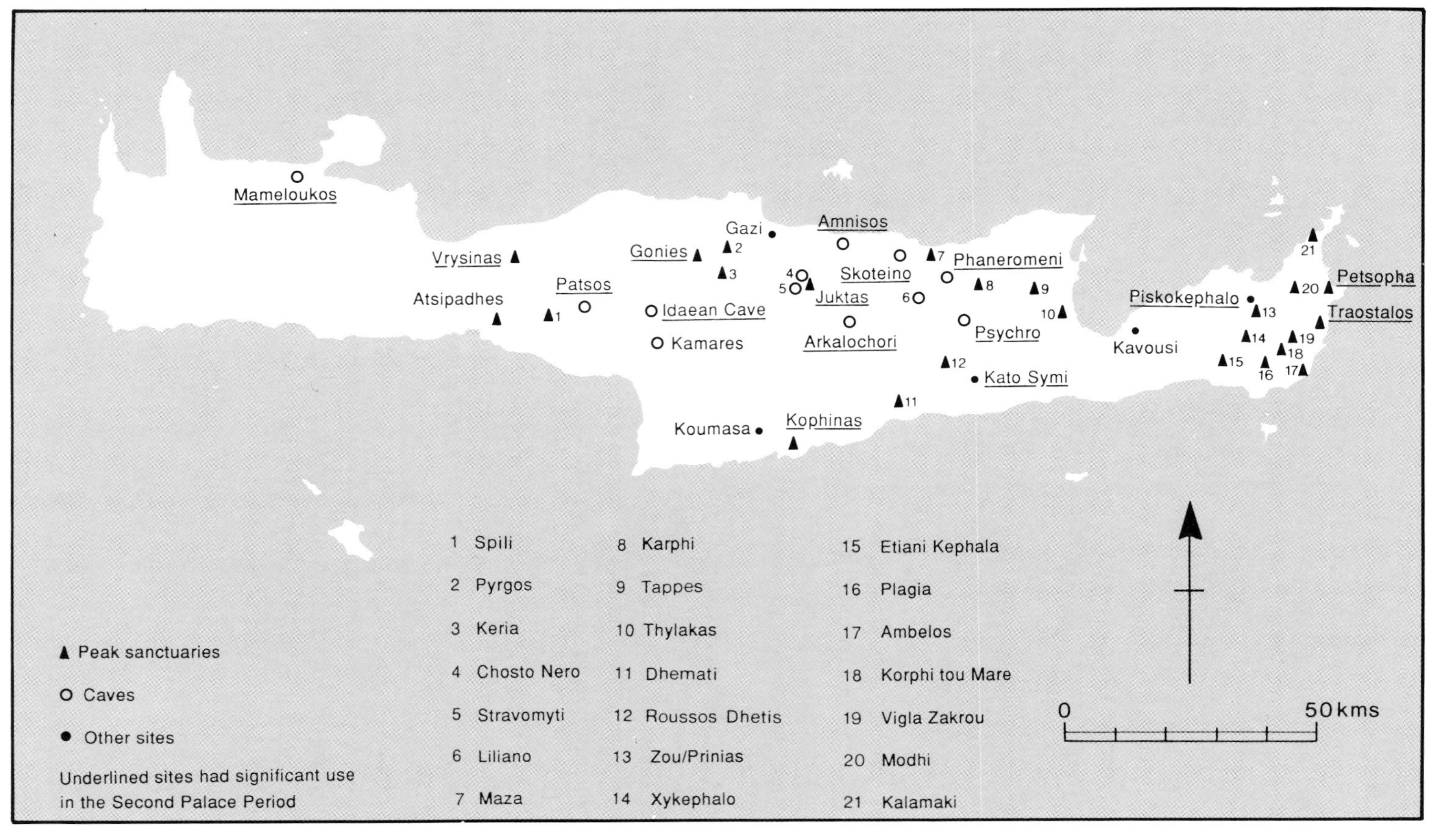

Fig. 8.2 The distribution of major types of cult site in Crete.

itself. Here Karetsou has noted a massive rise in offerings from 'MM IB', which could well suggest palace interest; this is to be expected with a major local religious centre, but is not the same thing as establishment or control, for which there is a better case in the Second Palace Period, as will be discussed below.

Accounts of peak sanctuaries tend to stress homogeneity in features and patterns of ritual activity. But caution is necessary, for the homogeneity may partly reflect what excavators choose to report; the most recently and extensively excavated example, Atsipadhes, departs from supposed norms in producing no evidence for fires or animal sacrifice and hardly any examples of 'votive limbs', but a preponderance of cattle figurines and many likely phalloi. The greatest, Juktas, seems to focus particularly on a unique feature, the 'Chasm', effectively lacks the beetle figurines popular at several other sites (Davaras 1988), but has produced hundreds of sea-shells. More detailed study of other sites would probably show up other such differences, which may reflect some distinctions in cult practice, even if the many shared features do represent a very similarly conducted cult.

Sites chosen for peak sanctuaries may be at varying heights, though within the range where vegetation is still present, and seem to have been picked for their visibility from and good view of the surrounding countryside; thus, they will not always be the highest peak on a mountain. Their arrangement varies greatly in details, but always seem to centre upon a natural rock terrace, which was a main focus of activity; often it was approached by one or more lower terraces. There might be a surrounding wall, which at Juktas was massively built, and some kind of altar-like structure; but neither has been found at Atsipadhes. Where buildings occur, as at Petsopha (Fig. 8.3), they seem a later feature. At Juktas a system of stone terrace walls and a row of five rooms was built, along with an elaborate stone altar (Fig. 8.4) and a major structure outside the sanctuary's north entrance (French 1990: 71), both beginning before the end of the First Palace Period, while lower down the slope, by the way up, the Anemospilia building was constructed, perhaps at much the same time (on the date of its destruction deposit see most recently Warren 1991b: 335). Apparent representations on stone vessels suggest that such buildings could be quite elaborate (Fig. 8.5).

Much the commonest ritual action indicated is the offering of clay items (Figs 5.36: 2–4, 6–7; 8.6: 2–4). Many appear to have been burnt in fires on the main terrace, apparently thrown in during major ceremonies which might have formed part of seasonal or annual festivals; since no evidence of fire was identified at Atsipadhes, Peatfield speculates that this may be a Second Palace Period development, but Warren argues against (in Peatfield 1992: 81). Others might be placed unburnt in rock fissures, and the perforations on one major class, the 'votive limbs', suggest that they might have been suspended within the sanctuary area, perhaps following individual visits, and cleared on the occasion of the fire ceremonies (alternatively, they could have been worn as amulets and brought for offering). Other rites may have taken place as part of the major ceremonies (cf.

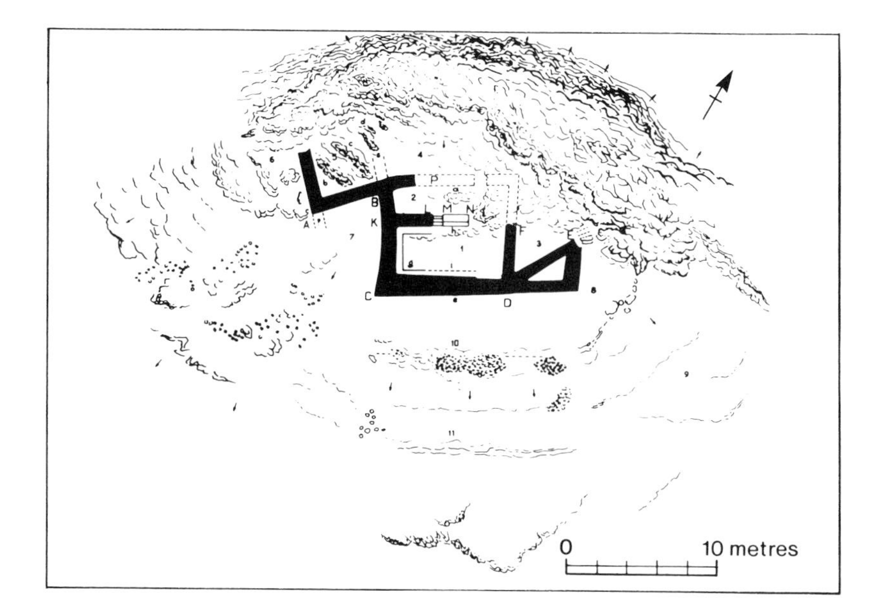

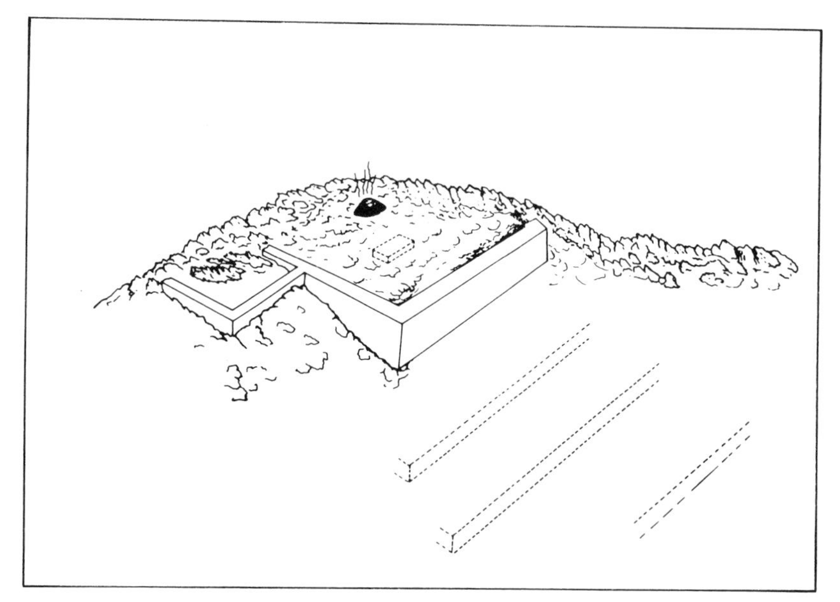

Fig. 8.3 Plan and reconstruction of the peak sanctuary at Petsopha. Courtesy of Prof. B. Rutkowski.

Peatfield 1992: 80 on rites, including libation, on the Atsipadhes Upper Terrace), or on separate occasions.

The purpose of offerings probably varied, as the items themselves do: they could be simple gifts, expressions of thanksgiving, fulfillments of vows, or appeals for help, for protection of humans or livestock, or for future good

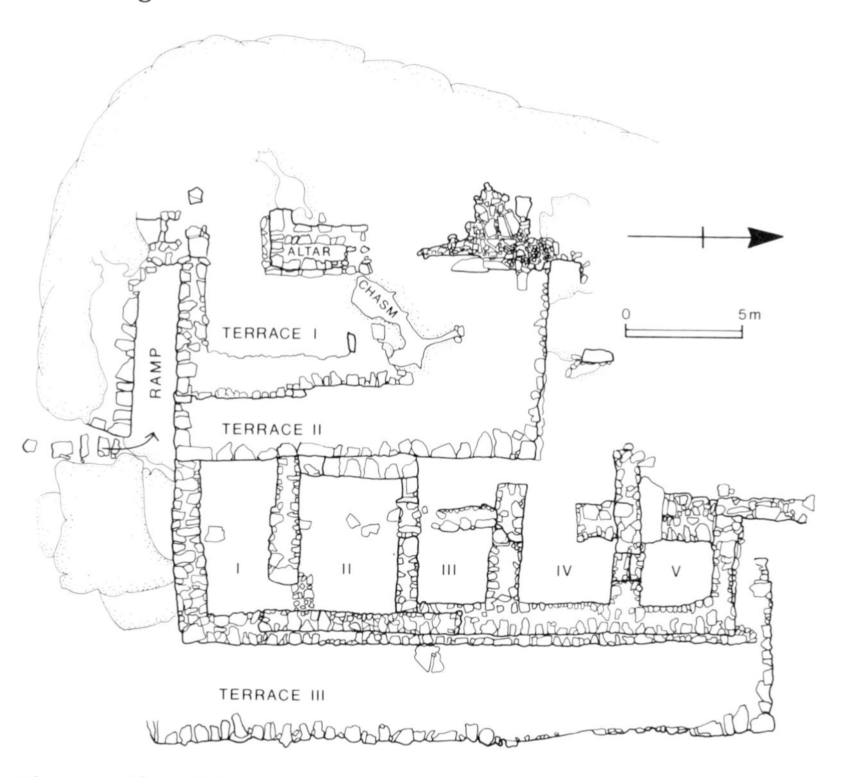

Fig. 8.4 Plan of the peak sanctuary at Juktas. Courtesy of Dr A. Karetsou.

fortune. Humans are often shown in poses of worship or invocation. Domestic animal figurines, ox heads, and models of loaves or fruit on plates seem to symbolise sacrifice or food offerings. 'Votive limbs', which include representations of detached heads, limbs and sections of the body, are best linked to appeals for healing in an afflicted part, which can sometimes be shown as diseased (Peatfield 1990: 122, 1992: 74; cf. Rutkowski 191: 32–4, 57). Some clay items may be sacred symbols, such as beetles, birds and snakes; some remain enigmatic, like balls and S-shaped coils. It seems most implausible that all this material should reflect the interests of a single group such as herders, as has been suggested; the offering of elaborately dressed and decorated figurines, examples of great size, and valuable items like metal objects is an indication of the participation of important members of society.

Shrines within buildings (Fig. 8.7: 1) include some with clearly palatial connections and associated with large open spaces, the first stages of the Central Palace Sanctuary, with which the Vat Room deposit should be associated (Panagiotaki 1992), and the Throne Room complex at Knossos, the Salle β and Quartier Mu complexes at Mallia, and the Upper and Lower West Court Shrines at Phaistos (Gesell 1985, nos 86–7, 102–3; Niemeier 1987: 163–4), also small structures in the towns at Gournia and Mallia (Fig. 8.7: 1) and on a hill at

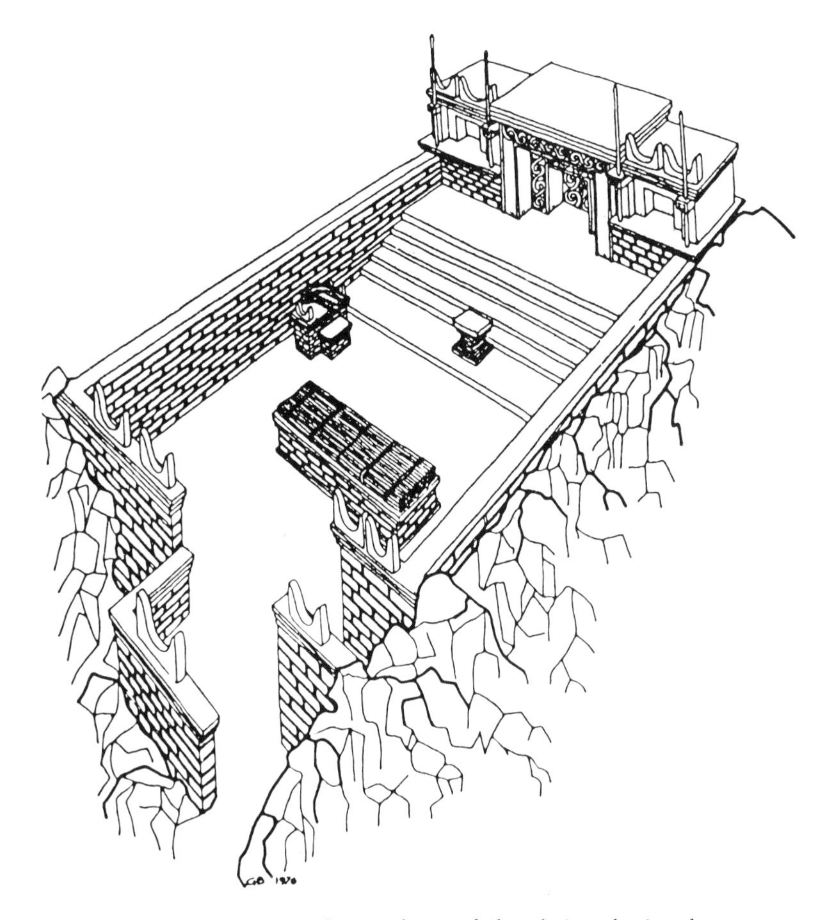

Fig. 8.5 Reconstruction by J. Shaw of the shrine depicted on a stone rhyton from Zakro. *AJA* 74 (1978) 434, fig. 8, courtesy of the Archaeological Institute of America.

Koumasa (Gesell 1985, nos 6, 70 (cf. also Rutkowski 1989), 76, ?77), and the Anemospilia building on Juktas, a late and unusually complex example (Sakellarakis 1991: 137–56). Some common features can be identified: they are generally approached through an anteroom, and often contain narrow bench-like platforms against one or more walls and centrally placed hearth-like features, sometimes sunk in the floor, for making offerings or cooking sacred meals. Probable offering vessels and 'libation tables' are commonly found in them or in associated rooms, which are often identified as for storage or food preparation; but it is hard to accept Marinatos's interpretation (1986: 19) of all the features of this kind at Anemospilia, of which there seems one in each part of the building, as solely for this purpose. They may rather have served for different rituals, or different stages in a single complex one (C. Sourvinou-Inwood, pers. commun.).

Marinatos has argued for associating these buildings particularly with rites of

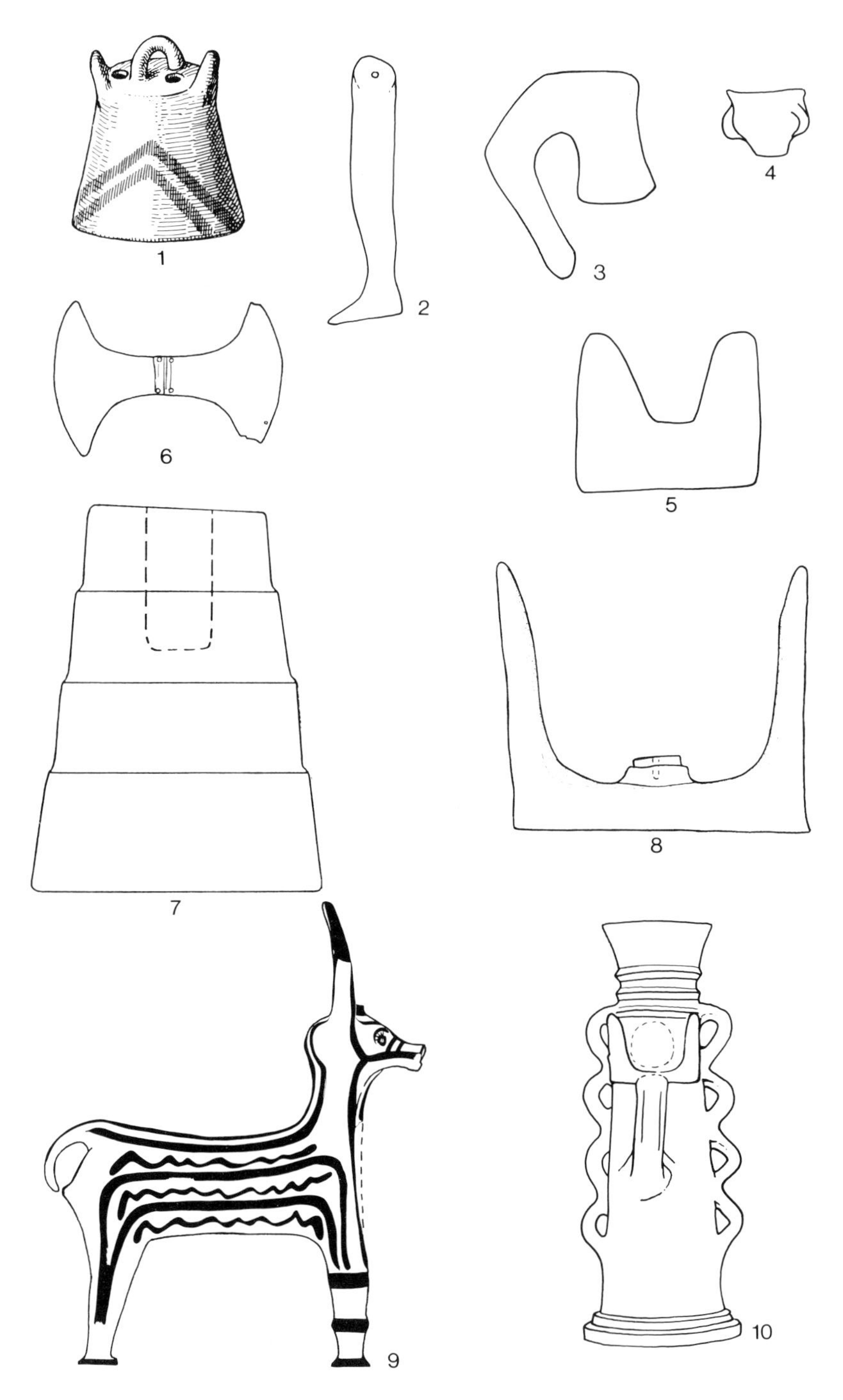

Fig. 8.6 Types of Minoan dedication and cult object. 1 'votive bell'/'horned mask'. 2, 3 'votive limbs', Petsopha. 4 miniature vessel, Petsopha. 5 miniature 'horns of consecration', Phaistos. 6 bronze double axe representation, Juktas. 7 stand for double axe, Palaikastro Block N. 8 LM III 'horns of consecration' with socket for ? double axe, Knossos. 9 wheelmade bovid figurine, Phylakopi. 10 'snake tube', Gournia. Scale of 1–5 1:3, of 6–10 1:6.

animal sacrifice in the open, followed by blood offering and sacred meals in the shrine (1986, especially 18–22, 37–8, 41); but it is less easy to associate such rites with the central 'lustral basins' at Knossos and Quartier Mu. She has also argued that at the palace sites the West Court was the setting for harvest festivals in the First Palace Period, associated with large-scale storage facilities (1987a: 135–8), which would emphasise the communal importance of the palace-based shrines; but this may not have been an original feature, for at Phaistos the Upper Shrine seems only to have been opened to the West Court in a second stage of its development, so may at first have been used by the palace personnel only.

It is unlikely that a single explanation will cover them all, but it is worth noting that shrines in buildings, including some of the tombs, differed significantly from open-air sites and probably from caves, in that parts of the ritual were apparently participated in by only a few people, not the whole of any gathering. This exclusiveness is what one would expect of an elite, whether secular or priestly; even in the West Court at Phaistos, the arrangements at the north end suggest that the 'theatre' was set aside for persons of special rank. The evidence of Anemospilia might indicate that this concealment of major elements in a ritual from any general congregation was spreading to rural sanctuaries, and the construction of buildings within the peak sanctuaries may represent a similar influence, although there is no certain evidence for their use in this way. But development was not all in one direction: towards the end of the First Palace Period, a ritual site was established at Kato Symi in the south-east, in a rural context and high above sea level, but not on a peak; the focus is likely to have been an abundant spring, near which a relatively small structure was built, but this is largely overlaid with an extremely complex series of later structural phases.

The Second Palace Period has always provided much of the data used for the reconstruction of Minoan religion, and its evidence has been basic to the arguments of those who would derive the dominant position of the palaces in Minoan society from their control of religion and treat the priesthood and ruling class as effectively identical (e.g. Marinatos 1984b: 167–8). There can be no denying the prominence of religion-related material. Scenes of ritual or religious symbolism have been widely identified, including on frescoes, metal seal-rings (Pl. 8.2), sealstones and relief-decorated stone vases, and skill and luxury materials were lavished on items evidently intended for ritual use. Complexes of rooms designed for rituals and ceremonies are identifiable in most important buildings, often approached through polythyra (Marinatos and Hägg 1986) and incorporating 'lustral basins' (Nordfeldt 1987), 'pillar crypts' (cf. Gesell 1985: 26–9), and also, in some cases, rooms argued to be for epiphany rituals (Hägg 1983). The constant association of these particular architectural types is a strong argument for their special significance, which is often enhanced further by the presence of frescoes or other features. It is impossible to doubt the religious function of the polythyron and 'lustral basin' complex in Xeste 3 at Akrotiri, or to ignore the fact that at Mallia the 'residential quarter' was built over the surely ritual Salle β complex, and if a ritual interpretation is appropriate in these cases so too, surely, should it be for comparable complexes. Some caution is still necessary, in that provision may be made for ceremonies that are not primarily religious, although they would almost certainly contain a religious element; further analysis may distinguish these from the purely religious settings. Evidence for the existence of small, one-room shrines, often in upper storeys, is even more widespread: 'town shrines' have been identified at Gournia and Pseira, and a whole complex of buildings that may have had ritual/ceremonial functions, facing onto a 'square' (plateia) is being uncovered at Palaikastro (cf. Fig. 4.13).

There is thus a significant quantity of evidence for the practice of religion in buildings within settlements, but many rural sites continued to be important ritual centres. Some of these may have been new foundations; certainly all the material from the Arkalochori cave seems to be of this period, apart from some very early EM, but the finds have never been fully published. But some previously significant sites evidently went into decline, if they were not completely abandoned, like most of the peak sanctuaries and the Kamares cave, which has produced only a little LM pottery. Peatfield places this development in the context of an extension of palatial control over religion: only certain peak sanctuaries, associated with palaces, major towns, or 'palatial areas' of high population, were patronised by the palaces, leading to the abandonment of those in more remote areas (1987: 92–3). The surviving peaks were, in his view, the primary sites for communal ritual, effectively united in one system with the palatial and town shrines, which he interprets more as sites for personal devotion and storage of ritual items. But there are difficulties in this view, not least that there are gaps in Peatfield's system (e.g. the Gulf of Mirabello towns, surely a 'palatial area', have no associated peak sanctuary) and that features which he uses to argue for palatial control can be found elsewhere: there was construction on a monumental scale at Kato Symi, and both here and in several caves valuable offerings and/or items inscribed in Linear A were found. Indeed, the inscriptions very often incorporate what seem stereotyped formulae (Karetsou *et al.* 1985), but this could as easily involve the repetition of standard phrases of dedication as of gods' names.

Moreover, it is hard to accept that all the evidence from buildings that has been mentioned relates purely to personal devotions, or that the elaborate vessels and even more the fine figures found in associated 'treasuries' were simply stored in them. The Palaikastro 'kouros' (Pl. 5.19) may well have been displayed (MacGillivray *et al.* 1991: 147) and the association of such items with successive phases of the Central Palace Sanctuary at Knossos (e.g. Pl. 5.18) strongly suggests use in it (Panagiotaki 1992). Others would also stress an extension of palatial control over religion, but place greatest importance on the rituals celebrated in or in association with the palaces (cf. especially Gesell 1987, Marinatos 1987a). The argument is that access to the ritual areas within the palaces was now restricted to an elite, and even if some rituals, especially in the courts, could have been witnessed by quite large audiences, their performance was the business of this elite. In the west courts, attention might have been focussed upon actions performed in the upper storey windows of the palace's west facade (Hägg 1987). It has even been suggested that the palaces were wholly temple complexes, and while this seems an exaggerated view, there is no denying that the palaces contain an impressive amount of evidence for the practice of religion.

This is particularly true of Knossos, where it has been argued that the fresco decoration largely reflects the conduct of important, multi-stage rituals for major festivals, involving large and small rooms in several parts of the palace (Cameron 1987). Figured frescoes in fact seem to be very largely concerned with ritual themes, and it is therefore interesting that they should be virtually absent from the other palaces, though found in lesser buildings. For the arguments for palatial control would work best if this control is envisaged as exercised from a single centre, Knossos. It would then be possible to explain the evidence in terms that would have good Near Eastern analogies, involving the celebration of the most important festivals at a capital, but provision in other centres of the state for rulers' residences where important types of ritual and ceremony could be celebrated, and patronage of the most significant local shrines by the ruler(s), as indicated by the presence of valuable offerings and inscribed items. It is even possible that the ruler(s) were expected to participate in festivals based at such local shrines. This still need not imply that the ruling elite and the priesthood were one and the same, but the domination of religious and ritual themes in art is very marked.

A striking feature of the evidence is the number of ritual complexes there can be in one building. In the Knossos palace, in particular (Fig. 5.26), one can cite the Central Palace Sanctuary, whose main part may now have been on the upper floor (Panagiotaki 1992), the Throne Room complex and East Hall, both of which are hypothesised to be for epiphany rituals, the Hall of the Double Axes, a polythyron complex which surely had at least ceremonial functions, and lesser rooms, such as that on the north which contained the Miniature Frescoes (cf. Cameron 1987). Several other Knossos buildings include comparable complexes (Gesell 1985, nos 42–56), especially the Royal Villa (Fig. 8.7: 2), House of the Chancel Screen, and High Priest's House, where rooms for epiphany rituals have been identified. There are similar complexes in the other palaces (and, at Mallia, in other buildings); even in the small example at Gournia, four shrines are identified in Soles' analysis (1991: 71–2). Taken together with the evidence for sometimes newly established town shrines and rural types of ritual site, this might seem massive over-provision for religious activity.

If, however, religion involved the worship of a number of important gods, 'national' and local, it could be readily explained. More than one god may have been summoned to epiphany, and the similarity of many of the complexes to each other would no more signify that they involved worship of the same god(s)

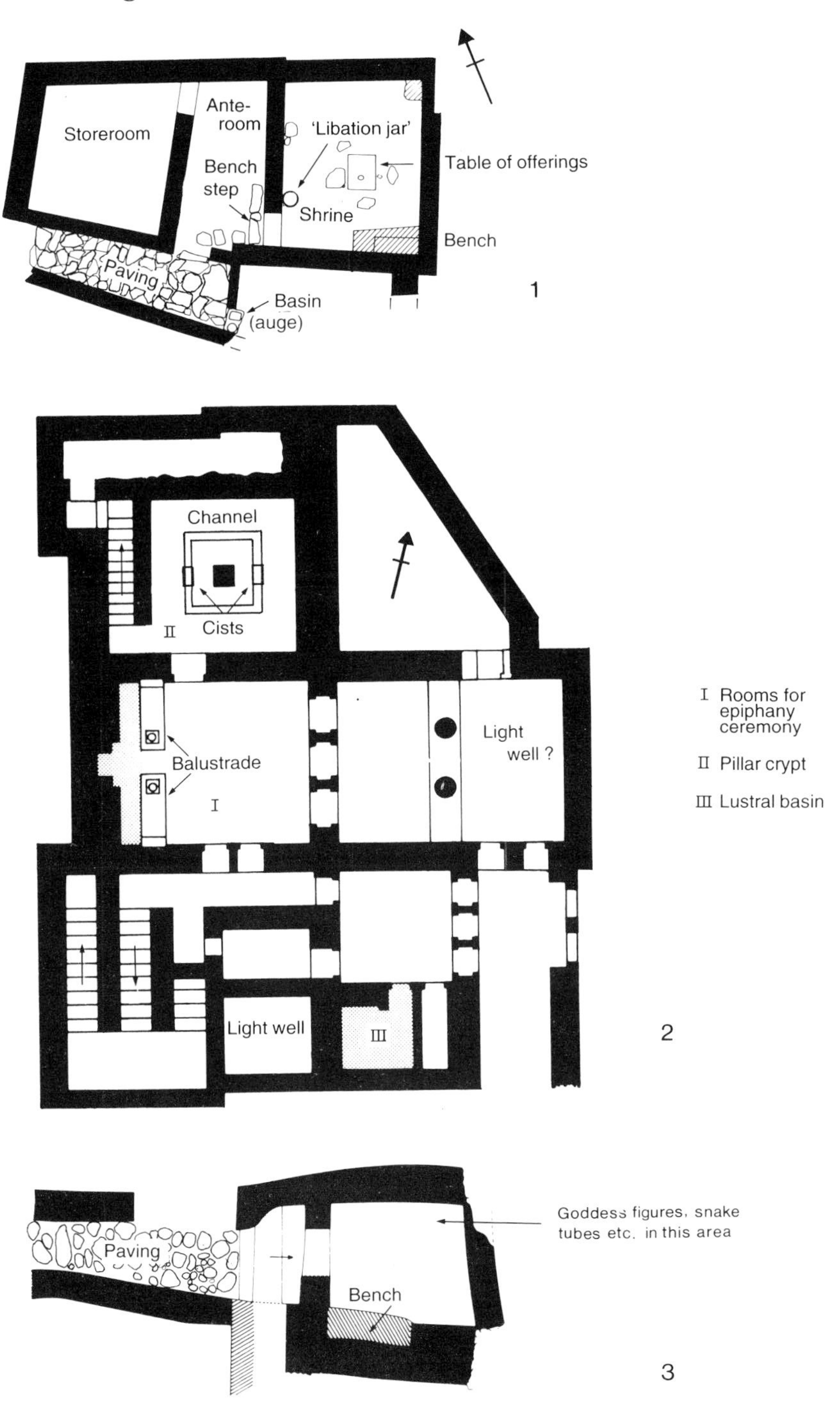

Fig. 8.7 Plans of Minoan built shrines. Scale c. 1:200.
1 the Mallia 'town shrine'. 2 the Royal Villa, Knossos. 3 the LM III shrine at Gournia. Courtesy of Prof. B. Rutkowski.

than the similarity of temples in the Near Eastern civilisations or later Greece. Some structures might indeed be linked through their use in multi-stage rituals, as Cameron suggested; but he was too ready to think in terms of worship of a single major deity. Knossos may have had exceptional provision because important gods of other territories had to be given a base in the capital (cf. Macqueen 1986: 122–3 for a Hittite parallel). It would follow that a palace was, if not entirely a temple complex, at least very much concerned with the practice of religion, and much of the storage, record-keeping and craftwork practised in it may have been tied to one or another cult.

Some attempt at creating a 'national religion' may well have been made in this period; this would provide a context for the unusual impressiveness of the Knossos palace's arrangements, since the local elites might have been expected to gather there to participate in important rites, such as may be shown on the Knossos Miniature Frescoes, in which the elaborate hair styles and sometimes jewellery of the audiences suggest their elite status. Certainly it is possible to document a growing convergence in practice, which may reflect attempts at harmonisation of beliefs. Not only are bronze worshipper figurines and stone 'libation tables' (Fig. 5.21: 12) found in many types of context; the double axe and 'horns of consecration' symbols are constantly used in representations and in reality (Fig. 8.6: 5–7), apparently to indicate a holy place, perhaps particularly one of animal sacrifice.

Yet there are still some very marked distinctions, especially in caves. From some nothing but pottery is reported, while others, especially Psychro, have produced a medley of items comparable to that from peak sanctuaries, including bronze worshipper figurines, double axe models (also some in gold and silver), weapons and weapon simulacra, stone 'libation tables', sealstones and jewellery. Arkalochori, which contained an exceptional wealth of metal offerings, but no figurines or 'libation tables', must surely be the base of a special cult. Kato Symi (Lebessi and Muhly 1990) is also remarkable for its wealth of offerings, which include not only some bronze figurines, but large numbers of stone vessels, especially 'libation tables', and of distinctive clay types, chalices and tubular stands (cf. Rutkowski 1986, figs 150, 152–7), presumably relating to the performance of special rituals. The sequence here was also individual, since a complex structure of many rooms was replaced during the Second Palace Period by an open-air enclosure, approached by a processional way and surrounding a massive podium, which was not an altar but was probably used for ceremonies (Fig. 8.8), and remained in use for a very long time though partly built over in later phases. The enclosure contained much evidence for animal sacrifice, followed, it seems, by a ritual meal, but probably not a burnt offering (Bergquist 1988).

The large amount of pictorial evidence belonging to this period offers the prospect of elucidating rituals reflected in the archaeological remains, but notoriously this material has its own problems of interpretation, and only a few

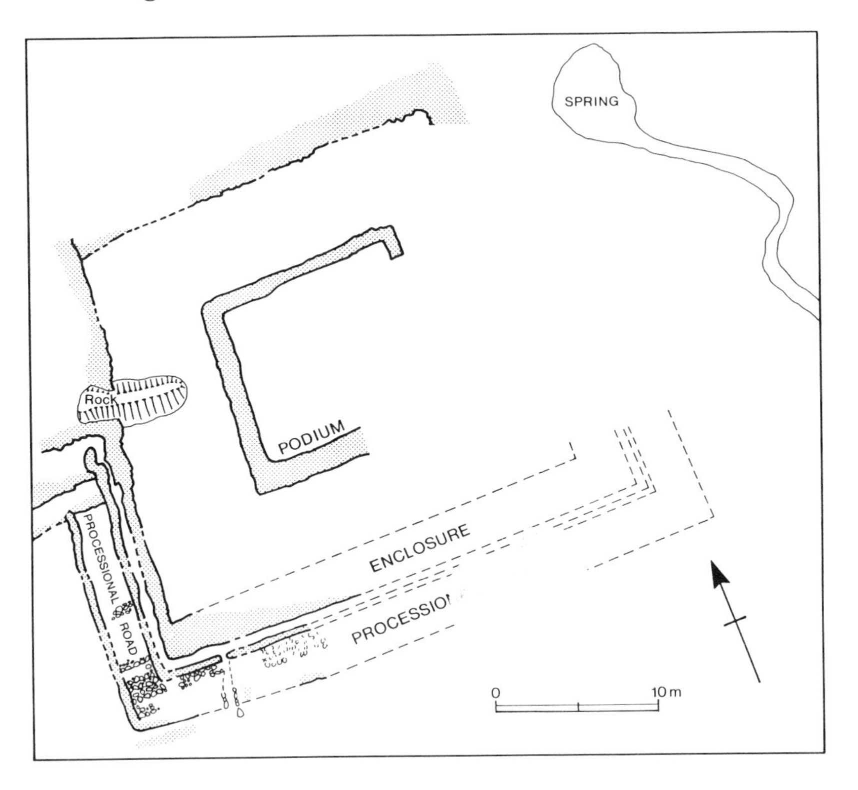

Fig. 8.8 Provisional plan of the podium at Kato Symi in its original form. Courtesy of Dr A. Lebessi.

comments will be made here. Most representations are small scale, and so must excerpt and allude in a way less necessary in a fresco, using conventions perfectly intelligible at the time that must now be reconstructed (cf. Marinatos 1986, Part II on allusions to animal sacrifice, and Sourvinou-Inwood 1989a). They may refer to a single stage in a ritual, or more generally to an important element of belief, religious symbolism or myth. Where settings are depicted, they are open-air, often apparently rural; though the exteriors of apparent shrine buildings may be shown, no scenes are clearly set within buildings or caves. Most often one to four figures are shown; only the Knossos Miniature Frescoes and Procession Fresco show considerably larger numbers, in the former case audiences of hundreds as well as a smaller group of performers. Sometimes figures shown in isolation, or accompanied by a mythical creature like the griffin, may be gods; sometimes, especially when carrying sacrificial instruments or wearing particular types of robes, they are probably priests or rulers in priestly guise. In contrast with the Near East, there seem to be no special forms of dress or attribute which distinguish gods; rather, they are shown as high-status humans (e.g. Figs 8.9: 3–5, 8.10), so identification is difficult. But figures larger than the rest among a group on the ground, or small figures, even birds, descending from the sky, have

Fig. 8.9 Probable Minoan deity representations.
1 the 'Lady of Myrtos'. 2 EM III/MM IA anthropomorphic vessel from Mochlos. 3 composite restoration of the 'Mountain Mother' sealing, Knossos. 4 reconstruction of the 'Priest-King' relief figure, Knossos, courtesy of Prof. W–D. Niemeier. 5 the 'Master Impression' central figure, Khania.

Fig. 8.10 The central figures in the Xeste 3 'Crocus Gatherers' fresco. Courtesy of Dr N. Marinatos.

reasonably been thought to represent gods about to make or having made an epiphany, or god-impersonators; several make a commanding gesture (Niemeier 1988: 240–1).

The complex iconography detected in the depictions and the elaboration of the reconstructed rituals and their architectural settings indicate the sophistication that Minoan religion had achieved by this time. It would be surprising if this religion did not exert influence on those of other Aegean cultures, as other aspects of Minoan civilisation did, but evidence of such influence is hard to find in the MBA. There are occasional finds of Minoan or Minoan-style figurines and other likely ritual items such as double axe models (French 1971: 148; Dickinson 1977: 35–6; Renfrew 1985: 376; Barber and Hadjianastasiou 1989: 129–30); but there is nothing evidently Minoan about the only substantial structure outside Crete, the 'temple' at Ayia Irini. This seems to date from the time of the site's refoundation in the mature MBA, and was a complex structure, originally two-roomed but soon extended eastwards for at least four more, the larger of which had benches along the walls. Later use of the building had badly damaged the earliest deposits, but rites of sacrifice and libation seem to have been practised throughout its history; these are too unspecific for the argument associating them with Dionysos (Caskey, M.E. 1981) to seem plausible, and it is perfectly possible that the building housed different cults. Minoan influence is more readily detectable in the Second Palace Period, but its incidence is more sporadic than brief summaries of the material tend to suggest. While Minoan types of ritual vessel, particularly rhytons, are widely found, figurines and other symbolic items are thinly scattered; there is a more substantial distribution of seal-rings and sealstones which show ritual themes or symbols in Minoan style, but these may be adapted or even misunderstood (cf. Niemeier 1990). The best evidence is provided by finds from Akrotiri, Ayia Irini and its neighbourhood, and the Apollo Maleatas site at Epidauros; Phylakopi has produced relatively little, but two 'pillar crypts' are notable, one of which contained a fresco which probably shows the robing ritual (Renfrew 1985: 375–7; Morgan 1990: 259 fig. 8). The evidence from Akrotiri is certainly the most impressive, including the use of the polythyron in the ashlar-faced Xeste buildings, which in Xeste 3 controls the approach to a 'lustral basin' complex, the depictions of Minoan-style rituals and religious themes in several frescoes within important buildings (notably Fig. 8.10), and examples of many types of religious paraphernalia (Marinatos 1984a, 1984b). This is only part of the larger body of evidence suggesting that there were strong similarities between the societies of Thera and Crete, of which the deduced age-grade systems, represented particularly in hair styles and probably linked to ritual, form an important part; female dress in ritual contexts also seems effectively identical to the Minoan. But it is worth pointing out that the decoration of a 'lustral basin' complex with symbolic and ritual scenes is not matched in Crete itself, and that the evidence perforce only relates to religious activity within the settlement; only a representation on a West House miniature fresco suggests the existence of something like a peak sanctuary. Marinatos is prepared to interpret the evidence in terms of syncretisation, rather than the adoption of purely Minoan cults (1990a), and this does, indeed, seem reasonable. The possibility that the evidence reflects the presence of a dominant body of Minoan settlers (Wiener 1990: 154) cannot be ruled out; but if so, this is likely to have been a local rather than pan-Cycladic phenomenon, for no buildings comparable to the Xestai have been identified elsewhere.

The large clay female figures in Minoan style from the 'temple' at Ayia Irini are also very striking, but their evidence should not be pressed too far. The 'temple' shows no other sign of being adapted to Minoan-style cult, although a bronze worshipper figurine was found (Caskey 1964: 328). The figures are argued to have been used to symbolise a ritual of epiphany of Minoan type, but no Minoan parallel is known for this yet, and the god or gods invoked could still have been local. Similarly, the possible shrine in House A (Cummer and Schofield 1984: 27–8, 39) has no very Minoan features, and a miniature fresco which includes a ceremonial procession from a room within the fortification is not markedly Minoan in content (Morgan 1990: 253–8). Even the nearby Troullos hill, which has produced another bronze worshipper figurine and two 'libation tables' (Davis 1984: 164–5) and seems clearly a ritual site, can hardly be called a peak sanctuary when it has produced no evidence of figurine deposition. In general, the evidence on Kea suggests that a Minoan veneer is being given to local cults, no doubt under cultural and perhaps political influence.

Finally, at the Epidauros site an open-air altar was established within an extensive terrace, on a hill site where there is no trace of previous cult, rather of an ordinary MH settlement (Lambrinudakis 1981; cf. also Hägg 1984: 120–1, Catling 1989: 27–8; on the lack of MH cult, Touchais 1989: 604). Rites evidently included animal sacrifice and the lighting of fires, to judge from extensive ash layers, and offerings included types that have clear Minoan connections, notably bronze double axe models and many conical cups (Wiener 1984: 21, n. 40). But other characteristic features of peak sanctuaries, notably the clay offerings, are absent; the site is closer in some ways to Kato Symi, but the dedication of weapons and double axe models can be paralleled at Arkalochori. In fact, as Hägg stresses, no complete Minoan cult pattern was taken over. Overall, the site raises many problems, not least its establishment as a major cult site so far from the major settlements of the Argolid on a site where there was no previous cult, and its evidence can hardly be used to argue for widespread Minoanisation on the mainland.

In the Third Palace Period, there were major changes. Many sites went out of use or show only a scatter of pottery, as at Arkalochori and Kamares (Kanta 1980: 80, 112). It is clear at Juktas and Kato Symi, and likely at Psychro, that there was no break in activity, but the same cannot be presumed for other sites from which both LM I and LM III types have been reported. Indeed, some peak sanctuaries apparently being used in LM III (Peatfield 1983: 278) have produced no LM I material; their revival may reflect the increasing provincialism in Crete that followed the destruction of the palace at Knossos, also perhaps perceptible in the foundation of many new LM III cult sites (some clearly LM IIIB). The continuing use of the Knossos palace involved the use of many of its rooms for ritual or ceremonial purposes, but overall polythyra, 'lustral basins', and 'pillar crypts' seem to have lost significance.

There is a similar picture in the evidence for rituals. Some types of item apparently ceased to be made, such as 'libation tables' and most stone ritual vessels, although older pieces could continue in use, as particularly in the Knossos Central Palace Sanctuary; this must have had an effect at sites like Kato Symi, where they had been common before. Yet there was also a considerable element of continuity: basic forms of ritual such as sacrifice, libation, and the offering of figurines and other items certainly continued. The clear evidence for animal sacrifice from Arkhanes T. A (Sakellarakis 1991: 76–7), best interpreted as part of the burial ritual for a special individual, seems to represent a continuation or adaptation of Minoan traditions rather than a newly introduced rite. The palace frescoes, a larnax from Knossos (Morgan 1987), the famous Ayia Triada sarcophagus with scenes of sacrifice and libation (Pl. 8.3), seal-rings and seal-stones all show rituals or religious themes in an essentially Minoan style. Similarly, in the Linear B texts concerning offerings of olive oil and other substances, the unspecific offerings to 'all the gods' or to apparently sacred places and shrines (most if not all close to Knossos, according to Killen 1987), and the

Pl. 8.3 The Ayia Triada sarcophagus: sacrifice scene. Peter Clayton.

prominence of 'priestesses of the winds' seem highly likely to preserve elements of the previous period, as does the occurrence of peculiar, apparently divine names here and elsewhere (Chadwick 1976: 100).

It is not clear how far any of the changes are attributable to the new 'Mycenaean' ruling class of Knossos. The survival or abandonment of major sites and the disappearance of inscribed dedications should reflect decisions at palace level. The term 'potnia', of patently Indo-European origin, meaning 'lady' or 'mistress', might have been introduced from the mainland, but no identifiably Greek divine names are prominent in the texts, although several occur once or twice; but the reference to 'Diktaian Zeus' is a noteworthy example of syncretism with a probably important local cult (particularly if Dikte was Petsopha, in a region generally thought to be outside the political control of the Knossos state). The griffins in the Throne Room fresco have been argued to reflect specifically Mycenaean iconography, but the general associations of the throne and frescoes seem Minoan (Niemeier 1987: 167). The prominence of males in the Procession Fresco may reflect a new social order, but they are led by, and are apparently paying respect to, female figures (cf. Boulotis 1987; Cameron 1987: 323 fig. 6). The overall impression gained, especially from the pictorial material, is of a wish to fit in with established traditions.

During the LM III phases there seems to be an increasing emphasis on built shrines, whether within a settlement or isolated (there is evidence for further building at Juktas and Kato Symi), and on open-air sanctuaries accessible from settlements, as at Ayia Triada (Gesell 1985: 76–7); their dating is often rather imprecise, for lack of sufficiently distinctive pottery, but many seem to be LM IIIB. The shrines have much in common with the older 'bench sanctuaries' (Fig. 8.7: 3), though there is no clear evidence that animal sacrifice was associated with them; but there is evidence for sacrifice, and for the dedication of animal figurines, at open-air sites, both old and new, and other types of dedication in bronze and clay were offered particularly at the Piazzale dei Sacelli site at Ayia Triada. The ritual items most commonly found associated with the built shrines (cf. Renfrew 1985: 366–8 for the best known), the 'goddess with upraised arms' figures and 'snake tubes' (Figs 8.13: 1–2, 8.6: 10) can be derived from older sources, although the figurine sequence is patchy and the apparent prototypes of the 'snake tubes' are virtually unique to Kato Symi and nearby Pyrgos (Gesell 1985, Figs 134–5). Yet both figures and tubes are commonly embellished with 'horns of consecration', birds and snakes, demonstrating the continuing vitality of these sacred symbols, and double axes survived, if less prominently (Gesell 1985: 53; but 'horns of consecration' like Fig. 8.6: 8 may well have held double axes).

Cave cults have been argued to become prominent in this period, in that many of those claimed to be cult sites have produced LM III material only. But this material has never been published in detail and interpretations relating to ordinary or 'refuge' occupation have sometimes been advanced. The cult interpretation seems safest where earlier evidence or the presence of clearly or plausibly ritual items corroborates it, as in fact in the Mameloukos cave, which has Second Palace Period ritual items, although LM IIIB material has been interpreted to represent a 'refuge site' (Tyree 1974: 58–9). Amnisos has the unique distinction of being apparently confirmed through the reference to Eileithyia's cave in Odyssey xix.188 and a Linear B record of an offering to *E-re-u-ti-ja*, both at Amnisos. The majority contain pottery and rarely figurines, but the range of offerings from Psychro and Patsos is as rich as before (cf. Tyree 1974, Ch. V).

'Goddess with upraised arms' figures do not seem to have been found in caves, but are otherwise one of the most characteristic ritual types of LM III Crete. They often occur in groups, which are basically similar though differing in details, and there is room for doubt whether they represent the same or different personalities. The discovery of at least seventeen in one LM IIIC deposit from Kavousi, along with many 'snake tube' fragments (French 1990: 73), suggests that perhaps they did represent only one goddess, whose image, along with an associated 'snake tube' which apparently supported an offering vessel, was replaced from time to time; alternatively, several may have been used simultaneously, as at Gazi (Gesell 1985: 69–71), perhaps by different communities who used the same site. They could still be interpreted as representing essentially local figures, the ancestors of the largely localised deities of later Crete like Britomartis, Diktynna and Eileithyia, though conceived in the same idiom.

This type did not spread to other parts of the Aegean, whereas the large wheelmade animal figurine, which seems to appear first in Crete, certainly did (Fig. 8.6: 9). This capacity to develop new types of ritual item, seen in other types of figurine, including groups and centaur-like figures, testifies to the continuing vitality of the Minoan religious tradition, although no class was mass-produced like the Mycenaean figurines. The survival of traditional symbols like the double axe and 'horns of consecration' also emphasises the strong link to the past. This amalgam of features continued into the Dark Age, when several of the ancient cult places continued or were revived, but by this time the Minoan tradition is being recognisably overlaid by new elements, although Cretan religion retained strong local features that may have preserved Minoan elements throughout antiquity.

The development of Mycenaean religion

Notoriously, evidence for MH religion is virtually non-existent, and the processes of development which led to a distinctively Mycenaean set of religious features are remarkably obscure. Hägg has suggested that libation was practised on the mainland from MH times (1990: 184), and that cults could have been established in caves and at open-air sites such as water sources, to become part of a 'popular' Mycenaean religion (1981a: 38); but the fact remains that, however inherently plausible such ideas seem, they are entirely hypothetical, and the identification of any 'Helladic' component among the practices at the Epidauros site (as in Hägg 1984: 121) must beg the question, since there is no evidence of cult activity here before LH I. But Hägg's argument that there was an eagerness to adopt Minoan symbols, practices and perhaps beliefs in the early Mycenaean period certainly seems to fit the evidence, although in the earliest phase this phenomenon may have been confined to the Argolid, where the only examples of Minoan-type ritual vessels in early contexts are found, and there is other evidence for emulation of Minoan high-status behaviour by the emerging elite (Dickinson 1989: 134–6). Yet it remains very difficult to link this early 'Minoanisation' to the undoubted Mycenaean practices and cult sites of the Third Palace Period, which have few if any obviously Minoan elements.

One of the earliest distinctively Mycenaean features is the figurine tradition, which had begun to develop before the end of LH II (cf. Cummer and Schofield 1984: 139); but while Minoan influences may be detected in this (French 1971: 105–6), the standard types have no very good LM analogues. They are far more frequent at Mycenae (cf. French in Hägg and Marinatos 1981: 48) than at other sites like Pylos and Nichoria, but many relatively early examples have been found in the south Peloponnese, and they are very widespread during the Third

Palace Period (see Ch. 5 (vi) for a discussion of types). Sites of figurine deposition, of which several have been noted (French 1971: 107; Hägg 1981a: 38–9; Kilian 1990: 185–90), may well prove to be one of the most characteristic features of Mycenaean religion. Some are separate from settlements, but one example has been identified in the Lower Citadel at Tiryns (Kilian 1981: 53; Catling 1984: 25), where the range of figurines and other goods suggests parallels with the shrines of Phylakopi, and figurine offering was practised at several sites together with other rites, as at Epidauros and the Ayia Irini 'temple', and may be represented in a Tiryns fresco (Immerwahr 1990: 114, cf. also 119). Clearly they could have a variety of functions, being found also as grave-goods and in domestic contexts, possibly as apotropaic items (Kilian 1988a: 148, using Tiryns evidence). It might well seem likely that the female figurines' popularity reflects that of at least one important goddess, but they could have been understood as references to several goddesses of varied, perhaps often only local significance, like the Syro-Palestinian figurines and plaques to which they have been compared (French 1971: 106; cf. Drower 1975: 157).

At the time that figurines were becoming popular, in the early Third Palace Period, ritual sites are still very hard to identify on the mainland, and in the Cyclades the only finds of significance come from the Ayia Irini 'temple'. Here the dedication of Mycenaean figurines, with the deposition of a group of these in a pit over House A (Cummer and Schofield 1984: 128–9, 139), indicates some Mycenaeanisation of local practice, while the construction of one large figure shows some attempt to keep up the earlier tradition. Much of the building continued in use till LH IIIC, with benches being replaced at higher levels, a feature paralleled in the shrine complex at Phylakopi, and at the end of the BA a small structure in a corner at the eastern end seems to have become a major focus of activity; but the later Dionysos cult, centring on the recovered head of one of the old figures, was based elsewhere.

Of the identifiable cult sites of the later Third Palace Period the most important by far are the complexes of buildings at Phylakopi, whose history goes back into LH IIIA (Fig. 8.11), and those in the Cult Centre at Mycenae, which appear to be entirely LH IIIB, although some finds are probably earlier (Fig. 8.12). In both cases there is a fairly complex series of building phases, involving extensions and rebuildings. It is characteristic of both that they have several different focusses of ritual activity, which frequently show significant distinctions in associated material and thus provide *prima facie* evidence that they were used for different cults; internal features seem to have been used largely for offering items of various kinds, while sacrifice and perhaps libation were more probably performed outside. The joining of several cults in one complex, presumably dominated by a chief god, may have been common; it certainly seems indicated by tablet Tn316 from Pylos (Boulotis 1990).

The material of these two sites has been analysed elsewhere in considerable detail and does not need extensive coverage here, but it is worth noting some

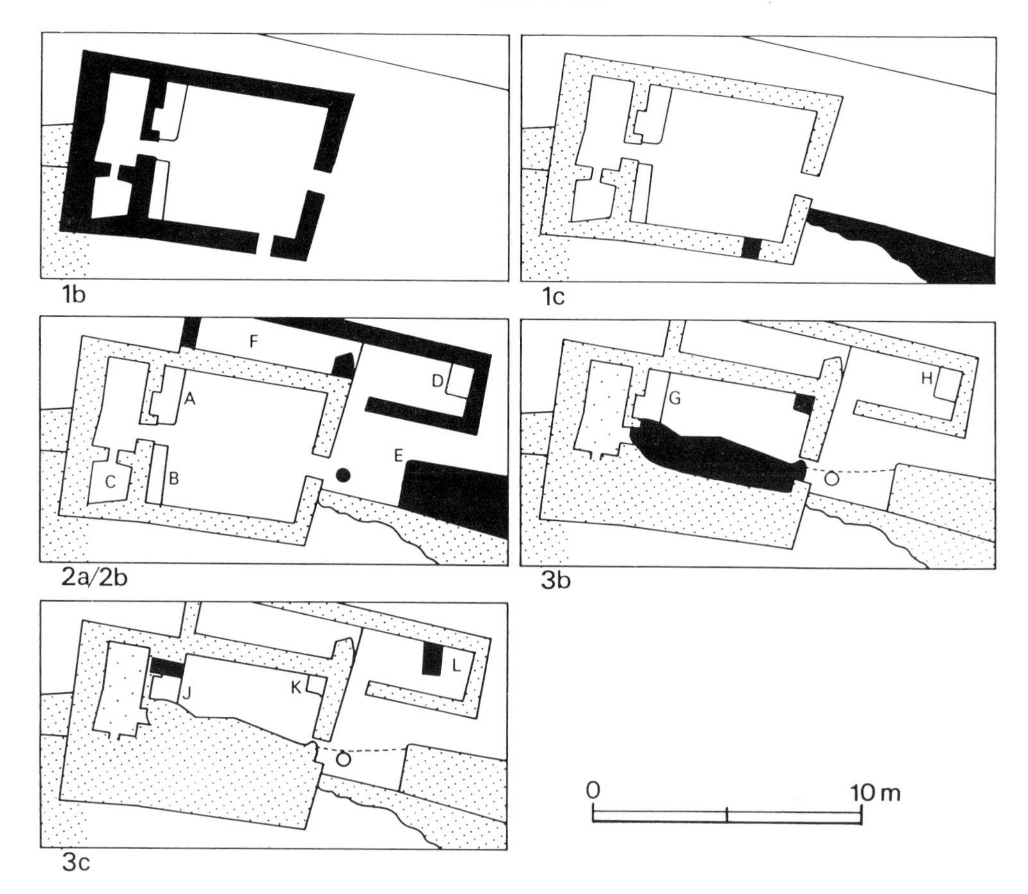

Fig. 8.11 The successive phases of the Phylakopi shrines. Courtesy of the Managing Committee of the British School at Athens and Prof. Lord Renfrew.

major differences, which hardly suggest much homogeneity of cult within the Mycenaean world. Phylakopi has no parallel for major features at Mycenae, such as the large figures, now interpreted as representations of worshippers rather than gods (Moore 1988), coiled snakes, and elaborate altars (Room of the Fresco, Tsountas House Shrine; the Court 92 altar at Pylos was also decorated). Conversely, the 'Lady', male figures (Fig. 8.13: 3, 5) and 'baetyl' of Phylakopi have no parallel at Mycenae, although there is other rather fragmentary evidence from the mainland for large clay figures that could have been cult images. Nor are the usual types of figurine very common among the Cult Centre material, as they are at Phylakopi. Neither complex, it may be noted, contains distinctively Minoan features, apart from the 'horns of consecration' depicted on the Room of the Fresco altar (Fig. 8.14).

Neither complex is particularly impressive in appearance, though the approaches to the Cult Centre's two levels at Mycenae have monumental features

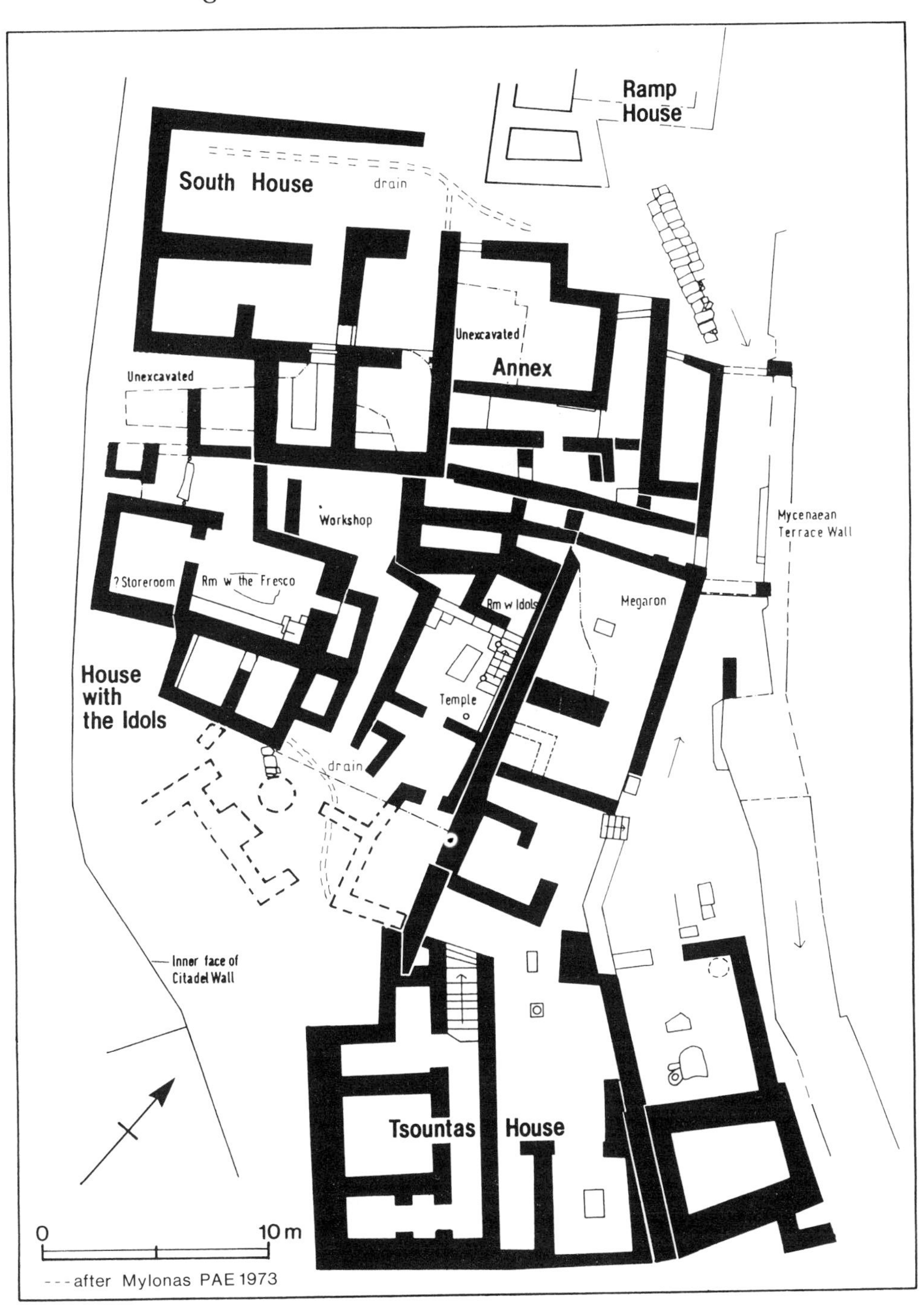

Fig. 8.12 Plan of the Mycenae Cult Centre. Courtesy of Drs E.B. French and K. Wardle.

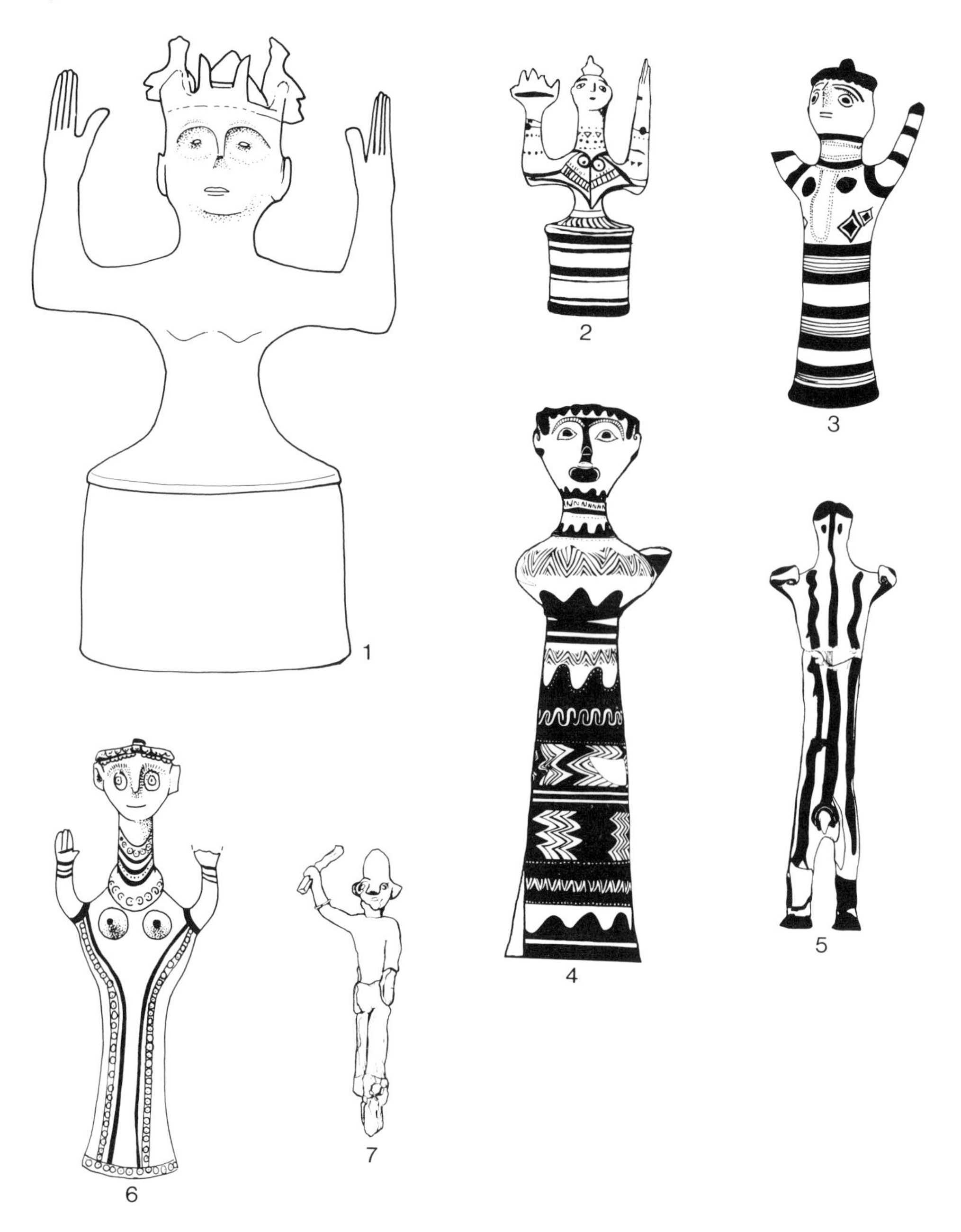

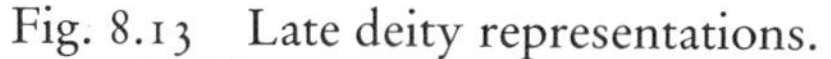

Fig. 8.13 Late deity representations.
1–3 'Goddesses with upraised arms' from the Gazi shrine, the Shrine of the Double Axes, Knossos, and 'Cult Centre' Room 31, Mycenae. 4 the 'Lady of Phylakopi'. 5 the largest male figure, Phylakopi. 6 figure from the Postpalatial shrine, Tiryns. 7 bronze 'smiting god', Phylakopi. Scale 1:6, except 7 (1:3).

and the layout at Phylakopi seems carefully structured, nor can any other impressive religious structures be recognised (on the claimed 'Mycenaean Telesterion' at Eleusis see Darcque 1981). It might be suggested that the palaces were the sites of important ceremonies, but the arguments for their religious use remain rather tentative. Certainly, the focussing of attention on the megaron suites and their massive, clearly ceremonial, hearths are suggestive, and taken with the presence of procession frescoes, clearly showing the bringing of offerings in several cases and at Pylos associated with the approach to the megaron, strongly suggest that there was some kind of cult activity in the palaces. But this might have been very specific, relating to the divine patrons of the citadel, the ruler(s) or the palace itself rather than those of the whole society. Unless the great courts were so used, the Mycenaean palaces certainly offer no place for a 'congregation' to gather.

Evidence from the Linear B texts, including those of Knossos, can now be used to supplement that of archaeology (see particularly Chadwick 1976, Ch. 6; Baumbach 1979), although it is patchy and often obscure. It is clear from the Pylos evidence that both males and females served as priests, presumably for gods of their respective sexes. Quite a number of divine names are known or suspected, but it is surely a mistake to lump them together as 'the Mycenaean pantheon'. Some names are recorded at more than one site, not only well-known names such as Zeus, Hera, Poseidon and Hermaias (Hermes), who might well be among the greater gods of the Mycenaean world, but figures unknown or totally obscure later such as Diwia, Marineus and *Ko-ma-we-te-ja* (Komawenteia?) (Chadwick 1976: 95, 99). The name/title Potnia, which appears universally, might refer to the leader of the pantheon, but only at Pylos is she clearly a figure of the highest importance; the often quoted examples of Potnia with an apparently local or specific epithet, and the offerings of oil made to Potnia and Wanax at different Pylian sites, seem to indicate that these titles could be applied to local figures (Hiller 1981: 122–5 interprets them as referring to the human king and queen, embodying divinities, but this does not explain why the palace should send offerings to them at minor sites). At Knossos there is much evidence for local cults, and another strong indication of localised pantheons is provided by the well-known Pylos tablet Tn316, which lists a series of gods receiving offerings of gold vessels and human beings at Pylos and the important religious centre of *Pa-ki-ja-ne* (Chadwick 1976: 89–96). Male gods are prominent in this text and generally in Linear B material, a notable contrast to their rarity in representations.

It remains impossible to relate the recorded names to the archaeological material. Even where representations are as specific as that in the Mycenae Room of the Fresco, which shows two goddesses facing one another, one with a long staff or sceptre, the other with a sword (Fig. 8.14; Marinatos 1988b), we cannot supply names, although the temptation to connect them with Hera and Athena, paired so often in Homer, is strong. But the inner room opening off the Room of

Fig. 8.14 Reconstruction of the fresco over an altar in the Room of the Fresco, Mycenae. Courtesy of Dr N. Marinatos.

the Fresco contains only one female figure, and with the possible exception of the 'shield goddess' on a painted stone tablet from the nearby Tsountas House (Immerwahr 1990, pls 62–3), there is no other representation of an armed goddess at this period, although two frescoes, one from the Mycenae Cult Centre, show females, who may be goddesses, wearing helmets (Morgan 1988, Pls 155, 157).

Overall, the impression given by the Mycenaean material of the Third Palace

Period is of a tradition distinct from and much simpler than the Minoan, from which it derived neither architectural features nor, with rare exceptions, many elements of ritual paraphernalia or symbolism: the 'horns of consecration' appear sometimes in representation or reality (examples in stone at Pylos and Gla, in clay on a brick 'house altar' at Tiryns, Catling 1981a: 15), while the double axe and tripartite shrine are each shown once on Tiryns frescoes (Immerwahr 1990: 204). But the basic rituals of the two traditions may have had many similarities, and in Postpalatial times there seems to be greater convergence: what look close to canonical 'bench sanctuaries' appear in the Lower Citadel at Tiryns, where female cult images in the upraised arms position were set up on the bench (Kilian 1981), and at Asine (Hägg 1981b), and the large barrel-bodied animals, apparently a Minoan type originally, become increasingly popular, especially at the Amyklaion, an apparently new open-air site (Demakopoulou 1982). Although some sites were abandoned, the material of the Postpalatial Period does not show great changes: the dedication of figurines continued to be very popular, although they may disappear from some parts of the Mycenaean world, and at Phylakopi old examples were reused, as well as other older ritual items. The occurrence of Near Eastern 'smiting god' figures (Fig. 8.13: 7) here and elsewhere might reflect a changing conception of one or more male gods, but this can only be suggested very tentatively.

But by the end of the BA the picture is very different. The figurine tradition had largely died out: females and small animals are no longer found, and barrel-bodied animals are barely attested outside Crete and Cyprus. This is evident even where continuity of cult activity is clear or plausible, as at Ayia Irini, the Amyklaion and Kalapodi. There were probable changes in the form of sacrifice (Marinatos 1988a; Bergquist 1988). Long-established sites of worship like the Phylakopi complex were abandoned; indeed, most major Greek cult sites outside Crete have no prehistoric predecessor, but begin in the Dark Age, often quite late (cf. Morgan, C. 1990: 12 (Argive Heraion), 14 (Eleusis), 22–3 (Olympia), 108, 148 (Delphi), 206 (Delos), 213 (Isthmia)). Some sites, divine names and, no doubt, ritual practices continued, as did the tradition that gods were normally served by priests of their own sex, but all the indications are that Aegean religion underwent great changes during the Dark Age.

Bibliography

For the most recent comprehensive collection of data see Rutkowski 1986; a useful discussion is Burkert 1985, Ch. I. The later LBA is focussed on particularly in Renfrew 1985, which addresses important theoretical issues in the Preface and Ch. 1, cf. also Renfrew 1972: 417–27 and, on questions of 'continuity', Sourvinou-Inwood 1989b. Goodison 1989 is a stimulating discussion of symbolism and the Prepalatial material particularly, and Hägg and Marinatos 1981 is an important collection of articles and discussions.

Minoan

I should record here my good fortune in being able to read, as External Examiner, an accomplished summary of many theories about Minoan religion in Zeimbekis 1991. Dr M. Panagiotaki has also kindly allowed me to refer to her important findings concerning the Central Court Sanctuary at Knossos (1992).

Warren 1987b is a brief survey, see also 1988. A full-scale work by N. Marinatos is expected shortly, and a major study of iconography by C. Sourvinou-Inwood is approaching completion.

Further references for some significant topics:

Built shrines: Hood 1977, Gesell 1983, 1985, 1987, Hägg 1987, Marinatos 1987a.

Caves: Tyree 1974; on the Idaean cave see also Catling 1985: 61; 1986: 91; 1987: 57.

Epiphany rituals: Hägg 1983, Hägg and Lindau 1984, Warren 1990 (baetyls).

Peak sanctuaries: Peatfield 1983, 1987, 1990, 1992 (which includes a detailed account of Atsipadhes) and Rutkowski 1988 (also on Juktas, Karetsou 1981; on Petsopha, Rutkowski 1991).

Sacrifice: Marinatos 1986.

Cycladic

On EC figurines see references cited for Ch. 5.

Keros: extensively discussed in Fitton 1984, see now Renfrew 1991: 100–1.

Akrotiri: Marinatos 1984a, 1984b, 1990a.

Ayia Irini 'temple': Caskey, M.E. 1981, 1986.

Phylakopi: Renfrew 1981, 1985.

Mainland

See generally Hägg 1981a, 1984, 1985b, and on figurines references cited in Ch. 5.

The Cult Centre at Mycenae: French 1981a, Mylonas 1981.

Near Eastern religions

I have relied particularly upon the relevant sections in *CAH* Vols I–II, Seltzer 1989, and Roaf 1990, also in Trigger *et al.* 1983, Kemp 1989 (Egyptian); Jacobsen 1976, Postgate 1977, Dalley 1984 (Mesopotamian/Syrian); Gurney 1977, 1990, and Macqueen 1986 (Anatolian/Hittite).

CHAPTER 9

CONCLUSIONS

A great deal of evidence has been surveyed in the preceding chapters; the time has come to discuss its overall significance. The starting point must be that at the height of the Aegean BA what may legitimately be called a civilisation, following the definition accepted by Renfrew (1972: 7), had become established. The obvious questions must be, how did this happen, why did this civilisation collapse, and did it leave much of a legacy to later Greek civilisation?

I have already suggested in the Introduction that explanations of cultural change which rely on theories of invasion and colonisation have largely lost plausibility. Not only do they depend upon tendentious interpretations of generally scanty archaeological material, but they resemble the Greek legends, on which they often draw, in failing to offer any rational motivation for such movements (cf. Dickinson 1977: 55). Why, to take an outstanding example (Bernal 1987, 1991), should Egyptians, whose whole life-style and culture depended upon residence along the Nile, show any interest in a region of completely different nature? What attraction could Greece's broken terrain have for any hypothetical group of 'northern' nomads (most recently, Diamant 1988), or, indeed, specialist charioteers (Drews 1988)? Undoubtedly the original spread of the farming economy often involved the colonisation of unpopulated land, and in times of decline, when relatively good land might again become empty or sparsely occupied, groups previously confined to poorer land might seize the opportunity to take it over. But in normal circumstances, the early farming populations could have no reason to be constantly on the move, and all that we know now about the nature and function of origin legends must argue against taking them at face value in the way that Thucydides did.

Theories that deploy the concept of 'influence' from a superior culture to explain change also tend to beg the question. Such influence should not be presented as the natural outcome of contact, affecting the recipient culture like a disease, but requires explanation by an analysis of that culture's development, which could show why foreign features might be adopted or adapted at that particular stage. For example, it is now clear that many MH sites were in contact with the more advanced Aegean cultures long before perceptible changes are detectable on the mainland; so more is needed to explain these changes than a simple appeal to 'influence from the Aegean'.

Explanations of major changes in terms of usually disastrous geological or meteorological events, such as earthquakes, erosion episodes or shifts in rainfall pattern, may seem more plausible, but invite further questions. Why, for example, should earthquakes cause permanent change at some stages of Aegean culture but purely temporary interruptions of development at others, and, more generally, do historical analogies suggest that any such natural events have really marked effects on historical development? The evidence supposed to indicate such events too often consists largely of the destructions and abandonments that they are intended to explain, so that the argument is dangerously close to being circular, and is in any case constantly subject to revision in the light of new evidence or reconstructions. A good example is the Thera eruption, which has now been firmly dissociated from the destruction horizon at the end of the Second Palace Period (Warren 1991a), while the reconstruction of the pre-eruption island's shape presented in several articles in Hardy 1990, Vol. 2, includes a smaller caldera-like bay, and thus renders all prevous calculations of the eruption's effects obsolete.

The arguments most likely to carry conviction will explain change in the Aegean as part of the general workings of cultural process, taking account of interactions within the Aegean and further afield; within this framework, particular events can figure as catalysts or contributory factors. But, as Wenke has pointed out, a general archaeological model of cultural development is still lacking (1984: 442–7). It remains difficult to identify the real 'prime movers' in change, if indeed there are any that will operate in all human cultures, and in an introductory work there seems no point in expending space on discussing the various theories. But these theories have drawn attention to factors likely to be of constant significance, which have been referred to frequently in preceding chapters and will underlie all that follows: the acquisition and mobilisation of resources, the competition for status, the roles of exchange and ideology and their use to underpin the power of elites. But the format of this account will remain a semi-historical narrative, which will inevitably focus on some fairly dramatic changes, but hope to present them as the outcome more of processes than of individual 'events'.

The period in which the BA cultures emerged from their Neolithic background is still rather obscure; but these clearly inherited not only a landscape already considerably opened up by agriculture, but networks of contacts, through which obsidian and other useful materials and items, probably also new ideas and techniques, were distributed. The settlement of the Aegean islands surely enhanced opportunities for exchanges of this kind and brought more materials into the distribution system, although as emphasised in Chapter 3 'trade' is unlikely to have been the primary reason for their settlement. The islanders developed an individual and relatively homogeneous culture, which might well offer an example of the effect of 'peer polity interaction', in which increasing contacts within a group of communities on a similar level can be a stimulus to development (Renfrew and Cherry 1986). But their capacity to influence other Aegean communities has probably been exaggerated, and although the wide distribution of the characteristic figurines and apparent recognition by several island communities of a common ritual centre on Keros imply a shared belief system, these communities do not otherwise seem as advanced as some were in Crete and the mainland, to judge from evidence for elaborate buildings, fortifications and tombs.

Nevertheless, it is possible to detect a common trend in the Aegean towards the development of ranked societies, from the occurrence in all parts of burials provided with more abundant and/or unusual burial goods, and otherwise singled out by the position or greater elaboration of their tombs and even by indications that ceremonies were performed at them. It is reasonable to suppose that this ranking was linked to successful leadership in various kinds of enterprise; but the provision of figurines and other likely ritual items as grave goods in many such cases suggests an extra element, linking ceremonial and ritual activity with rank. It is virtually impossible to establish which of these factors came into play first, whether those who became leading figures in their communities, for example by 'social storage' (Ch. 3, p. 36), claimed special ritual/ceremonial status as a result, or whether those who took prominent roles in these areas increasingly became general leaders of the community. It would be rash to argue that both factors operated together everywhere and in the same way, but evidence from the early Near East strongly suggests that those who claimed to lead would be expected to be the premier representatives of their communities in religion as in everything else. Such evidence also indicates that religion can motivate the large-scale mobilisation of resources, but it provides no explanation for the creation of these resources, merely for their concentration.

Here we encounter a phenomenon that recurs in Greek prehistory down to the emergence from the Dark Age, the capacity of a group of regions to generate wealth. The group varies somewhat in its membership at each recurrence, but includes the central and north-eastern parts of Crete, the north-east Peloponnese, Attica, Boeotia, central Euboea and Messenia sufficiently frequently to suggest the effect of underlying common factors, which might well include a favourable balance of natural resources, climate, and access to each other and the outside world. This wealth often, especially in the earliest stages of each development, takes the form of items made from valuable raw materials that were not available to all communities in the Aegean from local sources, if present at all; it implies, then, some form of exchange that extended beyond the Aegean to the Near East. The basis of exchange links between the Aegean and Near East and the possible motivation on the Near Eastern side have been discussed in Chapter 7; here it will simply be suggested that these were probably always involved in this process of wealth creation, and that this seems to be one of the basic features of Aegean cultural development, even if it cannot be clearly explained. It might well follow that the higher the level of cultural development in the Aegean, the more it depended on links with the Near East.

Certainly, in the Prepalatial Period knowledge of new forms of domesticated plant and animal, craft techniques, artefact types, and more complex features such as the seal's potential as an administrative tool all arrived in the Aegean from this direction, though probably by various routes: as seen in Chapter 7, only Crete has produced plausible evidence for links with anywhere further east than Anatolia. Near Eastern activity and Aegean expansion probably fed one another in a complicated process. It does not seem likely that very significant changes in the farming economy were taking place at this stage, and Runnels's argument (1985) that the increased distribution of millstones indicates specialised food production by some communities, which allowed greater craft specialisation and wealth creation in other communities through trade in the goods produced, has already been discounted in Chapter 7. But there may be a case for arguing that demand was increasing for items that gave prestige to the owner (cf. Wiencke 1989: 507), and that this competitiveness was a factor pushing development; the occurrence of rich and sometimes exotic grave-goods in relatively many graves at Mochlos, a not particularly large community, and in the Leukas R cemetery might be explained in this way. A desire to produce increasing quantities of goods for exchange could have stimulated the intensification of agricultural production that has been deduced from the spread of small farmstead-like sites on the mainland and in Crete, while the level of culture in the Cyclades may have depended partly upon that of exchange activity.

A very finely balanced situation of interconnections and, perhaps, interdependence between many communities could thus have developed, which might be vulnerable to upset by anything unforeseen, and may ultimately have placed too much pressure on society and the land itself. It has been plausibly argued that an episode of erosion in the south Argolid reflects the result of over-exploitation (Van Andel *et al.* 1986: 117, 125), and while this remains to be demonstrated for more central regions it is an attractive explanation for the marked and apparently abrupt decline on the mainland in the later stages of the EBA, which may have had a disastrous 'knock-on' effect on Cycladic culture in turn. Many features of the evidence anticipate those associated with the collapse of the Mycenaean palace societies much later: there was a severe decline in the number of sites, with apparent abandonment of some areas and the gathering of population into major nuclei, and previously homogeneous areas of material culture fragmented, but new types were also disseminated through continuing if less regular forms of exchange. The situation may well have been complicated by warfare and perhaps some population movement, which has been thought to explain the Anatolian features prominent in the 'Lefkandi I' and 'Kastri' groups and the subsequent establishment of the 'Lerna IV' assemblage in the north Peloponnese (cf. Wiencke 1989: 509). But even if these do represent population movements it is an essentially unimportant question whether either reflects the 'coming of the Greeks'; for the whole notion implicit in this phrase, of the arrival of a new people with institutions and qualities that had a profound effect on the direction of development in the Aegean Bronze Age, is outdated.

In fact, material culture on the mainland was to remain at village level for several centuries, achieving nothing of note; the general rarity of burial goods and narrow range of variation in graves suggest only minor differences of status in most communities. But after a period of obscurity, townlike settlements were established on several islands, with a lively level of exchange which included the nearest mainland settlements and increasingly those of Crete. The lack of information about this development is one of the most unfortunate gaps in Aegean prehistory, for despite the marked changes from the EC culture it was evidently indigenous, owing nothing to Cretan stimulus. It is not even possible to say what form of government these towns had, for no trace of a public building has been uncovered, but the existence of fortifications at some argues for some form of central authority, and also suggests somewhat disturbed conditions in the Aegean.

The troubles of the late EBA in the rest of the Aegean must have had some effect in Crete, but there is no suggestion of serious dislocation; rather, Cretan society continued to progress generally, although some communities, like Mochlos and Vasiliki, may have declined in importance. This may reflect the exceptional cohesion and stability of Cretan society which is implicit in the use of communal tombs over many generations. There is still evidence for considerable variation between different regions of Crete in some cultural features, such as burial customs, but there are also signs of increasing homogeneity, such as the spread of peak sanctuaries. As pointed out in Chapter 8, there is no good reason to link this with the foundation of the palaces, although it surely reflects the interests of local community leaders and might, again, be a product of 'peer polity interaction'. It is significant that it is a religious phenomenon, suggesting that the characteristically intimate connection between Minoan religion and the Minoan elite was already established.

Resources and people may well have been mainly mobilised through religion in Crete, but the establishment of the first palaces cannot clearly be explained in this light, or in any other. This is particularly frustrating, since they provide the clearest evidence of the development of states or polities in Crete comparable to those of the Near East, but it is an inevitable result of the fact that we still lack detailed knowledge about the immediately preceding period in the most important settlements, and often about the structural sequence on the palace sites themselves; for example, at Knossos the Hypogaeum, a remarkable rock-cut structure which may have been an early granary and would thus foreshadow the storage function of the palace, is hard to date, though evidently early (Momigliano 1991: 195–6). Branigan has laid stress on the early evidence that the palaces had an important storage function (1987b, 1988), particularly involving the *kouloures*, probable granaries, that were sunk in the West Courts at Knossos and Phaistos; this position suggests a significant relationship with the shrines in the west wings of the palaces, perhaps manifested in harvest festivals held in the West Court, as Marinatos has suggested (1987a). But at Mallia *kouloures* are lacking, though there is an important ritual/ceremonial complex beneath the later palace, and there is not only a second elaborate complex of buildings with many palatial features, Quartier Mu, but the unique 'Agora', which may have been a site for interaction between the community and its rulers. This emphasises the dangers of supposing that development at the different centres followed a uniform course.

While the theory linking the palaces' establishment to intensive Near Eastern influence is weakly based, both theoretically and in the available data, it remains possible to suggest that ruling groups at Cretan centres were drawing upon and emulating what they knew of expressions of power in the Near East to claim a comparable status (Cherry 1986: 39–41). But the degree to which this was done depends partly on the nature of these groups, which remains uncertain; as argued further below, there is a remarkable lack of evidence for any kind of ruling family. Whatever they were, it is very unlikely that they established at the beginning of the First Palace Period a position that remained unchanged for the next several hundred years. The development of the Minoan palace societies seems rather to have been a dynamic process, in which not only were the buildings expanded, perhaps taking on new functions, but their users adopted various Near Eastern features, both architectural and administrative, notably the use of writing and the seal for administrative purposes, perhaps also systems of weights and measures. There is every reason to suppose that this was a piecemeal process, in which the adoption of a feature at one centre was followed at others, again via 'peer polity interaction' (Cherry 1986: 42–3, cf. 33), and only gradually was a degree of homogeneity established.

The rise of the palaces was accompanied by a decline in the use of communal tombs of the old style, although some major examples continued, like T. B at Arkhanes. But it is not clear how markedly Minoan traditions changed in this respect, and how far this can be taken to indicate the extension of palace control over the population; for group burial continued to be practised on a lesser scale in other forms of tomb, such as the chamber tombs of the Knossos region, and the grouping of such tombs and of individual burials in cemeteries may be taken to reflect continued communal feeling. Similarly, it is not clear whether the signs of palace interest in sanctuaries, particularly Juktas, should be interpreted as evidence of control. The case for suggesting that the palaces played the major role in contacts with the Near East is better, but there is, frankly, no good evidence at present that from the beginning they held the central position in Minoan society attributed to them at their height.

Various cultural differences suggest at least five separate regions at this time in Crete, of which the polities based at Knossos, Phaistos, and Mallia are three (Cadogan 1990, especially on Mallia). The relations between them are not clear, though they evidently exchanged goods and ideas; such features as the road and guard post (?) system in the extreme east, the establishment of the Monastiraki complex west of Mt Ida, which has a very close relationship with Phaistos, and the tower and cisterns at Pyrgos, suggest that the major polities may have been attempting to extend their influence and been clashing with each other or local populations. Their relations with the rest of the Aegean do not seem particularly strong, overall, although the evidence for activity in the Cyclades increases over the First Palace Period and the incorporation of the Dodecanese and adjacent Anatolian coast within the area of Minoan culture seems to have been under way before its end. They may well have drawn on these regions as well as their own territories for commodities which could be exchanged for Near Eastern materials and artefacts, and their position as intermediaries for Near Eastern materials, techniques and ideas may have helped to increase their influence in the Aegean.

The end of the First Palaces in Crete has often been attributed to a severe earthquake, but here as in other cases it is necessary to query the presumption that deposits which look similar are literally contemporary, and whether the effects of any earthquake could be so severe over such a wide area. The possibility that they reflect a period of warfare within Crete, from which Knossos emerged as the leading centre, should not be discounted simply because it is dramatic. Cadogan has drawn attention to the disappearance of evidence for overseas contact at Mallia in the Second Palace Period, and linked the destructions in the Mallia territory to possible takeover by Knossos (1990: 174). During the Second Palace Period, but not necessarily simultaneously, palaces whose layout has much in common with that of Knossos were built at Mallia, Phaistos and Zakro, where the building seems not only to be an intrusion into the earlier town plan but to be partly walled off from it, also in a much smaller version at Gournia. It is remarkable that apart from Knossos these palaces contain little or nothing in the way of figured frescoes, in contrast with various 'villas', particularly in north central Crete, relatively close to Knossos, and that they contain less evidence for an administrative role than the 'villa' at Ayia Triada, which has been argued to be the administrative centre of the Mesara, and House A at Zakro. A relatively wide distribution of evidence for administrative activity, in the form of sealings or Linear A tablets, suggests that this was decentralised, and it may well be that the main importance of the palace complexes was ceremonial, although they also evidently served as storage centres.

It may more tentatively be suggested that the evidence from the sealings for links between different centres in Crete could reflect internal exchanges within a state dominated by Knossos, but perhaps consisting of a closely knit group of polities, like the Hittite state at its height. The exceptional elaboration of the arrangements for ritual and ceremonial in the Knossos palace and the number of other buildings which seem to have ritual/ceremonial purposes in the settlement would be appropriate to the capital of such a state, and its establishment would provide a good setting for a trend towards a 'national' religion and the evidence for palatial interest in major religious sites of all kinds. The evidence for this spreads outside the area of sealing interconnections, as far as Vrysinas, Kato Symi and Petsopha, which would suggest that the postulated state took in most of the significant regions of Crete. But there is still nothing to link Khania clearly to this system, and the existence of polities outside its control is quite plausible, although they could hardly have totally escaped its influence.

That such a state was created by a period of conquest comparable with those which produced the Egyptian state and various more short-lived 'empires' in Mesopotamia, Syria and Anatolia must remain a hypothesis. Certainly, there is no evidence that it was ruled by anything resembling a Near Eastern monarch. The characteristic depictions of the king in his military or religious role, and the public inscriptions reporting his acts and laws, are lacking; isolated and often dominant male and female figures in Minoan representations are more readily interpreted as gods, or humans impersonating gods (Davis, E.N. 1986a; cf. Fig. 8.9: 3–5). Admittedly, a similar case might be made from the representational evidence for the absence of Mycenaean monarchs, whose existence seems abundantly attested by other sources, notably the Linear B texts (Kilian 1988b; 300 n. 1 cites one possible representation); but the Mycenaean evidence includes a class of 'princely' tombs such as cannot be recognised in Crete.

Rather, the general impression given by the Cretan material is of an elite class, including both men and women. It surely must have had leaders, among whom one would expect to include the leading administrators whose sealing activities have been identified by Weingarten and the figures depicted as leading in rituals, especially those who may have impersonated gods; but if it centred on one family or a single ceremonial figure, there is nothing to single them out. It should also have included the persons based at some of the 'villas' and the audiences of the miniature frescoes of Knossos, which may show the class gathered for particularly important ceremonies. The age-grades differentiated by hair styles and dress, the initiation ceremonies these may reflect, and the special styles of dress shown in ritual/ceremonial contexts might be distinguishing features of this class alone, and the argument that access to ceremonies within the palaces was limited suggests that it was exclusive, perhaps hereditary. The fact that it is so frequently shown in scenes of ritual, and that in many 'villas' there were ritual/ceremonial rooms, suggests that it was largely through its religious status and activities that this class maintained its claim to rule. There is always the danger of reading too much into how an elite chooses to represent itself, but the near-total absence of weapons and military scenes from the representations (with the exception of the Chieftain Cup) strongly suggests that little emphasis was placed on the control of force. Given the remarkable prominence of ritual/ceremonial rooms in major buildings, and of ritual themes in representational art, including 'official' art like the decoration of palace walls and administrators' seals, and the use of Linear A equally for administration and for inscriptions on ritual offerings, one could well follow Marinatos in arguing for the identity of this class and the 'priestly class' identifiable in ritual scenes and in other ways. But it may be preferable to make a distinction between members of an elite who played leading roles in ritual as part of their duties, like kings and queens in the Near East, but also had administrative positions, and those whose duties were religious only, perhaps concerned with a single sanctuary, and who may not even have belonged to the elite.

Even if the rule of this class was based on a religious foundation rather than the monopoly of force, it does not follow that its rule was totally benevolent or accepted with complete willingness; its apparently increasing control of religion, which may have included the suppression of minor shrines, and the very existence of a single centre, could have caused strains within the postulated state which would not be visible archaeologically. But there is little evidence for truly centralised control, in comparison with what can be surmised of the position of the palace in the Third Palace Period. Rather, as noted above, the administration seems decentralised, but nevertheless able to support the level of culture achieved reasonably well; but this may have depended on a level of agricultural exploitation that came close to the limits.

Whether this postulated state, or any Cretan polity, exercised political control outside Crete and the Minoan culture sphere remains hotly debated. In the Second Palace Period Minoan cultural influence can be detected in many forms elsewhere in the Aegean, extending to some parts of the mainland, particularly the Argolid (Dickinson 1989: 135–6). It is easy to be overwhelmed by this evidence, but important to see it for what it is. This influence is extremely marked in Cycladic material culture, but the notable differences in town architecture and public buildings, even on Thera, from what is found in Crete may be cited as an argument against linking it with settlement by Minoans (for explanations in economic and social terms, cf. Davis 1984, Davis and Lewis 1985). Evidence for the use of Linear A in the Cyclades has to be balanced against a total absence of Cretan-style sealings (but no administrative building has yet been found at Akrotiri). In the field of religion, where, on the above analysis, one might expect Minoan control to show most clearly, the evidence is strikingly patchy: one does not find a constantly recurrent complex of Minoan features, but rather a random, often poorly represented selection. Only on Thera do the Xeste buildings and their polythyron complexes, unparalleled at other Cycladic sites, argue, along with other evidence, for quite substantial links with Minoan religion. Further, the existence of fortifications at a variety of sites from Kolonna on Aegina to Petras in eastern Crete, whose differing styles do not suggest that they were built at the instigation of a central authority, does not fit well with any idea of a *pax Minoica* prevailing throughout the Second Palace Period.

Overall, the case for suggesting that the strong Minoan cultural influence was matched by political control is not overwhelming, but that it reflects the wielding of considerable influence, including political, is likely enough. No doubt this was directed, among other things, to ensuring as far as possible that trading conditions were undisturbed, for, as indicated in Chapter 7 and above, exchange is likely to have been a major factor in increasing Aegean prosperity at this time. But it is not sufficient to argue that Crete's need for bronze, presumed from the large quantities found there, forced it to establish control of the routes by which copper and tin reached Crete, for the same argument could apply to Mycenae, where bronze is found in remarkable quantities.

As commented elsewhere (Dickinson 1989: 136), the emergence of Mycenae and other mainland centres of power remains hard to explain in detail, but the basic development seems clear enough: a ruling class, sprung from local roots, established itself in charge of principalities of varying size. Its features are of familiar type, in that its leaders show an evident interest in warfare and celebrated their status with lavish burials in a variety of newly developed tomb-types (Dickinson 1989: 133–4). It was able to accumulate considerable wealth, although the principalities were not as organised as the societies of Crete and the Aegean islands. Its emergence may partly represent a response to the stimulus of expanding Minoan influence in the Aegean, in which the evidence for a 'special relationship' between the Argolid and a Cretan palace, most probably Knossos, may be considered particularly significant (Dickinson 1977: 54–5, 1989: 136). A link may also be postulated with the growth of exchange, in which not only was the Near East showing increasing interest in the Aegean, but the south Aegean cultures were becoming active in the north Aegean and, still more, the central Mediterranean, both areas in which the mainlanders apparently played a major role. The importance of exchange to all the Aegean societies of this period is underlined by the prominence of lead weights in various contexts, and of sets of balances in some important Mycenaean graves, and its benefits are demonstrated by the masses of valuable materials found.

The eruption of Thera, which destroyed Akrotiri and made the island for a while uninhabitable, certainly did damage to some Cretan sites and could have had a marked psychological effect, perhaps causing the effectiveness of the elite in dealing with the gods to be questioned. But there is no indication that it caused any long-term deterioration in Minoan society, and it must certainly be dissociated from the destruction, and often subsequent decline or abandonment, of so many Second Palace Period sites of importance, especially in Crete, which still comes as a surprise. The standard explanations attributing these destructions to earthquake (most recently Warren 1991a: 36–7) or to a Mycenaean conquest of Crete (cf. Hood 1980) both lack plausibility, the former because the distribution pattern of seriously affected sites covers most of Crete but has puzzling gaps (relatively little evidence of damage at Knossos, none at Kommos), the latter because of the level of damage, which seems far in excess of what would be needed to establish control. Both also assume that the destructions were effectively contemporaneous, but the chronology of this period could easily accommodate their being spread over a decade or more, and having different causes; there do seem good reasons for suggesting an earthquake at Ayia Irini, for instance.

That warfare was involved seems likely enough: there may be traces of deliberate destruction at some sites (e.g. Pyrgos, where the 'villa' was burnt but not the settlement houses), and the major dislocations implied by the establishment of a new ruling class at Knossos, whose preferences in burial customs and some types of vessel have strong Mycenaean connections, and the subsequent marked decline of Minoan influence in the Aegean are unlikely to have occurred without serious disturbances. But the precipitating factor may well have been strain within Cretan society itself, arising from a drive to produce more in order to maintain and even increase the quantities of valuable materials being brought in; such a drive could even have been forced by a growing shortage of supplies or some other deterioration in previously favourable terms of exchange. The destructions and abandonments might then be a general reflection of a complex, if not chaotic, period of trouble, in the course of which a group of mainlanders took advantage of the situation to establish themselves in Crete.

But in many respects the period of the 'last palace' at Knossos marks a continuation of the old traditions: in religion and administration, much seems to have been preserved from the previous period, though much else was lost and what survived often underwent considerable adaptation. Study of the Linear B texts demonstrates a strongly centralised system of administration, with Knossos as the only 'first order' centre (Bennet 1987; 1988). Its territory evidently covered most of central and western Crete, but not apparently the east, so that if Petsopha was Dikte, Knossos was paying attention to an important shrine outside its control; other evidence, that of pottery style, suggests that Knossos exerted some influence throughout Crete at this time. As noted in Chapter 4, the texts display a level of agricultural exploitation, or at least of taxation of produce, that may have been more intensive than before, of which the purpose was surely to maintain the level of display seen in the 'burials with bronzes' and comparable graves. There are strong indications that the elite class represented by these graves was more male-dominated, and that there was now a monarch-like figure, the *wanax*, who apparently gave his name to the palace, *wanaktoron*, and whose name survived in Homeric Greek to signify a ruler but was later applied only to gods. But the very rich female burials in Ts. A and D at Arkhanes seem to receive honours in their own right, perhaps because of their importance in the state religion. Knossian society in this phase, then, may well have been a blending of old and new.

For a while the new regime at Knossos seems to have maintained a preeminent position in the Aegean, influencing its contemporaries on the mainland socially and in styles of display if not politically. The fine weapons and jewellery types produced by workshops at Knossos were adopted on the mainland, and so, more significantly, was the system of writing-assisted administration developed at Knossos. There continued to be significant contacts between Crete and the Near East, and Kommos was becoming a port of increasing importance in Mediterranean exchange, to judge from the range of foreign wares found there. But the Knossian state may not have had very stable foundations: the maintaining of considerable quantities of chariots and weapons suggests insecurity, and the somewhat ramshackle occupation and chequered history of the 'Unexplored

Mansion' may symbolise the history of the state as a whole; indeed, the period may have been turbulent in other parts of the Aegean (Catling 1989). Certainly, following a major destruction of the palace complex, plausibly the result of attack though its source could equally be local rivals or rebels, or an outside power, Knossos declined abruptly as both an inhabited centre and a source of influence in the Aegean; even though Linear B apparently continued in use in central Crete, the administrative centre that this implies was not necessarily Knossos itself. Pre-eminence in Crete seems to have passed to Khania; but the most important centres in the Aegean as a whole were now those of the Mycenaean mainland.

Already almost the last vestiges of independent cultural traditions in much of the Aegean had disappeared, and there was more cultural homogeneity than there had ever been; in fact, although Crete maintained its own traditions in some respects, its material culture and probably its society were very similar to those of the more purely Mycenaean areas. But there is no reason to suppose that this largely homogeneous 'Mycenaean' Aegean was united politically; although Mycenae in many ways seems the leading centre, the fact that, unlike those of Crete, all the major Mycenaean palaces were decorated with frescoes may symbolise their independence. Certainly, there is no hint in the Pylos archive or the more fragmentary material from Thebes of subordination to any superior. The argument for a major state in the Aegean, to be identified as the Ahhiyawā of the Hittite records, is thereby lessened (cf. Chapter 7, p. 253).

The salient impressions of this world given by the remains are of a generally stable and ordered society, with an established hierarchy, visually reflected in the positioning of the palace above the rest of the settlement. This society was headed, at least in the palace societies, by the *wanax*; another important functionary, the *lawagetas*, shares certain features with him, so that it is not absolutely certain that we have to do with a single monarch, although Kilian argues this (1988b). Certainly, parallels with the Near East are much closer in this society than in that of Minoan Crete. It seems less religion-dominated than Minoan society: there are no sites really comparable with the great rural sanctuaries of Crete, while the identifiable shrines in settlements conspicuously lack monumentality. The most impressive buildings, the palaces, contain far less evidence for the practice of ceremonies and rituals than Minoan palaces did, although the megaron suite may well have had such functions. But religion undoubtedly had an important role, and may well have been overseen at public level by the *wanax* and palace administration.

The complexities of Mycenaean palace society, as deduced particularly from the Pylos texts, have been discussed in Chapter 4. Unfortunately, with no knowledge of its laws, we still get only a very partial impression, but the texts imply that it was of a far more developed nature, closer to those of the Near Eastern civilisations, than that centring on individual chiefs or 'aristocratic' households which has been deduced from the Homeric epics (cf. Whitley 1991).

Authority was strongly centralised, and although the palace did not control every aspect of life in every community, it could if necessary gather detailed information in any part of the territory that it controlled. A hierarchy of officials indicates that these, rather than 'aristocrats', were the important figures, although there are signs of the existence of a major land-holding class, from whose ranks officials might well have been chosen. The land-holding texts suggest that there was a complex array of statuses, in which even those in the lowest levels apparently had considerable freedom of action in the equally complicated area of land-tenure; but the whole group involved in land-holding may have been a small proportion of the total population, the bulk of which may have been dependent on 'the state', or on individuals of varying importance, some being actually termed slaves. The holding of land seems to have rendered one liable to various services and obligations to the state, including perhaps military service. The arrangements for levying taxes and mobilising resources and personnel were quite sophisticated, giving an indication of how the massive public works at many major sites could be organised, and how, also, surplus was gathered to support this and other palace activities, which almost certainly included much of the exchange carried on, particularly that in valuable raw materials.

Unfortunately, this is one of the areas in which the Linear B texts are disappointingly uninformative. As already noted, there is a general impression that in the Second Palace Period systems of exchange were expanding within the Mediterranean, and this evidently continued into the Third Palace Period; but this may at best have maintained the situation at the same level, and the same process that, it has been suggested above, affected Minoan society adversely may have begun to affect the Mycenaean states. Well before the end of the fourteenth century there are signs that metals were not being used as lavishly as earlier, although other elaborate work involving much use of ivory, another presumably expensive imported raw material, was being produced. The process may have been retarded by the progressive elimination or reduction to insignificance of previously important consumers like Knossos, but by the thirteenth century the situation may have been deteriorating noticeably. One reaction may have been increasingly desperate attempts to produce, suggested particularly by the evidence that the palace at Pylos was being turned more and more into a perfumed oil factory (Shelmerdine 1985; 1987) and by the deficits in its taxation system, which may have been trying to extract more than the territory could produce. There could have been increasing tensions between the Mycenaean states as they tried to secure a share of diminishing resources, perhaps to be detected in the thirteenth-century destructions at various sites. A variety of factors, then, could have been negatively affecting the capacity of the Mycenaean states to support their way of life.

This, rather than overcentralisation or overspecialisation in the agricultural economy, may have been what ultimately caused 'systems collapse'. It is certainly better to think in terms of a process whose effects were cumulative and perhaps enhanced by some types of attempt to maintain the situation, than to search for a single precipitating event, natural or man-made, and unwise to attempt to reconstruct a sequence of events in any detail. Factors which contributed to the downward spiral, but were more probably local than general in their effect, could include wars and piracy, poor harvests, epidemics, episodes of erosion or flooding, even earthquakes that destroyed valuable stores. It remains unclear why in some regions, notably Messenia, there was an apparently wholesale abandonment of minor settlements without any of the evidence for nucleation of population at the major ones that can be identified in the Argolid, and this is one indication that the collapse was uneven in its effects. But over a period that might have covered a generation or more the world of the Third Palace Period effectively disintegrated: many major sites on the mainland were destroyed by fire and/or abandoned thereafter (Dickinson 1974 gives a detailed list, but needs updating on relative chronology), and there may have been trouble in other parts of the Aegean, especially Crete (Popham 1964: 9).

The recovery that has been detected in the Postpalatial Period was only partial: for example, no major centre replaced Pylos in Messenia, and although Thebes continued as a settlement there is no evidence that it was particularly important. The gathering of population in sites near the sea underlines the continuing significance of exchange, certainly evident in the exotic items found at some of these sites, but, as argued in Chapter 7, the old system could not be re-established, and what succeeded it was less stable. Despite Muhly's enthusiasm for this period (1992), in the Aegean it must be seen as one of at best fragile prosperity. There was still wealth at some centres, but its sources were not secure. It was a time of renewed emphasis on warfare, to judge from the popularity of warrior scenes on pottery, warrior burials and quite a number of destructions, partial or complete, at various sites, and this may have contributed to a degree of population mobility, which not only increased the sizes of old sites like Tiryns and Lefkandi, but resulted in apparently new foundations like Perati, and Emborio on previously non-Mycenaean Chios, perhaps also in migration to Crete. Ultimately, it may simply not have seemed worthwhile to traders to make what may have been an increasingly dangerous journey into the central Aegean; conditions deteriorated further, and many of the centres which had survived to the late twelfth century were abandoned or lost most of their importance.

Even greater mobility seems to have followed: groups moved to Cyprus and the Asia Minor coasts and islands. This could be interpreted as a movement born of despair at the situation in the mainland and central Aegean, and of hope for better things closer to the traditional centres of civilisation in the Near East. Such a period would be an appropriate setting for the movements on the mainland reported in the legends, which, it should be noted, nearly always involve movements *within* the boundaries of the Aegean cultures, and so need not have involved any major change in material culture, such as has been constantly but fruitlessly sought in the archaeological evidence. But there is no good reason to explain the movements overseas as caused by such 'invasions', an interpretation for which the legends in fact provide little support, nor need the changes that were taking place in many areas of Aegean life, such as religion and burial customs, at the end of the BA have anything to do with them.

To sum up, it is still not possible to give wholly satisfactory explanations to the questions propounded at the beginning. But it does seem that the Aegean populations' capacity to form organised societies, under whatever motivation, was an important factor in enabling them to participate in exchange with the Near East at a level sufficient to provide wealth. This wealth consists in large measure of the prestigious materials used by the ruling elites; but they were also able to fund the construction of major architectural complexes, and presided over considerable populations whose standard of living was quite reasonable for the period. But the need to maintain this level of exchange with the Near East may ultimately have caused strain within these societies, both on social bonds and quite possibly on the capacity of the land to produce. Stable conditions in the Near East were also required, and when the political and exchange systems there became severely dislocated, those of the Aegean seem to have been unable to maintain themselves. Thus, although the Aegean as a whole survived the Minoan collapse, it could not survive the Mycenaean collapse, because of the severe troubles at more or less the same time in the Near East.

This ushered in a long period, lasting to the dawn of Greek history, in which traditional culture was transformed by the incorporation of many new elements, so absolutely basic to the later Greeks' way of life that, as their legends show, they could not imagine the past without them. Crete survived through the Dark Age in a more prosperous state than other regions, and probably for this reason preserved more of its BA heritage in fields like religion and, for a considerable time, burial customs. Individual settlements also survived elsewhere, like Argos and Athens, but there was very considerable dislocation in patterns of settlement, burial customs and religious practice, and so, surely, in social structure. The traditions that were preserved of a great past were encapsulated in a setting that bore little resemblance to that past's actuality by the time that we can recognise them in the Homeric epics, just as, in my view, the religion of the Greeks may have preserved BA elements in a largely transformed context. On the evidence available, the Dark Age and not any earlier time saw the true birth of 'the Greeks'.

Bibliography

Obviously, works cited in the General Bibliography are bound to discuss the themes of this chapter. Shorter but more up-to-date discussions of many important topics can be found in Krzyszkowska and Nixon 1983, Hägg and Marinatos 1984, 1987, French and Wardle 1988, Laffineur 1989a (many have been cited above); see also Cadogan 1986 on the EBA, Wiencke 1989 on EH, Warren 1985 and Cherry 1986 on Minoan developments. For recent discussions of the end of the Third Palace Period see Betancourt 1976, Sandars 1978, Ch. 8; Snodgrass 1971 is the most thoughtful account of the Dark Age.

BIBLIOGRAPHY

To conserve space, bibliographical details have been kept to a minimum, and in the interests of uniform presentation Roman numerals have mostly been converted, authors have always been cited with the same initials, and Greek citations have all been written in the revised orthography.

(1) General works

(These have been picked as useful surveys and/or good sources of illustrations, although information and interpretations are outdated in many cases.)

Barber, R.L.N. 1987. *The Cyclades in the Bronze Age*. London: Duckworth.

Branigan, K. 1970a. *The Foundations of Palatial Crete*. London: Routledge and Kegan Paul.

Cadogan, G. 1976. *Palaces of Minoan Crete*. London: Barrie and Jenkins.

Caskey, J.L. 1971. Greece, Crete, and the Aegean islands in the Early Bronze Age. *CAH* I:2, Ch. XXVI(a). Cambridge: Cambridge University Press.

1973. Greece and the Aegean islands in the Middle Bronze Age. *CAH* II:1, Ch. IV(a). Cambridge: Cambridge University Press.

Chadwick, J. 1976. *The Mycenaean World*. Cambridge: Cambridge University Press.

Christopoulos, G.A. (ed.) 1974. *History of the Hellenic world I: prehistory and protohistory*. Athens: Ekdotike Athenon.

Demakopoulou, K. (ed.) 1988. *The Mycenaean world*. Athens: Greek Ministry of Culture.

Dickinson, O.T.P.K. 1977. *The origins of Mycenaean civilisation*. *SIMA* 49. Göteborg: Åström.

Higgins, R.A. 1973. *The archaeology of Minoan Crete*. London: Bodley Head.

1981. *Minoan and Mycenaean art* (2nd edition). London: Thames and Hudson.

Hood, M.S.F. 1967. *The home of the heroes: the Aegean before the Greeks*. London: Thames and Hudson.

1971. *The Minoans*. London: Thames and Hudson.

1978. *The arts in prehistoric Greece*. London: Penguin.

Hooker, J.T. 1977. *Mycenaean Greece*. London: Routledge and Kegan Paul.

Hope Simpson, R. 1981. *Mycenaean Greece*. Park Ridge, N.J.: Noyes Press.

Hutchinson, R.W. 1962. *Prehistoric Crete*. London: Penguin.

Marinatos, S. and Hirmer, M. 1960. *Crete and Mycenae*. London: Thames and Hudson.

1976. *Kreta, Thera und das mykenische Hellas* (3rd edition). Munich: Hirmer.

Mylonas, G.E. 1966. *Mycenae and the Mycenaean Age*. Princeton: Princeton University Press.

Platon, N. 1968. *Crete*. Geneva: Nagel (Archaeologia Mundi).

Renfrew, C. 1972. *The emergence of civilisation: the Cyclades and the Aegean in the third millennium B.C.* London: Methuen.

Snodgrass, A.M. 1971. *The Dark Age of Greece*. Edinburgh: Edinburgh University Press.

Taylour, Lord William, 1983. *The Mycenaeans* (2nd edition). London: Thames and Hudson.
Theocharis, D.R. (ed.) 1973. *Neolithic Greece*. Athens: Bank of Greece.
Treuil, R., Darcque, P., Poursat, J-C. and Touchais, G. 1989. *Les civilisations égéennes*. Paris: presses universitaires de France.
Vermeule, E. 1972. *Greece in the Bronze Age*. Chicago: University of Chicago (5th printing, with new introduction).
Warren, P.M. 1989. *The Aegean civilisations* (2nd edition). Oxford: Phaidon.
Weinberg, S.S. 1970. The Stone Age in the Aegean. *CAH* I:1, Ch. 10. Cambridge: Cambridge University Press.

(2) *Other cited works*

Åkerström, Å. 1968. A Mycenaean potter's factory at Berbati near Mycenae. In *Atti e memorie del primo congresso internazionale di micenologia*, 48–53. Incunabula Graeca 25. Rome: Edizioni dell' Ateneo.
1987. *Berbati vol. 2: the pictorial pottery*. Stockholm: Swedish Institute at Athens.
Allen, S.H. 1990. Trade and migration? Grey burnished wheelmade wares of the eastern Mediterranean. *AJA* 94, 298.
Angel, J.L. 1971. *Lerna II: the people*. Princeton: Princeton University Press.
Aschenbrenner, S. 1972. A contemporary community. In McDonald and Rapp 1972, 47–63.
Åström, P. 1977. *The cuirass tomb and other finds at Dendra I. SIMA* 4. Göteborg: Åström.
1980. Cyprus and Troy. *OpAth* 13, 23–8.
(ed.) 1987. *High, Middle or Low? Parts I–II. SIMA* pocketbooks 56, 57. Göteborg: Åström.
Atkinson, T.D., Bosanquet, R.C., Edgar, C.C., Evans, A.J., Hogarth, D.G., Mackenzie, D., Smith, C. and Welch, F.B. 1904. *Excavations at Phylakopi on Melos*. London: Macmillan.
Avila, R.A.J. 1983. *Bronzene Lanzen- und Pfeilspitzen der griechischen Spätbronzezeit* (*Prähistorische Bronzefunde* V.1). Munich: Beck.
Bailey, G.N. (with others) 1986. Palaeolithic investigations at Klithi: preliminary results of the 1984 and 1985 seasons. *BSA* 81, 7–35.
Banks, E. 1967. The Early and Middle Helladic small objects from Lerna. PhD thesis, Cincinnati. Ann Arbor: University Microfilms International.
Barber, E.J.W. 1991. *Prehistoric textiles*. Princeton: Princeton University Press.
Barber, R.L.N. and Hadjianastasiou, O. 1989. Mikre Vigla: a Bronze Age settlement on Naxos. *BSA* 84, 63–162.
Barber, R.L.N. and MacGillivray, J.A. 1980. The Early Cycladic period: matters of definition and terminology. *AJA* 84, 141–57.
Barfield, L. 1991. Wessex with and without Mycenae: new evidence from Switzerland. *Antiquity* 65, 102–7.
Bass, G.F. 1967. *Cape Gelidonya: a Bronze Age shipwreck*. Philadelphia: Transactions of the American Philosophical Society, 57, part 8.
1986. A Bronze Age shipwreck at Ulu Burun (Kaş): 1984 campaign. *AJA* 90, 269–96.
1987. Splendors of the Bronze Age. *National Geographic Magazine* 172 (6), 693–732.
1991. Evidence of trade from Bronze Age shipwrecks. In Gale 1991, 69–82.
, Pulak, C., Collon, D. and Weinstein, J. 1989. The Bronze Age shipwreck at Ulu Burun: 1986 campaign. *AJA* 83, 1–29.
Baumbach, L. 1979. The Mycenaean contribution to Greek religion. *SMEA* 20, 143–60.
Baurain, C. 1987. Les nécropoles de Malia. In Laffineur 1987, 61–72.

Becker, M.J. 1975. Human skeletal remains from Kato Zakro. *AJA* 79, 271–6.
Bennet, J. 1987. Knossos and LM III Crete: a post-palatial palace? In Hägg and Marinatos 1987, 307–12.
1988. 'Outside in the distance': problems in understanding the economic geography of Mycenaean palatial territories. In Olivier and Palaima 1988, 19–41.
Benzi, M. 1984. Evidence for a Middle Minoan settlement on the acropolis at Ialysos (Mt Philerimos). In Hägg and Marinatos 1984, 93–105.
Bergquist, B. 1988. The archaeology of sacrifice: Minoan–Mycenaean versus Greek. In Hägg, Marinatos and Nordquist 1988, 21–34.
Bernal, M. 1987, 1991. *Black Athena: the Afro-Asiatic roots of Classical civilisation*, vols I, II. New Brunswick: Rutgers University Press/London: Free Association Books.
Betancourt, P.P. 1976. The end of the Greek Bronze Age. *Antiquity* 50, 40–7.
1979. *Vasilike ware. SIMA* 56. Göteborg: Åström.
1985. *The history of Minoan pottery*. Princeton: Princeton University Press.
1987. Dating the Aegean Late Bronze Age with radiocarbon. *Archaeometry* 29, 45–9.
and Davaras, C. 1988. Excavations at Pseira, 1985 and 1986. *Hesperia* 57, 207–25.
Bietak, M. 1992. Minoan wall-paintings unearthed at ancient Avaris. *Egyptian Archaeology. Bulletin of the Egyptian Exploration Society* 2, 26–8.
Bintliff, J.L. 1977. *Natural environment and human settlement in prehistoric Greece*. Oxford: *BAR* S28.
1984. Structuralism and myth in Minoan studies. *Antiquity* 58, 33–8.
Blackburn, E.T. 1970. Middle Helladic graves and burial customs with special reference to Lerna in the Argolid. PhD thesis, Cincinnati. Ann Arbor: University Microfilms International.
Blackman, D. and Branigan, K. (ed.) 1977. An archaeological survey of the lower catchment of the Ayiopharango valley. *BSA* 72, 13–84.
1982. The excavation of an Early Minoan tholos tomb at Ayia Kyriaki, Ayiofarango, southern Crete. *BSA* 77, 1–57.
Blasingham, A.C. 1983. The seals from the tombs of the Messara: inferences as to kinship and social organisation. In Krzyszkowska and Nixon 1983, 11–21.
Blegen, C.W. 1921. *Korakou: a prehistoric settlement near Corinth*. Boston: American School of Classical Studies.
1928. *Zygouries: a prehistoric settlement in the valley of Cleonae*. Cambridge, Mass.: Harvard University Press.
1937. *Prosymna: the Helladic settlement preceding the Argive Heraeum*. Cambridge: Cambridge University Press.
and Haley, J. 1928. The coming of the Greeks. *AJA* 32, 141–54.
and Rawson, M. 1966. *The palace of Nestor at Pylos in western Messenia*, Vol. I. Princeton: Princeton University Press.
, Rawson, M., Taylour, Lord William and Donovan, W.P. 1973. *The palace of Nestor at Pylos in western Messenia*, Vol. III. Princeton: Princeton University Press.
Blitzer, H. 1990a. ΚΟΡΩΝΕΪΚΑ: storage-jar production and trade in the traditional Aegean. *Hesperia* 59, 675–711.
1990b. Pastoral life in the mountains of Crete. *Expedition* 32, 34–41.
1991. Middle to Late Helladic chipped stone implements of the southwest Peloponnese, Greece. Part I: the evidence from Malthi. *Hydra* 9, 1–73.
n.d. Olive cultivation and oil production in Minoan Crete. In Amouretti, M-C. and Brun, J-P., *La production du vin et de l'huile en Mediterranée de l'âge du bronze à la fin du XVIème siècle de notre ère* (forthcoming as *BCH* Supplement).
Boardman, J. 1970. *Greek gems and finger rings, Early Bronze Age to late Classical*. London: Thames and Hudson.

Boulotis, C. 1987. Nochmals zum Prozessionsfresko von Knossos: Palast und Darbringung von Prestige-Objekten. In Hägg and Marinatos 1987, 145–56.

1990. *Synnaoi theoi*: a cult phenomenon of the Aegean Late Bronze Age. In Hägg and Nordquist 1990, 199–200.

Boyd Hawes, H. (with others) 1908. *Gournia, Vasiliki and other prehistoric sites on the isthmus of Hierapetra, Crete*. Philadelphia: American Exploration Society.

Branigan, K. 1968a. *Copper and bronze working in Early Bronze Age Crete. SIMA* 19. Göteborg: Åström.

1968b. A transitional phase in Minoan metallurgy. *BSA* 63, 185–203.

1970b. *The tombs of Mesara*. London: Duckworth.

1971. Cycladic figurines and their derivatives in Crete. *BSA* 66, 57–78.

1972. Minoan settlements in east Crete. In P.J. Ucko, R. Tringham and G.W. Dimbleby (eds), *Man, settlement and urbanism*, 751–9. London: Duckworth.

1974. *Aegean metalwork of the Early and Middle Bronze Age*. Oxford: Clarendon Press.

1975. The round graves of Levkas reconsidered. *BSA* 70, 37–49.

1983. Crafts specialization in Minoan Crete. In Krzyszkowska and Nixon 1983, 23–32.

1987a. The economic roles of the first palaces. In Hägg and Marinatos 1987, 245–9.

1987b. Body-counts in the Mesara tholoi. In *ΕΙΛΑΠΙΝΗ, Festschrift for Prof. N. Platon*, 299–309. Herakleion: Vikelaia Vivliothiki.

1988. Some observations on state formation in Crete. In French and Wardle 1988, 63–71.

1989. Minoan foreign relations in transition. In Laffineur 1989a, 65–71.

Braudel, F. 1972. *The Mediterranean and the Mediterranean world in the age of Philip II*. London: Collins.

Broodbank, C. 1989. The longboat and society in the Cyclades in the Keros–Syros culture. *AJA* 85, 319–37.

(forthcoming). The Neolithic labyrinth. Social change at Knossos before the Bronze Age. To appear in *JMA* 5(1).

and Strasser, T.F. 1991. Migrant farmers and the Neolithic colonization of Crete. *Antiquity* 65, 233–45.

Bryce, T.R. 1989. Ahhiyawans and Mycenaeans – an Anatolian viewpoint. *OJA* 8, 297–310.

Buchholz, H-G. 1962. Die Pfeilglätter aus dem VI. Schachtgrab von Mykene und die helladischen Pfeilspitzen. *JdAI* 77, 1–58.

Burkert, W. 1985. *Greek religion*. Oxford: Blackwell.

Cadogan, G. 1971. Was there a Minoan landed gentry? *BICS* 18, 145–8.

1978. Pyrgos, Crete 1970–77. In *AR* 1977–78, 70–84.

1983. Early Minoan and Middle Minoan chronology. *AJA* 87, 507–18.

(ed.) 1986. *The end of the Early Bronze Age in the Aegean*. Leiden: Brill.

1988. Some Middle Minoan problems. In French and Wardle 1988, 95–9.

1990. The Lasithi area in the Old Palace period. *BICS* 37, 172–4.

Cameron, M.A.S. 1987. The 'palatial' thematic system in the Knossos murals. Last notes on Knossos frescoes. In Hägg and Marinatos 1987, 320–8.

, Jones, R.E. and Philippakis, S.E. 1977. Scientific analyses of Minoan fresco samples from Knossos. *BSA* 72, 121–84.

Carothers, J. and McDonald, W.A. 1979. The size and distribution of the population in Late Bronze Age Messenia: some statistical approaches. *JFA* 6, 433–53.

Carpenter, M. 1983. ki-ti-me-na and ke-ke-me-na at Pylos. *Minos* 18, 81–8.

Caskey, J.L. 1964. Excavations in Keos, 1963. *Hesperia* 33, 314–35.

Caskey, M.E. 1981. Ayia Irini, Kea: the terracotta statues and the cult in the temple. In Hägg and Marinatos 1981, 127–35.
1986. *Keos II,i. The temple at Ayia Irini: the statues*. Princeton: Princeton University Press.
1990. Thoughts on Early Bronze Age hearths. In Hägg and Nordquist 1990, 13–21.
Catling, H.W. 1964. *Cypriot bronzework in the Mycenaean world*. Oxford: Oxford University Press.
1968a. Late Minoan vases and bronzes in Oxford. *BSA* 63, 89–131.
1968b. A Mycenaean puzzle from Lefkandi. *AJA* 72, 41–9.
1970. A bronze plate from a scale-corslet found at Mycenae. *AA* 1970, 441–9.
1977. Excavations at the Menelaion, Sparta. *AR* 1976–77, 24–42.
1973, 1976, 1978, 1979, 1980, 1981a, 1982, 1984, 1985, 1986, 1987, 1988, 1989. Archaeology in Greece, 1972–73 etc., to 1988–89. In *AR* 1972–73, 3–32; 1975–76, 3–33; 1977–78, 3–69; 1978–79, 3–42; 1979–80, 3–53; 1980–81, 3–48; 1981–82, 3–62; 1983–84, 3–70; 1984–85, 3–69; 1985–86, 3–101; 1986–87, 1–61; 1987–88, 3–85; 1988–89, 3–116.
1989. Some problems in Aegean prehistory, c. 1450–1380 B.C. (fourteenth J.L. Myres Memorial Lecture). Oxford: Leopard's Head Press.
1991. A Late Cypriot import in Rhodes. *BSA* 86, 1–7.
and Catling, E.A. 1981b. 'Barbarian' pottery from the Mycenaean settlement at the Menelaion, Sparta. *BSA* 76, 71–82.
and MacGillivray, J.A. 1983. An Early Cypriot III vase from the palace at Knossos. *BSA* 78, 1–8.
Cavanagh, W.G. 1978. A Mycenaean second burial custom? *BICS* 25, 171–2.
and Laxton, R.R. 1981. The structural mechanics of the Mycenaean tholos tomb. *BSA* 76, 109–37.
and Laxton, R.R. 1982. Corbelled vaulting in the Late Minoan tholos tombs of Crete. *BSA* 77, 65–77.
and Mee, C. 1978. The re-use of earlier tombs in the LH IIIC period. *BSA* 73, 31–44.
and Mee, C. 1990. The location of Mycenaean chamber tombs in the Argolid. In Hägg and Nordquist 1990, 55–64.
Charles, J.A. 1968. The first Sheffield plate. *Antiquity* 42, 278–85.
Cherry, J.F. 1979. Four problems in Cycladic prehistory. In Davis and Cherry 1979, 22–47.
1986. Polities and palaces: some problems in Minoan state formation. In Renfrew and Cherry 1986: 19–45.
1988. Pastoralism and the role of animals in the pre- and protohistoric economies of the Aegean. In C.R. Whittaker (ed.), *Pastoral economies in Classical antiquity*, 6–34. Cambridge: Philological Society.
1990. The first colonization of the Mediterranean islands: a review of recent research. *JMA* 3, 145–221.
and Davis, J.L. 1982. The Cyclades and the Greek mainland in LC I: the evidence of the pottery. *AJA* 86, 333–41.
Chryssoulaki, S. and Platon, L. 1987. Relations between the town and palace of Zakros. In Hägg and Marinatos 1987, 77–84.
Cline, E. 1987. Amenhotep III and the Aegean: a reassessment of Egypto-Aegean relations in the 14th century BC. *Orientalia* 56, 1–36.
1991. Monkey business in the Bronze Age Aegean: the Amenhotep II faience figurines from Mycenae and Tiryns. *BSA* 86, 29–42.
Coldstream, J.N. and Huxley, G.L. (eds) 1972. *Kythera, excavations and studies*. London: Faber and Faber.

and Huxley, G.L. 1984. The Minoans of Kythera. In Hägg and Marinatos 1984, 107–12.

Coleman, J.E. 1977. *Keos I. Kephala: a Late Neolithic settlement and cemetery*. Princeton: Princeton University Press.

1985. 'Frying pans' of the Early Bronze Age Aegean. *AJA* 89, 191–219.

Crossland, R.A. and Birchall, A. (eds) 1973. *Bronze Age migrations in the Aegean. Archaeological and linguistic problems in Greek prehistory*. London: Duckworth.

Crouwel, J.H. 1981. *Chariots and other means of land transport in Bronze Age Greece*. Amsterdam: Allard Pierson Museum.

Cummer, W.W. and Schofield, E. 1984. *Keos III. Ayia Irini: House A*. Mainz: von Zabern.

Cunliffe, B. (ed.) 1987. *Origins*. London: BBC Books.

Dalley, S. 1984. *Mari and Karana: two Old Babylonian cities*. Harlow: Longman.

Darcque, P. 1980. *L'architecture domestique mycénienne*. Thèse du III° cycle, Paris.

1981. Les vestiges mycéniens découverts sous le Télestérion d'Eleusis. *BCH* 105, 593–605.

and Poursat, J-C. (eds) 1985. *L'iconographie minoenne* (*BCH* Supplement 11). Athens: French School at Athens.

and Treuil, R. (eds) 1990. *L'habitat égéen préhistorique* (*BCH* Supplement 19). Athens: French School at Athens.

Davaras, C. 1971. Πρωτομινωικόν νεκροταφείον Άγιας Φωτίας Σητείας. *AAA* 4, 392–7.

1975. Early Minoan jewellery from Mochlos. *BSA* 70, 101–14.

1980. A Minoan pottery kiln at Palaikastro. *BSA* 75, 115–26.

1988. A Minoan beetle-rhyton from Prinias Siteias. *BSA* 83, 45–54.

David, A.R. 1982. *The ancient Egyptians. Religious beliefs and practices*. London: Routledge.

Davidson, D. and Tasker, C. 1982. Geomorphological evolution during the late Holocene. In Renfrew and Wagstaff 1982, 82–94.

Davis, E.N. 1977. *The Vapheio cups and Aegean gold and silver ware*. New York: Garland.

1986a. The political use of art in the Aegean: the missing ruler. *AJA* 90, 216.

1986b. Youth and age in the Thera frescoes. *AJA* 90, 399–406.

1987. The Knossos miniature frescoes and the function of the central courts. In Hägg and Marinatos 1987, 157–61.

Davis, J.L. 1978. The mainland panelled cup and panelled style. *AJA* 82, 216–22.

1979. Late Helladic I pottery from Korakou. *Hesperia* 48, 234–63.

1984. Cultural innovation and the Minoan thalassocracy at Ayia Irini, Keos. In Hägg and Marinatos 1984, 159–66.

1986. *Keos V. Ayia Irini: period V*. Mainz: von Zabern.

and Cherry, J.F. (eds) 1979. *Papers in Cycladic prehistory*. Los Angeles: University of California, Los Angeles, Institute of Archaeology.

and Lewis, H.B. 1985. Mechanization of pottery production: a case study from the Cycladic islands. In Knapp and Stech 1985, 79–92.

, Schofield, E., Torrence, R. and Williams, D.F. 1983. Keos and the eastern Aegean: the Cretan connection. *Hesperia* 52, 361–6.

Day, P.M. 1988. The production and distribution of storage jars in Neopalatial Crete. In French and Wardle, 1988, 499–508.

Demakopoulou, K. 1982. Τό μυκηναικό ιερό στό Αμυκλαίο καί η ΥΕ ΙΙΙΓ περίοδος στή Λακωνία (with English summary). PhD thesis, Athens.

1990. The burial ritual in the tholos tomb at Kokla, Argolis. In Hägg and Nordquist 1990, 113–23.

and Crouwel, J.H. 1984. Some Mycenaean pictorial pottery from Thebes. *BSA* 79, 37–48.

Detournay, B., Poursat, J-C. and Vandenabeele, F. 1980. *Fouilles executées à Mallia. Le Quartier Mu, II.* Etudes Crétoises 26. Paris: French School at Athens.

Diamant, S. 1974. A prehistoric figurine from Mycenae. *BSA* 69, 103–8.

1988. Mycenaean origins: infiltration from the north? In French and Wardle 1988, 153–9.

Dickinson, O.T.P.K. 1974. 'Drought and the decline of Mycenae': some comments. *Antiquity* 48, 228–30.

1983. Cist graves and chamber tombs. *BSA* 78, 55–67.

1984. Cretan contacts with the mainland during the period of the Shaft Graves. In Hägg and Marinatos 1984, 115–18.

1986a. Homer, the poet of the Dark Age. *Greece and Rome* 33, 20–37.

1986b. Early Mycenaean Greece and the Mediterranean. In Marazzi *et al.* 1986, 271–6.

1989. 'The origins of Mycenaean civilisation' revisited. In Laffineur 1989a, 131–6.

Dietz, S. 1991. *The Argolid at the transition to the Mycenaean age.* Copenhagen: National Museum.

and Divari-Valakou, N. 1990. A Middle Helladic III/Late Helladic I grave group from Myloi in the Argolid (oikopedon Manti). *OpAth* 18, 45–62.

and Papachristodoulou, I. (eds) 1988. *Archaeology in the Dodecanese.* Copenhagen: National Museum.

Doumas, C. 1977. *Early Bronze Age burial habits in the Cyclades. SIMA* 48. Göteborg: Åström.

(ed.) 1978, 1980. *Thera and the Aegean World*, I, II. London: Thera Foundation.

1983. *Thera: Pompeii of the ancient Aegean.* London: Thames and Hudson.

1987. Early Cycladic society: the evidence from the graves. In Laffineur 1987, 15–18.

1992. *The wall-paintings of Thera.* Athens: Thera Foundation.

Drews, R. 1988. *The coming of the Greeks. Indo-European conquests in the Aegean and Near East.* Princeton: Princeton University Press.

Driessen, J. and Macdonald, C.F. 1984. Some military aspects of the Aegean in the late 15th and early 14th centuries BC. *BSA* 79, 49–74.

Driessen, J. and MacGillivray, J.A. The Neopalatial period in east Crete. In Laffineur 1989a, 99–110.

Drower, M.S. 1975. Canaanite religion and literature. In *CAH* II:1, Ch. 21, section 5.

Du Boulay, J. 1974. *Portrait of a Greek mountain village.* Oxford: Clarendon Press.

Easton, D.F. 1990. Reconstructing Schliemann's Troy. In W.M. Calder III and J. Cobet, *Heinrich Schliemann nach hundert Jahren*, 431–48. Frankfurt: Victorio Klostermann.

Evans, A.J. 1905. The prehistoric tombs of Knossos. *Archaeologia* 59, 391–562.

1921–35. *The Palace of Minos at Knossos I (1921), II (1928), III (1930), IV (1935).* London: Macmillan.

Evans, J.D. and Renfrew, C. 1968. *Excavations at Saliagos near Antiparos.* London: Thames and Hudson.

Evely, D. 1988a. The potter's wheel in Minoan Crete. *BSA* 83, 83–126.

1988b. Minoan craftsmen: problems of recognition and definition. In French and Wardle 1988, 297–415.

Felsch, R.S.C. 1981. Mykenischer Kult im Heiligtum bei Kalapodi? In Hägg and Marinatos 1981, 81–9.

Felten, F. 1986. Early urban history and architecture of ancient Aigina. In Hägg and Konsola 1986, 21–8.

Fitton, L. (ed.) 1984. *Cycladica. Studies in memory of N.P. Goulandris*. London: British Museum.
1989. *Cycladic art*. London: British Museum.
Forsdyke, E.J. 1927. The Mavro Spelio cemetery at Knossos. *BSA* 28, 243–96.
1956. *Greece before Homer*. London: Max Parrish.
Foster, K.P. 1979. *Aegean faience of the Bronze Age*. New Haven and London: Yale University Press.
French, D.H. 1972. *Notes on prehistoric pottery groups from central Greece*. Privately circulated.
French, E.B. 1971. The development of Mycenaean terracotta figurines. *BSA* 66, 101–87.
1981a. Cult places at Mycenae. In Hägg and Marinatos 1981, 41–8.
1981b. Mycenaean figures and figurines, their typology and function. In Hägg and Marinatos 1981, 173–8.
1990, 1991. Archaeology in Greece 1989–90, 1990–91. *AR* 1989–90, 3–82; 1990–91, 3–78.
and Wardle, K.A. (eds) 1988. *Problems in Greek prehistory*. Bristol: Bristol Classical Press.
Gale, N.H. (ed.) 1991. *Bronze Age trade in the Mediterranean. SIMA* 90. Göteborg: Åström.
and Stos-Gale, Z.A. 1986. Oxhide ingots in Crete and Cyprus and the Bronze Age metals trade. *BSA* 81, 81–100.
Gallis, K.J. 1985. A Late Neolithic foundation offering from Thessaly. *Antiquity* 59, 20–4.
Gamble, C. 1986. *The Palaeolithic settlement of Europe*. Cambridge: Cambridge University Press.
Gates, C. 1989. Iconography at the crossroads: the Aegina Treasure. In Laffineur 1989a, 215–24.
Georgiou, H.A. 1983. Minoan coarse wares and Minoan technology. In Krzyszkowska and Nixon 1983, 75–92.
1986. *Keos VI. Ayia Irini: specialised domestic and industrial pottery*. Mainz: von Zabern.
Gesell, G.C. 1983. The place of the goddess in Minoan society. In Krzyszkowska and Nixon 1983, 93–9.
1985. *Town, palace, and house cult in Minoan Crete. SIMA* 67. Göteborg: Åström.
1987. The Minoan palace and public cult. In Hägg and Marinatos 1987, 123–8.
Getz-Preziosi, P. 1985. *Early Cycladic sculpture: an introduction*. Malibu: Getty Museum.
Gill, M.A.V. 1985. Some observations on representations of marine animals in Minoan art, and their identification. In Darcque and Poursat 1985, 63–81.
Goldman, H. 1931. *Excavations at Eutresis in Boeotia*. Cambridge, Mass.: Harvard University Press.
Goodison, L. 1989. *Death, women and the sun*. Institute of Classical Studies, Bulletin Supplement 53. London: London University.
Graham, J.W. 1987. *The palaces of Crete* (2nd edition). Princeton: Princeton University Press.
Graziadio, G. 1988. The chronology of the graves of Circle B at Mycenae: a new hypothesis. *AJA* 92, 343–72.
1991. The process of social stratification at Mycenae in the Shaft Grave period: a comparative examination of the evidence. *AJA* 95, 403–40.
Gurney, O.R. 1977. *Some aspects of Hittite religion*. The Schweich Lectures 1976. Oxford: University Press.

1990. *The Hittites* (revised 2nd edition). London: Penguin.
Hägg, R. 1981a. Official and popular cults in Mycenaean Greece. In Hägg and Marinatos 1981, 35–9.
1981b. The house sanctuary at Asine revisited. In Hägg and Marinatos 1981, 91–4.
1983. Epiphany in Minoan ritual. *BICS* 30, 184–5.
1984. Degrees and character of the Minoan influence on the mainland. In Hägg and Marinatos 1984, 119–21.
1985a. Pictorial programmes in the Minoan palaces and villas? In Darcque and Poursat 1985, 209–17.
1985b. Mycenaean religion: the Helladic and the Minoan components. In Morpurgo Davies and Duhoux 1985, 203–25.
1987. On the reconstruction of the west facade of the palace at Knossos. In Hägg and Marinatos 1987, 129–34.
1990. The role of libations in Mycenaean ceremony and cult. In Hägg and Nordquist 1990, 177–84.
and Konsola, D. 1986. *Early Helladic architecture and urbanization. SIMA* 76. Göteborg: Åström.
and Lindau, Y. 1984. The Minoan 'snake frame' reconsidered. *OpAth* 15, 67–77.
and Marinatos, N. 1981. *Sanctuaries and cults in the Aegean Bronze Age*. Stockholm: Swedish Institute in Athens.
and Marinatos, N. 1984. *The Minoan thalassocracy: myth and reality*. Stockholm: Swedish Institute in Athens.
and Marinatos, N. 1987. *The function of the Minoan palaces*. Stockholm, Swedish Institute in Athens.
, Marinatos, N. and Nordquist, G. 1988. *Early Greek cult practice*. Stockholm: Swedish Institute in Athens.
and Nordquist, G.C. 1990. *Celebrations of death and divinity in the Bronze Age Argolid*. Stockholm: Swedish Institute in Athens.
Hallager, B. 1985. Crete and Italy in the Late Bronze Age III period. *AJA* 89, 293–305.
Hallager, E. 1977. *The Mycenaean palace at Knossos*. Stockholm: Medalhavsmuseet.
1983. The Greek–Swedish excavations at Kastelli, Khania 1980. The Linear B inscriptions. *AAA* 16, 58–73.
1985. *The Master Impression. SIMA* 69. Göteborg: Åström.
1988. The roundel in the Minoan administrative system. In French and Wardle 1988, 101–12.
Halstead, P. 1977. The Bronze Age demography of Crete and Greece – a note. *BSA* 72, 107–11.
1981a. Counting sheep in Neolithic and Bronze Age Greece. In Hodder *et al.* 1981, 307–39.
1981b. Review of Hourmouziadis 1979 in *JHS* 99, 206–7.
1987a. Man and other animals in later Greek prehistory. *BSA* 82, 71–83.
1987b. Traditional and ancient rural economy in Mediterranean Europe: plus ça change? *JHS* 107, 77–87.
1988. On redistribution and the origin of Minoan–Mycenaean palatial economies. In French and Wardle 1988, 519–30.
1989. The economy has a normal surplus: economic stability and social change among early farming communities of Thessaly, Greece. In P. Halstead and J. O'Shea (eds), *Bad year economics: cultural responses to risk and uncertainty*, Ch. 5. Cambridge: Cambridge University Press.
Hankey, V. 1974. A Late Bronze Age temple at Amman: I. The Aegean pottery. II. Vases and objects made of stone. *Levant* 6, 131–78.

1979. Crete, Cyprus and the south-eastern Mediterranean, 1400–1200 B.C. In *Acts of the International Archaeological Symposium 'The relations between Cyprus and Crete, ca. 2000–500 B.C.'*, 144–57. Nicosia: Department of Antiquities, Cyprus.
1988. Pyrgos. The communal tomb in Pyrgos IV (Late Minoan I). *BICS* 33, 135–7.
Hansen, J.M. 1988. Agriculture in the prehistoric Aegean: data versus speculation. *AJA* 92, 39–52.
Harding, A. 1984. *The Mycenaeans and Europe*. London: Academic Press.
and Hughes-Brock, H. 1974. Amber in the Mycenaean world. *BSA* 69, 145–72.
Hardy, D.A. (ed., with others) 1990. *Thera and the Aegean world III* (3 vols.). London: Thera Foundation.
Haskell, H.W. 1983. From palace to town administration: the evidence of coarse-ware stirrup-jars. In Krzyszkowska and Nixon 1983, 121–8.
1984. Pylos: stirrup jars and the international oil trade. In Shelmerdine and Palaima 1984, 97–107.
1990. Late Bronze Age trade: transport stirrup jars. *AJA* 94, 298.
Hayden, B.J. 1987. Crete in transition: LM IIIA–B architecture, a preliminary study. *SMEA* 26, 199–233.
Heltzer, M. 1988. Trade relations between Ugarit and Crete. *Minos* 23, 7–13.
1989. The trade of Crete and Cyprus with Syria and Mesopotamia and their eastern tin-sources in the XVIII–XVII century B.C. *Minos* 24, 7–27.
Hiesel, G. 1990. *Späthelladische Hausarchitektur*. Mainz: von Zabern.
Higgins, R.A. 1979. *The Aegina Treasure, an archaeological mystery*. London: British Museum.
1980. *Greek and Roman jewellery* (2nd edition). London: Methuen.
1987. A gold diadem from Aegina. *JHS* 107, 182.
Hiller, S. 1981. Mykenischer Heiligtümer: das Zeugnis der Linear B-Texte. In Hägg and Marinatos 1981, 95–125.
1989. On the origins of the Shaft Graves. In Laffineur 1989a, 137–44.
Höckmann, O. 1980. Lanze und Speer im spätminoischen und mykenischen Griechenland. *JRGZM* 27, 13–158.
Hodder, I., Isaac, G. and Hammond, N. (eds) 1981. *Pattern of the past*. Cambridge: Cambridge University Press.
Hood, M.S.F. 1977. Minoan town-shrines? In K.H. Kinzl (ed.), *Greece and the eastern Mediterranean in ancient history and prehistory*, 158–72. Berlin: de Gruyter.
1980. Traces of the eruption outside Thera. In Doumas 1980, 681–90.
1983. The 'country house' and Minoan society. In Krzyszkowska and Nixon 1983, 129–35.
and de Jong, P. 1952. LM warrior graves from Ayios Joannis and the New Hospital site at Knossos. *BSA* 47, 243–77.
and Smyth, D. 1981. *Archaeological survey of the Knossos area*, London: Thames and Hudson.
Hooker, J.T. 1980. *Linear B: an introduction*. Bristol: Bristol Classical Press.
Hope Simpson, R. and Dickinson O.T.P.K. 1979. *A gazetteer of Aegean civilization in the Bronze Age*, Vol. I: *The mainland and islands*. *SIMA* 52. Göteborg: Åström.
Hourmouziadis, G. 1979. *Τὸ νεολιθικὸ Διμήνι*. Volos: Society for Thessalian Studies.
Hurwit, J. 1979. The Dendra Octopus Cup and the problem of style in the fifteenth century Aegean. *AJA* 75, 413–26.
Iakovidis, S.E. 1969. *Περατή. Τὸ νεκροταφεῖον* (with English summary). Athens: Archaeological Society.
1977. On the use of Mycenaean 'buttons'. *BSA* 72, 113–19.

1980. *Excavations of the necropolis at Perati.* Los Angeles: University of California, Los Angeles.
1983. *Late Helladic citadels on mainland Greece.* Leiden: Brill.
1990. Mycenaean roofs: form and construction. In Darcque and Treuil 1990, 147–60.
Immerwahr, S.A. 1985. A possible influence of Egyptian art in the creation of Minoan wall painting. In Darcque and Poursat 1985, 41–50.
1990. *Aegean painting in the Bronze Age.* Philadelphia: Pennsylvania State University Press.
Jacobsen, Th. 1976. *The treasures of darkness.* New Haven: Yale University Press.
Jacobsen, T.W. 1981. Franchthi cave and the beginning of settled village life in Greece. *Hesperia* 50, 303–19.
Jarman, M.R., Bailey, G.B. and Jarman, H.N. (eds) 1982. *Early European agriculture.* Cambridge: Cambridge University Press.
Jones, R.E. 1986. *Greek and Cypriot pottery. A review of scientifc studies.* Athens: British School at Athens.
Kanta, A. 1980. *The Late Minoan III period in Crete. A survey of sites, pottery, and their distribution. SIMA* 58. Göteborg: Åström.
1983. Minoan and traditional Crete: some parallels between two cultures in the same environment. In Krzyszkowska and Nixon 1983, 155–62.
Karetsou, A. 1981. The peak sanctuary of Mt Juktas. In Hägg and Marinatos 1981, 137–53.
, Godart, L. and Olivier, J-P., 1985. Inscriptions en linéaire A du sanctuaire de sommet du mont Iouktas. *Kadmos* 24, 89–147.
Karo, G. 1930–33. *Die Schachtgräber von Mykenai.* Munich: Bruckmann.
Keller, D.R. and Ruipp, D.W. (eds) 1983. *Archaeological survey in the Mediterranean.* Oxford: British Archaeological Reports S155.
Kemp, B.J. 1989. *Ancient Egypt: anatomy of a civilization.* London: Routledge.
and Merrillees, R.S. 1980. *Minoan pottery in second millennium Egypt.* Mainz: von Zabern.
Kienast, H. 1987. Neue Forschungen im Kopais-Becken. In Hägg and Marinatos 1987, 121–2.
Kilian, K. 1981. Zeugnisse mykenische Kultausübung in Tiryns. In Hägg and Marinatos 1981, 49–58.
1986. The circular building at Tiryns. In Hägg and Konsola 1986, 65–71.
1987a. Zur Funktion der mykenischen Residenzen auf dem griechischen Festland. In Hägg and Marinatos 1987, 21–38.
1987b. L'architecture des résidences mycéniennes: origine et extension d'une structure du pouvoir politique pendant l'âge du bronze. In E. Lévy (ed.), *Le système palatial en Orient, en Grèce et à Rome*, 203–17. Strasbourg: université des sciences humaines de Strasbourg.
1988a. Mycenaeans up to date, trends and changes in recent research. In French and Wardle 1988, 115–52.
1988b. The emergence of *wanax* ideology in the Mycenaean palaces. *OJA* 7, 291–302.
1988c. Mycenaean architecture. In Demakopoulou 1988, 30–4.
1990. Patterns in the cult activity in the Mycenaean Argolid. In Hägg and Nordquist 1990, 185–96.
Kilian-Dirlmeier, I. 1985. Noch einmal zu den 'Kriegergräber' von Knossos. *JRGZM* 32, 196–214.
1986. Beobachtungen zu den Schachtgräbern von Mykenai und zu den Schmuckbeigaben mykenischer Mannergräber. *JRGZM* 33, 159–98.

1988. Jewellery in Mycenaean and Minoan 'warrior graves'. In French and Wardle 1988, 161–71.
Killen, J.T. 1979. The Linear B tablets and economic history: some problems. *BICS* 26, 133–4.
1985. The Linear B tablets and the Mycenean economy. In Morpurgo Davies and Duhoux 1985, 241–305.
1987. Piety begins at home: place-names on Knossos records of religious offerings. In P.H. Ilievski and L. Crepajac (eds), *Tractata Mycenaea*. Skopje: Macedonian Academy of Arts and Sciences.
Kitchen, K.A. 1987. The basics of Egyptian chronology in relation to the Bronze Age. In Åström 1987, 37–55.
Knapp, A.B. 1990. Ethnicity, entrepreneurship, and exchange: Mediterranean inter-island relationships in the Late Bronze Age. *BSA* 85, 115–53.
and Stech, T. (eds) 1985. *Prehistoric production and exchange*. Los Angeles: University of California, Los Angeles.
Koehl, R.B. 1986. The Chieftain Cup and a Minoan rite of passage, *JHS* 106, 99–110.
Konsola, D. 1984. Beobachtungen zum Wegenetz in Frühhelladische Siedlungen. *AA* 1984, 197–210.
1986. Stages of urban transformation in the Early Helladic period. In Hägg and Konsola 1986, 9–17.
1990. Settlement size and the beginning of urbanisation. In Darcque and Treuil 1990, 463–71.
Korres, G.S. 1976. Τύμβοι, θόλοι, καί ταφικοί κύκλοι τής Μεσσηνίας. In *Proceedings of the first international conference of Peloponnesian studies*, Vol. 2, 337–69. Athens: Society for Peloponnesian Studies.
1984. The relations between Crete and Messenia in the late Middle Helladic and early Late Helladic period. In Hägg and Marinatos 1984, 141–52.
Koutsouflakis, G. 1990. Trade mechanisms in the Early Bronze Age. *Hydra* 7, 27–39.
Kroll, H. 1984. Zum Ackerbau gegen Ende der mykenischen Epoche in der Argolis. *AA* 1984, 210–22.
Krzyszkowska, O. 1988. Ivory in the Aegean Bronze Age: elephant tusk or hippopotamus ivory? *BSA* 83, 209–34.
1991. The Enkomi head reconsidered. *BSA* 86, 107–20.
and Nixon, L. (eds) 1983. *Minoan society*. Bristol: Bristol Classical Press.
Laffineur, R. (ed.). 1987. *Thanatos. Les coutûmes funéraires en Egée à l'Age du Bronze (Aegaeum 1)*. Liège: University of Liège.
1988. Réflexions sur le trésor de Tôd. *Aegaeum* 2, 17–30.
(ed.) 1989a. *Transition. Le monde égéen du Bronze Moyen au Bronze Récent (Aegaeum 3)*. Liège: University of Liège.
1989b. Mobilier funéraire et hiérarchie sociale aux cercles des tombes de Mycènes. In Laffineur 1989a, 227–38.
1990. Grave Circle A at Mycenae: further reflections on its history. In Hägg and Nordquist 1990, 201–5.
Lambert, N. 1972. Grotte d'Alépotrypa. *BCH* 97, 845–71.
Lambrinudakis, V. 1981. Remains of the Mycenaean period in the sanctuary of Apollon Maleatas. In Hägg and Marinatos 1981, 59–65.
Larsen, T.M. 1976. *The Old Assyrian city-state and its colonies*. Copenhagen: Akademisk Forlag.
Lauter, H. 1989. Die protomykenische burg auf Kiapha Thiti in Attika. In Laffineur 1989a, 145–9.

Laviosa, C. 1968. Una forma minoica per fusione a cera perduta. *ASAtene* 45/46, 499–510.

1984. The Minoan thalassocracy, Iasos and the Carian coast. In Hägg and Marinatos 1984, 183–5.

Lebessi, A. and Muhly, P. 1990. Aspects of Minoan cult. Sacred enclosures. The evidence from the Syme sanctuary (Crete). *AA* 1990, 315–36.

Lejeune, M. 1976. Analyse du dossier Pylien Ea. *Minos* 15, 81–115.

Levi, D. 1976. *Festòs e la civiltà minoica*. Rome: Edizioni dell' Ateneo.

Littauer, M.A. 1972. The military use of the chariot in the Aegean in the Late Bronze Age. *AJA* 76, 145–57.

Long, C.R. 1974. *The Ayia Triadha sarcophagus. A study of Late Minoan and Mycenaean funerary practices and beliefs. SIMA* 41. Göteborg: Åström.

1978. The Lasithi dagger. *AJA* 82, 35–46.

Lo Schiavo, F., Macnamara, E. and Vagnetti, L. 1985. Late Cypriot imports to Italy and their influence on local bronzework. *Papers of the British School at Rome* 53, 1–71.

Lukermann, F. and Moody, J. 1985. The wild country west of Idha; the prehistory of the Khania nomos. *AJA* 89, 340.

Macdonald, C.F. 1987. A Knossian weapon workshop in Late Minoan II and IIIA. In Hägg and Marinatos 1987, 293–5.

and Driessen, J.M. 1988. The drainage system of the domestic quarter in the palace at Knossos. *BSA* 83, 235–58.

MacGillivray, J.A. 1984a. Cycladic jars from Middle Minoan III contexts at Knossos. In Hägg and Marinatos 1984, 153–8.

1984b. The relative chronology of Early Cycladic III. In MacGillivray and Barber 1984, 70–7.

1986. The end of the Old Palaces in Crete. Unpublished paper delivered at the Mycenaean Seminar, London, 23 April 1986.

1987. Pottery workshops and the Old Palaces in Crete. In Hägg and Marinatos 1987, 273–9.

MacGillivray, J.A. and Barber, R.L.N. (eds) 1984. *The prehistoric Cyclades*. Edinburgh: Edinburgh University Press.

, Day, P.M. and Jones, R.E. 1988. Dark-faced incised pyxides and lids from Knossos: problems of date and origin. In French and Wardle 1988, 91–4.

and Sackett, L.H. 1984. An archaeological survey of the Roussolakkos area at Palaikastro. *BSA* 79, 129–59.

, Sackett, L.H., Driessen, J. and Smyth, D. 1989. Excavations at Palaikastro, 1988. *BSA* 84, 135–54.

, Sackett, L.H., Driessen, J., Farnoux, A. and Smyth, D. 1991. Excavations at Palaikastro, 1990. *BSA* 86, 121–47.

Macqueen, J.G. 1986. *The Hittites and their contemporaries in Asia Minor* (2nd edition). London: Thames and Hudson.

Mancz, E.A., 1989. An examination of changing patterns of animal-husbandry of the Late Bronze and Dark Ages of Nichoria in the southwestern Peloponnese. PhD thesis, Minnesota. Ann Arbor: University Microfilms International.

Manning, S. 1988. The Bronze Age eruption of Thera: absolute dating, Aegean chronology, and Mediterranean cultural interrelations. *JMA* 1, 17–82.

1990. The Thera eruption: the Third Congress, and the problem of the date. *Archaeometry* 32, 91–100.

and Weninger, B. 1992. Archaeological wiggle matching and chronology in the Aegean Late Bronze Age. *Antiquity* 66, 636–63.

Marangou, L. (ed.) 1990. *Cycladic culture: Naxos in the 3rd millennium BC*. Athens: Goulandris Foundation.

Marazzi, M., Tusa, S. and Vagnetti, L. 1986. *Traffici micenei nel Mediterraneo*. Taranto: Istituto per la storia e l'archeologia della Magna Grecia.

Marinatos, N. 1984a. *Art and religion in Thera*. Athens: Mathioulakis.

1984b. Minoan threskeiocracy on Thera. In Hägg and Marinatos 1984, 167–78.

1986. *Minoan sacrificial ritual. Cult practice and symbolism*. Stockholm: Swedish Institute in Athens.

1987a. Public festivals in the west courts of the palaces. In Hägg and Marinatos 1987, 135–43.

1987b. Role and sex division in ritual scenes of Aegean art. *JPR* 1, 23–34.

1988a. The imagery of sacrifice: Minoan and Greek. In Hägg, Marinatos and Nordquist 1988, 9–20.

1988b. The fresco from Room 31 at Mycenae: problems of method and interpretation. In French and Wardle 1988, 245–51.

1990a. Minoan–Cycladic syncretism. In Hardy 1990, 370–6.

1990b. Review of P.M. Warren, *Minoan religion as ritual action*, in *JPR* 3–4, 68–9.

and Hägg, R. 1983. Anthropomorphic cult images in Minoan Crete? In Krzyszkowska and Nixon 1983, 185–201.

and Hägg, R. 1986. On the ceremonial function of the Minoan polythyron. *OpAth* 16, 57–73.

Marinatos, S. 1957. Excavations near Pylos, 1956. *Antiquity* 31, 97–100.

Marketou, T. 1988. New evidence on the topography and site history of prehistoric Ialysos. In Dietz and Papachristodoulou 1988, 27–33.

Marthari, M. 1987. The local pottery wares with painted decoration from the volcanic destruction level of Akrotiri, Thera. *AA* 1987, 359–79.

Martín de la Cruz, J.C. 1990. Die erste mykenische Keramik von der Iberischen Halbinsel. *PZ* 65, 49–52.

Matson, F.R. 1972. Ceramic studies. In McDonald and Rapp 1972, 200–24.

Matthäus, H. 1980. *Die Bronzegefässe der kretisch-mykenisch Kultur* (*Prähistorische Bronzefunde* II.1). Munich: Beck.

McDonald, W.A. 1975. Excavations at Nichoria in Messenia. *Hesperia* 44, 69–141.

and Rapp, G., Jr. (ed.) 1972. *The Minnesota Messenia Expedition*. Minneapolis: University of Minnesota Press.

and Thomas, C.G. 1990. *Progress into the past: the rediscovery of Mycenaean civilisation*. Bloomingon: Indiana University Press.

and Wilkie, N.C. (eds) 1992. *Excavations at Nichoria in southwest Greece*, Vol II. *The Bronze Age occupation*. Minneapolis: University of Minnesota Press.

McEnroe, J. 1982. A typology of Minoan Neopalatial houses. *AJA* 86, 3–19.

McGeorge, P.J.P. 1988. Health and diet in Minoan times. In R.E. Jones and H.W. Catling (eds), *New aspects of archaeological science in Greece*, 47–54. Athens: British School at Athens.

McNeal, R.A. 1975. Helladic prehistory through the looking-glass. *Historia* 24, 385–401.

Mee, C.B. and Cavanagh, W.G. 1984. Mycenaean tombs as evidence for social and political organisation. *OJA* 3, 45–64.

and Cavanagh, W.G. 1990. The spatial distribution of Mycenaean tombs. *BSA* 85, 225–43.

Melas, E.M. 1985. *The islands of Karpathos, Saros and Kasos in the Neolithic and Bronze Ages*. *SIMA* 68. Göteborg: Åström.

1988a. Minoans overseas: alternative models of interpretation. *Aegaeum* 2, 47–70.

1988b. Exploration in the Dodecanese: new prehistoric and Mycenaean finds. *BSA* 83, 283–311.

Mellaart, J. 1979. Egyptian and Near Eastern chronology: a dilemma? *Antiquity* 53, 6–18.

Miller, D. 1981. The relationship between ceramic production and distribution in a central Indian village. In H. Howard and E.L. Morris (eds) 1981, *Production and distribution: a ceramic viewpoint*, 221–8. Oxford: *BAR* S120.

Mitchell, S. 1990. Archaeology in Asia Minor 1985–1989. In French 1990, 83–131.

Momigliano, N. 1991. MM IA pottery from Evans' excavations at Knossos: a reassessment. *BSA* 86, 149–271.

Moody, J. 1983. Khania archaeological site survey. In Keller and Rupp 1983, 301–2.

Moore, A. 1988. The large monochrome terracotta figures from Mycenae: the problem of interpretation. In French and Wardle 1988, 219–28.

Morgan, C. 1990. *Athletes and oracles. The transformation of Olympia and Delphi in the eighth century B.C.* Cambridge: Cambridge University Press.

Morgan, L. 1987. A Minoan larnax from Knossos. *BSA* 82, 171–200.

1988. *The miniature wall paintings from Thera: a study in Aegean culture and iconography*. Cambridge: Cambridge University Press.

1990. Island iconography: Thera, Kea, Milos. In Hardy 1990, Vol. I, 252–66.

Morpurgo Davies, A. and Duhoux, Y. 1985. *Linear B: a 1984 survey*. Louvain-la-Neuve: Institut de Linguistique de Louvain.

Morris, I. 1987. *Burial and ancient society*. Cambridge: Cambridge University Press.

Mountjoy, P-A. 1976. Late Helladic IIIB 1 pottery dating the construction of the South House at Mycenae. *BSA* 71, 77–112.

1984. The Marine Style pottery of LMIB/LHIIA: towards a corpus. *BSA* 79, 161–220.

1986. *Mycenaean decorated pottery*. *SIMA* 73. Göteborg: Åström.

, Jones, R.E. and Cherry, J.F. 1978. Provenance studies of the LMIB/LHIIA Marine Style. *BSA* 73, 143–72.

Muhly, J.D. 1992. The crisis years in the Mediterranean world: transition or cultural disintegration? In W.A. Ward and M.S. Joukowsky (eds), *The crisis years: the 12th century B.C.* Dubuque: Kendall/Hunt.

Müller, S. 1989. Les tumuli helladiques: où? quand? comment? *BCH* 113, 1–42.

Musgrave, J. 1990. Dust and damn'd oblivion: a study of cremation in ancient Greece. *BSA* 85, 271–99.

Mylonas, G.E. 1973. *Ο τάφικος κύκλος Β τών Μυκηνών* (with English summary). Athens: Archaeological Society.

1975–6. *Τό δυτικόν νεκροταφείον τής Ελευσίνος* (with English summary). Athens: Archaeological Society.

1981. The cult centre of Mycenae. *Proceedings of the British Academy* 67, 307–20.

Mylonas Shear, I. 1987. *The Panaghia Houses at Mycenae*. Philadelphia: the University Museum, University of Pennsylvania.

Negbi, O. 1988. Levantine elements in the sacred architecture of the Aegean. *BSA* 83, 339–58.

Niemeier, W-D. 1982. Mycenaean Knossos and the age of Linear B. *SMEA* 23, 219–87.

1985. *Die Palaststilkeramik von Knossos: Stil, Chronologie und historischer Kontext*. Berlin: Mann 1985.

1986. Creta, Egeo e Mediterraneo agli inizi del bronzo tardo. In Marazzi *et al.* 1986, 245–70.

1987. On the function of the 'Throne Room' in the palace at Knossos. In Hägg and Marinatos 1987, 163–8.

1988. The 'Priest King' fresco from Knossos. A new reconstruction. In French and Wardle 1988, 235–44.

1990. Cult scenes on gold rings from the Argolid. In Hägg and Nordquist 1990, 165–70.

1991. Minoan artisans travelling overseas: the Alalakh frescoes and the painted plaster floor at Tel Kabri (western Galilee). In R. Laffineur and L. Basch, *Thalassa. L'Egée préhistorique et la mer (Aegaeum 7)*. Liège: University of Liège.

Nilsson, M.P. 1950. *The Minoan–Mycenaean religion and its survival in Greek religion* (2nd edition). Lund: Kungl. Humanistiska Vetenskapssamfundet.

Nordfeldt, A-C. 1987. Residential quarters and lustral basins. In Hägg and Marinatos 1987, 187–94.

Nordquist, G.C. 1987. *A Middle Helladic village. Asine in the Argolid. BOREAS* 16. Uppsala: University of Uppsala.

1990. Middle Helladic burial rites: some speculations. In Hägg and Nordquist 1990, 35–41.

Olivier, J-P. 1984. Administration at Knossos and Pylos: what differences. In Shelmerdine and Palaima 1984, 11–18.

1989. Les écritures crétoises. In Treuil *et al.* 1989, Book 2, Ch. 2.

and Palaima, T.G. 1988. *Texts, tablets and scribes. Minos* Supplement 10. Salamanca: University of Salamanca.

Orme, B. 1981. *Anthropology for archaeologists*. London: Duckworth.

Overbeck, J.C. 1989. *Keos VII. Ayia Irini: Period IV. Part 1: the stratigraphy and the find deposits*. Mainz, von Zabern.

Palaima, T.G. 1987. Preliminary comparative textual evidence for palatial control of economic activity in Minoan and Mycenaean Crete. In Hägg and Marinatos 1987, 301–6.

1988a. The development of the Mycenaean writing system. In Olivier and Palaima 1988, 269–342.

1988b. The development of the Mycenaean script and literacy. *BICS* 35, 166–7.

Palyvou, C. 1986. Notes on the town plan of Late Cycladic Akrotiri, Thera. *BSA* 81, 179–94.

1987. Circulatory patterns in Minoan architecture. In Hägg and Marinatos 1987, 195–203.

Panagiotaki, M. 1992. The 'Central Palace Sanctuary' area at Knossos. Unpublished paper delivered at the Mycenaean Seminar, London, May 1992.

Papathanasopoulos, G. 1971. Σπήλαια Διρού: Αί ανασκαφαί τού 1970–71. *AAA* 4, 12–26.

Payne, S. 1985. Zoo-archaeology in Greece: a reader's guide. In N.C. Wilkie and W.D.E. Coulson (eds), *Contributions to Aegean archaeology*, 212–44. Minneapolis: University of Minnesota, Center for Ancient Studies.

Peacock, D.P.S. 1982. *Pottery in the Roman world*. New York: Longman.

Peatfield, A.A.D. 1983. The topography of Minoan peak sanctuaries. *BSA* 78, 273–9.

1987. Palace and peak: the political and religious relationship between palaces and peak sanctuaries. In Hägg and Marinatos 1987, 89–93.

1990. Minoan peak sanctuaries: history and society. *OpAth* 18, 117–31.

1992. Rural ritual in Bronze Age Crete: the peak sanctuary at Atsipadhes. *CAJ* 2, 59–87.

Pelon, O. 1976. *Tholoi, tumuli et cercles funéraires*. Paris: French School at Athens.

1988. L'autel minoen sur le site de Malia. *Aegaeum* 2, 31–46.

Peltenburg, E.J. (ed.) 1989. *Early society in Cyprus*. Edinburgh: Edinburgh University Press.

1991. Greeting gifts and luxury faience: a context for Orientalising trends in late Mycenaean Greece. In Gale 1991, 162–79.

Pendlebury, J.D.S. 1939. *The Archaeology of Crete. An introduction.* London: Methuen.

Perlès, C. 1988. New ways with an old problem: chipped stone assemblages as an index of cultural discontinuity in early Greek prehistory. In French and Wardle 1988, 477–88.

1990. L'outillage de pierre taillée Néolithique en Grèce: approvisionnement et exploitation des matières premières. *BCH* 104, 1–42.

1992. Production strategies and exchange systems in Neolithic Greece. Research Seminar, Department of Archaeology, University of Durham, February 1992.

Persson, A.W. 1931. *The royal tombs at Dendra near Midea.* Lund: Kungl. Humanistiska Vetenskapssamfundet.

1942. *New tombs at Dendra near Midea.* Lund: Kungl. Humanistiska Vetenskapssamfundet.

Pierpont, G. de 1987. Réflexions sur la destination des édifices de Chrysolakkos. In Laffineur 1987, 79–93.

Pini, I. 1968. *Beiträge zur minoischen Gräberkunde.* Wiesbaden: Steiner.

Piteros, C., Olivier, J-P. and Melena, J.L. 1990. Les inscriptions en Linéaire B des nodules de Thèbes (1982): la fouille, les documents, les possibilités d'interpretation. *BCH* 114, 103–84.

Platon, N. 1971. *Zakros: the discovery of a lost palace of ancient Crete.* New York: Scribner.

Popham, M.R. 1964. *The last days of the palace at Knossos. Complete vases of the Late Minoan IIIB period. SIMA* 5. Göteborg: Åström.

1970. *The destruction of the palace at Knossos. Pottery of the Late Minoan IIIA period. SIMA* 12. Göteborg: Åström.

1979. Connections between Crete and Cyprus between 1300–1100 B.C. In *Acts of the International Archaeological Symposium 'The relations between Cyprus and Crete, ca. 2000–500 B.C.'*, 178–91. Nicosia: Department of Antiquities, Cyprus.

1984. *The Minoan Unexplored Mansion at Knossos.* London: Thames and Hudson.

, and Catling, E.A. and H.W. 1974. Sellopoulo Tombs 3 and 4, two Late Minoan graves near Knossos. *BSA* 69, 195–257.

and Sackett, L.H. (ed.) 1968. *Excavations at Lefkandi, Euboea 1964–66.* London: Thames and Hudson.

Postgate, N. 1977. *The first empires.* London: Elsevier Phaidon.

Poursat, J-C. 1977. *Les ivoires mycéniens.* Paris: French School at Athens.

1980. Reliefs d'applique moulés. In Detournay *et al.* 1980, Ch. 4, B.

1983. Ateliers et sanctuaries à Malia: nouvelles données sur l'organisation sociale à l'époque des premiers palais. In Krzyszkowska and Nixon 1983, 277–81.

Pritchard, J.P. (ed.) 1974. *Ancient Near Eastern texts relating to the Old Testament* (4th edition). Princeton: Princeton University Press.

Protonotariou-Deilaki, E. 1990a. Burial customs and funerary rites in the prehistoric Argolid. In Hägg and Nordquist 1990, 69–83.

1990b. The tumuli of Mycenae and Dendra. In Hägg and Nordquist 1990, 85–106.

Pulak, C. 1988. The Bronze Age shipwreck at Ulu Burun, Turkey: 1985 campaign. *AJA* 92, 1–37.

Pullen, D.J. 1986. A 'House of Tiles' at Zygouries? The function of monumental Early Helladic architecture. In Hägg and Konsola 1986, 79–84.

1990. Early Helladic burials at Asine and Early Bronze Age mortuary practice. In Hägg and Nordquist 1990, 9–12.

1992. Ox and plow in the Early Bronze Age Aegean. *AJA* 96, 45–54.

Rackham, O. 1982. Land use and the native vegetation of Greece. In M. Bell and S.

Limbrey (ed.), *Archaeological aspects of woodland ecology*, 177–98. Oxford: *BAR* S146.
1983. Observations on the historical ecology of Boeotia. *BSA* 78, 291–351.
Rapp, G., Jr. and Aschenbrenner, S.E. (eds) 1978. *Excavations at Nichoria in southwestern Greece*, Vol. I. *Site, environment and techniques*. Minneapolis: University of Minnesota Press.
Re, L. 1986. Importazioni di ceramica d'uso corrente sull'isola di Vivara. In Marazzi *et al.* 1986, 162–4.
Renfrew, C. 1967. Cycladic metallurgy and the Aegean Early Bronze Age. *AJA* 63, 1–20.
1979. Terminology and beyond. In Davis and Cherry 1979, 51–63.
1981. The sanctuary at Phylakopi. In Hägg and Marinatos 1981, 67–79.
1985. *The archaeology of cult. The sanctuary at Phylakopi*. London: Thames and Hudson.
1986. The Goulandris Museum of Cycladic and ancient Greek art. *AR* 1985–86, 134–41.
1989. *Archaeology and language: the puzzle of Indo-European origins*. London: Penguin.
1991. *The Cycladic spirit*. London: Thames and Hudson.
and Cherry, J.F. (eds) 1986. *Peer polity interaction and socio-political change*. Cambridge: Cambridge University Press.
, Doumas, C. and Marangou, L. 1989. Amorgos and Keros: recent researches in the Cycladic Early Bronze Age. Lecture delivered to the Society of Antiquaries of London, 14 December 1989.
and Wagstaff, M. (eds) 1982. *An island polity. The archaeology of exploitation on Melos*. Cambridge: Cambridge University Press.
Renfrew, J.M. 1973. *Palaeoethnobotany*. Cambridge: Cambridge University Press.
1982. Early agriculture in Melos. Ch. 12 in Renfrew and Wagstaff 1982.
Ridley, C. and Wardle, K.A. 1979. Rescue excavations at Servia 1971–1973: a preliminary report. *BSA* 74, 185–230.
Riley, J.A. 1983. The contribution of ceramic petrology to our understanding of Minoan society. In Krzyszkowska and Nixon 1983, 283–92.
Roaf, M. 1990. *Cultural atlas of Mesopotamia and the ancient Near East*. Oxford: Facts on File.
Robkin, A.H.L. 1979. The agricultural year, the commodity *SA* and the linen industry of Mycenaean Pylos. *AJA* 83, 469–74.
Runnels, C.N. 1985. Trade and the demand for millstones in southern Greece in the Neolithic and Early Bronze Age. In Knapp and Stech 1985, 30–43.
Rutkowski, B. 1986. *The cult places of the Aegean*. New Haven and London: Yale University Press.
1988. Minoan peak sanctuaries: the topography and architecture. *Aegaeum* 2, 71–98.
1989. Minoan sanctuaries at Christos and Koumasa, Crete: new field research. *Archäologisches Korrespondenzblatt* 19, 47–51.
1991. *Petsophas. A Cretan peak sanctuary*. Warsaw: Art and Archaeology.
Rutter, J.B. 1979a. *Ceramic change in the Aegean Early Bronze Age*. Los Angeles: University of California, Los Angeles.
1979b. Stone vases and Minyan ware: a facet of Minoan influence on Middle Helladic Laconia. *AJA* 83, 464–9.
1983. Fine gray-burnished pottery of the Early Helladic III period: the ancestry of Gray Minyan. *Hesperia* 52, 327–55.
1985. An exercise in form vs. function: the significance of the duck vase. *TUAS* 10, 16–41.

1988. Early Helladic III vasepainting, ceramic regionalism, and the influence of basketry. In French and Wardle 1988, 73–89.
1990. Pottery groups of the end of the Middle Bronze Age from Tsoungiza. *Hesperia* 59, 375–458.
and Zerner, C. 1984. Early Hellado-Minoan contacts. In Hägg and Marinatos 1984, 175–83.
Sakellarakis, E. and J. 1984. The Keftiu and the Minoan thalassocracy. In Hägg and Marinatos 1984, 197–202.
Sakellarakis, J. 1976. Mycenaean stone vases. *SMEA 17*, 173–87.
Sakellarakis, J. and E. 1991. *Archanes*. Athens: Ekdotike Athenon.
Sali-Axioti, T. 1990. The lightwell of the House of the Ladies and its structural behaviour. In Hardy 1990, Vol. I, 437–40.
Sampson, A. 1984. The Neolithic of the Dodecanese and Aegean Neolithic. *BSA* 79, 239–49.
1986. Architecture and urbanization in Manika, Chalkis. In Hägg and Konsola 1986, 47–50.
1987. The Early Helladic graves of Manika: contributions to the socioeconomic conditions of the Early Bronze Age. In Laffineur 1987, 19–28.
1988. Early Helladic contacts with the Cyclades during the EBA 2. In *Aegaeum* 2, 5–9.
Sandars, N.K. 1961. The first Aegean swords and their ancestry. *AJA* 65, 17–29.
1963. Later Aegean bronze swords. *AJA* 67, 117–53.
1978 (2nd edition 1985). *The Sea Peoples*. London: Thames and Hudson.
Sapouna-Sakellaraki, E. 1987. New evidence from the Early Bronze Age cemetery at Manika, Chalkis. *BSA* 82, 233–64.
1990. Archanès à l'époque mycénienne. *BCH* 114, 67–102.
Schilardi, D.U. 1984. The LH IIIC period at the Koukounaries acropolis, Paros. In MacGillivray and Barber 1984, 184–206.
Seltzer, R.M. (ed.) 1989. *Religions of antiquity*. New York: Macmillan.
Shaw, J.W. 1971. Minoan architecture: materials and techniques. *ASAtene* 33, 5–256.
1978. Akrotiri as a Minoan settlement. In Doumas 1978, 429–36.
1986. Excavations at Kommos (Crete) during 1984–85. *Hesperia* 55, 219–69.
1987. The Early Helladic II 'corridor house'. *AJA* 91, 59–74.
1990. Bronze Age Aegean harboursides. In Hardy 1990, Vol. I, 420–36.
and Shaw, M.C. (eds) 1985. *A great Mediterranean triangle in southcentral Crete: Kommos, Ayia Triada, Phaistos (Scripta Mediterranea 6)*. Toronto: Society for Mediterranean Studies.
Shelford, P. The geology of Melos. In Renfrew and Wagstaff 1982, 74–81.
Shelmerdine, C.W. 1985. *The perfume industry of Mycenaean Pylos. SIMA* pocketbook 34. Göteborg: Åström.
1987. Architectural change and economic decline at Pylos. *Minos* 20–22, 557–68.
and Palaima, T.G. 1984. *Pylos comes alive. Industry + administration in a Mycenaean palace*. New York: Fordham University.
Sherratt, A.G. 1981. Plough and pastoralism: aspects of the secondary products revolution. In Hodder *et al.* 1981, 261–305.
1987a. Warriors and traders: Bronze Age chiefdoms in central Europe. In Cunliffe 1981, ch. 5.
1987b. Cups that cheered. In W.H. Waldren and R.C. Kennard, *Bell beakers of the western Mediterranean*, 81–103. Oxford: *BAR* S331.
Sherratt, E.S. 1980. Regional variation in the pottery of Late Helladic IIIB. *BSA* 75, 175–202.
1985. The development of Late Helladic IIIC. *BICS* 32, 161.

1990. 'Reading the texts': archaeology and the Homeric question. *Antiquity* 64, 807–24.
and Crouwel, J.H. 1987. Mycenaean pottery from Cilicia in Oxford. *OJA* 6, 325–52.
Sinos, S. 1971. *Die vorklassischen Hausformen in der Ägäis*. Mainz: von Zabern.
Smith, J.S. 1991. Bronzeworkers at Pylos: their place in Mycenaean economy and industry. *AJA* 95, 316.
Snodgrass, A.M. 1985. The New Archaeology and the Classical archaeologist. *AJA* 89, 31–7.
Soles, J.S. 1973. The Gournia house tombs: a study of the architecture, chronology and use of the built rectangular tombs of Crete. PhD thesis, Pennsylvania. Ann Arbor: University Microfilms International.
1979. The early Gournia town. *AJA* 75, 149–67.
1988. Social ranking in Prepalatial cemeteries. In French and Wardle 1988, 49–61.
1991. The Gournia palace. *AJA* 95, 17–78.
1992. *The Prepalatial cemeteries at Mochlos and Gournia and the house tombs of Bronze Age Crete*. *Hesperia* Supplement 24. Princeton: Princeton University Press.
and Davaras, C. 1990. Theran ash in Minoan Crete: new excavations at Mochlos. In Hardy 1990, Vol. III, 89–95.
Sourvinou-Inwood, C. 1989a. Space in Late Minoan religious scenes in glyptic – some remarks. In W. Müller (ed.), *Corpus der minoischen und mykenischen Siegel, Beiheft 3*, 241–57. Berlin: Mann.
1989b. Review of B.C. Dietrich, *Tradition in Greek religion*, in *CR* 39, 51–8.
Stos-Gale, Z.A. and Gale, N.H. 1984. The Minoan thalassocracy and the Aegean metal trade. In Hägg and Marinatos 1984, 59–64.
Symeonoglou, S. 1973. *Kadmeia I. Mycenaean finds from Thebes, Greece. Excavations at 14 Oedipus Street. SIMA* 35. Göteborg: Åström.
1985. *The topography of Thebes from the Bronze Age to modern times*. Princeton: Princeton University Press.
Televantou, C.A. 1990. New light on the West House wall-paintings. In Hardy 1990, Vol. I, 309–24.
Themelis, P.G. 1984. Early Helladic monumental architecture. *AthMitt* 99, 335–51.
Torrence, R. 1986. *Production and exchange of stone tools. Prehistoric obsidian in the Aegean*. Cambridge: Cambridge University Press.
Touchais, G. 1980, 1985, 1989. Chronique des fouilles et découvertes archéologiques en Grèce en 1979, 1984, 1988, in *BCH* 105, 561–688; 109, 759–862; 113, 581–700.
Tournavitou, I. 1988. Towards an identification of a workshop space. In French and Wardle 1988, 447–67.
1989. Mycenae, the Wace and West Houses: function and status. Mycenaean Seminar, London, January 1989.
1990a. Enclave colonies model – true or false? *BSA* 85, 415–19.
1990b. Aspects of trade and production in Mycenaean Greece. *Hydra* 7, 76–86.
Trigger, B.G., Kemp, B.J., O'Connor, D. and Lloyd, A.B. 1983. *Ancient Egypt: a social history*. Cambridge: Cambridge University Press.
Tsountas, C. and Manatt, J.I. 1897. *The Mycenaean age*. London: Macmillan.
Tyree, E.L. 1974. Cretan sacred caves: archaeological evidence. PhD thesis, Missouri – Columbia. Ann Arbor: University Microfilms International.
Tzavella-Evjen, H. 1985. *Lithares, an Early Bronze Age settlement in Boeotia*. Los Angeles: University of California, Los Angeles, Institute of Archaeology.
Tzedakis, Y. and Chryssoulaki, S. 1987. Neopalatial architectural elements in the area of Chania. In Hägg and Marinatos 1987, 111–15.
, Chryssoulaki, S., Voutsaki, S. and Veniéri, Y. 1989. Les routes minoennes: rapport

préliminaire. Défense de la circulation ou circulation de la défense? *BCH* 113, 43–75.
Chryssoulaki, S., Veniéri, Y. and Avgouli, M. 1990. Les routes minoennes. – Le poste de Χοιρόμανδρες et la contrôle des communications. *BCH* 114, 43–62.
Vagnetti, L. and Jones, R.E. 1988. Towards the identification of local Mycenaean pottery in Italy. In French and Wardle 1988, 335–48.
and Lo Schiavo F. 1989. Late Bronze Age long distance trade in the Mediterranean: the role of the Cypriots. In Peltenburg 1989, 217–43.
Van Andel, T.H., Runnels, C.N. and Pope, K.O. 1986. Five thousand years of land use and abuse in the southern Argolid, Greece. *Hesperia* 55, 103–28.
and Runnels, C.N. 1987. *Beyond the acropolis: a rural Greek past*. Stanford: Stanford University Press.
and Runnels, C.N. 1988. An essay on the 'emergence of civilisation' in the Aegean world. *Antiquity* 62, 234–47.
and Shackleton, J.C. 1982. Late Palaeolithic and Mesolithic coastlines of Greece and the Aegean. *JFA* 9, 449–54.
Vandenabeele, F. 1987. L'influence égéenne dans les coutumes funéraires chypriotes. In Laffineur 1987, 227–34.
Van Effenterre, H. and M. 1969. *Fouilles exécutées à Mallia. Le centre politique I. L'Agora (1960–66)*. Etudes crétoises 17. Paris: French School at Athens.
Van Effenterre, H. 1980. *Le palais de Mallia et la cité minoenne*. Rome: Edizioni dell'Ateneo.
Van Leuven, J.C. 1981. Problems and methods of Prehellenic naology. In Hägg and Marinatos 1981, 11–25.
Vasilakis, A.S. 1989. Ο Πρωτομινωικός οικισμός Τρυπητής (with English summary). *ΑΡΧΑΙΟΛΟΓΙΑ* 30, 52–6.
Ventris, M. and Chadwick, J. 1973. *Documents in Mycenaean Greek*. Cambridge: Cambridge University Press.
Verlinden, C. 1984. *Les statuettes anthropomorphes crétoises en bronze et en plomb du IIIe millénaire au VIIe siècle av. J.C.* Providence, R.I.: Brown University, Center for Old World Archaeology and Art.
Vermeule, E.T. 1975. *The art of the Shaft Graves of Mycenae*. Norman, Oklahoma: University of Oklahoma Press.
Von den Driesch, A. 1987. Haus- und Jagdtiere im vorgeschichtlichen Thessalien. *PZ* 61, 1–21.
and Boessneck, J. 1990. Die Tierreste von den mykenischen Burg Tiryns bei Nauplion/ Peloponnes. In J. Weisshaar *et al.*, *Tiryns Forschungen und Berichte XI*, 878–164. Mainz: von Zabern.
Wace, A.J.B. 1921. The rhyton well. *BSA* 24, 20–9.
1923. Mycenae. Report of the excavations of the British School at Athens 1921–23. *BSA* 25, *passim*.
1932. Chamber tombs at Mycenae. *Archaeologia* 82, *passim*.
1949. *Mycenae: an archaeological history and guide*. Princeton: Princeton University Press.
Wachsmann, S. 1987. *Aegeans in the Theban tombs*. Leuven: Peeters.
Walberg, G. 1976. *Kamares: a study of the character of palatial Middle Minoan pottery*. *BOREAS* 8. Uppsala: University of Uppsala.
1983. *Provincial Middle Minoan pottery*. Mainz: von Zabern.
1987. Palatial and provincial workshops in the Middle Minoan period. In Hägg and Marinatos 1987, 281–5.
Wall, S.M., Musgrave, J.H. and Warren, P.M. 1986. Human bones from a Late Minoan IB house at Knossos. *BSA* 81, 333–88.

Walter, H. and Felten, F. 1981. *Alt-Ägina III, 1. Die vorgeschichtliche Stadt: Befestigungen, Häuser, Funde*. Mainz: von Zabern.
Wardle, D.E.H. 1988. Does reconstruction help? A Mycenaean dress and the Dendra suit of armour. In French and Wardle 1988, 469–76.
Wardle, K.A. 1969. A group of Late Helladic IIIB 1 pottery from within the citadel at Mycenae. *BSA* 64, 71–93.
Warren, P.M. 1969. *Minoan stone vases*. Cambridge: Cambridge University Press.
1972. *Myrtos. An Early Bronze Age settlement in Crete*. London: Thames and Hudson.
1973a. The beginnings of Minoan religion. In *Antichità cretesi: studi in onore di Doro Levi Vol. I*, 137–47. Catania: Università di Catania, Istituto di Archeologia.
1973b. Crete, 3000–1400 B.C.: immigration and the archaeological evidence. In Crossland and Birchall 1973, 41–50.
1979. The stone vessels from the Bronze Age settlement at Akrotiri, Thera. *AE* 1979, 82–113.
1980. Problems of chronology in Crete and the Aegean in the third and earlier second millennium B.C. *AJA* 84, 484–99.
1984a. The place of Crete in the thalassocracy of Minos. In Hägg and Marinatos 1984, 39–44.
1984b. Circular platforms at Minoan Knossos. *BSA* 79, 307–23.
1985. Minoan palaces. In *Scientific American* 253, 94–103.
1987a. The genesis of the Minoan palace. In Hägg and Marinatos 1987, 47–56.
1987b. The Minoans and their gods. In Cunliffe 1987, ch. 3.
1988. *Minoan religion as ritual action*. Göteborg: Göteborg University.
1990. Of baetyls. *OpAth* 18, 193–206.
1991a. The Minoan civilisation of Crete and the volcano of Thera. *Journal of the Ancient Chronology Forum* 4, 29–39.
1991b. A new Minoan deposit from Knossos, c. 1600 B.C., and its wider relations. *BSA* 86, 319–40.
and Hankey, V. 1989. *Aegean Bronze Age chronology*. Bristol: Bristol Classical Press.
and Tzedakis, J. 1974. Debla. An Early Minoan settlement in western Crete. *BSA* 69, 299–342.
Watrous, L.V. 1982. *Lasithi. A history of settlement on a highland plain in Crete. Hesperia* Supplement 18. Princeton: Princeton University Press.
1984a. Ayia Triada: a new perspective on the Minoan villa. *AJA* 88, 123–34.
1984b. The Late Bronze Age pottery from Kommos as evidence for the history of Crete. *BICS* 31, 216.
1991. The origins and iconography of the Minoan painted larnax. *Hesperia* 60, 285–307.
Weingarten, J. 1986a. *The Zakro Master and his place in prehistory. SIMA* pocket book 26. Göteborg: Åström.
1986b, 1988. The sealing structures of Minoan Crete: MM II Phaistos to the destruction of the palace at Knossos. Part I: the evidence until the LM IB destructions. *OJA* 5, 279–98. Part II: the evidence from Knossos until the destruction of the palace. *OJA* 7, 1–17.
1989. Old and new elements in the seals and sealings of the Temple Repository, Knossos. In Laffineur 1989a, 39–51.
1991. Late Bronze Age trade within Crete: the evidence of seals and sealings. In Gale 1991, 303–24.
Weisshaar, J. 1990. Die Keramik von Talioti. In J. Weisshaar *et al.*, *Tiryns Forschungen und Berichte XI*, 1–34.

Wenke, R.J. 1984. *Patterns in prehistory*. Oxford: Oxford University Press.
Whitelaw, T.M. 1983. The settlement at Fournou Korifi, Myrtos and aspects of Early Minoan social organization. In Krzyszkowska and Nixon 1983, 323–45.
1986. The absolute chronology of the Aegean Early Bronze Age: a reassessment of the radiocarbon dates from Fournou Korifi, Myrtos. *AJA* 90, 178.
Whitley, J. 1991. Social diversity in Dark Age Greece. *BSA* 86, 341–65.
Wiencke, M.H. 1970. Banded pithoi of Lerna III. *Hesperia* 39, 94–110.
1989. Change in early Helladic II. *AJA* 85, 495–509.
Wiener, M.H. 1984. Crete and the Cyclades in LM I: the tale of the conical cups. In Hägg and Marinatos 1984, 17–26.
1987. Trade and rule in palatial Crete. In Hägg and Marinatos 1987, 261–6.
1990. The isles of Crete? The Minoan thalassocracy revisited. In Hardy 1990, Vol. I, 128–60.
Wilson, D.E. 1985. The pottery and architecture of the EM IIA West Court house at Knossos. *BSA* 80, 281–364.
Wilson, R.J.A. 1988. Archaeology in Sicily 1982–1987. In *AR* 1987–88, 103–50.
Wright, J.C., Cherry, J.F., Davis, J.L., Mantzourani, E., Sutton S.B. and Sutton, R.F., Jr. 1990. The Nemea Valley Archaeological Project, 1984–1987. *Hesperia* 59, 579–659.
Xanthoudides, S. 1924. *The vaulted tombs of Mesarà*. London: Hodder and Stoughton. Reprinted with introduction by K. Branigan 1971; Farnborough: Gregg International.
Xenaki-Sakellariou, A. 1985. *Οί θαλαμώτοι τάφοι τών Μυκηνών* (with French summary). Paris: Boccard.
and Chatziliou, C. 1989. *Peinture en metal à l'epoque mycénienne*. Athens and Paris: Ekdotike Athenon/Boccard.
Younger, J.G. 1973. Towards the chronology of Aegean glyptic in the Late Bronze Age. PhD thesis, Cincinnati. Ann Arbor: University Microfilms International.
1979a. The Rhodian Hunt Group. In Davis and Cherry 1979, 97–105.
1979b. Semi-precious stones to the Aegean. *Archaeological News (Tallahassee, Florida)* 8, 40–4.
1985. Aegean seals of the Late Bronze Age: stylistic groups IV. Almond- and dot-eye groups of the fifteenth century B.C. *Kadmos* 24, 34–73.
1989. Bronze Age seals in their middle period. In Laffineur 1989a, 53–64.
1991. Seals? from Middle Helladic Greece. *Hydra* 8, 35–54.
Yule, P. 1980. *Early Cretan seals: a study in chronology*. Mainz: von Zabern.
Zaccagnini, C. 1986. Aspects of copper trade in the eastern Mediterranean during the Late Bronze Age. In Marazzi *et al.* 1986, 413–24.
Zachos, K. 1990. The Neolithic period in Naxos. In Marangou 1990, 29–32.
Zapheiropoulou, P. 1984. The chronology of the Kampos group. In MacGillivray and Barber 1984, 31–40.
Zeimbekis, M.A. 1991. The priesthood in Crete: a Minoan perspective. Bristol, MA dissertation.
Zerner, C.W. 1978. The beginning of the Middle Helladic period at Lerna. PhD thesis, Cincinnati. Ann Arbor: University Microfilms International.
1986. Middle Helladic and Late Helladic I pottery from Lerna. *Hydra* 2, 58–74.
1988. Middle Helladic and Late Helladic I pottery from Lerna: Part II, shapes. *Hydra* 4, *passim*.
Zois, A. 1976. *Βασιλική I*. Athens: Archaeological Society.

INDEX

(References to the Aegean, Crete, and chronological and cultural terms are too numerous and, often, insignificant for all to be indexed; only the more notable have been selected. To conserve space, words that appear rarely and have a common feature, e.g. types of stone, and those hardly referred to outside a single section, e.g. types of ornament, have sometimes been grouped under an appropriate general heading)